How
Psychotherapists
Develop

How Psychotherapists Develop

A Study of Therapeutic Work and Professional Growth

David E. Orlinsky
Michael Helge Rønnestad

and the Collaborative Research Network of the
Society for Psychotherapy Research

With Contributions by

Hansruedi Ambühl, Ulrike Willutzki, John D. Davis,
Paul Gerin, Thomas A. Schröder, Hadas Wiseman,
Marcia L. Davis, Jean-François Botermans, Alice Dazord,
Manfred Cierpka, and others

American Psychological Association
Washington, DC

Second Printing, March 2009

Published by
American Psychological Association
750 First Street, NE
Washington, DC 20002
www.apa.org

To order
APA Order Department
P.O. Box 92984
Washington, DC 20090-2984
Tel: (800) 374-2721
Direct: (202) 336-5510
Fax: (202) 336-5502
TDD/TTY: (202) 336-6123
Online: www.apa.org/books/
E-mail: order@apa.org

In the U.K., Europe, Africa, and the Middle East, copies may be ordered from
American Psychological Association
3 Henrietta Street
Covent Garden, London
WC2E 8LU England

Typeset in Goudy by World Composition Services, Inc., Sterling, VA

Printer: Book-Mart Press, North Bergen, NJ
Cover Designer: Naylor Design, Washington, DC
Technical/Production Editors: Emily Leonard and Harriet Kaplan

The opinions and statements published are the responsibility of the authors, and such opinions and statements do not necessarily represent the policies of the American Psychological Association.

Library of Congress Cataloging-in-Publication Data

Orlinsky, David E. (David Elliot), 1936–
    How psychotherapists develop : a study of therapeutic work and professional growth / by David E. Orlinsky and M. Helge Rønnestad.
        p. cm.
    Includes bibliographical references and index.
    ISBN 1-59147-273-3 (alk. paper)
    1. Psychotherapists—Attitudes. 2. Psychotherapists—Psychology.
3. Psychotherapists—Training of. 4. Self-actualization (Psychology) I. Rønnestad, Michael Helge. II. Title.

RC480.5.O747   2005
616.89'14—dc22   2004025345

British Library Cataloguing-in-Publication Data
A CIP record is available from the British Library.

Printed in the United States of America
First Edition

CONTENTS

CONTRIBUTORS

Nicoletta Aapro, MD, Psychiatrist and Psychotherapist (FMH), Consultant in Psychotherapy, Department of Psychiatry, University Hospitals of Geneva, Geneva, Switzerland

Hansruedi Ambühl, PhD, Senior Psychotherapist and Supervisor, Private Practice, Bern, Switzerland

Alejandro Ávila Espada, MD, PhD, Professor of Clinical Psychology and Chair of Psychotherapy, Complutense University, Madrid, Spain

Sue Hyun Bae, PhD, Assistant Professor of Psychology, Illinois School of Psychology, Argosy University, Chicago, IL

Larry E. Beutler, PhD, McInnes Distinguished Professor of Psychology, Pacific Graduate School of Psychology, Palo Alto, CA

Jean-François Botermans, PhD, Senior Psychotherapist and Supervisor, Private Practice, Brussels, Belgium

Peter Buchheim, Professor of Psychiatry and Psychotherapy, Technical University of Munich, Munich, Germany

Isabel Caro Gabalda, PhD, Associate Professor of Psychology, University of Valencia, Valencia, Spain

Manfred Cierpka, MD, Professor and Director, Department of Family Therapy and Research, University of Heidelberg, Heidelberg, Germany

Christine Davidson, PhD, Associate Professor of Psychiatry, University of Illinois at Chicago, Chicago, IL

John D. Davis, PhD, Senior Lecturer in Psychology, University of Warwick, Coventry, England

Marcia L. Davis, PhD, Consultant Clinical Psychologist, North Warwickshire NHS Primary Care Trust, Nuneaton, England

Alice Dazord, MD, PhD, Research Director (Directeur de Recherche), National Institute of Health and Medical Research (INSERM), Lyon, France

Salvatore Freni, MD, Psychiatrist Psychoanalyst (IPA), Associate Professor in Psychotherapy, Università degli Studi di Milano, Milan, Italy

Alessandra Gabrielli, PhD, Psychoanalyst, Private Practice, Milan, Italy

Paul Gerin, MD, Research Director (Directeur de Recherche), National Institute of Health and Medical Research (INSERM), Lyon, France

Eunsun Joo, PhD, Associate Professor of Psychology, Duksung Women's University, Seoul, South Korea

Erik Friis Jørgensen, MA, Associate Professor of Psychology, University of Copenhagen, Copenhagen, Denmark

Horst Kächele, MD, Professor and Chair, Department of Psychosomatic Medicine and Psychotherapy, University of Ulm, Ulm, Germany

Ekaterina Kalmykova, PhD, Senior Research Scientist, Institute of Psychology, Russian Academy of Sciences, Moscow, Russia

Anna von der Lippe, PhD, Professor of Clinical Psychology, University of Oslo, Oslo, Norway

Jan Meyerberg, PhD, Licensed Psychologist and Psychotherapist (Psychologischer Psychotherapeut), Private Practice, Karlsruhe, Germany

John C. Norcross, PhD, Professor of Psychology, University of Scranton, Scranton, PA

Terry Northcut, PhD, Director, Doctoral Program, School of Social Work, Loyola University Chicago, Chicago, IL

David E. Orlinsky, PhD, Professor of Human Development and Social Sciences, University of Chicago, Chicago, IL

Barbara K. Parks, PhD, Visting Scholar, Committee on Human Development, University of Chicago, Chicago, IL

Michael Helge Rønnestad, PhD, Professor of Clinical Psychology, University of Oslo, Oslo, Norway

Michael Rosander, PhD, Senior Lecturer in Behavioral Sciences, Linköping University, Linköping, Sweden

Seth Rubin, PhD, Director of Research, C. G. Jung Institute, San Francisco, CA

Elena Scherb, PhD, Psychotherapist and Clinical Researcher, Fundación AIGLE, Buenos Aires, Argentina

Thomas A. Schröder, PhD, Consultant Clinical Psychologist, Derbyshire Mental Health Services NHS Trust and University of Derby, Derby, England

Gaby Shefler, PhD, Director, Sigmund Freud Center for Study and Research in Psychoanalysis and Professor of Psychology, Hebrew University, Jerusalem, Israel

Manuel S. Silverman, PhD, Governing Council, American Academy of Psychotherapists, Licensed Clinical Psychologist, Private Practice, Chicago, IL

David P. Smith, PhD, Licensed Clinical Psychologist and Visiting Scholar, Committee on Human Development, University of Chicago, Chicago, IL

Dan Stiwne, PhD, Associate Professor of Clinical Psychology, Linköping University, Linköping, Sweden

Scott Stuart, MD, Professor of Psychiatry, University of Iowa, Iowa City, Iowa

Margarita Tarragona, PhD, Professor of Psychology, Universidad de las Américas, Grupo Campos Eliseos, Mexico City, Mexico

António Branco Vasco, PhD, Associate Professor of Psychology, University of Lisbon, Lisbon, Portugal

Ulrike Willutzki, PD, PhD, Associate Professor of Psychology, Ruhr University-Bochum, Bochum, Germany

Hadas Wiseman, PhD, Senior Lecturer in Counseling, Faculty of Education, University of Haifa, Haifa, Israel

I
THE STUDY

1

THE DEVELOPMENT
OF PSYCHOTHERAPISTS

DAVID E. ORLINSKY, MICHAEL HELGE RØNNESTAD, PAUL GERIN,
JOHN D. DAVIS, HANSRUEDI AMBÜHL, MARCIA L. DAVIS,
ALICE DAZORD, ULRIKE WILLUTZKI, NICOLETTA AAPRO,
JEAN-FRANÇOIS BOTERMANS, AND THOMAS A. SCHRÖDER

PSYCHOTHERAPY *AND* PSYCHOTHERAPISTS

Many justifications can be offered for a study of psychotherapists, not the least of which is the fact that therapists seem to be rather interesting people. When the developmental psychologist Paul Baltes and his colleagues (e.g., Baltes & Smith, 1994) chose to study the nature of wisdom, they selected psychotherapists as a group they expected to exhibit it—a choice that might elicit a wry if appreciative smile in many therapists. The hallmarks of wisdom that Baltes and Smith (1994) thought might be found among psychotherapists included the following: rich factual knowledge; rich procedural knowledge; life span contextualism, or knowledge about the contexts of life and their temporal relationships; relativism, or knowledge about differences in values, goals, and priorities; and uncertainty, or knowledge about the relative indeterminacy and unpredictability of life and ways to manage it.

When a team of sociologists led by Robert Bellah (Bellah, Madsen, Sullivan, Swidler, & Tipton, 1985) undertook to investigate "the pursuit of happiness" in contemporary America, they too thought it important to include psychotherapists among their key informants. In their book *Habits of the Heart: Individualism and Commitment in American Life*, they explored the following aspects of private life: "finding oneself," love and marriage, "reaching out," and individualism. Evidently, the experiences and opinions of psychotherapists were considered meaningful as resources for understanding these topics.

Others have been interested in the profession of psychotherapy as well, although more critically. When the moral philosopher Alasdair MacIntyre (1981) sought to describe the emblematic occupational roles in modern society that embody the self-based ethic of *emotivism*, he focused on therapists (whom he viewed as "technicians" of private life) as well as managers (the "technicians" of corporate life). The profession has also been faulted for promoting a "therapeutic sensibility" that has purportedly contributed to the decline in traditional values and in their place fostered a "culture of narcissism" (Lasch, 1979). Collectively, therapists are nearly as much praised or blamed for the varied ills of modern society as their colleagues in the teaching profession. Individually, they are nearly as often expected to help cure those ills.

If we psychotherapists are of interest to scholars and critics beyond our profession, we are (and should be) at least as interesting to ourselves. All modern therapeutic approaches are based on the notion, variously expressed, that self-understanding contributes importantly to professional effectiveness, rational self-management, and personal well-being. To facilitate that self-understanding, we rely individually on our supervisors, our colleagues, and our own psychotherapists; but we also need to understand ourselves collectively, as a profession (or, more accurately, as a set of related professions). To supervise ourselves as a profession, and to develop optimally as a profession, we need accurate knowledge concerning who we are, what we do, and how well we do it. Although our teachers, supervisors, and personal therapists can help to increase and refine our individual self-knowledge, the only real path to reliable collective self-knowledge is through systematic empirical research.

Reliance on systematic empirical research for the understanding and improvement of *psychotherapeutic procedures*, of course, has been long established and is increasingly accepted (e.g., Aveline & Shapiro, 1995; Beutler & Clarkin, 1990). Scientific research on psychotherapy and counseling has been a continuous and growing enterprise for more than half a century (Hill & Corbett, 1993; Orlinsky & Russell, 1994; Strupp & Howard, 1992), and by the 1980s had become truly international in scope (e.g., Beutler & Crago,

1991). Those who wish to trace that development can do so conveniently by consulting successive editions of the authoritative *Handbook of Psychotherapy and Behavior Change* (Bergin & Garfield, 1971, 1994; Garfield & Bergin, 1978, 1986; Lambert, 2004).

Much less consistent attention has been given by psychotherapy researchers over the years to the professional and personal characteristics and contributions of *psychotherapists*. As a rule, the study of psychotherapies has been favored over the study of psychotherapists—as if therapists, when properly trained, are more or less interchangeable. There are exceptions to this rule, represented by major projects ranging from the early contributions that focused on training (Holt & Luborsky, 1958; Kelley & Fiske, 1951), through a few broader studies of therapists' characteristics and careers (e.g., Henry, Sims, & Spray, 1971, 1973; Norcross & Prochaska, 1982, 1983, 1988), to a more recent qualitative study of psychotherapist development (Skovholt & Rønnestad, 1995) and an anthropological study of American psychiatrists (Luhrmann, 2000). Nevertheless, these works stand out like islands in a relatively empty sea when compared with the amply settled ocean of studies on therapeutic processes and outcomes that have filled professional journals for years.

We think that one reason for this relative paucity of research on psychotherapists is an implicit bias in thinking about therapy leading to the assumption that it is basically a set of methods, techniques, or procedures that are efficacious, in and of themselves, in curing or ameliorating psychological and psychiatric disorders (Orlinsky, 1989). This bias is supported by a scientific culture of modernity that prizes and emphasizes rationality, objectivity, and mechanisms conceived as impersonal processes (e.g., Berger, Berger, & Kellner, 1973; Lakoff & Johnson, 1980; Toulmin, 1990) and that views the personal element or the subjective equation in human experience and relations as a source of error in research to be minimized or controlled (e.g., the placebo effect).[1] Following this approach, it seems only natural for researchers to have focused primarily on therapies rather than therapists. Typically, in experimental studies, patients—but not therapists—are randomly assigned to different treatment or control groups and, on the basis of the results, conclusions are drawn about the relative efficacy of *treatments* or the relative contribution of *treatment components* to patients' outcomes. Few researchers have recognized or tried to deal with the fact that the lack of random assignment of therapists (as well as patients) to different treatment

---

[1] As often happens, the one-sidedness of this bias has generated a corrective but equally limited and one-sided cultural reaction prizing faith, spirituality, and charisma; however, these are contextual issues beyond the scope of the present work (but see Lakoff & Johnson, 1980; Orlinsky, 2004).

groups makes it impossible to separate the effects attributable to treatments from those attributable to therapists (Elkin, 1999).[2]

An alternative and more balanced conception, in our judgment, is to view psychotherapy basically as a professional–personal relationship, in which properly qualified (and relevantly distressed) individuals interact respectively in the roles of therapist and patient to alleviate the distress and improve the well-being of those in the patient role (e.g., Derlega, Hendrick, Winstead, & Berg, 1991; Orlinsky & Howard, 1987). Certainly, these goals are accomplished in large part through the expert interventions of therapists functioning to mobilize and enhance the resources that patients bring to therapy—but this must occur through the establishment and maintenance of a vital *personal* connection between the individuals involved. We do not deny the significant impact of specific therapeutic procedures (cf. Orlinsky, Rønnestad, & Willutzki, 2004). However, the weight of scientific evidence[3] favors viewing therapy as a professional relationship in which the quality

---

[2] This brings to mind the concluding lines of W. B. Yeats's (1952) famous poem, "Among School Children": "O body swayed to music, O brightening glance, How can we know the dancer from the dance?" (p. 214).
[3] Although research evidence indicates that a patient's clinical outcome depends most directly on what the patient brings to, and experiences in, therapy, it is also clear that what a patient experiences in therapy depends largely on the characteristics and quality of the therapist's participation (Orlinsky, Grawe, & Parks, 1994; Orlinsky, Rønnestad, & Willutzki, 2004). Comparative outcome research and process–outcome research on psychotherapy have shown that the personal connection experienced by patients with their therapists consistently has a vital influence on the benefit that patients receive. Several lines of evidence lead to this conclusion. First, differences among treatment groups in controlled clinical trials typically are neither great nor consistent, generally showing a tendency to favor the treatment to which the researchers conducting the study are committed (Elliott, Greenberg, & Lietaer, 2004, p. 509; Luborsky et al., 1999). Furthermore, variations in outcome among patients in such studies is often as great or greater *within* each particular treatment group than it is *among* different treatment conditions (e.g., Howard, Krause, & Vessey, 1994; Wampold, 2001). Third, the design of comparative clinical trials calls for the random assignment of patients to treatments but rarely, if ever, for the random assignment of therapists to treatments, with the inevitable but typically overlooked consequence that comparisons of treatment groups do not really compare treatment groups as such but Treatment × Therapist interactions (Elkin, 1999). Last, these findings converge strongly with the results of a half-century of process–outcome research (in its earlier Rogerian phase of studying warmth and empathy and its more recent embodiment in studying the therapeutic alliance) that massively documents the importance of the patient's experience of the therapeutic relationship—a finding that is highly robust in the sense that it is consistent across many studies and with frequently large effect sizes (see Orlinsky, Grawe, et al., 1994; Orlinsky, Rønnestad, & Willutzki, 2004). The criteria of wisdom studied by Baltes and Smith (1994) also suggest the importance of personal and professional characteristics of psychotherapists as distinct from the methods or techniques that define particular types of treatment. Congruent with this conception, we think that virtually all psychotherapists, when effective, do the following for their patients, in various measures according to the varying needs of their patients (Stiles, 1988): They listen facilitatively, that is, attentively and respectfully (although not always with respect for patients' self-imposed and self-defeating limitations); they provide support, helping to calm, comfort, and console; they help solve patients' problems by reframing those problems, by proposing effective problem-solving strategies, or by exploring possible alternative solutions; and they offer counsel, providing information, instruction, or advice. That is also what most patients hope to find in a psychotherapist: someone well equipped and ready to listen well, provide needed support, help solve problems, and counsel wisely. Patients may also find in therapists a model of maturity whose internalization strengthens them (e.g., Orlinsky & Geller, 1993).

of personal relatedness between patient and therapist as individuals is a key factor in strengthening (or limiting) the impact of therapeutic procedures. According to this view, research on the abilities and experiences of psychotherapists should be seen as a relevant and valuable complement to those areas of research that focus on therapeutic processes and outcomes, and the lives and problems of patients.

AIMS OF THE PRESENT STUDY

The study we describe in this book focuses broadly on the formative experiences, practices, and development of psychotherapists at all career levels. It was initiated in 1989 as a cooperative enterprise by the Society for Psychotherapy Research's (SPR) Collaborative Research Network (CRN), and it includes a large number of therapists from different countries, different professional backgrounds, and different theoretical orientations. Its long-term goals initially centered on four general questions:

1. To what extent, and in what respects, do professional psychotherapists develop over the course of their careers?
2. What professional and personal circumstances and factors influence, positively or negatively, the development of psychotherapists?
3. How does the development of psychotherapists, in turn, influence their therapeutic work and personal and professional lives?
4. To what extent are patterns of therapeutic work and professional development, and the factors that influence them, broadly similar for all therapists, and to what extent do they differ by profession, theoretical persuasion, nationality, or other characteristics (e.g., gender)?

Each of the foregoing questions gives rise to a series of more specific questions,[4] but an even broader set of questions emerged as our study got

---

[4]First, how much do therapists develop, when viewed from various perspectives? Does development appear to be unidimensional, or does it occur along several dimensions? Does therapeutic development appear to be a continuous process, or can critical turning points and sequential stages be discerned? What is the range of individual differences in development? Do therapists develop at significantly different rates, and along diverse paths, or is there a broadly common course of development in terms of which therapists may be described? Is therapeutic development basically the same at all times, or do therapists at different points in their careers develop in different ways or at different rates? Second, what factors do therapists themselves view as facilitating or impeding their development? Among the correlates of therapeutic development, how much do the traditional elements of therapeutic training—academic coursework, case supervision, and personal psychotherapy—contribute to development? How much does the therapist's personal life influence professional development? Are there types of work environments that stimulate development or provoke deterioration? Do the amount and type of therapeutic work that therapists do affect the rate

underway. Who actually practices psychotherapy in different countries? What training do they receive? Where, when, with whom, and how much do they practice? What treatment modalities do they use in practice? We quickly had to recognize that very little systematic data are available regarding the basic characteristics of psychotherapists practicing in different countries. Thus, we undertook to ask those questions, and others as well. For example, how do therapists view their work with patients? What treatment goals do therapists typically seek to attain with patients? What types of skill do therapists use, what types of difficulty do they encounter, and how do they cope with those difficulties? What satisfactions and stresses do therapists experience in their work, and how do these affect them personally? Indeed, what are therapists like as people? How well or poorly do they get along in their own personal lives? Many practitioners have written interestingly and insightfully on these questions based on their individual experiences, but so far relatively little solid knowledge has been generated by systematic research.

Gathering such basic knowledge about psychotherapists can have value in many fields other than the group of disciplines that are collectively referred to as *mental health professions*. Those would include the comparative and historical sociology of professions (e.g., Abbott, 1988; Kurzweil, 1989; Macdonald, 1995; Parsons, 1964; Turkle, 1978), the study of professional education and training (e.g., Gartner, 1976; Green, Grosswald, Suter, & Walthall, 1984; Houle, 1980; Hughes, Thorne, DeBaggis, Gurin, & Williams, 1973), the economics of mental health manpower (e.g., Albee, 1959; Bonacci, 2000), and the study of adult socialization and personality (e.g., Becker & Strauss, 1956; Henry, 1954; Light, 1980; Lowenthal, Thurnher, & Chiriboga, 1975; Roe, 1954; Smelser & Erikson, 1980; White, 1975). Closer to home, we believe that better knowledge about psychotherapists per se is essential for researchers who seek to understand the nature of therapists' influence on therapeutic process and outcome (e.g., Beutler, Machado, & Neufeldt, 1994; Beutler et al., 2004; Crits-Christoph et al., 1991). Our study aimed to extend and deepen the findings of previous studies about psychotherapists, which we review only briefly here.

---

or extent or direction of their professional development? Do these influences on development differ at different stages of the therapist's career? Third, do patterns of development differ by profession, theoretical orientation, and nationality, or is development generally the same for therapists in different countries, orientations, and professions? Do psychoanalysts in Germany, France, and other countries differ significantly, as Kurzweil (1989) suggested? Do American therapists trained in psychology resemble their counterparts in Germany, Portugal, Switzerland, and other countries? Within each country, how much do medically and psychologically trained therapists resemble each other, or their less frequently studied colleagues trained in social work, counseling, nursing, or the ministry? To what extent do historic lines of division among therapeutic guilds and schools and national cultures exert a formative impact on the development of psychotherapists? Alternatively, are any signs to be found that a new international profession has begun to emerge, as forecast 30 years ago (e.g., Henry et al., 1971; Holt, 1971)?

PREVIOUS STUDIES

Despite its intermittent nature, the study of psychotherapists' characteristics, training, and performance is nearly as old as research on psychotherapy in general (e.g., Fiedler, 1950; Holt & Luborsky, 1958; Kelley & Fiske, 1951; Strupp, 1955a, 1955b; see also Orlinsky & Russell, 1994), yet the study of psychotherapists seems to slip from view again and again, as implicitly recognized by the journal *Clinical Psychology Science and Practice*, which recently devoted a special section to "The Therapist as a Neglected Variable in Psychotherapy Research" ("Therapist," 1997).

After the 1950s, one finds only a few major studies (e.g., Henry et al., 1971, 1973; Rønnestad & Skovholt, 2003; Skovholt & Rønnestad, 1995), one landmark anthology (Gurman & Razin, 1977), periodic reviews of research on therapist effects in treatment (Beutler, Crago, & Azrimendi, 1986; Beutler et al., 1994; Beutler et al., 2004; Parloff, Waskow, & Wolfe, 1986), and reviews of research on therapist training (Matarazzo, 1971, 1978; Matarazzo & Patterson, 1986), along with a number of interesting qualitative accounts (e.g., Dryden & Spurling, 1989; Guy, 1987; Kottler, 1993).

With some notable exceptions (e.g., Crits-Christoph et al., 1991; Davis, Elliott, et al., 1987; Dent & Furse, 1978; Dlugos & Friedlander, 2001; Geller, Lehman, & Farber, 2002; Gerin & Vignat, 1984; Henry et al., 1971, 1973; Norcross & Guy, 1989; Orlinsky & Howard, 1975, 1977; Prochaska & Norcross, 1983a; Skovholt & Rønnestad, 1995), most research involving psychotherapists has dealt with specific practical concerns rather than the essential characteristics and development of the psychotherapist.

There is, for example, a substantial literature on therapist burnout and stress (e.g., Brady, Guy, Poelstra, & Brokaw, 1999; Deutsch, 1984, 1985; Farber, 1983; Farber & Heifetz, 1981; Guy & Liaboe, 1986; Guy, Poelstra, & Stark, 1989; Holmqvist & Andersen, 2003; Kramen-Kahn & Hansen, 1998; Maslach & Leiter, 1997; Maslach, Schaufeli, & Leiter, 2000; Menninger, 1991; Murtagh & Wollersheim, 1997; Norcross, Geller, & Kurzawa, 2001; Norcross & Prochaska, 1986a, 1986b; Norcross, Prochaska, & DiClemente, 1986; Pines & Maslach, 1978; Raquepaw & Miller, 1989; van der Ploeg, van Leeuwen, & Kwee, 1990). Another specialized area is the study of therapists' personal psychotherapy (e.g., Deutsch, 1985; Geller, Norcross, & Orlinsky, 2005; Guy, Stark, & Poelstra, 1988; MacDevitt, 1987; McNamara, 1986; Macran, Stiles, & Smith, 1999; Norcross, Strausser, & Faltus, 1988; Norcross, Strausser-Kirtland, & Missar, 1988; Pope & Tabachnick, 1994).

Other studies have focused on important practical issues, such as therapists' ethical standards and conduct (e.g., Borys & Pope, 1989; Pope, Keith-Spiegel, & Tabachnick, 1986; Pope & Tabachnick, 1994; Pope, Tabachnick, & Keith-Spiegel, 1987, 1988; Pope & Vetter, 1991); the distribution of health care personnel and services (e.g., Knesper, Wheeler, & Pagnucco, 1984; West et al., 2001); and the selection, training, and supervision of student therapists (e.g., Bernard & Goodyear, 2004; Crits-Christoph et al., 1998; Gurman & Razin, 1977; Holt & Luborsky, 1958; Kivlighan, Schuetz, & Kardash, 1998; Ladany, Hill, Corbett, & Nutt, 1996; Light, 1980; Matarazzo, 1971, 1978; Matarazzo & Patterson, 1986; Norcross & Prochaska, 1982; Rønnestad & Orlinsky, 2000; Rønnestad, Orlinsky, Parks, & Davis, 1997; Rønnestad & Skovholt, 1993; Stoltenberg & Delworth, 1987).

Of somewhat more general interest are studies of the effects of training and professional experience (e.g., Anthony, 1967; Auerbach & Johnson, 1977; Berman & Norton, 1985; Botermans, 1996; Hill, Charles, & Reed, 1981; Kopta, Newman, McGovern, & Angle, 1989; Mallinckrodt & Nelson, 1991; Nerdrum & Rønnestad, 2002, 2003; Tracey, Hays, Malone, & Herman, 1988; Tyler & Clark, 1987; Watkins, Lopez, Campbell, & Himmell, 1986) and of variations in therapists' theoretical orientations (e.g., Ambühl & Orlinsky, 1995, 1999; Arthur, 2000; Elliott, Orlinsky, Klein, Amer, & Partyka, 2004; Guest & Beutler, 1988; Hill & O'Grady, 1985; Jensen & Bergin, 1988; Jensen, Bergin, & Greaves 1990; Keinan, Almagor, & Ben-Porath, 1989; Kopta, Newman, McGovern, & Sandrock, 1986; Lehman & Salovey, 1990; Mahoney & Craine, 1991; McGovern, Newman, & Kopta, 1986; Norcross & Prochaska, 1983, 1988; Norcross & Wogan, 1982, 1983, 1987; Prochaska & Norcross, 1983a; Sundland, 1977; Vasco & Dryden, 1997). However, most of these studies are limited by the fact that they were conducted only in the United States, had only psychologists as subjects, or focused mainly on psychotherapy trainees rather than experienced practitioners.

ORGANIZATION OF THIS BOOK

This book draws on part of the data collected by the SPR CRN thus far to focus on psychotherapists' experiences of their therapeutic work, their professional development, and the interrelations among them.[5] The book is divided into four sections.

In Part I, we introduce the aims and background of the study (chap. 1); describe the methodology of the study, including the Development of Psychotherapists Common Core Questionnaire (DPCCQ), which is its main

---

[5] Other aspects of the data have been reported elsewhere (e.g., Orlinsky, Norcross, Rønnestad, & Wiseman, 2005; Orlinsky & Rønnestad, 2003; Orlinsky, Rønnestad, Willutzki, Wiseman, & Botermans, 2005; Rønnestad et al., 1997; Schröder & Orlinsky, 2003; Smith & Orlinsky, 2004; Wiseman & Orlinsky, 2003), and still more data are being collected and analyzed for future presentation. Among those are volumes on the diverse theoretical orientations and approaches of therapists and one on the personal and spiritual lives of psychotherapists.

instrument (chap. 2); and summarize the professional, demographic, and practice characteristics of the therapists who provided the data that we analyzed (chap. 3). Two appendixes support the chapters of Part I: Appendix A, a personal narrative of the origins of the SPR CRN and its project, and Appendix B, which comprises statistical cross-tabulations of sample characteristics as a context for the interpretation of research findings.

In the chapters in Part II we present our analyses of therapists' experiences of psychotherapeutic work. First, the varied aspects of therapeutic work surveyed by the DPCCQ are analyzed separately to provide a detailed account of therapists' experiences (chap. 4). Next, building on these detailed analyses, we explore the broader dimensions and determinants of therapeutic work experience (chap. 5). Finally, we use therapists' individual profiles on those broad dimensions to generate an empirical typology of therapeutic work practice patterns, and we explore the distribution of those patterns in terms of the therapists' characteristics (chap. 6). These chapters are supported by detailed statistical analyses that will be primarily of interest to other researchers (Appendix C).

The nature of psychotherapeutic work is a natural starting point for our exploration of psychotherapists' development. From the psychotherapist's perspective, therapeutic work is a skilled service performed as gainful employment, an activity through which one earns one's living. However, it is clear that for most therapists, doing therapy is not only a job but also a calling, or vocation, a worthy profession that is chosen at least in part to provide a sense of meaningful activity and personal fulfillment. Parks (1996, p. 12), summarizing various writers, noted:

> Accounts by psychotherapists of their professional [work] suggest that the feelings they experience while practicing therapy are very important in motivating their therapeutic work and that, generally, therapists enjoy working with patients and derive a deep sense of personal satisfaction from doing therapy (Dryden & Spurling, 1989; Guy, 1987). That these feelings are intrinsically satisfying, and not a reward on a par with money or professional prestige, is evident from the terms that therapists use. Working with patients is described as "interesting" and "fascinating" (Bloomfield, 1989), "nourishing" (Thorne, 1989), "meaningful" and "stimulating" (Heppner, 1989), "exciting" (Fransella, 1989), and "sustaining" (Street, 1989). Some consider it a "privilege" (Mahoney, 1989) or a "creative art" (Burton, 1972a), while others liken it to a "religious," "generative," or "magical" experience (Thorne, 1989; Heppner, 1989; Chaplin, 1989). It clearly represents a part of life which has serious personal meaning and value and which therapists would be most reluctant to give up (Fransella, 1989).

Therapeutic work is not only the core of the therapist's professional experience but also the vital point of contact between patients and therapists, the field of action on which patients thrive, or fail to thrive, in their search for help. Understanding the various ways in which therapists experience their work with patients should provide an essential perspective on the therapeutic process, to be compared and synthesized ultimately with the patients' perspective (e.g., Orlinsky & Geller, 1993; Orlinsky, Geller, Tarragona, & Farber, 1993; Orlinsky & Howard, 1975) and with the external perspective of researchers who view therapeutic processes from the outside looking in.

The chapters in Part III are devoted to the psychotherapists' experience of professional development, which is the central concern of the CRN study. First, we translate the concept of development into four empirical–methodological perspectives, focused respectively on currently experienced development, overall career development, cross-sectional comparisons of therapist cohorts at different career levels, and longitudinal studies of therapists over extended periods of time (chap. 7). The first three of these are examined in successive chapters: currently experienced growth and depletion and their correlates (chap. 8); cumulative career development and its sources (chap. 9); and career-level cohorts in which we compare six groups of therapists, ranging from inexperienced novices to exceptionally experienced seniors (chap. 10). These chapters also demonstrate the close reciprocal relationship between therapeutic work and professional development.

We know from the history of this project (recounted in Appendix A) that "development" as a concept is highly valued and evidently very meaningful to all sorts of psychotherapists. We know this, first, from the informal discussions in 1989 that led to the formation of the CRN at the European SPR conference in Bern, Switzerland, in which we were joined by a surprising number of colleagues interested in the topic. We know this, too, from the large number of psychotherapists with research interests, encountered in many countries, who subsequently joined the CRN to translate our new research instrument into their languages and collect data for the project, freely contributing their own time, materials, and labor. We know this, finally, from the fact that several thousand psychotherapists found it meaningful to give an hour or two of their time to participate in our study. And indeed, subsequent systematic analyses of our data confirm these informal observations of the great significance attributed to development by psychotherapists (chap. 7). Detailed statistical analyses reported in Appendix D support these chapters.

In Part IV, we conclude the book with a theoretical integration of the findings that provides a detailed conceptual model of psychotherapeutic development (chap. 11) and a series of recommendations to students and teachers, supervisors, and practitioners of psychotherapy based on our empirical findings and their conceptual integration (chap. 12). To support the practical implementation of these recommendations, we present two very brief instruments based on the DPCCQ that can be used by students, supervisors, and practitioners to assess therapeutic work (Appendix E) and professional development (Appendix F). Finally, the book concludes with a brief description of continuing research in the CRN project and the formulation of a key hypothesis about the relation of the psychotherapist's perspective on therapy to other perspectives—those of patients, supervisors, and external observers—which we expect to constitute a major focus of future studies (chap. 13).

However, to start at the beginning, we turn next to a description of the research instrument and procedures with which our data were gathered and analyzed, and of the many therapists who shared their experiences with us.

2

STUDY METHODS

DAVID E. ORLINSKY, MICHAEL HELGE RØNNESTAD, PAUL GERIN,
JOHN D. DAVIS, HANSRUEDI AMBÜHL, ULRIKE WILLUTZKI,
MARCIA L. DAVIS, ALICE DAZORD, CHRISTINE DAVIDSON,
NICOLETTA AAPRO, JEAN-FRANÇOIS BOTERMANS,
THOMAS A. SCHRÖDER, AND HADAS WISEMAN

In this chapter we present the methods we used to gather and analyze the data of our collaborative, international study of the development of psychotherapists. Details of these procedures need to be known, particularly by our research colleagues, if the strengths and limitations of our study are to be correctly understood. Thus, we describe here the instrument we designed to present to psychotherapists, the procedures we followed in collecting data with it, and the methods we followed in conducting the data analyses presented in chapters 4 through 10.

THE DEVELOPMENT OF PSYCHOTHERAPISTS
COMMON CORE QUESTIONNAIRE

Although data about psychotherapists and their development can be obtained from various perspectives, it seemed most logical and most practical to start with the psychotherapist's own perspective. Therapeutic work involves therapists not only as participant–observers of their clients' personal

15

struggles to develop but also as reflectively observing participants in their own professional growth (Skovholt & Rønnestad, 1995). Indeed, judging from their own extensive use of personal therapy (e.g., Geller, Norcross, & Orlinsky, 2005; Norcross, Strausser-Kirtland, & Missar, 1988; Pope & Tabachnick, 1994; Prochaska & Norcross, 1983b), therapists may well be the foremost modern practitioners of the Delphic oracle's injunction to "Know thyself." Observations and ratings of therapists from the external perspectives of supervisors, colleagues, or patients might well show therapists in a different light and are methodologically clearly of great importance. On the other hand, it would be difficult to imagine, and hard to justify, a large-scale study of psychotherapists that did not include the therapists' own perspective as a primary point of reference.

There are also good practical reasons to begin a study of psychotherapists' development with analyses of data collected from the psychotherapists' perspective. In the first chapter of Part III, we outline four empirical frameworks for collecting data about development, two of which depend directly on the therapist's perspective: therapists' retrospective views of their careers to date and therapists' contemporaneous views of their own current development. The other two frameworks—longitudinal and cross-sectional—can also make use of data collected from therapists' reports, or from the reports of "external" observers. It would, of course, have been meaningful and possible to collect direct first-person reports by interviewing therapists, as Skovholt and Rønnestad did in their Minnesota Study of Counselor and Therapist Development (Rønnestad & Skovholt, 1991; Skovholt & Rønnestad, 1992)—but, unlike their project, which was designed as an intensive qualitative study, the Collaborative Research Network (CRN) study was constructed as an extensive quantitative survey (Orlinsky, Ambühl, Rønnestad, et al., 1999). With limited resources of time and very limited funding, the use of self-report questionnaires promised a greater return.

Given persuasive reasons for starting in this way, a team consisting of clinician–researchers from different countries, professions, and theoretical orientations worked to formulate a set of self-administered questionnaires that would enable therapists to describe themselves professionally and personally in some detail and would include information directly assessing and indirectly reflecting their professional development as well as the experiences that might have facilitated or hindered that development.

At various times, the team of collaborators who constructed the questionnaire included (in alphabetical order): Nicoletta Aapro, of Geneva, Switzerland; Hansruedi Ambühl, of Bern, Switzerland; Wouter Backx, of The Hague, the Netherlands; Jean-François Botermans, of Brussels, Belgium; Christine Davidson, of Chicago; John Davis and Marcia Davis, of Warwick, England; Alice Dazord, Paul Gerin, and Jean-François Iahns, of Lyon, France; David Orlinsky, of Chicago; Thomas Schröder, of Derby, England;

and Ulrike Willutzki, of Bochum, Germany. The professions represented by this group included medicine, psychology, and social work. The theoretical orientations included were behavioral, cognitive, experiential, interpersonal, psychoanalytic, systemic, and integrative.

The work of designing a suitable questionnaire extended for more than 18 months during 1990 and 1991, mainly during in-person meetings at international and regional Society for Psychotherapy Research conferences in England, France, Switzerland, and the United States, supplemented (in those days before e-mail) by faxed correspondence. The process effectively consisted of a focus group that met recurrently over an extended duration. At these meetings, the group worked together for long hours, then cooked together, dined together, and went back to work. The creativity and conviviality of these initial meetings remain a prized and vivid memory.

Basic concepts of development and how to measure it were freely debated until a consensus of views was achieved. The range and depth of information about therapists and their practices that was needed to properly understand the evidence on development and its sources was intensively discussed and continually reviewed. A constant effort was made to ensure that the questions we asked of therapists actually fit the experiences that we ourselves had as therapists, so that they would seem to grow from a collegial rapport between us and the therapists whose experiences we sought to know. At the same time, an effort was made to conceptualize each of the facets of experience surveyed to ensure systematic coverage of the subject matter. These organizing concepts are introduced in chapter 4 for aspects of therapeutic work experience and in chapter 6 for the spheres of professional development.

The final result of our 18-month joint effort was a research instrument (or, more precisely, a package of instruments) that was called the *Development of Psychotherapists Common Core Questionnaire* (DPCCQ). The final version agreed on in 1991 was used for most of that decade, with a few modifications based on initial psychometric analyses made for data collections in 1998 and after. Unless otherwise indicated, the findings reported in this book are based on items from the 1991 version that have been retained in later variants.[1]

Content

The various sections of the DPCCQ include a total of 392 items. Most of the items were designed as structured-response scales or checklists, for

---

[1] Readers can obtain a sample copy of the DPCCQ in English or several other languages by writing to David Orlinsky, University of Chicago, 5555 South Everett Avenue, Chicago, IL 60637, or by e-mail at d-orlinsky@uchicago.edu.

standardization and ease of response, but a number of open-ended questions were also included. The sections were made into a booklet that we did our best to ensure would be experienced by respondents as the written equivalent of an interview among colleagues. Specific items will be introduced as they are used in the successive chapters of this book; however, to orient readers to the range and types of information to be used, we present here an overview of the DPCCQ's organization and content.

The first section of the DPCCQ (5 items) requests information to identify the respondent without revealing his or her actual identity: a personal code devised by respondents from the letters of their father's first and mother's maiden names, date of birth, gender, and date on which the DPCCQ was answered.

The second section (23 items) explores psychotherapists' professional identification, qualifications, and organizational affiliations; amount and type of academic preparation; past and current supervision; and training in specific therapeutic methods.

The third section (21 items) gathers information about the duration and types of clinical experience the therapist has had in different settings, with varied patient groups, using different treatment modalities (e.g., individual, couple, family, group), as well as experience treating and supervising other therapists.

Section 4 (51 items) solicits therapists' retrospective estimates of their overall career development, including both direct ratings and indirect measures based on estimates of initial and current skill levels. It also asks about therapists' initial theoretical orientation and the experiences that positively and negatively influenced their development.

The fifth section (23 items) asks therapists about their attitude toward and experiences in their own personal therapy. Space is provided for therapists to report on the type, intensity, and duration of up to four separate courses of therapy, as well as the reasons for undertaking each treatment and a rating of its personal value or outcome.

Section 6 (52 items) explores therapists' current theoretical orientation, including the extent to which they used varied theoretical frameworks to guide their practice, their typical treatment goals, and their ideal manner of relating to patients.

Section 7 (36 items) focuses on therapists' sense of their current professional development, the experiences that are having a positive or negative influence on their development, and their feelings during recent therapy sessions with patients.

The eighth section (43 items) gathers information about therapists' current practice: the type and number of settings where they do therapeutic work (inpatient and outpatient, institutional and private practice); the number and types of patients they see (by age, diagnosis, and severity of disturbance); the number of cases they currently have in each of several treatment modalities; and the extent of professional autonomy, support, and satisfaction they experience in their main work setting.

Section 9 (96 items) assesses the frequency with which therapists currently experience various types of difficulty when working with patients and the frequency with which they use each of various coping strategies when they encounter difficulties. This section also surveys the therapists' flexibility or strictness in managing the boundaries of the treatment situation, their interpersonal style or manner in relating to patients, and several open-ended questions about their salient strengths and limitations as therapists.

The tenth section (42 items) asks therapists about their personal characteristics: their marital, minority, and immigration status (supplementing data on age, sex, and country of residence noted in Section 1); their general levels of life satisfaction and stress, along with specific aspects of emotional well-being; their interpersonal style or manner in close personal relationships (personal self-concept); and the extent to which their development as therapists has been influenced by their motivation to explore and resolve their own personal problems.

Finally, to accommodate therapists who prefer to give a narrative account rather than simply respond to structured-response questions, the DPCCQ ended with an optional item asking therapists to "describe the main factors that have led you to become the therapist you are at present" and to address any other issues they consider important in their work and development as psychotherapists that had not been adequately covered in the preceding pages.

The length of the DPCCQ was dictated partly by the complexity of the subject matter itself and partly by a need to collect extensive descriptive information about therapists in different countries. Because of its length, the DPCCQ generally requires an hour or two of the therapist's time and thus may deter some potential respondents. However, it also affords some advantages that briefer, single-issue questionnaires do not, the chief among these being that those who do complete and return the DPCCQ can be viewed as seriously motivated respondents. Another major advantage is that, although each item represents a bit of information in its own right, it can also be analyzed in conjunction with a great deal of other information about the respondent. Thus, the data can be viewed in depth (i.e., in a variety of related contexts) and can be understood in terms of broader patterns in a manner analogous to clinical inference. It is possible to read through the responses of a single (anonymous) individual and gain a clear sense of the person who gave them, demonstrating the instrument's strength with regard to *reconstructivity*—defined as the capacity to generate "a clinically meaningful gestalt from distinct bits of coded information" (Pinsof, 1986, p. 220).

Translations

The DPCCQ was composed originally in English (by a multilingual group of American, Belgian, Dutch, English, French, German, Italian, and Swiss researchers), with care taken to use terms and phrases that would translate well into other languages. The questionnaire has been translated into Arabic, Chinese, Danish, Dutch, Finnish, French, German, Greek, Hebrew, Hungarian, Italian, Japanese, Korean, Malay, Norwegian, Polish, Portuguese, Russian, Spanish, and Swedish, in addition to separate English versions following North American and British usage. To ensure the greatest comparability in meaning among different versions of the questionnaire, each translation was submitted for evaluation to two independent bilingual colleagues before being used in data collection. Each judge rated each question and set of instructions on 4-point scales for exactness of translation and for correctness of expression (1 = *excellent*, 2 = *good*, 3 = *marginal*, 4 = *poor*). Translations were accepted when the both judges rated each item and instruction *good* or *excellent* in both respects. Items and instructions that were not approved were revised until these criteria were met. Translations of single-term adjective scales (e.g., "accepting," "warm") were further checked by having them independently translated back to English.

DATA COLLECTION: FINDING AND QUESTIONING PSYCHOTHERAPISTS

The systematic collection of data on therapists requires a satisfactory answer to the question "Who is and who is not a psychotherapist?" Unfortunately, the population of psychotherapists at large is difficult to define precisely, even within a single country, and is all the more difficult to define in an international context. Although there are many professional psychotherapists, there is no single profession of psychotherapy whose members, even within a single country, belong to one national organization or professional society. Instead, psychotherapy is typically practiced by some but not all members of several different professions, and the organizations that represent them are varied and often conflict over matters of professional jurisdiction and economic advantage (Abbott, 1988). Within these professions, members often also divide into rival theoretical camps, making the situation even more complex. Besides, there are informal channels through which persons of talent sometimes succeed in becoming established as psychotherapists without conventional professional training. In an international study, one must also take account of local differences regarding which professions are allowed to practice, which orientations are popular, and which types of therapy are supported by national or private health insurance.

DATA COLLECTION STRATEGIES: GENERALITY VERSUS GENERALIZABILITY

Representative sampling poses insoluble problems when the parent population cannot be clearly defined, especially when it is unclear whether one or several populations must be considered. Given this situation, two alternative data collection strategies seemed possible for the present study. One involved asking colleagues in each of several countries to collect data from a broad range of persons who are locally accepted as therapists, counselors, or similar practitioners. The aim of this strategy is to gather a heterogeneous database whose size and internal diversity permits disaggregation into meaningful subgroups. In this case, the question of *generalizability* from the sample to its parent population would remain moot, but the *generality* of findings across diverse professional and demographic groups of therapists could be assessed. Collection of detailed descriptive data regarding the therapists in the study would allow for a tentative generalization, or *transferability*, of findings to other therapists with similar professional and demographic characteristics (Lincoln & Guba, 1985).

The second alternative involved seeking representative samples from various psychotherapy associations (e.g., associations advocating specific theoretical orientations) and from regional or national professional associations in which many members are known to engage in therapy, counseling, or cognate practices. In this case, although the samples might be more surely *generalizable* to members of the specific groups from which they were drawn, the results of each would have unknown *generality*, in the sense that they might not apply beyond the specific groups that were studied. Thus, findings based on a representative sample of psychologists could not be assumed to apply to psychiatrists or social workers or counselors. Similarly, findings based on a representative sample of psychodynamic therapists could not be assumed to apply to cognitive–behavioral, systemic, or humanistic psychotherapists.

Because each approach had its strengths and limitations, we decided that the best solution for our discovery-oriented study was to pursue a mixed model of data collection using various strategies as circumstances allowed. One strategy involved solicitation of attendees at professional workshops and conferences (e.g., the annual "Lindau Psychotherapy Weeks" in Germany). A second involved cooperation with professional societies to survey their members either through random sampling (e.g., American Psychological

Association Division 29, Psychotherapy) or, if the membership were small, through requesting all to participate (e.g., the American Academy of Psychotherapists). A third approach involved collaboration with training programs in which the availability of faculty, supervisors, and graduates as well as current trainees ensured the inclusion of a wide range in therapist experience levels. A fourth procedure depended on individual collegial networks and involved having CRN members ask therapists they knew personally to complete the questionnaire and to request their colleagues to do the same. A fifth method of data collection involved contacting individuals who listed themselves in classified telephone directories as providers of counseling or therapy services to the public. The resulting sample of therapists in our study (described in chap. 3) is, in effect, an aggregate database containing information collected by all of these methods. Of course, the method by which each batch of data was collected was recorded so that their possible impact on the findings could subsequently be assessed.

The responsiveness of psychotherapists to these varied approaches is indicated by the large number who completed and returned an obviously lengthy questionnaire, without compensation for their time and sometimes even for the cost of postage. Various data collections have been made in different countries since 1991, and new ones continue to be made as opportunities arise and as new colleagues become interested in joining the project. The data collected by these means have been aggregated in successive stages to make a single, continually expanding database for use by the CRN team as a group in pursuit of the study's main aims and by individual CRN members in return for their contributions to the project.

Several types of research questions can be validly pursued with a large and varied database, even when sample-to-population generalizability is unknown. Strong hypotheses of the form "All or most therapists have Characteristic X" or "Few if any therapists show Quality Y" can be falsified by demonstrating that only moderate numbers of therapists have Characteristic X or that a fairly large number show Quality Y. Findings that a very high proportion of therapists share certain characteristics despite marked differences in other respects can also be made. The size and heterogeneity of the CRN database also make it possible to conduct certain types of data analyses with strong internal validity (through controlled comparisons using multiple covariates with adequate statistical power, or through replication across internally defined subgroups) and with partial external validity (emphasizing generality as well as generalizability). Questions of generalizability also can be addressed indirectly in several ways: by detailed descriptions of therapists' professional and demographic characteristics, so that findings may be tentatively generalized to other therapists with similar characteristics; by comparing the characteristics of therapists in the CRN database with published reports of therapist samples in other studies; and by supplementing the current database with random samples of members from specific therapeutic organizations.

INDUCTIVE STEPS AND LEVELS
OF CONCEPTUAL GENERALITY

Each section of the DPCCQ contains a series of items that are of interest in their own right, as direct reflections of the therapists' perceptions and judgments, and that are also capable of yielding information reflecting deeper processes of which therapists are likely to be unaware. Our step-by-step approach to data analysis, done with SPSS software, was designed to systematically explore these different levels of conceptual generality.

At the first and most basic level, the responses that therapists made to the specific questions posed in the DPCCQ are tabulated using standard measures of central tendency, variability, and percentages of endorsement. This level of analysis most directly reflects the therapists' consciously reported experiences.

The next step in our analytic procedure used factor analysis to define the psychologically meaningful dimensions underlying the specific responses given by therapists to the items *within* each of the distinguishable facets of work experience and professional development. Item responses within each facet were intercorrelated, and then factors were extracted from the correlation matrix by principal-components analysis. The resulting factors were rotated by the varimax method, with the number of factors to be rotated set by the conventional criterion (eigenvalue ≥ 1). The stability of the factor solution was typically checked by rotating one more and then one fewer factor than indicated by the conventional criterion, but the standard eigenvalue criterion was used unless otherwise noted in reporting a particular analysis. Interpretations of the resulting factor dimensions were based, in the usual way, on the content of items with loadings ≥ 0.35, giving relatively greater conceptual emphasis to those items with the highest or most salient loadings.

Multiple-item scales were then constructed to represent the factorial dimensions by summing and averaging the significant items defining that dimension, after testing for reliability or internal consistency using Cronbach's alpha. In cases where a particular item loaded significantly on more than one factor, it typically was used in scaling the factorial dimension on which it was most highly loaded so long as that exceeded by 0.10 its loadings on other factors. When items loaded significantly on more than one factor but did not meet the differential 0.10 criterion, those items were retained in subsequent analyses as individual item-level scales. On occasion, an item that loaded significantly on a factorial dimension had the effect of lowering the reliability of the dimensional scale as assessed by Cronbach's alpha, and when this happened it was not used in computing the multiple-item dimension (as noted in the relevant data tables).

In this way, scores were constructed for a relatively small number of dimensional scales that effectively summarize the meaning underlying myriad individual questionnaire items. This allowed us to better define the ways in which therapists differed from one another in their responses to each set of related items. Aside from the great economy achieved, these dimensions reflect a level of meaningfulness that is a step beyond the respondents' immediate awareness. Therapists would normally be fully conscious of their intentions as they responded to each specific questionnaire item, but without making a special effort to do so would not be aware of the patterns among the answers that they gave to a long series of questions.

The next step in our data analytic procedure was to examine the broader dimensions that emerge *across* the several facets of work experience and professional development. We did this by intercorrelating and factor analyzing therapists' scores on the facet dimension scales constructed in the preceding step. The factor analytic procedures and criteria described above (extraction by principal-components analysis and rotation of factors with eigenvalues ≥ 1 by the varimax method) were also used in this step. The result was a set of meaningful, higher-level factor dimensions that more concisely reflect the overall patterns underlying the respondents' general experiences of therapeutic work and professional development. On the basis of this level of analysis, new scales were constructed that most broadly reflected the dimensions of meaningful variation in therapists' experiences—empirical measures reflecting patterns that can be viewed as more deeply embedded, and thus further away from, the therapists' immediate awareness and intentions in responding to individual DPCCQ items.

Following this, two further steps could be taken to explore the range and depth of therapists' responses to the questions asked of them, each leading to a higher level of induction. First, types of therapist could be distinguished on the basis of the scores they had on the final set of general factor dimensions by dividing each dimension at a meaningful midpoint such that therapists were either "high" or "low" (or "high," "middle," or "low") on that dimension and then creating a profile across the relevant dimensions. For example, a typology of four distinct patterns of experience would be created by dividing two dimensions each into high and low ranges, with therapists being categorized as high/high, high/low, low/high, or low/low. The number of distinctive patterns to be defined would be determined partly by their conceptual meaningfulness and partly by considerations of their utility in statistical analyses (e.g., the number of therapists in each category) when comparing the different types of psychotherapist that were defined.

The final step of data analysis we report focuses on the correlates and potential determinants of the broad dimensions of therapeutic work experience and professional development. To control for redundancy among the many possible correlates to be explored, we typically have used multiple regression analyses (MRAs) after initially finding the significant linear correlates of each dimension. When employing this procedure in exploratory analyses simply to partial out the shared variance in a set of significant linear correlates, we used stepwise MRAs. When our intention was to determine the effects of a specific variable controlling for other differences among therapists (e.g., professional background or nationality), we used hierarchical MRAs. The relevant procedures are specified in reporting particular analyses.

The general strategy of our study can be described as conceptually organized, systematic exploratory research. It is not a hypothesis-testing study, because theories of therapeutic work experience and professional development have not yet been elaborated to a point from which hypotheses can be logically derived. Instead, our study seeks to answer a number of broader questions on those topics by gathering reliable empirical data from which such theories can eventually be formed. By working inductively and drawing judiciously on our clinical understanding, we aim to offer qualitatively meaningful interpretations for the results of systematic quantitative analyses of a rich body of data on the experiences reported to us by a large number of fellow therapists.

3

THE PSYCHOTHERAPISTS

DAVID E. ORLINSKY, MICHAEL HELGE RØNNESTAD,
NICOLETTA AAPRO, HANSRUEDI AMBÜHL,
ALEJANDRO ÁVILA ESPADA, SUE HYUN BAE, LARRY E. BEUTLER,
JEAN-FRANÇOIS BOTERMANS, PETER BUCHHEIM, ISABEL CARO
GABALDA, MANFRED CIERPKA, JOHN D. DAVIS, MARCIA L. DAVIS,
ALICE DAZORD, SALVATORE FRENI, ERIK FRIIS JØRGENSEN,
ALESSANDRA GABRIELLI, PAUL GERIN, EUNSUN JOO,
HORST KÄCHELE, EKATERINA KALMYKOVA, ANNA VON DER LIPPE,
JAN MEYERBERG, JOHN C. NORCROSS, TERRY NORTHCUT,
BARBARA K. PARKS, MICHAEL ROSANDER, SETH RUBIN,
ELENA SCHERB, THOMAS A. SCHRÖDER, GABY SHEFLER,
MANUEL S. SILVERMAN, DAVID P. SMITH, DAN STIWNE,
SCOTT STUART, MARGARITA TARRAGONA, ANTÓNIO BRANCO
VASCO, ULRIKE WILLUTZKI, AND HADAS WISEMAN

In this chapter, we introduce readers to the varied groups of psychotherapists who participated in our study. In doing this, we have two aims in mind. The first is to provide a context for understanding variations in responses to the questions posed in the Development of Psychotherapists Common Core Questionnaire. Psychotherapists share certain basic characteristics, but they also differ in many ways from one another. A detailed description of our therapists' varied characteristics will help readers appreciate both how much therapists do have in common and what the differences among them really mean.

A second aim served by providing a detailed portrait of a large number of psychotherapists is simple curiosity. Psychotherapists are interesting people. Psychologically troubled and emotionally distressed people seek their help. Society recognizes their profession and licenses its practitioners as experts who are qualified to help disturbed and disturbing individuals. Therapists have become familiar figures as characters in novels, dramas, films, and television. One wants to know what psychotherapists are really like.

This chapter provides an overview of the nearly 5,000 psychotherapists who accepted our invitation to answer the questions set forth in the Development of Psychotherapists Common Core Questionnaire. As we explained in chapter 2, we make no claim that those who participated in our study are representative of all psychotherapists, at all times and places, for the simple reason that a sufficiently clear definition of *psychotherapy* (and, thus, of *psychotherapists*) is impossible to formulate. Those definitions vary across professions and orientations, eras and cultures. However, the samples of therapists available in our study are so large and diverse that we can learn a great deal about those who define themselves and are generally accepted as psychotherapists in their own communities. In the following sections, we provide a general overview of their professional characteristics, the nature of their professional practices, and their demographic and personal characteristics. (For interested colleagues and fellow researchers, in Appendix B we analyze those characteristics differentially by therapists' professions, theoretical orientations, career levels, and countries.)

PROFESSIONAL CHARACTERISTICS

Psychotherapists are generally described in terms of their professional training and identification, their theoretical orientation, and their career level. For example, one might be a relatively inexperienced, psychodynamically oriented psychiatrist; another might be a moderately experienced cognitive–behavioral psychologist; and a third might be a highly experienced systemically oriented social worker.

Professional Background

Although there are many professional psychotherapists, there is as yet no single profession of psychotherapist; instead, some of the members of several different professions acquire varying amounts of additional training in order to practice psychotherapy as a specialty or subspecialty. The medical profession has traditionally been a major source of psychotherapists through the training of specialists in psychiatry (or, in Germany, the field of psychosomatics and psychotherapy)—although currently, in America at least, there is a reduced emphasis on psychotherapy in psychiatric training (Luhrmann, 2000). Additionally, a large number of professional psychotherapists are trained in psychology, and often hold doctoral or comparable university-level degrees, but only some psychologists are clinical or counseling psychologists, and only some of those work as psychotherapists. The professions of social work, nursing, and others also are sources of trained psychotherapists, and in some countries it is still possible for talented individuals to receive training as lay therapists or analysts without having had prior training in one of the usual mental health professions.

The psychotherapists in our sample were asked the following question about their professional background: "What is your professional identity? That is, how do you refer to yourself in professional contexts?" Their answers as summarized in Table 3.1 (row 1): Some 57% identified themselves as psychologists, 28% identified themselves as psychiatrists (or, in Germany, as *psychosomatic physicians*), 6% identified themselves as social workers, 2% identified themselves as counselors, 2% identified themselves as nurses, and 5% identified themselves as lay therapists or as therapists trained in some other field. It is obvious that clinical social workers are seriously underrepresented in our current sample, as are psychiatric nurses and others (e.g., pastoral therapists trained initially in religious ministry) who have not yet been included in the Collaborative Research Network study. Nevertheless, both psychologists and psychiatrists are amply (if perhaps not proportionately) represented, and they are typically among the largest groups of professional therapists in most countries.

Theoretical Orientations

Therapists were also asked to describe their theoretical orientations. This was done by asking them to rate the influence that each of five characteristically different treatment models have on their current practice. Six-point scales (ranging from 0 = *not at all* [influenced] to 5 = *very greatly*) were provided for each of the following orientations: analytic–psychodynamic, behavioral, cognitive, humanistic, systemic, and an optional open-ended scale for respondents to specify an "other" orientation. For the purpose of descriptive analysis, therapists were considered to have a strong, or *salient* orientation if they rated the influence of that orientation on their practice as a 4 or a 5 on the 0–5 scale. Because therapists could rate several orientations as salient, the figures shown in Table 3.1 (row 2) add to more than 100%. In fact, nearly half (46%) of the therapists indicated that their practice was saliently influenced by two or more types of theoretical orientation, reflecting a rather extensive amount of eclecticism.

TABLE 3.1
Therapists' Professional, Personal, and Practice Characteristics

Characteristics		n	%
Professional background	Psychology	2,810	57.3
	Medicine	1,378	28.1
	Social work	280	5.7
	Counseling	97	2.0
	Nursing	91	1.9
	Lay therapist[a]	145	3.0
	Other	107	2.2
Salient theoretical orientation[b]	Analytic–dynamic	2,784	57.6
	Behavioral	688	14.2
	Cognitive	1,154	23.9
	Cognitive–behavioral[c]	593	10.7
	Humanistic	1,507	31.2
	Systemic	1,008	20.9
	Other	580	13.4
	No salient orientation	403	8.4
	2+ salient orientations	2,200	45.5
Years in practice		$M = 11.2$	$SD = 8.9$
Career cohort	Novice (< 1.5 years)	534	11.3
	Apprentice (1.5–< 3.5 years)	549	11.6
	Graduate (3.5–< 7 years)	774	16.4
	Established (7–< 15 years)	1,429	30.2
	Seasoned (15–< 25 years)	1,074	22.7
	Senior (25–53 years)	373	7.9
Gender	Female	2,580	53.0
	Male	2,288	47.0
Age		$M = 42.4$	$SD = 10.6$
Marital status	Single	833	17.9
	Living with partner	777	16.7
	Married	2,608	56.0
	Separated/divorced	395	8.5
	Widowed	44	0.9
Nation	United States	844	17.3
	Germany	1,059	21.7
	Switzerland	263	5.4
	Norway	804	16.5
	Denmark	158	3.2
	Sweden	117	2.4
	Portugal	188	3.8
	Spain	182	3.7
	Belgium	132	2.7
	France	117	2.4
	Russia	110	2.3
	Israel	100	2.0
	South Korea	538	11.0
	Other	272	5.6
Social status	Non-native	423	10.9
	Minority	457	10.5

(continued)

TABLE 3.1   *(Continued)*

Characteristics		*n*	%
Current caseload[d]		*M* = 16.5	*SD* = 14.5
Practice setting	Any inpatient	1,400	28.4
	Any outpatient	2,801	43.1
	Any independent practice	2,165	44.0
	Only independent practice	1,235	25.1
	Works in > 1 setting	2,178	44.2
Treatment modality	Individual	4,250	93.3
	Couple	1,533	34.1
	Family	1,269	27.9
	Group	1,551	34.1
	Other	420	9.2
	Uses only individual therapy	1,380	30.5
	Uses > 1 modality	2,905	63.8
Client age groups (years)	Children (≤ 12)	1,131	25.1
	Adolescents (13–19)	2,058	45.7
	Adults (20–49)	3,927	87.1
	Older adults (50–64)	2,479	55.0
	Seniors (65+)	858	19.0
	Treats > 1 age group	3,366	72.3
Patient impairment levels	Absent or minimal symptoms	901	19.2
	Transient, situational symptoms	1,872	39.9
	Mild but enduring symptoms	2,986	63.5
	Moderate symptoms	3,249	69.1
	Serious symptoms	3,224	68.6
	Significant impairment	2,095	44.6
	Serious impairment	1,265	26.9
	Real danger to self or others	1,000	21.3

Note. N = 4,923. *N*s vary slightly because of omitted questions or missing data.
[a]Includes respondents who described themselves as psychotherapists or psychoanalysts without also listing a core profession. [b]An orientation was considered *salient* if it was rated 4 or 5 on 0–5 scale of influence on therapeutic practice; the total exceeds 100% because multiple ratings were allowed. [c]Subset of therapists who rated both behavioral and cognitive orientations as salient. [d]Total number of cases, summing across treatment modalities.

The type of orientation most commonly rated as salient by the therapists in our sample was analytic–psychodynamic (58%). This was followed by the humanistic (31%), cognitive (24%), systemic (21%), and behavioral (14%) orientations. The fact that 11% of our therapists reported as salient both cognitive and behavioral orientations shows that half of those with salient cognitive orientations were not strongly behavioral, whereas most of those with salient behavioral orientations said they were cognitive–behavioral. A small group of therapists in our sample (8%) reported having no salient orientation (i.e., did not rate any orientation higher than 3 on the 0–5 scale). In contrast to these, another small but interesting group of therapists (5% of the total sample) reported having more than three salient orientations and accordingly were labeled *broad-spectrum* therapists.

Career Levels

The therapists in our sample represent every career level, with experience in therapeutic practice ranging from a few months to more than 50 years. Half of the therapists had practiced therapy for more than 10 years (the median level), with the average or mean just over 11 years (and a standard deviation just under 9 years), as shown in Table 3.1 (row 3). To further explore the distribution of experience levels, we divided the sample into six career cohorts. Empirically based literature on the professional development of psychotherapists is scarce. To define career cohorts, we were guided partly by the related literature on supervision, which focuses predominantly only on the early professional years (Grater, 1985; Hess, 1987; Stoltenberg & Delworth, 1987) and partly our own clinical experience. Our closest model for the definition of cohorts was the conception of two successive student cohorts and four successive postgraduate cohorts used by Skovholt and Rønnestad (1995) in their study of counselor and psychotherapist development.

After examining the distribution of therapists in our own data, we defined the following as psychologically meaningful and statistically viable cohorts: *novices*, who had practiced therapy for less than 1.5 years; *apprentices*, who had 1.5 to less than 3.5 years of experience; *graduates*, including those who had practiced therapy for 3.5 to 7 years (most of whom would have completed their basic professional training); *established* therapists, who had practiced for 7 years to 15 years; *seasoned* therapists (Goldberg, 1992), with 15 to 25 years of experience; and *senior* therapists, who had practiced from 25 to 53 years.

As shown in Table 3.1 (row 4), the largest career cohort in our sample (30%) consisted of established therapists, whose range of 7 to 15 years of experience brackets the average for the entire sample. Novice and apprentice therapists who, with less than 3.5 years of experience, would still be trainees or supervisees in most professions, jointly comprise about one quarter of our sample. At the other extreme, seasoned and senior therapists together made up nearly one third of the sample.

PERSONAL AND DEMOGRAPHIC CHARACTERISTICS

Age and Sex

Our overall sample is fairly evenly divided between men and women (see Table 3.1, row 5), although the percentages vary from country to country and from one profession to another (see Appendix B). The mean age of therapists was about 42 (Table 3.1, row 6); this was also the median (i.e., half the sample was older than 42, and half was younger). Nevertheless, there was a very broad range of ages, from as young as 21 to as old as 90.

When age and sex were combined into categories, we noted that women were somewhat overrepresented in the two youngest groups of therapists (86% for those under age 25, and 56% for those between ages 25 and 35), with proportionately more men among the two oldest groups (65% for those aged 65–75, and 75% for those 75 and older). The association is statistically significant but relatively small, and it probably reflects differences in professional background as much as a possible historical trend, because the two youngest groups include a significant number of American social workers.

Marital Status

Nearly three quarters of the therapists in our sample were either currently married (56%) or living with a partner (17%). Table 3.1 (row 7) shows that fewer than 1 in 5 were single, and fewer than 1 in 10 were separated, divorced, or widowed. However, there are clear differences in marital status between male and female therapists, even when controlling for differences in age. Four fifths (81%) of the men, but only two thirds (66%) of the women, were currently married or living with a partner. Proportionally more women than men were single (21% vs. 14%), and more women than men were separated or divorced (12% vs. 5%). The reasons for this are not clear, but the fact should be borne in mind when interpreting differences among other factors that may be associated with marital status.

Nationality

The therapists in our study live and work in many countries. However, three countries at present account for the largest numbers. Table 3.1 (row 8) shows that between one fourth and one fifth of the sample (22%) live in Germany. About one sixth of the total (17%) live in the United States, and a similar number (17%) are from Norway. These three countries account for slightly over half of the therapists in the present sample. Other substantial groups of therapists are South Korean ($n = 538$), Swiss ($n = 263$), Portuguese ($n = 188$), and Spanish ($n = 182$), with smaller representations from Denmark ($n = 158$), Sweden ($n = 117$), Belgium ($n = 132$), France ($n = 117$), Russia ($n = 110$), and Israel ($n = 100$). In addition, there were groups of fewer than 100 from Argentina, Austria, India, Italy, Mexico, the United Kingdom, and a few eastern European countries. (More recently, substantial data collections have continued in several countries, e.g., Austria, Canada, Greece, New Zealand, and the United Kingdom.)

Social Status

Professional psychotherapists would be viewed by sociologists as having middle-class status by virtue of their education and occupation, although variations in income and lifestyle would undoubtedly place some in the category of upper middle class. Other marks of social standing in a community include minority status and immigrant status, either of which can lead an individual to be seen as an outsider. Table 3.1 (row 9) shows that, overall, about 90% were native born, and 90% said they would not be viewed as members of a social, cultural, or ethnic minority. The overwhelming majority (83%) of therapists in our sample were both native born and majority status members of the countries in which they live. This contrasts markedly with the emphasis on cultural marginality reported by Henry, Sims, and Spray (1971) in their survey of American psychotherapists, suggesting that their findings may have been specific to the country and historical period of their study.

PRACTICE CHARACTERISTICS

A further understanding of the therapists in our sample depends on knowing something about the kinds of professional practice in which they engage.

Caseload

Our therapists vary greatly in the number of treatment cases they carry, with the standard deviation being nearly as large as the mean (see Table 3.1, row 10). When we computed quartiles to get a clearer idea of the distribution, we found that one fourth of the therapists were currently treating between 1 and 5 cases, another fourth had between 6 and 12 cases, another fourth had between 13 and 22 cases, and the last fourth were treating 23 or more cases. (Because couple, family, and group psychotherapies involve multiple patients, these caseload figures somewhat underestimate the number of separate patients whom the therapists were treating.)

Practice Setting

Table 3.1 (row 11) shows that nearly half (44%) of the therapists in our sample practiced therapy in more than one type of setting. About the same percentages treated at least some of their patients in public or private outpatient settings (43%) or in independent private practice (44%), and a substantial fraction of the sample (25%) did therapy exclusively in private practice. Slightly more than one fourth of our therapists (28%) treated any psychotherapy patients in public or private inpatient settings.

Treatment Modalities

Individual psychotherapy of one type or another was by far the most prevalent treatment modality, with more than 9 out of 10 therapists reporting they had at least one individual therapy case (see Table 3.1, row 12). In fact, nearly one third of the therapists were practicing only individual therapy. However, the predominant pattern of practice was to combine individual therapy with one or more other treatment modalities, either group therapy (34%) or couple therapy (34%) and family therapy (28%). Less than one tenth of the therapists reported using some other therapeutic modality.

Client Age Groups

The therapists in our sample were also largely treating adult patients, as shown in Table 3.1 (row 13). About 9 out of 10 treated adults in the 20- to 49-year-old age range, and over half also treated older adults of 50 to 64 years of age—although a minority of the therapists treated seniors aged 65 or more. Adolescents (aged 13–19) were present in the practices of less than half of the therapists, and only one fourth of our therapists treated children 12 or younger.

Impairment Levels

Therapists were asked "How disturbed or impaired are the patients you are currently treating in psychotherapy?" They were requested to indicate in response how many patients in their practice were currently functioning at each of eight levels of impairment (based on Axis V of the *Diagnostic and Statistical Manual of Mental Disorders* system; American Psychiatric Association, 1994). Table 3.1 (row 14) shows that just over two thirds of our therapists reported treating patients with moderate symptoms (e.g., occasional panic attacks) or moderate difficulty in social, occupational, or school functioning, and virtually the same proportion reported treating patients with serious symptoms (e.g., suicidal ideation, severe obsessional rituals) or serious impairment in social, occupational, or school functioning (e.g., no friends, inability to keep a job).

We note that four out of five therapists were not treating so-called worried well patients, that is, those with absent or minimal symptoms who are socially effective, generally satisfied with life, and have no more than everyday problems or concerns. In fact, more were treating patients at the other end of the severity spectrum. More than one fourth of the therapists had some patients who were seriously impaired in communication or judgment (e.g., considerably influenced by delusions or hallucinations) or unable to function in almost all areas, and one out of five were treating patients considered to be in real danger of harming themselves or others (e.g., suicide attempts, recurrent violence), or patients so grossly impaired that they could not communicate or maintain minimal personal hygiene.

SUMMARY AND PROSPECT

The diversity of the therapists in our sample does not lend itself to summarization by describing a "typical" or "average" psychotherapist, which all approximate to some extent. Most of our therapists were trained in psychology or medicine, but a number of other professions are also (if still insufficiently) represented. The work of many therapists is saliently influenced by psychodynamic models of treatment, but large numbers are also influenced by humanistic, cognitive, behavioral, and systemic theories of therapy—and many are influenced by more than one theory. Moreover, our sample also includes substantial numbers of therapists at all career levels, from novices to seniors.

Despite these diverse professional characteristics, there are some commonalities in practice. Most therapists treat their patients on an outpatient basis, either in public or private institutions or in independent private practice, and many conduct therapy in more than one type of setting. Most therapists practice some form of individual psychotherapy, either alone or in combination with other treatment modalities. Most psychotherapists also treat adult patients, although many treat adolescents, too. Most therapists treat patients with significant levels of emotional disturbance and psychological impairment.

In terms of demographic and social characteristics, there are both differences and commonalities in our therapist sample. There are major differences in nationality, although most of our therapists live in North American and western European countries that are broadly similar in culture. Also, most of the therapists in our sample are native born, nonminority, and (by virtue of their education and occupation) middle- or upper middle class members of their societies. Most live in settled domesticity with spouses or partners. In general, our therapists seem to be members of the mainstream of society rather than outsiders within it.

At this point, we warn readers again not to view the therapists in our sample as representative of all therapists at large but to generalize cautiously on the basis of the degree of similarity to our therapists' professional, personal, and practice characteristics. Readers should also bear in mind that many of the characteristics summarized in this chapter are not evenly distributed across therapists but rather tend to be confounded with one another. This is partly due to the nature of the therapeutic professions (e.g., social workers most often are women) and partly to the vicissitudes of data collection (e.g., few of our American or Norwegian therapists are psychiatrists). What this means is that the various groups of therapists in our sample differ from one another in more than one way, making it difficult to interpret any between-group differences that may be found unless relevant statistical controls are used. For example, differences that might be observed between therapists of different countries might be due not to nationality per se but rather to the fact that the proportions of therapists' professions, theoretical orientations, or gender differ from one country to another. To correct for this, we have made extensive use of statistical controls in our data analyses. By the same token, however, this heterogeneity in our sample permits stronger inferences about observed commonalities between groups, because these are found despite the fact that the groups differ in multiple ways.

II

THERAPEUTIC WORK

4

FACETS OF PSYCHOTHERAPEUTIC WORK

DAVID E. ORLINSKY, MICHAEL HELGE RØNNESTAD,
HANSRUEDI AMBÜHL, JOHN D. DAVIS, MARCIA L. DAVIS,
EUNSUN JOO, JAN MEYERBERG, BARBARA K. PARKS,
THOMAS A. SCHRÖDER, AND ULRIKE WILLUTZKI

Psychotherapeutic work is a therapist's daily occupation, source of livelihood, and personal professional commitment. It involves listening and talking to patients, forming relationships with them, and exercising on their behalf the specialized training, skills, and capacities that therapists have acquired and refined over time. Because professional development reflects the progressive enhancement of these skills and capacities, we direct our attention initially to therapists' experiences of their therapeutic work. In this chapter, we focus on the various aspects of what it is like to engage patients in a psychotherapeutic process. In the next two chapters, we analyze the broader dimensions that organize the experience of therapeutic work and examine the practice experience patterns resulting from variation among therapists on those dimensions. Then, in Part III of the book, we examine the reciprocal influences that exist between therapeutic work experience and the professional development of psychotherapists.

ORGANIZATION OF THERAPEUTIC WORK FACETS

The sections and items of the Development of Psychotherapists Common Core Questionnaire (DPCCQ) were derived by the original team of clinician–researchers for the most part through a two-step process: first, by induction, through free-ranging discussion and gradual explication of our practice-based tacit knowledge as therapists, and by consulting previous empirical studies as relevant; and second, by reflecting on the conceptual organization implicit in the material thus generated, with appropriate additions and revisions to ensure a conceptually systematic coverage of item domains. However, because relevant theoretical models were available for two facets of therapeutic work, these were used to guide the construction of DPCCQ items for relational manner and in-session feelings (as described below).

With respect to the facets of therapeutic work, the DPCCQ items generated surveyed the following:

- the *goals* that typically guide therapists in their work with patients;
- the clinical *skills* that therapists exercise to reach those goals;
- the *difficulties* that therapists may encounter in working with patients;
- the *coping strategies* that therapists use when difficulties arise;
- the general experience of *relational agency* that therapists have in pursuing their work, as a result of pursuing treatment goals with varying degrees of skill, difficulty, and coping;
- their person-to-person *relational manner* with patients as they participate together in therapeutic work; and
- the therapists' personal *feelings* during sessions with patients.

Table 4.1 presents the conceptual organization of these work experience facets. Two columns show the traditional differentiation of therapists'

TABLE 4.1
Conceptual Analysis of Therapist Work Experience Components

Aspects of behavior	Psychotherapist's actions	
	Therapeutic interventions	Therapeutic relationship
Task–instrumental aspect	Treatment goals Clinical skills Difficulties in practice Coping strategies	Relational agency
Social–emotional aspect	Therapist's in-session feelings	Relational manner

actions into *therapeutic interventions* and the *therapeutic relationship*. Two rows show the venerable analytic distinction between *task–instrumental* and *social–emotional* aspects of interpersonal behavior (Parsons & Bales, 1953). Four cells defined by the intersection of these two behavioral aspects with the two spheres of therapist action classify the facets of work experience.

Given the fact that therapy is a contractual involvement deliberately undertaken to alter the psychological status of one party (Orlinsky & Howard, 1987), it seems appropriate that the task–instrumental aspect of therapeutic interventions is the most highly differentiated cell, containing four of the seven work-related DPCCQ sections: goals, skills, difficulties, and coping strategies. For the therapist as an actor in the relationship, these culminate in an experience of more or less successful agency, which Bandura (1997, p. 3) defined as "the power to make things happen" through "acts done intentionally"—found in the cell described as the task–instrumental aspect of therapeutic relationship. This is complemented by the social–emotional aspect of the therapeutic relationship, most commonly described in terms of the therapist's style or manner in relating to patients. That, in turn, is complemented by the social–emotional aspect of therapeutic interventions, viewed here in terms of the therapist's affective reactions in the course of working sessions.

Each of the foregoing sections of the DPCCQ contain 12 to 30 items, typically presented as 4- or 6-point Likert-type scales, which we will introduce sequentially when describing the characteristic qualities of therapeutic work as experienced by the participants in our study.

Conceptually Based Facets

Relational Manner

The psychotherapist's ability to work helpfully with patients presupposes the creation and maintenance of a relationship that is both the context in which the work of therapy takes place and an important healing influence in its own right (Orlinsky, Rønnestad, & Willutzki, 2004). These considerations prompted the team to focus carefully on therapists' experiences of relating to patients. As an overall question, therapists were asked "How would you describe yourself as a therapist, that is, your actual style or manner with patients?" The question was to be answered by rating a series of relational adjectives suggested by the well-known model of interpersonal behavior developed by Leary and his colleagues (e.g., Leary, 1957).

Leary's (1957) systematic analysis takes the form of a compasslike circular organization, or *circumplex*, which has two orthogonal bipolar axes, one vertical and one horizontal (see Figure 4.1). In this model, the vertical axis is one of hierarchy or social control, with a positive (upper) pole representing dominance or control and a negative (lower) pole representing

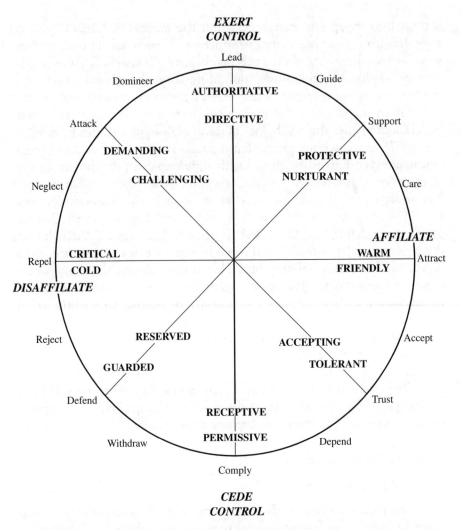

EXERT
CONTROL

Lead

Domineer   Guide

AUTHORITATIVE

DIRECTIVE

Attack   Support

DEMANDING   PROTECTIVE

CHALLENGING   NURTURANT

Neglect   Care

AFFILIATE

CRITICAL   WARM
Repel   Attract
COLD   FRIENDLY

DISAFFILIATE

Reject   Accept

RESERVED   ACCEPTING

GUARDED   TOLERANT

Defend   Trust

RECEPTIVE

Withdraw   PERMISSIVE   Depend

Comply

CEDE
CONTROL

Figure 4.1. The circumplex model of interpersonal behavior (based on Leary, 1957).

compliance or submission. The cross-cutting horizontal axis is one of solidarity or social cohesion, with a positive (right) pole representing affiliation or attraction and a negative (left) pole representing rejection or aversion.[1] Thus, social hierarchy and social solidarity are viewed as the basic coordinates of interpersonal behavior, more or less consciously following the analysis

---

[1]Leary's model has been effectively integrated with other social and psychological theories by Carson (1969), and generally similar but more highly elaborated systems have been further developed by Benjamin (1974, 1996), Horowitz et al. (1988), and Kiesler and his associates (Kiesler, 1983; Kiesler et al., 1985; Kiesler & Watkins, 1989).

of social structure offered by sociologist Emile Durkheim (1897/1951, 1893/1964).

Behavior expressing attraction–affiliation generally is warm and friendly, and behavior expressing rejection–aversion is cold and critical, with a midpoint of neutrality or indifference. Likewise, behavior expressing dominance–control is authoritative and directive, and behavior expressing compliance–submission is obedient and receptive, with a midpoint of independence. It is important to note that in this scheme each participant's interpersonal behavior simultaneously expresses both a certain degree of attraction or rejection and a certain degree of dominance or compliance toward the other.

A further virtue of this frequently validated scheme is that the regions between adjacent poles or cardinal points also have meaning. Thus, the region between attraction–affiliation and dominance–control reflects varying degrees of caregiving; the region between attraction–affiliation and compliance–submission reflects varying degrees of acceptance and receptivity; the region between dominance–control and rejection–aversion reflects varying degrees of challenge and attack; and the region between rejection–aversion and compliance–submission reflects varying degrees of evasion and resistance. Two scales were constructed to represent each octant of Leary's (1957) circumplex, yielding a systematic set of 16 items.

In-Session Feelings

The feelings that therapists have as they work with patients during therapy sessions reflect the therapists' personal response to the vicissitudes of therapeutic work. Items reflecting this aspect of therapeutic work were based on the theoretical and empirical analyses of optimum experience and intrinsic motivation developed by Mihaly Csikszentmihalyi (1990, 1996). Csikszentmihalyi's initial model distinguished three basic subjective states depending on the relative balance of challenge and skill an individual experiences in a particular situation. Feelings of anxiety are expected to the extent that situational challenge exceeds the skills at a person's command. On the other hand, feelings of boredom are expected to the extent that a situation fails to challenge a person's skills. The optimum state of involvement is expected when a situational challenge closely matches a person's skills and demands that they be exercised fully, and at times stretched to new levels. The subjective state characteristic of this situation (referred to as *flow*) is one of intense absorption, finely calibrated responsiveness, and keenly felt satisfaction, generally accompanied by a withdrawal of awareness from extraneous situational cues and a diminution of reflective self-consciousness. Four scales were constructed for each of the three affective states responsive to the balance between situational challenge and relevant skill.

One way to compare the broad variety of social relationships is to contrast those that occur naturally on the basis of biosocial ascription (e.g., kinship relations and ethnic solidarity) or on the basis of mutual attraction (e.g., friendships and love relationships) and those that are undertaken intentionally on the basis of goal-relevant needs and qualifications to achieve a specific purpose. In the former, *affectional* type of relationship, the attachment itself is primary and the functions served by the relationship are secondary, even though those functions may be numerous and important. In the latter, *purposive* type of relationship, which has one dominant or preeminent function, the success of its means-to-end progress is primary and the attachment that forms between participants as they work together is secondary (although potentially also important).

Instrumental Aspects of Work Experience

It is clear that psychotherapy is a relationship of the latter (purposive) type, undertaken deliberately by patients and therapists with the specific goal of improving patients' well-being and life satisfaction insofar as those are related to the patients' mental health status. In this, the therapist's role is defined mainly as being the source or catalyst of therapeutic change, an expert qualified to guide and help implement the means–end process leading to improvement in the patient's mental health status. For the therapist, that entails four closely related instrumental facets of work experience: goals, skills, difficulties, and coping strategies.

Typical Treatment Goals

Treatment goals define the strategic focus of therapeutic work as well as the criteria for evaluating its success. The goals surveyed in this section of the DPCCQ include a broad variety based on the emphases of different theoretical orientations. Therapists were asked to select 4 specific goals from a list of 15 that they judged "to be generally most important" for their patients. The full list of treatment goals and the percentage of endorsement for each are shown in Appendix C (Table C.1).

Despite the range of options on the list and the diversity of orientations among our therapists, a broad consensus emerged somewhat unexpectedly regarding one goal: Three fifths (60%) of the therapists chose helping patients "have a strong sense of self-worth and identity" as one of the four main aims of treatment. This was the first-ranked choice of therapists in most countries in our sample (United States, Germany, South Korea, Switzerland, and Portugal), the second-ranked choice in one (Norway), and the fourth-ranked in one (Spain). More significantly, this was also the most highly endorsed goal by therapists of all theoretical orientations, ranging from 66% and 64%, respectively, for strongly humanistic and systemic therapists, to 56% for strongly cognitive and behavioral therapists.

Two other treatment goals were widely held to be important, but by less than a majority of therapists. One was helping patients to "improve the quality of their relationships" (44%), which was the leading choice of our Norwegian therapists (62%) and the second- or third-ranked choice by our American, Swiss, Portuguese, and Spanish therapists. Among the different theoretical orientations, it was the second most highly endorsed by strongly systemic therapists (51%), analytic–psychodynamic therapists (47%), humanistic therapists (44%), and cognitive therapists (40%)—but was ranked only sixth by strongly behavioral practitioners (32%), for whom the second most frequently chosen goal was "learning to behave effectively in problematic situations" (42%).

The other highly endorsed goal was helping patients to "understand their feelings, motives, and/or behavior" (41%). This was ranked first by our Spanish therapists (59%) and third or fourth by our American, Norwegian, German, Korean, Portuguese, and other therapists.

What the commonly endorsed therapeutic goals seem to have in common is a focus on the patient's self-experience and intimate involvements as an individual, both of which are distinctive characteristics of the peculiarly modern cultural sphere of "personal life" (Ariès, 1962; Berger, Berger, & Kellner, 1973; Orlinsky, 2004; Prost & Vincent, 1991). Most in this culture simply assume that every individual has a right to a personal life and, in fact, that the cultivation of one's personal life is virtually an ethical obligation (so we enjoin those who seem stuck or regressed in their development to "get a life"). The themes associated with this sphere of personal life constitute the very stuff and business of psychotherapy: individualism, inwardness, the ethic of self-actualization, romantic love, and marital and familial intimacy (Bellah, Madsen, Sullivan, Swidler, & Tipton, 1985; Cushman, 1995; Gay, 1986; Lasch, 1979; Orlinsky, 1989; Prost & Vincent, 1991; Rieff, 1966; Taylor, 1989). From this perspective, the modern professional psychotherapies themselves appear to be a central part of modern culture—the part that ministers to the pathologies and quality-of-life issues of persons living in an individualistic, secular, urban, and global mass society.

Therapeutic Skills

Practitioners pursue the varied aims of therapeutic work through the application of their clinical skills. Although common sense as well as two earlier studies (Elizur, Kretsch, Spaizer, & Sorek, 1994; Najavits & Strupp, 1994) suggest that a one-to-one correspondence should not be expected between self-ratings and other indexes of therapeutic skill, our study of therapists' work experiences would hardly be complete—in fact, would be seriously lacking—if these had not been surveyed. We asked therapists to rate themselves on a variety of clinical skills that they perceive themselves to have and exercise in their current practice. Current levels on 12 specific clinical skills each were rated on a 6-point Likert-type scale. The list of current skills,[2] with means, standard deviations, and results of a factor analysis, are shown in Appendix C (Table C.2).

Therapists overall showed considerable confidence in their skills, rating themselves most often in the upper half of the 0–5 scale (averaging a rating of 3.6 across all 12 skills). With regard to specific skills, as many as four fifths (81%) gave themselves a high rating of 4 or 5 on feeling "natural (authentically personal) . . . while working with patients," as did nearly as many (77%) on being "effective . . . at engaging patients in a working alliance" and "effective . . . in communicating . . . understanding and concern to [their] patients" (73%). Two thirds (68%) also gave themselves a high rating on being "good . . . at grasping the essence of [their] patients' problems." These were linked through factor analysis with another scale concerning "how empathic [they] are in relating to patients with whom [they] had relatively little in common," although only 58% gave themselves a high rating on this. All these jointly defined a dimension identified as consisting of *Basic Relational Skills*.

Comparatively fewer therapists (53%) gave themselves high ratings on "how much mastery [they] have of the techniques and strategies involved in practicing therapy," "how skillful [they] are at getting . . . patients to play their part in therapy," and "how well [they] understand what happens moment-by-moment during therapy sessions." Fewer still (47%) rated themselves as high on "how much precision, subtlety and finesse [they] have attained in . . . therapeutic practice." These mostly defined a dimension identified through factor analysis as *Technical Expertise*.

For descriptive purposes, factor analyses of the 12 current skills suggest that the most satisfactory description of this domain includes three dimensions: the two already described plus a third identified as consisting of *Advanced Relational Skills*. The latter was defined principally

---

[2] To establish an indirect measure of career development, we asked therapists in a separate section of the DPCCQ to rate themselves on the same clinical skills when they first started to practice. The factor analysis of therapists' initial skills clearly distinguished two dimensions. One reflected *Basic Relational Skills* (being natural or genuine with patients, being empathic, being able to establish a working alliance, being able to communicate understanding and concern), which approximately one third (32%) of our therapists felt they possessed strongly from the outset. However, only a small minority (10%–15%) of our therapists rated themselves highly on the other initial skill dimension, which combined *Technical Expertise* and *Advanced Relational Skills* (mastery of technique and strategies, moment-by-moment understanding of process in sessions, ability to detect and deal with patients' emotional reactions to them, ability to make constructive use of their own personal reactions to patients).

by two items on which three fifths of our therapists gave themselves high ratings: "How well are you able to detect and deal with your patients' emotional reactions to you?" and "How good are you at making constructive use of your personal reactions to patients?" These inquiries focus on therapists' skills with the often-elusive nuances and emotional subtleties of the therapeutic relationship—or, in psychoanalytic terminology, with *transference* and *countertransference* phenomena.

Although each of the three current skill factors could be made into a reliable multiple-item scale, they also proved to be highly positively inter-correlated,[3] indicating the presence of one second-order dimension of *Current Skillfulness* that can be used as an overall measure for many purposes. However, use of the three specific current skill dimensions in some contexts can be more revealing. For example, when analyzed by career cohorts,[4] mean levels of Technical Expertise are significantly different at each career level, rising from 2.6 (on the 0–5 scale) for novices, to 3.1 for apprentices, 3.3 for graduates, 3.7 for established therapists, 3.9 for seasoned therapists, and 4.0 for senior therapists. Yet in a similar analysis of Basic Relational Skills significant differences were found only between novices (3.4), apprentices (3.7), and graduates (3.8) but no longer among established, seasoned, and senior therapists (who, at 4.0, 4.1, and 4.1, respectively, were all significantly higher than the three junior cohorts). Moreover, although a similar mid-career peaking was found for Advanced Relational Skills, the mean levels were consistently lower at each career level than those for Basic Relational Skills (2.9 rather than 3.4 for novices, 3.3 rather than 3.7 for apprentices, and on up to 3.8 rather than 4.0 for established and seasoned therapists).

Difficulties in Practice

The challenges in therapeutic work that patients present are often, but not always, well met by the various skills that therapists can bring to their task. When those skills fail, or when therapists are unsure how to use them, minor or major difficulties in practice are experienced. Despite the overall high level and increasing levels of confidence in their therapeutic skills, difficulties too are an integral part of therapeutic work experience.

To assess therapists' difficulties, items were composed for the DPCCQ based on a qualitative study of the subject previously published by members of our Collaborative Research Network (Davis, Elliott, et al., 1987). Their analyses of numerous descriptions by therapists of their difficulties in practice

---

[3] The intercorrelations were .67, .70, and .72, which reflect between 45% and 50% of variance shared between them. Although largely overlapping, they are not redundant in meaning. The question about the actual number of current skill dimensions was finally clarified when separate factor analyses were conducted for each of several career cohorts (see chap. 9).
[4] See chapter 10 and Appendix D (Table D.23) for details.

revealed 10 distinct types or clusters, for each of which two quantitative scales were constructed. The twenty 6-point Likert-type scales are shown in Appendix C (Table C.3) together with their item statistics and factor structure.

The frequency with which therapists experienced each difficulty was assessed on a 0–5 scale (0 = *never*, 5 = *very frequently*), with the overall average falling between 1 and 2. Considering that ratings of 1 indicated *rarely*, the following difficulties were experienced more than rarely (i.e., were rated 2 or higher) by a substantial majority of therapists: being "unsure how best to deal effectively with a patient" (76%), feeling "distressed by [their] powerlessness to affect a patient's tragic life situation" (59%), and "lacking in confidence that [they] can have a beneficial effect on a patient" (58%). Other difficulties experienced more than rarely by many therapists included feeling "unable to generate sufficient momentum to move therapy in a constructive direction" (47%), feeling "irritated with a patient who is actively blocking [their] efforts" (47%), feeling "demoralized by [their] inability to find ways to help a patient" (43%), and feeling "bogged down with a patient in a relationship that seems to go nowhere" (41%). These generally reflect failings or limitations that therapists find in themselves.

By contrast, the difficulties least often experienced by therapists were being "unable to find something to like or respect in a patient" (15% rated this as happening more than rarely) and feeling "afraid that [they] are doing more harm than good in treating a patient" (17% rated this as happening more than rarely). The former reflects a general capacity among therapists to be accepting toward individuals who tend to be rejecting of themselves and are often rejected by others. The latter reveals a general attitude among therapists of confidence in the positive nature of their work; they may not always be able to help or know how to help, but they do not often fear having a negative impact.[5]

Factor analyses of the scales revealed three dimensions of therapists' difficulties that were identified, respectively, as *Professional Self-Doubt*, *Frustrating Treatment Case*, and *Negative Personal Reaction*. The first consists in varying measure of feeling unsure how best to deal effectively with a patient, lack of confidence in one's ability to have a beneficial effect on a patient, feeling unable to generate momentum to move therapy forward, feeling

---

[5] This does not contradict the presence of negative effects in psychotherapy, which has long been a concern of researchers (e.g., Strupp, Hadley, & Gomes-Schwartz, 1977). Lambert and Ogles (2004), in a comprehensive review of outcome studies, noted that "a relatively consistent portion of individuals (5 to 10%) deteriorate while participating in treatment" (p. 158). Although some of those undoubtedly may be "harmed through the inept application of treatments, negative attitudes, or poor combinations of treatment technique and patient problem" (Lambert & Ogles, 2004, p. 181), it seems likely that many whose conditions deteriorate in therapy do so despite the best efforts of their therapists rather than because their therapists have (as the DPCCQ item states) done "more harm than good in treating [the] patient."

demoralized by an inability to help a patient, and feeling unable to comprehend the essence of a patient's problems. Professional Self-Doubt was the most commonly experienced type of difficulty.

Having a Frustrating Treatment Case was defined by feeling distressed at one's powerlessness to affect a patient's tragic life situation, feeling bogged down with a patient in a relationship that seems to go nowhere, feeling angered by factors in a patient's life that make a beneficial outcome impossible, and feeling conflicted about how to reconcile obligations to a patient with equivalent obligations to others.

The least frequently experienced type of difficulty was having a Negative Personal Reaction to a patient. The items defining this dimension are feeling unable to withstand a patient's emotional neediness, feeling unable to have much empathy for a patient's experience, feeling uneasy that one's personal values make it difficult to maintain an appropriate attitude toward a patient, and feeling unable to find something to like or respect in a patient.

Despite the meaningful differences among these dimensions, moderately high correlations among them ($r = .60$) led again to a two-level interpretation in which the three types of difficulty are viewed as particular aspects of a higher order dimension of overall difficulty. Therefore, we constructed a scale called *Total Difficulties* to supplement the three specific difficulty scales; which of these we used in subsequent analyses was determined by what seemed most useful in each context.

Coping Strategies

When difficulties arise in practice, therapists may rely on a variety of coping strategies, intentionally or unintentionally, helpfully or otherwise. To ascertain the types and frequency of coping strategies used by therapists, we started again from a qualitative study of therapists' narratives by members of the team that had previously studied therapists' difficulties. By analyzing those narratives, Davis, Francis, Davis, and Schröder (1987) formulated 13 coping strategies, and we constructed two 6-point Likert-type scales for each. The 26 scales are shown in Appendix C (Table C.4) with their item statistics and factor structure.

The coping strategy scales were presented in a section of the DPCCQ as possible responses to the question "When in difficulty, how often do you . . . ?" Alternatives ranged from 0 (*never*) to 5 (*very often*), and strategies rated as 4 or 5 were considered to be those on which therapists often relied. By this standard, a majority of our therapists reported often resorting to four coping methods: (a) to "review privately with yourself how the problem has arisen" (58%) and (b) "try to see the problem from a different perspective" (54%), or (c) to "discuss the problem with a colleague" (56%) and (d) "consult about the case with a more experienced therapist" (53%).

Therapists' most likely first responses to difficulty thus appear to be calling on their own resources or on the advice of a trusted colleague.

Other coping strategies often used by many therapists were to "just give yourself permission to experience difficult or disturbing feelings" (49%) and to "see whether you and your patient can together deal with the difficulty" (42%). Both involve remaining within the bounds of the therapeutic relationship, either passively accommodating one's own distress or actively enlisting one's patient in a problem-solving process.

The responses to difficulty used by the fewest number of therapists were "criticize a patient for causing you trouble" (< 1%), "show your frustration to the patient" (3%), "seriously consider terminating therapy" (4%), and "explore the possibility of referring the patient on to another therapist" (6%). In other words, therapists are least often inclined to turn against the patient or away from the patient.

Other rare responses were to "avoid dealing with the problem for the present" (4%) and "simply hope that things will improve eventually" (7%) or else to "make changes in your therapeutic contract with a patient" (7%) and "step out of the therapist role in order to take some urgent action on a patient's behalf" (5%). Most therapists appear to reject the two extreme alternatives of either doing nothing but hope or doing more than the therapist role normally allows.

Factor analyses of the 26 scales led to the identification of six interpretable dimensions. The dimension that included the most frequently used coping strategies was identified as *Exercising Reflective Control*, which involves reviewing privately how a problem has arisen, trying to see the problem from a different perspective, attempting to contain one's own troublesome feelings, interpreting the patient's resistant or troublesome behavior, and setting limits to maintain an appropriate therapeutic frame.

The other common recourse when in difficulty was to *Seek Consultation*, reflecting a tendency to consult a more experienced therapist, discussing the problem with a colleague, involving another professional or agency in the case, consulting relevant articles or books, and signing up for a conference or workshop that might bear on the problem.

The foregoing represent constructive approaches to coping with difficulties, as does the third factorial dimension, which was identified as *Problem Solving With Patient*. In this strategy, therapists gave themselves permission to experience their difficult or disturbing feelings, shared their experience of the difficulty with the patient, and attempted to work jointly with their patients to deal with the difficulty.

The fourth coping dimension, *Reframing the Helping Contract*, seems on the other hand to reflect the therapists' recognition that the difficulty is beyond their ability to resolve within the limits of therapy as usual. Although not very common, this approach to coping involved making changes in the therapeutic contract with a patient and modifying one's therapeutic stance or approach with a patient—for example, stepping out of the therapist role to take some action on a patient's behalf, perhaps by seeking collaboration from a patient's friends or relatives or postponing therapy to care for a patient's more immediate needs.

By contrast, the last two coping factors showed therapists retreating from therapeutic goals rather than searching for some way to still attain them. In *Seeking Alternative Satisfactions*, therapists compensated for the difficulties they encountered by looking for some form of satisfaction away from therapy, or by expressing their upset feelings to somebody close to them. Worse yet—but fortunately quite rarely—therapists engaged in a countertherapeutic pattern identified as *Avoiding Therapeutic Engagement*. This involved therapists avoiding dealing with the problem altogether and simply hoping that the difficult situation will eventually improve, as well as considering terminating therapy or referring the patient to another therapist, or even showing their frustration to the difficult patient and criticizing a patient for causing trouble.

Because the positive coping dimensions were positively intercorrelated, we also constructed a single scale called *Constructive Coping* to contrast with the negative dimension of Avoiding Therapeutic Engagement. This was done conceptually by combining the most positive aspects of Exercising Reflective Control, Seek(ing) Consultation, and Problem Solving With the Patient (see Appendix C, Table C.4). The number of therapists who often engaged in Constructive Coping when they experience difficulties in practice proved to be 10 times that of those who often engaged in Avoiding Therapeutic Engagement.

Personal Aspects of Work Experience

The foregoing facets of therapeutic work experience focus primarily on the means–ends aspects of the work itself. Nevertheless, despite the primary emphasis on goals and goal attainment in a purposive relationship such as therapy, those who participate in it (both patients and therapists) do so as persons and experience themselves vis-à-vis one another as persons in it. For the therapist, this entails three further aspects of work experience: (a) an overall experience of relational agency as a source and catalyst of therapeutic change, (b) an overall experience of their relational manner in the bonds that they form with their patients, and (c) an experience of personal affective responsiveness while interacting with patients.

Relational Agency

Psychotherapists are agents of change in the therapeutic relationship and thus a facet of their work experience inevitably focuses on their agentic qualities. A dozen 4-point Likert-type scales were included in the DPCCQ to assess these qualities, which were selected by the clinician–researchers who designed the DPCCQ on the basis of their relevance to clinical experience. These are listed in Appendix C (Table C.5) along with descriptive item statistics and factor structure.

Given that the responses for these scales ranged from 0 (*not at all*) to 3 (*very much*), it is unclear whether to use ratings of 2 and 3 (the higher half of the scale) as indicating a high endorsement level or just the extreme rating of 3. By the latter, more stringent criterion, none of the agentic quality scales were checked by a majority of therapists. However, when the first criterion is used, a high positive experience of agency is very widespread. A great majority of therapists experienced themselves in therapy as highly committed (86%), involved (84%), intuitive (80%), skillful (72%), and effective (72%). Smaller but still clear majorities also experienced themselves as pragmatic (61%), determined (59%), organized (56%), and not neutral (58%).

Even with this strongly positive tilt, however, some therapists were either honest enough or pessimistic enough to report themselves as highly unhelpful (9%) or confused (6%). Indeed, using a less stringent criterion (≥ 1) to indicate "somewhat," many of our therapists confessed to experiencing themselves as at least somewhat confused (43%) and at least somewhat unhelpful (48%). As might be expected, 61% of our novice therapists (< 1.5 years of experience) reported being at least somewhat confused, with a significant monotonic decrease across career cohorts, but some confusion was also experienced by more than one fourth (28%) of our senior therapists (≥ 25 years experience).

The trend across cohorts was much less pronounced (and was not linear) with respect to therapists' experiencing themselves as unhelpful: Some 52% of the novices said they were at least somewhat unhelpful, but as many as 48% of the senior therapists also reported experiencing themselves as at least somewhat unhelpful. Evidently, greater understanding by therapists of what they are doing does not necessarily translate into a more effective experience as agents of therapeutic change—which is perhaps only another reflection of the fact that how much help patients receive depends to a large extent on the resources that they bring to therapy (Orlinsky, Grawe, & Parks, 1994; Orlinsky, Rønnestad, & Willutzki, 2004).

Factor analysis of the scales used to assess instrumental agency in relating to patients revealed three independent dimensions of relational agency. Most therapists clearly experience themselves as personally *Invested* in therapeutic work, that is, as involved, committed, intuitive, and not neutral. Most therapists generally also experienced themselves as *Efficacious* in therapeutic work: that is, as skillful, organized, effective, subtle, pragmatic, and determined. These are the two main, reliably scorable dimensions of agency. On the negative side, therapists also sometimes experienced themselves as *Baffled* (confused, unhelpful) when working with patients—but this third dimension was not reliably scorable.

Relational Manner

The participants in therapy interact and work together specifically through their reciprocal social roles as patient and therapist, but they are also present to one another as persons; that is, as individuals having a variety of other traits and characteristics not officially relevant to their roles in therapy. They are each of a certain age, gender, ethnicity, marital status, and cultural background, and each has a certain physical appearance, style of dress, vocal quality, personal mannerism, and so forth. These are manifest in the therapeutic situation in varying degrees and contribute to the creation of a purely interpersonal or person-to-person context for their therapeutic work. This is not so much a matter of what patient and therapist *do* together as it is of how they *are* together. Researchers have typically referred to this element as the therapeutic *bond* (e.g., Bordin, 1979; Orlinsky & Howard, 1987) and have consistently shown it to have an important impact on the success attained in therapeutic work (Orlinsky, Rønnestad, & Willutzki, 2004).

Relational manner is the facet of therapeutic work experience that reflects therapists' perceptions of their characteristic contribution to the therapeutic bond: how they typically relate to patients on a person-to-person basis. The general rationale for constructing scales to assess therapists' relational manner for use in the DPCCQ (described earlier in this chapter) was based on Leary's (1957) circumplex model of interpersonal behavior. Sixteen 4-point Likert-type scales were derived by selecting two adjectives for each octant of the Leary circumplex. These are listed in Appendix C (Table C.6) with their descriptive item statistics and factor structure.

Using the same criterion for high endorsement as we did for relational agency (i.e., upper half of the 0–3 scales), these traits were seen as highly characteristic of their relational manner by impressively great majorities of therapists: accepting (96%), tolerant (91%), warm (89%), and friendly (89%). Many also rated their relational manner as receptive (73%), nurturant (68%), and permissive (56%). By contrast, relatively few therapists saw their manner as highly cold (5%), detached (15%), or critical (21%).

These results are consistent across nationality, gender, and profession. For example, with respect to being highly accepting, the figures by country were as follows: United States, 99%; Norway, 99%; Denmark, 97%; Sweden, 97%; Germany, 97%; Switzerland, 97%; Portugal, 94%; Spain, 97%; Belgium, 97%; France, 95%; Russia, 93%; Israel 99%; and South Korea, 91%. Actually, more than 50% of therapists in these countries saw themselves as *very highly* accepting (a rating of 3 on the 0–3 scale), with just the following exceptions: Germany (48%), Belgium (44%), and South Korea (38%).

Similarly, 97% of female therapists and 96% of male therapists reported experiencing themselves as highly accepting, as did 98% of psychologists, 94% of psychiatrists, and 96% of respondents of other professional backgrounds. Comparable although somewhat less extreme results were found across nationality, gender, and profession for the scales rating warmth, friendliness, and tolerance.

These findings replicate and greatly extend the results previously reported for a preliminary sample (Orlinsky et al., 1996), which linked these very common aspects of therapists' relational manner to the common factors that are viewed as the main source of similar outcome rates among different forms of therapy (e.g., Frank & Frank, 1991) and are often held accountable for the greatest share of variance in therapy's contribution to patient change (e.g., Lambert, 1992; Lambert & Ogles, 2004). Even if patients and external observers were less sanguine than therapists about how *very* accepting, tolerant, warm, and friendly they generally are, these qualities would almost certainly pervade the atmosphere of therapeutic work and frequently allow amenable patients to experience therapy as a positive "holding environment" (Winnicott, 1965).

Factor analysis of the scales used to assess therapists' relational manner revealed four independent dimensions. The qualities of acceptance, warmth, tolerance, and friendliness defined a dimension of basic *Affirming* style toward patients that might well be described as the quintessential therapeutic attitude. This warmly accepting attitude of active welcome evidently typifies the therapist's professional persona and is an aspect of the helping role that transcends differences in academic background, theoretical orientation, career level, gender, and nationality.

Therapists also frequently saw themselves as *Accommodating* in their relational manner, that is, as permissive, receptive, nurturant, and protective. As might be expected, we found a moderate but significantly positive correlation ($r = .36$) between this and the preceding dimension, but the fact that the factor analysis showed they were clearly separate dimensions suggests that therapists can be Affirming without also being Accommodating.

Therapists were more evenly divided in the extent to which they experienced themselves as *Dominant*—that is, as challenging, authoritative, and directive and, to a lesser extent, as demanding and critical. The least frequently endorsed items—being guarded, reserved, detached, and cold— defined a dimension of *Reserve* in therapists' relational manner.

The therapist's gender made only the slightest difference with respect to these dimensions, accounting for less than 1% of the variance in each. (Women were a shade more Affirming and Accommodating, and men were a trace more Dominant and Reserved.) Much the same is true for therapists' experience level, although more senior therapists were slightly more Affirming and less Reserved in relating to patients (rs = .15 and −.15, respectively).

Therapists' theoretical orientations were more clearly associated with their typical relational manner. The most striking correlations were between having a Dominant manner and a behavioral or cognitive orientation (rs = .23 and .19, respectively), whereas analytic–psychodynamic therapists tended generally to be less Dominant (r = −.14). Humanistically oriented therapists tended to be somewhat more Affirming and Accommodating (rs = .18 and .14, respectively). Systemically oriented therapists also tended generally to be more Affirming but also more Dominant (rs = .13 for both). These correlations are relatively low but—because of the large sample size—statistically highly significant and are consistent with those orientations' general approach to therapeutic work.

In-Session Feelings

The feelings that therapists experience during the process of working with patients were surveyed in the DPCCQ by asking: "Recently in sessions with patients, how often have you found yourself feeling . . . ?" This heading was followed by a set of twelve 4-point Likert-type scales representing aspects of Flow, Boredom, and Anxiety as defined in Csikszentmihalyi's (1990) previously described model. The 12 items, with scales ranging from 0 (*not at all*) to 3 (*very often*), are listed in Appendix C (Table C.7), which also includes their basic item statistics and factor structure.

Factor analysis of therapists' feelings confirmed the existence of the three affect dimensions theoretically posited. The great majority of therapists reported recently having high levels of *Flow* feelings: stimulated (80%), engrossed (80%), inspired (79%), and challenged (70%). By contrast, few therapists felt *Boredom*—with only small percentages often feeling absent (9%), inattentive (9%), drowsy (14%), or bored (15%). Frequent feelings of *Anxiety* also were relatively rare, the most common among therapists being feeling pressured (25%) or overwhelmed (19%), with fewer feeling overtly anxious (14%) or trapped (12%).

Despite the predominance of Flow in their work experience, neither Boredom nor Anxiety were strangers to these therapists. This is especially clear when the criterion of note is changed from "often" (≥ 2) to "occasionally" (≥ 1). With respect to Anxiety, clear majorities of therapists felt occasionally pressured (74%), overwhelmed (64%), anxious (64%), and trapped (63%). With regard to Boredom, clear majorities of therapists reported occasionally feeling inattentive (70%), absent (66%), drowsy (63%), and bored (61%). Geller (1994) provided an interesting clinical and theoretical account of this affect.

The fact that therapists were willing to report significant levels of negative feelings makes their common report of very frequent positive feelings all the more credible. The fact that Anxiety was reported significantly more often by new therapists (< 1.5 years in practice) than by all other career cohorts, and that apprentice and graduate therapists in turn reported Anxiety significantly more often than established, seasoned, and senior therapists, adds further to the credibility of these reported in-session feelings. This is consistent with the high level of anxiety reported by many beginning therapists in a qualitative study of American psychotherapists conducted by Rønnestad and Skovholt (2003). Finally, it may also be reassuring for clinicians to know that senior therapists (≥ 25 years in practice) experience Flow even more often than their younger colleagues.

COMMON ELEMENTS IN THERAPEUTIC WORK EXPERIENCE

A composite portrait of how psychotherapists typically experience their therapeutic work with patients can be drawn by reviewing the most common salient elements found for each of the seven facets. These are summarized in Table 4.2 using a 55% majority of therapists as a criterion of commonality.

One treatment goal stands out as common to the work of most psychotherapists: that of helping their patients gain a strong sense of self-worth and identity. Toward this end, most deploy a variety of clinical skills, especially of the kind that were identified as Basic and Advanced Relational Skills: being genuinely personal, able to engage the patient in an alliance, effective at communicating understanding and concern, being alert to transference issues, and being constructive in using their own personal reactions to patients. The difficulties in practice that therapists most commonly experience focus on their uncertainty about how best to deal effectively with a patient and on the limits that a patient's life situation or condition impose on their ability to help bring about improvement. As strategies for coping with difficulties, therapists most commonly rely on their ability to concentrate on and understand how the problem arose and on discussing the problem with a clinical colleague.

Overall, as agents and catalysts of therapeutic change, almost all therapists experience themselves as highly involved and committed; as operating with intuitive skillfulness; and, for the most part, as effective. Therapists almost uniformly experience their manner of relating to patients as strongly Affirming—that is, as accepting, tolerant, friendly, and warm—which, even if only partially experienced in the same way by their patients, very probably contributes to the effectiveness that therapists sense in their work. The intense involvement and sense of efficacy that therapists experience in their

TABLE 4.2
Common Elements in Therapeutic Work Experience

Work element	Items	%
Treatment goals	Strong sense of self-worth and identity	60
Current skills[a]	Natural (personally authentic) while working with patients	81
	Effective at engaging patients in a working alliance	77
	Effective at communicating understanding and concern to patients	73
	Good at grasping the essence of patients' problems	68
	Good general theoretical understanding of therapy	62
	Able to detect and deal with patients' emotional reactions to you	60
	Good at making constructive use of personal reactions to patients	59
	Empathic in relating to patients different from oneself	58
Difficulties in practice[b]	Unsure how best to deal effectively with a patient	76
	Distressed by powerlessness to affect a patient's tragic situation	59
	Lacking confidence about having a beneficial effect on a patient	58
Coping strategies[a]	Review privately how the problem arose	58
	Discuss the problem with a colleague	56
Relational agency[c]	Committed	86
	Involved	84
	Intuitive	80
	Effective	73
	Skillful	72
	Pragmatic	61
	Determined	60
	(Not) neutral	58
	Organized	56
Relational manner[c]	Accepting	97
	Tolerant	91
	Warm	89
	Friendly	89
	Receptive	73
	Nurturant	68
	Permissive	56
Feelings in sessions[c]	Engrossed	80
	Inspired	79
	Stimulated	77
	Challenged	70

[a]Percentage of respondents who gave a rating of "high" (≥ 4 on a 0–5 scale). [b]Percentage of respondents who gave a rating of "more than rarely" (≥ 2 on a 0–5 scale). [c]Percentage of respondents who gave a rating of "much" or "very much" (≥ 2 on a 0–3 scale).

work is confirmed by the *flow* states that they commonly feel in therapy sessions, indicating how intrinsically rewarding their work is to them.

Of course, this composite portrait based on common tendencies must be qualified by recalling that negative and stressful aspects were also present in therapists' work experience. Moreover, in addition to their central tendencies, the several work experience facets were characterized by dimensions of between-therapist variation. Those dimensions represent threads of distinctive coloration that are woven together variously in the design of therapists' overall work experience. We consider these patterns in the chapters that follow.

5

DIMENSIONS OF
WORK INVOLVEMENT

DAVID E. ORLINSKY AND MICHAEL HELGE RØNNESTAD

In the last chapter, we focused separately on seven conceptually distinguishable facets of psychotherapists' work experience. Through the factor analysis of six of those facets, 22 dimensions were identified on which therapists vary in their work experience (listed together here, for convenience, in Table 5.1). These work facet dimensions were likened to threads of different hue and texture from which whole tapestries of work experience are woven. Each therapist's score on each one of those dimensions represents a different nuance of experience, but because the facets of experience are just aspects of a complex totality, the design or pattern of the whole becomes apparent only when all the threads are viewed in combination.

The design of each individual tapestry—that is, the shape of each therapist's experience—is reflected in a configuration or profile of scores across all facet dimensions. However, rather than dealing with 22 discrete scores, a simpler way to trace the individual shape of work experience is to conduct a second-level factor analysis of the 22 facet dimension scores. The resulting second-level dimensions constitute a "double distillation" of therapists' responses, reflecting a broadened view of work experience that nevertheless remains firmly grounded in the many specific impressions that

TABLE 5.1
Summary of Work Facet Dimensions

Work experience facet	Work facet dimensions	M	SD
Current skills[a]	Basic Relational Skills	3.83	0.66
	Technical Expertise	3.49	0.80
	Advanced Relational Skills	3.54	0.76
	Current Skillfulness (combined scale)	3.61	0.65
Difficulties in practice[a]	Professional Self-Doubt	1.72	0.77
	Frustrating Treatment Case	1.48	0.80
	Negative Personal Reaction	1.07	0.69
	Total Difficulties (combined scale)	1.37	0.62
Coping strategies[a]	Exercise Reflective Control	3.10	0.73
	Seek Consultation	2.79	0.96
	Problem Solving With Patient	3.00	0.87
	Reframing the Helping Contract	1.71	0.84
	Seeking Alternative Satisfactions[c]	—	—
	Avoiding Therapeutic Engagement	1.22	0.65
	Constructive Coping (conceptual scale)	2.98	0.71
Relational agency[b]	Invested	2.20	0.57
	Efficacious	1.66	0.53
	Baffled[c]	—	—
Relational manner[b]	Affirming	2.36	0.47
	Accommodating	1.70	0.55
	Dominant	1.11	0.49
	Reserved	0.82	0.53
In-session feelings[b]	Flow	2.00	0.62
	Boredom	0.84	0.53
	Anxiety	0.91	0.61

[a]Scales range from 0 to 5. [b]Scales range from 0 to 3. [c]No scale was constructed.

they recorded, item by item, when completing the Development of Psychotherapists Common Core Questionnaire (DPCCQ).

In addition to making the number of dimension scores more manageable by identifying dimensions that cut across work experience facets, the results of a second-level factor analysis provide a view of therapeutic work that penetrates more deeply to the underlying structures of experience than is possible by conscious reflection alone, because no respondent could keep in mind all of the answers he or she gave to questions on the many pages of the DPCCQ or consciously compute the complex relations among those responses. However, our step-by-step inductive strategy (presented in chap. 2) explores the organization of those responses and, by analyzing the pooled experiences of many therapists, should result in findings that resonate with the lived experience of individuals.[1]

---

[1]Our ability as researchers to recognize patterns in therapists' experience of which therapists themselves may be unaware parallels the therapists' own ability to recognize patterns latent in a

BROADER DIMENSIONS OF WORK EXPERIENCE

The correlation matrix for our second-level factor analysis included therapists' scores on the reliable first-level dimension scales for relational manner (Affirming, Accommodating, Dominant, and Reserved), relational agency (Invested and Efficacious), and in-session feelings (Flow, Boredom, and Anxiety), as well as scales for current skillfulness (Basic Relational Skills[2] and difficulties (Frequent Difficulties). It also included scales for positive and negative coping strategy dimensions (Avoiding Therapeutic Engagement and the composite scale for Constructive Coping).[3] Three second-level factors emerged (see Table 5.2) and were respectively labeled *Healing Involvement*, *Stressful Involvement*, and *Controlling Involvement*.

Healing Involvement

The first broad factor underlying therapeutic work experience was identified as *Healing Involvement*. This was defined by scales representing the therapist as personally Invested (involved, committed) and Efficacious (effective, organized) in relational agency, as Affirming (accepting, friendly, warm) and Accommodating (permissive, receptive, nurturant) in relational manner, as currently Highly Skillful, as experiencing Flow states (stimulated, inspired) during therapy sessions, and as using Constructive Coping strategies when dealing with difficulties.

---

patient's experiences. In clinical work, a therapist's interpretive comments can draw a patient's attention to a relationship between aspects of experience that the patient had never noticed when reporting the experiences separately, which can result in a moment of insight and deepened understanding. In the same way, our analyses can make manifest relations among the particular aspects of what our therapists reported and may thus enhance our understanding of therapeutic work experience.

[2] We chose Basic Relational Skills to represent current skillfulness because it is already present at high levels among beginning therapists (Orlinsky, Botermans, & Rønnestad, 1998) and to eliminate overlap with Technical Skills and Advanced Relational Skills, which figure as components of cumulative career development (see chap. 9).

[3] The manner of selecting typical treatment goals did not lend itself to the generation of first-level facet dimensions and thus could not be included directly in the second-level factor analysis. After the second-level factors were determined, however, we computed the correlations of each with each of the goals. Most were close to naught, but the following statistically significant correlations of .10 or more may be noted. For Healing Involvement, $r = -.13$ for "Think realistically about their lives," $r = -.11$ for "Moderate their excessive, inappropriate or irrational emotional reactions," and $r = -.10$ for "Evaluate themselves realistically." These negative correlations imply that therapists who aim to help patients become more realistic tend to experience less Healing Involvement. For Stressful Involvement, no correlations with treatment goals were as high as .10. For a Dominant relational manner, the core variable defining Controlling Involvement, $r = .15$ for "Learn to behave effectively in problematic situations," and $r = -.12$ for "Allow themselves to experience feelings fully." These goals suggest that behavioral therapists are somewhat more likely, and dynamic or humanistic therapists are somewhat less likely, to experience therapeutic work as a Controlling Involvement— an impression supported by subsequent findings cited in this chapter.

TABLE 5.2
Dimensions of Work Involvement

Second-level factors	First-level factors	Factor		
		I	II	III
I. Healing I. Involvement				
	Invested (Relational agency)	.76		
	Affirming (Relational manner)	.71		
	Flow (In-session feelings)	.69		
	Constructive Coping (Coping strategies)	.62		
	Accommodating (Relational manner)	.49		
	Basic Relational Skills (Current skills)	.48	−.52	
II. Stressful Involvement				
	Total Difficulties (Difficulty in practice)		.81	
	Anxiety (In-session feelings)		.65	
	Avoiding Therapeutic Engagement (Coping strategies)		.62	.35
	Boredom (In-session feelings)		.52	
III. Controlling Involvement				
	Dominant (Relational manner)			.77
	Reserved (Relational manner)			.55
	Efficacious (Relational agency)	.50	−.30	.55
	Cronbach's α	.74	.66	.43

Note. Items in boldface type were scored on a dimension scale. The scale for Controlling Involvement was not computed because of a low alpha value.

Therapists who experience therapeutic work as a Healing Involvement clearly are not the detached practitioners of impersonal techniques that therapists are sometimes thought to be. Images of the latter sort are based partly on Freud's (1912/1958) often-quoted and often-misunderstood[4] recommendation to physicians to "model themselves during psycho-analytic treatment on the surgeon, who puts aside all his own feelings, even his human sympathy, and concentrates his mental forces on the single aim of performing the operation as skillfully as possible" (p. 115). Freud meant here to warn beginners ("young and eager psycho-analysts") who want to be helpful to their patients that effective therapeutic work requires more than personal interest and kindheartedness, it necessitates a professional

---

[4]The extent to which Freud himself departed from this therapeutic model was nicely documented by Lohser and Newton (1996).

discipline that keeps an appropriate boundary between the personal and professional aspects of caring. (That boundary was expressed in a seeming paradox by T. S. Eliot [1952], who ended his poem "Ash Wednesday" with the prayer "Teach us to care and not to care" [p. 67].) Indeed, if the therapist "concentrates his mental forces on the single aim of performing the operation as skillfully as possible," that quality of concentration actually is typical of the absorbed involvement one experiences in states of Flow. It should also be remembered that "the operation" that Freud (1912/1958) recommended therapists perform requires a deep inner responsiveness in which "evenly hovering attention" allows the analyst to participate in "unconscious-to-unconscious communication" with the patient.

Most of the therapists in our sample were already beyond the "young and eager" level of development and had practiced long enough to internalize the explicit rules of the sort that Freud (1912/1958) set forth, whatever model of treatment they might follow. Once well learned, the procedural rules and norms of the therapist's role become effectively embedded in his or her natural and spontaneous responsiveness to patients. Without seeming imposed, they implicitly provide the structural frame and modus operandi for therapists' healing involvements with their patients.

Stressful Involvement

The second broad dimension of therapeutic work experience, identified as *Stressful Involvement*, reflects a different side of therapeutic work experience. This factor was defined most saliently by the therapist's experiences of Frequent Difficulties in practice, accompanied by feelings of Anxiety and Boredom during sessions and a tendency to cope with difficulties by Avoiding Therapeutic Engagement (avoiding the problem, hoping it will disappear, considering transferring or terminating the patient). Perceptions of total current therapeutic skill and sense of efficacy loaded negatively on this dimension, reinforcing the impression of this dimension as one in which the therapists feel their skills are inadequate to the task confronting them.

Being as human as their patients, therapists inevitably bring limitations and vulnerabilities with them into therapy. Some of the limitations may be due to the therapist's failings (as reflected in the dimension of difficulties identified as Professional Self-Doubt), whereas others may be due to the enormity of the task presented by the patient's condition or life situation (reflected in the difficulties dimension Frustrating Treatment Case). In certain situations, these limitations and vulnerabilities may render therapists ineffective and subject them to emotional distress.

The fact that this emerges clearly in our data—as it has in various ways in previous research (e.g., Farber & Heifetz, 1981; Holmqvist & Andersen, 2003; Kramen-Kahn & Hansen, 1998; Menninger, 1990, 1991;

Murtagh & Wollersheim, 1997; Raquepaw & Miller, 1989)—reflects well on the frankness of our therapists as well as the ability of the DPCCQ to detect negative as well as positive experiences. However, it is also worth noting that Stressful Involvement is not simply the opposite of Healing Involvement. The relative independence of the two dimensions ($r = -.13$) implies that it is quite possible for therapists to experience them concurrently. Therapists can perceive and feel that they are helping their patients even while experiencing the stressfulness of therapeutic work.

Controlling Involvement

The third factor revealed in this analysis appeared to reflect a dimension of variation primarily in the therapist's relational manner with patients, because it was most prominently defined by the extent to which therapists experience themselves as Dominant—that is, as directive, demanding, and challenging. This dimension, which we identified as *Controlling Involvement*, does, however, gain some interesting nuances through the significant but secondary loadings of a Reserved relational manner (being guarded, reserved, detached) and the tendency to cope with difficulties by Avoiding Therapeutic Engagement, despite being also linked to an experience of Efficacy (skillful, effective) in relational agency. The therapist's effort to control what is happening seems primarily focused on maintaining the upper hand, but the nuances prompt us to wonder whether therapists who score highly on this dimension are not also trying to control themselves, perhaps fearing to lose control of the therapeutic process. If one views the dimension as a defensive reaction, the sense of Efficacy in it may amount to a bit of reassuring self-deception by the therapist. In partial support of this idea, we note that the feeling of Efficacy in this case is *not* accompanied by a concomitant sense of Current Skillfulness.

On the other hand, the linkage of Dominant and Reserved styles of relating observed here, combined with the feeling of being Efficacious, might lead some to view Controlling Involvement as the kind of authoritative detachment that many people have associated with Freud's (1912/1958) image of the "surgical" analyst: a commanding presence, aloof yet technically masterful. It may also characterize therapists whose theoretical model is more directive. For example, the correlations of a Dominant relational manner and therapists' ratings of their theoretical influences were .23 with behavioral and .19 with cognitive. These correlations are statistically significant but not very strong, yet they reflect the degrees of procedural directiveness associated with those orientations.

The ambiguity we perceive here is expressed in English by the difference between the adjectives *authoritative* and *authoritarian*. *Authoritative* suggests control of the therapeutic process combined with a sense of therapeutic skill; *authoritarian*, on the other hand, is suggestive of situations in which therapists redouble their efforts at control because they feel it slipping away and so become more insistently directive. Both the authoritative and authoritarian qualities of experience are covered by the broader notion of a Controlling Involvement, but at the same time they make it an ambiguous, if not ambivalent, configuration of experience. That may be the reason why the factorial dimension exhibits low internal consistency (α = .43) even though it recurrently emerged as a minor factor in the multiple analyses we present below.

GENERALITY OF THE WORK INVOLVEMENT DIMENSIONS

Before using our reliable scales of Helpful Involvement and Stressful Involvement in further analyses, we ought to ask how well they represent the varied groups of therapists in our large, internally heterogeneous database. One way to assess the generality of those dimensions across different groups of therapists is to repeat the second-level factor analysis for each of the main subgroups in our sample. The results of these comparative analyses are summarized in Appendix C (Tables C.8–C.12).

Professions

We conducted separate second-level factor analyses for therapists with backgrounds in psychology (n = 2,810) and medicine (n = 1,378) as well as our much smaller groups of social workers (n = 280); nurses (n = 91); and lay therapists, analysts, and counselors who specified no professional affiliations other than those labels (n = 214). The smaller subgroups were included for the sake of comparison, although factor analytic solutions for them are less stable than for the larger groups.

Despite some variation in detail, comparison of the professional subgroups shows a general consistency in factor solutions. In each case, three or four factors had eigenvalues greater than 1, and the two largest factors were essentially the same as those identified in the analysis of the total sample. Across all professions, the dimension of Healing Involvement was defined by therapists being Invested, relating to patients in an Affirming manner, experiencing Flow in sessions, and using Constructive Coping strategies to deal with difficulties. Experiencing their work as currently skillful was also significantly associated with this factor either as a primary or secondary loading, and a sense of Efficacy tended to have a secondary loading here as well.

The dimension of Stressful Involvement was always defined by Frequent Difficulties; in-session feelings of Boredom, and usually Anxiety, too; and coping with difficulties by Avoiding Therapeutic Engagement. Computations of Cronbach's alpha for these two dimensions in each of the professional subgroups showed that measurements of reasonable internal consistency could be made. In no case did alphas for the third (or fourth) factors reach acceptable levels.

Theoretical Orientations

We also conducted separate second-level factor analyses for six groups of therapists of different theoretical orientations. These were constructed as nonoverlapping groups, although this meant excluding approximately 20% who were either too divergent or too overlapping in the theoretical influences they reported. They were saliently analytic–dynamic ($n = 1,508$), mainly cognitive–behavioral ($n = 528$), mainly humanistic ($n = 744$), mainly systemic ($n = 393$), and broad-spectrum eclectics ($n = 241$), plus a number of therapists with no salient orientation ($n = 545$) who did not check 4 or 5 on any of the 0–5 scales of orientation.

Factor analyses of these orientation-based groups yielded generally consistent results in which the dimensions of Healing Involvement and Stressful Involvement were always the two largest factors and always generated reliable, internally consistent measures. Across all orientation groups, Healing Involvement was defined by therapists perceiving themselves as relating to patients as Affirming, as Invested, and generally also Accommodating in manner, along with in-session Flow, and use of Constructive Coping strategies to deal with difficulties. Feeling Efficacious was significantly associated with this dimension as a secondary loading in four of the six groups, as was Current Skillfulness in three of the groups. Similarly, Stressful Involvement was always defined by primary (or occasionally by secondary) loadings of Total Difficulties in practice, by feeling Boredom and Anxiety, and by coping with difficulties by Avoiding Therapeutic Engagement.

Career Cohorts

We also repeated the second-level factor analysis separately for groups of therapists at different career levels, defined as follows: novices who had less than 1.5 years in practice ($n = 534$); apprentices who had 1.5 to less than 3.5 years of experience ($n = 549$); graduates, with 3.5 to less than 7 years of experience ($n = 774$); established therapists, with 7 to less than 15 years of experience ($n = 1,429$); seasoned therapists, who had 15 to less than 25 years of experience ($n = 1,074$); and senior therapists, who had practiced for 25 years or more ($n = 375$).

The results for therapists at these different levels of professional experience show the same broadly consistent pattern seen in the profession and orientation subgroups. Healing Involvement was consistently defined by experiences of being Affirming, being Invested, and generally also Accommodating, feeling Flow during sessions, and using Constructive Coping strategies to deal with difficulties. Stressful Involvement was consistently defined by Total Difficulties in practice, feelings of Boredom and Anxiety, and the habit of dealing with difficulties by Avoiding Therapeutic Engagement. Alpha levels demonstrate the usefulness of the corresponding scales to each career level.

Gender

We conducted separate factor analyses for male and female therapists, which showed that the work experiences of the women and men in our sample are similarly organized, principally in terms of Healing Involvement and Stressful Involvement as independent, reliably scorable dimensions. The variables defining those dimensions are essentially the same as in previous analyses.

Nationality

Finally, we conducted separate factor analyses for the therapists from countries having sufficiently large numbers in our sample—the United States (n = 844), Germany (n = 1,059), Norway (n = 804), and South Korea (n = 538)—with results basically similar to those of the other analyses. As a way of including therapists from other countries, we also computed Cronbach's alpha to test the consistency of the Healing Involvement and Stressful Involvement scales for countries represented by at least 100 therapists. The results suggest that the two broad dimensions of work experience apply adequately to therapists from all countries, with the exception of the small subgroup from France.

Taken together, these repeated analyses of professional and demographic subgroups demonstrate an impressive degree of generality in the structure of therapeutic work experience, with surprisingly few exceptions and relatively minor variations. The experience of therapeutic work was consistently organized by the two main independent dimensions of Healing Involvement and Stressful Involvement, together with a minor, apparently stable but internally inconsistent dimension reflecting the degree to which therapists experience their work as a Controlling Involvement. With this assurance, we next explore the correlates of Healing Involvement and Stressful Involvement.

CORRELATES OF WORK INVOLVEMENT DIMENSIONS

When one examines the correlates of various therapist and practice characteristics with Healing Involvement and Stressful Involvement, some correlates may be plausibly interpreted as their determinants, others as their consequences, and still others simply as causally unrelated concomitants. The design of our study precludes tests of causal hypotheses, although careful consideration of the findings may lead to formulations that can be fruitful for future research.

A second problem with interpreting the correlates of Healing Involvement and Stressful Involvement using our heterogeneous database stems from the fact that particular therapist and practice variables are often confounded. For example, our most senior therapists are disproportionately psychologists, our social workers are primarily American, most of the Korean therapists are psychiatrists, and so on (see Appendix B).

However, our data are well suited to the use of multiple regression analysis (MRA), which offers an efficient way to explore the simultaneous effects of several therapist characteristics while controlling statistically for their overlapping influences. This is partly because our very large sample provides great statistical power and enables us to use many variables simultaneously without excessive loss of degrees of freedom. Moreover, categorical variables as well as continuous variables can be used as predictors by reconfiguring them as dummy variables. Still another advantage of MRA is that it provides estimates of the incremental predictive power of each therapist and practice characteristic.

The initial step in using MRAs involves deciding which variables to include as predictors in the analyses. When testing a theory, the selection can be made on conceptual grounds, but in a wide-ranging, discovery-oriented study such as ours there simply are too many variables to include in each analysis. The method of selection that seemed most appropriate to us was to compute simple correlations for Healing Involvement and Stressful Involvement for a broad range of variables and then to choose those that showed at least moderate correlations with either or both. To be consistent with our discovery orientation, we set as a minimal criterion for inclusion in the MRAs a bivariate correlation of $r = .10$. This means that a variable would potentially share at least 1% of its variance with Healing Involvement or Stressful Involvement.

The bivariate correlations between each of several therapist and practice characteristics and the scales assessing the two broad dimensions of therapeutic work are shown in Appendix C (Table C.13). In general, Healing Involvement was more strongly predicted than Stressful Involvement by the characteristics we surveyed. Healing Involvement was positively correlated with duration of therapeutic practice ($r = .17$) and with a measure of depth and breadth of therapeutic experience ($r = .36$) that reflects the number of cases a therapist has treated in various therapy modalities (individual, couple, family, group). In our sample, Healing Involvement was also correlated positively with a professional background in psychology ($r = .23$) and negatively with medicine ($r = -.32$). In terms of training experience, Healing Involvement was positively correlated with having previously had personal therapy ($r = .25$), with total years of formal supervision ($r = .20$), and with total years of academic instruction ($r = .17$). Theoretical orientation was positively correlated with Healing Involvement, mainly in terms of the therapist's breadth or number of salient orientations ($r = .34$) but also, to some extent, with influence by systemic theories ($r = .20$), humanistic theories ($r = .15$), and cognitive theories ($r = .12$).

In terms of practice conditions, Healing Involvement also was positively correlated with the therapists' sense of support in and satisfaction with their main work setting ($r = .33$) and with their sense of Professional Autonomy ($r = .26$). Other positive correlates included the size of a therapist's caseload ($r = .15$) and whether he or she had some amount of full- or part-time private practice ($r = .17$). On the other hand, having any inpatient practice was negatively correlated with Healing Involvement ($r = -.15$).

Demographically, Healing Involvement was positively correlated with age ($r = .22$)—which, of course, is confounded with practice duration—as well as with gender and nationality. Female therapists appeared to experience Healing Involvement somewhat more than men ($r = .20$), as did American therapists ($r = .11$) and Norwegian therapists ($r = .14$), whereas lower scores on Healing Involvement were observed for the few French therapists ($r = -.10$) and especially for the Korean therapists in our sample ($r = -.45$).

Some of the same variables also correlated negatively with Stressful Involvement: feeling satisfaction and support in one's main work setting ($r = -.18$), feeling a sense of Professional Autonomy ($r = -.18$), having some amount of independent practice ($r = -.14$), age ($r = -.12$), years in practice ($r = -.10$), and being a psychologist ($r = -.10$). However, our sample of medically trained therapists tended to experience higher levels of Stressful Involvement ($r = .12$) and lower levels of Healing Involvement. Our German therapists tended to manifest higher levels of Stressful Involvement ($r = .16$), whereas the Danish and Portuguese had slightly lower levels ($r = -.10$).

Although all the correlations cited are statistically significant, their magnitude is generally small, and the variables involved clearly overlap in ways that make it difficult to say which of them are really related to the main dimensions of therapeutic work. Conducting MRAs with these variables will indicate which of the several correlated variables are independent predictors and will aggregate their predictive power into a single measure.

Our procedure in this was as follows. The MRA for each dimension was done first for the total sample using a two-stage hierarchical MRA model. The first stage consisted of a block of dummy variables identifying the national subgroups of therapists that had bivariate correlations of .10 or more (Korea, Norway, France, and the United States). The second stage consisted of all the professional, practice, and personal characteristics of therapists that had bivariate correlations of .14 or more. Within each block, a stepwise entry procedure was followed to identify variables that significantly contributed to the overall prediction. In tabulating the results (see Appendix C, Tables C.14–C.20), we noted the step on which a variable entered the equation (within its block) by putting the step number in parentheses. The amount of incremental variance accounted for by the variable entered is also shown, along with a sign derived from the beta weights indicating the direction of association between the predictor and target variables.

Healing Involvement

The aggregate joint prediction of Healing Involvement for the total sample yielded a substantial multiple correlation ($R = .63$) that accounted for nearly 40% of the variance (see Appendix C, Table C.14). However, more than half of that amount (22%) was attributable to differences in therapists from Korea (about 21%) and France (about 1%). The Korean therapists in our sample (who were predominantly less experienced psychiatrists) on average had notably lower scores on Healing Involvement.

Of more substantive interest are the professional, personal, and practice characteristics of therapists that significantly predict therapists' levels of Healing Involvement when the influence of nationality is statistically controlled. Approximately 18% of the variance over and above nationality was predicted by 14 statistically significant therapist and practice characteristics, but clearly the most important of these was the therapists' Theoretical Breadth (8%) and, beyond that, their sense of Work Setting Support and Satisfaction (3%). These two variables alone account for nearly two thirds of the variance remaining after the influence of nationality was excluded. Variables adding smaller increments to the prediction of Healing Involvement were the therapists' gender (2%) and Breadth and Depth of Case Experience (2%). Each of the 10 further variables that were statistically significant accounted for just a fraction of 1% of additional variance, and all together they accounted for less than 3%. It is interesting that some variables with significant bivariate correlations (see Table C.13) failed to make statistically significant contributions to the MRA. Those included the therapists' caseload, conduct of inpatient therapy, and systemic orientation.

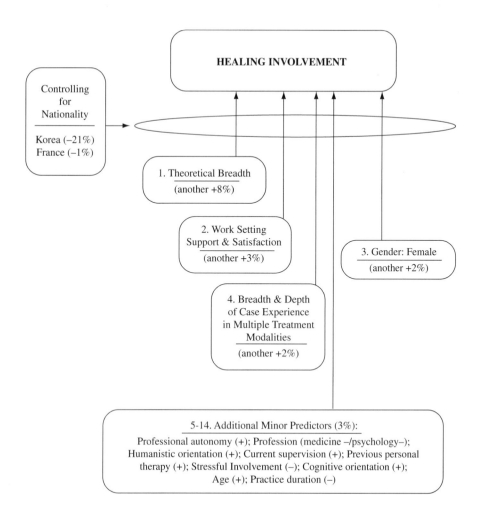

Figure 5.1. Predictors of Healing Involvement (total sample multiple regression analysis).

These results are summarized graphically in Figure 5.1.[5] The quality of Healing Involvement was most prominent in the therapeutic work experience of therapists who use multiple theoretical perspectives in treating patients, who feel most support and satisfaction in their main work setting, who have the broadest experience in different treatment modalities, and

---

[5] The findings at this stage of induction undergo reformulation in chapter 11, in which the MRA is recomputed with dimensions of current and career development included as predictors. Readers are advised to consider both sets of results in the contexts most suitable to each.

who are women. By contrast, Healing Involvement was least frequently experienced by therapists who have no salient theoretical orientation, who feel least support and satisfaction in their main work setting, who have practiced only in one treatment modality, and who are men.

Because our analysis showed substantial effects of national differences with respect to Healing Involvement, we decided to test the generality of findings about the other predictor variables by computing separate stepwise MRAs for the countries in our database with substantial numbers of therapists; that is, the United States, Germany, Norway, and South Korea, as well as the composite group of therapists from "other" countries (see Appendix C, Table C.15). Multiple correlations ranged from $R = .44$ in Germany and in "other" countries, $R = .50$ in Norway, and $R = .57$ in Korea, to $R = .61$ for the United States; that is, 18% to 20% of the variance in Healing Involvement was successfully predicted for German and "other" therapists, 24% for Norwegian therapists, 31% for Korean therapists, and 34% for American therapists.

Theoretical Breadth—the number of salient theoretical orientations used by therapists in their practice—was the leading predictor of Healing Involvement among German, Norwegian, and Korean therapists, as well as therapists from "other" countries, and it was the third leading predictor for American therapists. It was especially potent for our Korean sample, by itself predicting 23% of the variance and accounting for more than two thirds of the total predictive power.

Work Setting Support and Satisfaction was the second leading predictor of Healing Involvement for all national subgroups except the Norwegians, for whom it was the third leading predictor.

Breadth and Depth of Case Experience was the leading predictor of Healing Involvement for the American therapists. It ranked as the third leading predictor for therapists from "other" countries, as fourth for the Germans, and as eighth for the Norwegians.

Therapist gender also proved to be a consistent predictor of Healing Involvement, and among the Norwegian therapists a substantial one as well. Other things being equal, women were more likely to experience Healing Involvement in all national subgroups except South Korea.

Theoretical Breadth, Work Setting Support and Satisfaction, and Breadth and Depth of Case Experience were among the four most predictive variables in the MRA of the total sample when variance due to nationality is excluded, and they show an impressive degree of consistency in the MRAs of separate national subgroups. They were more potent predictors of Healing Involvement than career level, profession, specific theoretical orientation, type of practice setting, amount of didactic training, supervision, or personal therapy. This implies that intrinsic qualities of the therapist (breadth in theoretical perspective and in clinical experience) and qualities of the therapist's work milieu (social support) strongly and consistently influence levels of Healing Involvement.

Although correlational findings do not normally permit causal inference, it is hard to imagine that the opposite relation might hold; that is, that therapists' experiences of Healing Involvement could cause them to have broad experience across treatment modalities, would lead them to have multiple theoretical orientations, or would cause their work milieu to be supportive.

Breadth in theoretical perspective and in treatment experience suggest qualities of conceptual and practical flexibility, which therapists high on Healing Involvement bring to their work. Breadth in theoretical perspective and in treatment experience suggests an openness to experience, which Rønnestad and Skovholt (1991) noted is a prerequisite for optimal professional development, in contrast to a sense of stagnation due to premature closure.

Also, our finding regarding the importance of having a supportive work milieu suggests that therapists' ability to provide a secure "holding environment" for their patients may depend on their own sense of having a holding environment in the work situation.

Table C.15 (in Appendix C) highlights differences as well similarities among therapists from different countries. For example, our American therapists were distinctive with respect to the influence of Breadth and Depth of Case Experience on Healing Involvement. Similarly, therapist gender ranked a strong second for the Norwegians. The Korean therapists in our sample differed most notably with respect to the negative prediction of Korean nationality for levels of Healing Involvement, but another striking difference is the very high positive predictive value of Theoretical Breadth in this group which had seven to eight times the proportion of therapists with no salient orientation than did the other main national subgroups.

Theoretical Breadth (i.e., number of salient orientations) predicted 23% of the variance in Healing Involvement among Korean therapists, in contrast to 9%, 8%, 7%, and 4%, respectively, for Norwegian, German, "other," and American therapists. Also worth noting is the fact that, among our Korean therapists, neither age, nor gender, nor profession, predicted level of Healing Involvement, although the Korean sample had the highest proportion of young male psychiatrists of any national subgroup. Although being young, male, and a psychiatrist are negatively predictive of Healing Involvement in the total sample, and in some national subgroups, they are not so in the Korean sample. That fact makes it more difficult to attribute the generally lower scores of our Korean therapists on Healing Involvement to the higher proportion of young male psychiatrists among them.

There were other variables that we had expected to be significant predictors but were not, or were so only to a minor degree. The most surprising in this regard was the fact that Healing Involvement was only weakly predicted by a therapist's experience level (measured by years in therapeutic practice), both in the total sample MRA and the analyses of the nationality subgroups. This was in marked contrast to Breadth and Depth of Case Experience, which was a more consistent predictor in the MRAs of Healing Involvement. This implies that it is not simply the amount of time a therapist has been in practice that is important but rather what the therapist has experienced during that time.

Stressful Involvement

The MRA results for Stressful Involvement in the total sample confirm much of what was shown by the initial bivariate correlations (see Appendix C, Table C.16). There were fewer significant predictors in the total sample analysis ($R = .30$), accounting for a much smaller percentage of the variance (9%, in contrast to 43% for Healing Involvement). Just under half that amount (4%) is attributable to differences among national subgroups. German therapists as a group had somewhat higher scores, and Danish and Portuguese therapists had slightly lower scores on Stressful Involvement.

Figure 5.2 summarizes graphically the results of this analysis. With nationality controlled, most of the variance attributable to other characteristics was due to situational variables. High Stressful Involvement was associated with therapists' feeling little Work Setting Support and Satisfaction (3%), having no independent private practice (1%), and experiencing little Professional Autonomy (0.4%). Thus, by implication, therapists who feel supported and satisfied in their main work setting, who have a large measure of Professional Autonomy, and who spend at least some time in independent private practice are less likely to experience therapeutic work as a Stressful Involvement.

No professional characteristics were associated with Stressful Involvement, meaning that therapists of different professions, theoretical orientations, and career levels were about equally likely to experience Stressful Involvement. However, younger (although not less experienced) therapists were slightly more likely to experience therapeutic work as stressful.

We used the same professional, personal, and practice characteristics in separate MRAs for our therapists from the United States, Germany, Norway, South Korea, and "other" countries (see Appendix C, Table C.17). Work Setting Support and Satisfaction was the only significant predictor for American therapists, the leading predictor for German and Norwegian therapists, and the second- or third-leading predictor, respectively, for therapists from Korea and "other" countries. In each case, low support and satisfaction predicted a tendency to experience therapeutic work as a Stressful Involvement.

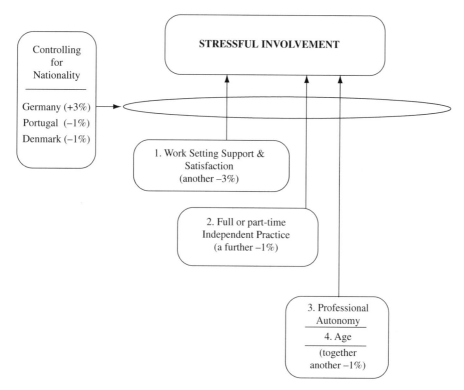

Figure 5.2. Predictors of Stressful Involvement (total sample multiple regression analysis).

Lack of Professional Autonomy was the leading predictor of Stressful Involvement among therapists from "other" countries and the second leading predictor among German therapists. Thus, Stressful Involvement among therapists in most places is predominantly reflective of situational or practice characteristics.

Controlling Involvement

Because of inadequate internal consistency, a sufficiently reliable scale could not be constructed for Controlling Involvement, the third broad dimension of therapeutic work experience. However, the main variable defining that dimension was the therapist's Dominant relational manner, and a reliable multi-item scale was constructed for that first-level facet dimension, including therapists' descriptions of themselves as directive, demanding, authoritative, challenging, and critical. Consequently, we used this key first-level dimension to assess Controlling Involvement.

The bivariate correlates of therapists' Dominant manner are included in Appendix C (Table C.13). The largest number of correlates were with theoretical orientations, with therapists who rated behavioral and cognitive theories as strong influences appearing to be the most directive and challenging in relating to patients, and those with analytic–psychodynamic orientations tending to be less Dominant. Male therapists also appeared slightly more likely to describe themselves as Dominant, as did those with greater Breadth and Depth of Case Experience, those with greater Theoretical Breadth, and those from Germany. Because these were mostly small correlations, and because we had found a parallel factor of Dominant relating in analyzing therapists' reports of their close personal relationships (Orlinsky & Rønnestad, 2003), we decided to include the latter in the list of potential correlates and found that being Dominant in therapy is much more highly correlated with being Dominant in personal relationships ($r = .46$) than it is with any of the professional, demographic, or practice characteristics of our therapists.

We conducted a second-level hierarchical MRA for a Dominant relational manner in the total sample with nationality in the first block and other variables in the second, using the stepwise method of entry within each block. There was a large multiple correlation ($R = .55$), accounting for an aggregate of 29% of the variance (see Appendix C, Table C.18). With nationality controlled, the therapists' description of themselves as Dominant in personal relationships was by far the strongest predictor, by itself accounting for 19% or half of the remaining variance.

There was still a notable impact of theoretical orientation over and above personal disposition and nationality. Being strongly behavioral in orientation predicted a substantial portion (5%) of additional variance in Dominant relational manner, with further nuances predicted by the degree of cognitive, systemic, and (negatively) analytic–psychodynamic orientations. Nuances were also predicted by Breadth and Depth of Case Experience, and therapist gender (being male).

We again tested the generality of these findings by computing separate MRAs for our therapists from the United States, Germany, Norway, South Korea, and "other" countries (see Appendix C, Table C.19). In each group, being Dominant in personal relationships was by far the strongest predictor of being Dominant in relating to patients. The percentage of variance attributable to this one variable ranged from a minimum of 14% for American therapists and 16% for Norwegians to 20% for Germans, and 22% for South Koreans, to as much as 25% for therapists from "other" countries.

Theoretical orientation was generally the second (although far less influential) predictor but was variable across national subgroups. Being strongly influenced by cognitive theories was the second leading predictor for American therapists (8% of variance), German therapists (2%), and South Korean therapists (1%). Being strongly influenced by behavioral theories was the second leading predictor for Norwegian therapists (2% of variance) and for therapists from "other" countries (6%). These are independent of the therapist's tendency to be Dominant in personal relations, the correlations of the latter with behavioral orientation being only $r = .06$ and $r = .04$ with cognitive orientation.

CONCLUDING COMMENT

Three integrative dimensions of therapeutic work experience were identified in this chapter through a factor analysis of the first-level facet dimensions identified previously. A configuration of experience called *Healing Involvement* centered on therapists' investment in their work, affirmative manner with patients, sense of skillfulness and efficacy, and constructive coping with difficulties when they arise. Another configuration of experience, called *Stressful Involvement,* focused on therapists' frequent difficulties in practice, feelings of anxiety or boredom in sessions, and coping by avoidance of issues. The third configuration of experience converged on therapists' Dominant relational manner and was called *Controlling Involvement.*

The correlates of the three dimensions imply that they are each determined by different types of variables. With nationality controlled, the main predictors of Healing Involvement were intrinsic therapist qualities such as theoretical breadth and breadth and depth of case experience across treatment modalities, rather than extrinsic characteristics such as profession, experience level, or theoretical orientation. In contrast, the main predictors of Stressful Involvement were basically situational conditions: feeling little support and satisfaction in one's main work setting, having little professional autonomy, and having no independent practice, rather than extrinsic therapist characteristics such as profession, experience level, or theoretical orientation. Finally, the variable used as a proxy for the unscaled dimension of Controlling Involvement (dominant relational manner) was associated primarily with the therapists' tendency to be dominant in their personal relationships and only secondarily with theoretical allegiance to a directly interventionist therapeutic orientation.

Overall, our findings indicate that therapeutic work is experienced most favorably by therapists who have a broad theoretical perspective and have worked in multiple treatment modalities, who feel supported and satisfied in their main work setting, and who have professional autonomy. Contrarily, therapeutic work is experienced least favorably by therapists who have little commitment to any theoretical orientation, who have worked in just one or two treatment modalities, who feel unsupported and dissatisfied in their main work setting, and who have little professional autonomy. Thus, the qualities that therapists bring to their work and the complex conditions of therapeutic practice all influence the way these broad dimensions evolve into distinctive patterns of work experience.

6

WORK PRACTICE PATTERNS

DAVID E. ORLINSKY AND MICHAEL HELGE RØNNESTAD

Three broad strands of involvement interweave to shape therapists' experiences of therapeutic work: Healing Involvement, Stressful Involvement, and Controlling Involvement. Of these, the last reflects variations mainly in the therapist's personal style and theoretical allegiance but apparently not in more clinically significant aspects of treatment.[1] Healing Involvement and Stressful Involvement, on the other hand, seem to reflect the warp and woof of therapeutic work—the therapist's absorbed, affirmative investment as an agent or catalyst of improvement in patients' lives, with greater or lesser success and satisfaction. These two constitute our focus in this chapter, both because they are more clinically interesting and because

---

[1] *Controlling Involvement* was defined primarily by the therapist's Dominant manner of relating to patients (being directive, authoritative, challenging) and secondarily by a combined sense of being instrumentally Efficacious and relationally Reserved (guarded, reserved, detached), with an additional hint of Avoiding Therapeutic Engagement when confronting difficulties. The pattern mainly reflects the therapist's heightened sense of control in the therapeutic situation, which on one side can be linked to a sense of effectiveness but on the other hand is also a way of limiting personal contact. Although descriptively and conceptually interesting, the level of internal consistency among its defining elements was too low to combine into a single scale of *Controlling Involvement*. The central element in *Controlling Involvement*—a Dominant manner in relating to patients—was most prominent among therapists who rated themselves as dominant in their close personal relationships and among therapists committed to directive theoretical orientations (mainly behavioral but also cognitive and systemic).

Healing Involvement and Stressful Involvement were the two broad strands of work experience that yielded reliable multifacet dimension scales.

The strand of Healing Involvement emphasizes the therapist's Affirming and Attending manner in relating to patients, his or her sense of being Invested and Efficacious instrumentally, as having Current Skillfulness, generating Flow feelings in therapy sessions, and meeting any difficulties that arise with Constructive Coping. This was clearly the modal work experience in our large, heterogeneous sample, as reflected in the relatively high average and low level of variation for more than 4,200 therapists (M = 10.2 and SD = 1.7 on a 0–15 scale).

The strand of Stressful Involvement, by contrast, emphasizes therapists' experiences of low Current Skillfulness, high Total Difficulties, Avoiding Therapeutic Engagement in the face of difficulties, and tending to feel Anxiety and Boredom during therapy sessions. Although many therapists in our sample experienced some degree of Stressful Involvement, the average level and variability were relatively low (M = 4.1 and SD = 1.7 on a 0–15 scale, n > 4,000).

PRACTICE PATTERNS

Healing Involvement and Stressful Involvement are basically independent dimensions of therapeutic work,[2] which means that neither one alone gives an adequate view of what a therapist experiences in practice. A more balanced representation of a therapist's practice experience requires constructing a profile of two scores. For each therapist, one must ask about both the level of Healing Involvement and the level of Stressful Involvement, which together represent a distinctive pattern of practice experience.

To construct distinctive categories of practice experience, one must first divide the continuous scales of Healing Involvement and Stressful Involvement into meaningful segments. For example, by dividing each scale in two—high versus low—one would generate four profile patterns (high–low, high–high, low–high, low–low); by dividing each scale in three—high, medium, and low—one would generate nine patterns; and so on. The initial

---

[2] There is a slight negative correlation between the two (r = −.11). This small proportion of shared variance (just over 1%) is likely to affect only the extreme ends of their distributions, as a tendency for therapeutic work that is very stressful to be experienced as less than very healing and for therapeutic work that is experienced as very healing not to feel very stressful. Within these wide limits, a therapist may be high or low on Healing Involvement and, separately, high or low on Stressful Involvement. It is interesting that each of these negatively correlated dimensions is positively though slightly correlated with the key element of Controlling Involvement (a Dominant manner in relating to patients). Those correlations (r = .14 with Healing Involvement, r = .22 with Stressful Involvement) emphasize the ambiguity and ambivalence of Controlling Involvement as a strand of therapeutic work experience.

question, then, is how many patterns are useful and meaningful to distinguish. After some trial and deliberation, we settled on four as a reasonable first approximation to the delineation of individual work practice patterns. It might eventually be useful to distinguish a larger number of patterns, but in an exploratory study already richly supplied with information it seemed wise to begin simply.

The next question was how to divide each dimension. A conventional procedure is to divide each distribution at the median so that half of the persons are in each category (high vs. low). However, the median value on Healing Involvement for our sample was quite high (10.3), well above the scale midpoint of 7.5. Similarly, the median value on Stressful Involvement was quite low (4.0 on the 0–15 scale), well below the scale midpoint of 7.5. Thus, dividing distributions at their medians would lead to a situation in which the group deemed low on Healing Involvement would contain many therapists whose scale scores were actually quite high, and the group deemed high on Stressful Involvement would include many therapists whose scale scores were quite low.

The best compromise seemed to be one that balanced the actual distribution of therapists with the conceptual meaning of the scale values. Examination of the distribution of therapists on Healing Involvement led to the choice of 9.55 on the 0–15 scale as a reasonable criterion for separating those experiencing "much" Healing Involvement (> 9.55) from those experiencing "not much" (≤ 9.55). Similarly, examination of the actual distribution on Stressful Involvement led to the choice of 4.75 on the 0–15 scale as a reasonable criterion for separating therapists experiencing "little" Stressful Involvement (≤ 4.75) from those experiencing "more than a little" (> 4.75) Stressful Involvement. These values fall between the median and the midpoint on each scale, within one standard deviation of the mean. Our procedure resulted in classifying approximately two thirds of the therapists in our sample as experiencing much Healing Involvement and little Stressful Involvement.[3]

Combining therapists' classification as experiencing "much" or "not much" Healing Involvement with their classification as experiencing "little" or "more than a little" Stressful Involvement resulted in defining the four practice patterns shown in Table 6.1. These were identified as *Effective Practice, Challenging Practice, Disengaged Practice*, and *Distressing Practice*. (Table C.20 in Appendix C specifies the parameters of each pattern on the constituent dimensions.)

---

[3] The proportion of therapists assigned to different practice patterns obviously depends on the cutoff scores chosen for the two constituent dimensions. We have tried to select empirically and clinically meaningful cutoff scores for each dimension, but we recognize that different cutoffs (e.g., a simple median split) would result in somewhat different findings.

TABLE 6.1
Patterns of Therapeutic Work Experience for Western Countries

	Stressful Involvement[b]	
Healing Involvement[a]	Little	More than a little
Much	Effective Practice (*n* = 1,802, 50%)	Challenging Practice (*n* = 821, 23%)
Not much	Disengaged Practice (*n* = 629, 17%)	Distressing Practice (*n* = 377, 10%)

Note. Involvement dimension scales range from 0 to 15; *n* = 3,629. Percentages that include the South Korean sample are as follows: Effective Practice, 46%; Challenging Practice, 21%; Disengaged Practice, 20%; and Distressing Practice, 13%.
[a]For Healing Involvement, much = > 9.55, not much = ≤ 9.55.
[b]For Stressful Involvement, little = ≤ 4.75, more than a little = > 4.75.

Effective Practice was the most common pattern embodied in therapists' reports of their overall work experience, including an estimated 50% of the therapists in Western countries.[4] These therapists showed much Healing Involvement and little Stressful Involvement in their practice. They were personally Invested in their work, were Affirming and Accommodating in relating to patients, experienced Flow feelings during sessions, felt themselves to be currently skillful and efficacious, and used Constructive Coping to deal with difficulties in practice. At the same time, those difficulties were rarely experienced, and the therapists rarely felt either Boredom or Anxiety during sessions. From the psychotherapist's perspective, at least, this is a picture of therapeutic process at its best.

A second pattern portrayed a more *Challenging Practice*, characterized by much Healing Involvement but also by more than a little Stressful Involvement. Almost one quarter of the therapists in Western countries (23%) experienced themselves as somewhat besieged but generally prevailing in their work with patients. Despite encountering more Frequent Difficulties, having some doubts about their skillfulness, and experiencing distressing

---

[4]The exclusion of South Korean therapists from these overall figures is based on the fact that they clearly represent a different distribution of practice patterns. Table C.21 (Appendix C) shows that distribution to be only 8% for Effective Practice and only 4% for Challenging Practice, with correspondingly high figures for Disengaged Practice (48%) and Distressed Practice (41%). Table C.21 further shows that this discrepancy is due primarily to the fact that the South Koreans have much lower scores on Healing Involvement (*Mdn* = 7.7, compared to 11.3 for Americans, 10.6 for Norwegians, 9.9 for Germans, and 10.4 for other countries), whereas median scores on Stressful Involvement did not differ much. How much this discrepancy is due to general cultural differences, specific differences in South Korean social and mental health institutions, sampling contingencies (e.g., the unusually large proportion of relatively inexperienced, predominantly male, medically trained therapists in the current sample), or some combination of these, is unclear at present. Resolution of these questions will require separate and deeper study in a broader sample of South Korean therapists, grounded in work that has already started (Bae, Joo, & Orlinsky, 2004; Bae & Orlinsky, 2003; Joo & Kim, 2000; Joo, Kim, & Orlinsky, 1995).

feelings during sessions, they managed to use Constructive Coping strategies (e.g., Problem Solving With Patient, Seeking Consultation) when difficulties arose. They also remained Invested in their work and related to patients in an Accommodating, Affirming manner.

By contrast, a minority of therapists (10%) experienced therapeutic work as a personally *Distressing Practice*, characterized by more than a little Stressful Involvement and not much Healing Involvement. They had Frequent Difficulties with their patients and tended to cope with those difficulties by Avoiding Therapeutic Engagement (e.g., simply hoping for an eventual improvement, or giving serious thought to terminating therapy or transferring the patient). Therapists also felt Boredom and Anxiety more frequently during sessions, did not experience Flow, felt neither skillful nor Efficacious, were not much Invested in working with their patients, and were not very Affirming or Accommodating toward them. This pattern seems to present a picture of psychotherapy gone painfully wrong.[5]

The fourth pattern of work experience was one of generally *Disengaged Practice*, which included 17% of the therapists in Western countries. For these therapists, therapeutic work entailed not much Healing Involvement but also little Stressful Involvement. They were not necessarily more detached than other therapists in relating to patients[6] but rather seemed detached from the work itself. Perhaps the most that can be said for this pattern is that therapists neither feel they are causing harm to their patients nor that they themselves are being greatly stressed or harmed. Unfortunately, they also do not feel they are providing much benefit for their patients; neither do they feel Invested in what they do. This raises potentially uncomfortable questions about why they are doing psychotherapy and what they are actually doing with their patients.

PRACTICE PATTERNS, PRACTICE CONDITIONS, AND THERAPIST CHARACTERISTICS

Half of the therapists in our study experienced their therapeutic work as an Effective Practice, and another quarter found themselves in a Challenging Practice, facing but apparently overcoming difficulties. The remaining quarter of our sample included a relatively small group of therapists for whom

---

[5]The percentage of therapists in this practice pattern is broadly similar to the percentage estimated by Lambert and Ogles (2004) of patients having a negative therapeutic outcome. How closely related they are in fact remains to be determined.

[6]On average, only 13% of Disengaged Practice therapists experienced themselves as highly detached when relating to patients, compared with 25% of Distressed Practice therapists and 15% of Challenging Practice therapists. Only the Effective Practice group had a smaller proportion of therapists who experienced themselves as highly detached (8%).

therapeutic work was a rather Disengaged Practice that did not seem to affect them (or their patients) either positively or negatively. It also included an even smaller number for whom therapeutic work was actually a Distressing Practice; in effect, a group of helpers who appear to need help themselves. But which therapists were most likely to be in each of these groups? How do they differ from one another?

In principle, we already know the answer from results reported in chapter 5, because the four practice patterns are jointly defined by variations in Healing Involvement and Stressful Involvement, and we identified the predictors of those dimensions through statistically controlled analyses. Therapists who had broad case experience in several treatment modalities, who had considerable autonomy in their work, and who drew on a broad range of theoretical approaches were the ones most likely to experience much Healing Involvement. On the other hand, those with limited case experience in a single treatment modality, little professional autonomy, and a monotheoretic approach tended to have not much of that experience. Similarly, therapists who experienced considerable support and satisfaction in their main work setting, and who had some independent practice, were likely to experience little Stressful Involvement in doing therapy, whereas those who felt unsupported and had no independent practice found more than a little Stressful Involvement in their work.

Yet a richer, more finely detailed picture can be drawn of the therapists in each group by using more of the descriptive information collected in the Development of Psychotherapists Common Core Questionnaire (DPCCQ). To be sure, this must be done cautiously, because many of those descriptive variables are confounded or covary—which was the reason we did statistically controlled multiple regression analyses (MRAs) in the first place. Moreover, although our sample is large and diverse, we do not know how representative our therapists are of others who declined to participate in the study or had no chance to participate.[7] However, with these caveats clearly in mind, we venture to report which of our therapists experienced each practice pattern.

Professional Characteristics

Analyses of the four practice patterns by the professional background, experience level, and theoretical orientation of therapists from Western countries (using the chi-square statistic) are presented in Table 6.2.

---

[7] See chapter 3 for a discussion of the differences between the *generalizability* and *generality* of research findings.

TABLE 6.2
Practice Patterns in Western Therapist Samples: Professional Characteristics

Characteristics	n	Effective Practice	Challenging Practice	Disengaged Practice	Distressing Practice
Total sample	3,629	49.7	22.6	17.3	10.4
Profession[a]					
Psychology	2,189	**54.6**	22.3	**15.5**	**7.6**
Medicine	901	**35.1**	22.3	**24.5**	**18.1**
Other background	535	**53.8**	24.5	**12.9**	8.8
Experience level[b]					
< 5 years	964	**40.4**	22.4	**21.0**	**16.3**
5 to 15 years	1,667	50.0	23.6	17.1	**9.4**
> 15 to 50 years	931	**57.7**	22.0	**14.0**	**6.3**
Experience level × Profession[c]					
Psychology					
< 5 years	450	45.8	20.7	20.2	13.3
5 to 15 years	1,037	**53.8**	23.2	16.2	6.8
> 15 to 50 years	667	**60.4**	22.8	**11.4**	5.4
Medicine					
< 5 years	298	**28.9**	24.5	**25.2**	**21.5**
5 to 15 years	413	**35.8**	22.8	**23.0**	**18.4**
> 15 to 50 years	171	43.3	18.7	**26.3**	11.7
Other professions					
< 5 years	215	44.7	23.3	16.7	15.3
5 to 15 years	216	**58.3**	26.9	**10.2**	4.6
> 15 to 50 years	91	**64.8**	22.0	9.9	3.3
Theoretical orientation[d]					
No salient orientation	237	**34.2**	19.4	**25.3**	**21.1**
Salient analytic–psychodynamic	1,182	**43.4**	**19.6**	**24.3**	**12.7**
Mainly cognitive–behavioral	386	**54.7**	**17.4**	17.4	10.6
Mainly humanistic	552	**53.4**	23.4	**14.5**	**8.7**
Mainly systemic	331	48.9	**29.0**	**13.9**	8.2
Broad-spectrum integrative/eclectic	180	**65.6**	27.2	**4.4**	**2.8**

Note. Unless otherwise noted, all table values are percentages. Numbers in boldface type indicate an adjusted standardized residual ≥ 2.
[a]$\chi^2(6, N = 3,625) = 158.2, p < .0000.$ [b]$\chi^2(6, N = 3,562) = 91.6, p < .0000.$ [c]$\chi^2(24, N = 3,558) = 238.6, p < .0000.$ [d]$\chi^2(15, N = 2,868) = 144.4, p < .0000.$

Profession

With respect to profession, therapists trained initially in medicine were significantly more likely than therapists trained in psychology or other professions to experience therapeutic work as a Disengaged Practice or as a Distressing Practice, and they were less likely to find themselves in an Effective Practice. Effective Practice was still the most common pattern for medically trained therapists, but only for one third of them, in contrast to more than one half of the psychologists and other therapists.

Experience Level

Similarly, with regard to experience level, therapists with less than 5 years in practice were significantly more likely than others to experience therapeutic work as a Disengaged Practice or as a Distressing Practice, and they were less likely to find themselves in an Effective Practice—although, again, Effective Practice was the single most common pattern. In contrast, therapists with more than 15 years in practice were more likely than their juniors to experience work with patients as an Effective Practice, were less likely to have a Disengaged Practice, and only rarely found themselves caught in a Distressing Practice.

Also presented in Table 6.2 is an analysis of practice patterns by experience level and profession, because in our data the two variables were somewhat conflated. One can see that rates of Effective Practice increase with seniority in each profession, even though the rates in general are lower for the medically trained therapists. In a similar manner, the incidence of Distressing Practice decreases with seniority in each profession despite overall differences in level.

Overall, Effective Practice was found significantly more often among the most highly experienced psychologists and therapists of other professions (60% and 65%, respectively) and among "other" therapists with moderate (5–15 years) experience levels (58%). It occurred least frequently among inexperienced and moderately experienced psychiatrists (29% and 36%, respectively).

By contrast, Distressing Practice was found significantly more often among the least experienced and moderately experienced psychiatrists (22% and 18%, respectively), as well as the least experienced psychologists (13%) and those of other professions (15%). Least likely to be in a Distressing Practice were moderately experienced and highly experienced therapists trained in psychology (7% and 5%, respectively) and in "other" professions (5% and 3%, respectively).

The fact that approximately one fourth of the medically trained therapists at all levels of experience showed evidence of a Disengaged Practice (and were significantly higher than other groups in this respect) suggests that this pattern may reflect a distinctive professional style and not just a personal characteristic of therapists. Appendix C (Table C.20) makes clear that levels of Healing Involvement are more than twice that of Stressful Involvement even in a Disengaged Practice. The apparently distant, impersonal, "objective" manner of physicians trained to deal calmly with intimate bodily dysfunctions and distressing life-or-death emergencies may carry over into the work of many who later engage in psychotherapeutic practice. However, that notion also points to the fact that such a manner serves as a form of emotional armor and that a Disengaged Practice can reflect a personally defensive posture on the part of a therapist.

Theoretical Orientation

Besides profession and experience level, a main distinguishing characteristic of psychotherapists is their theoretical orientation. The data in Table 6.2 show a number of significant differences in this regard. Significantly higher proportions of humanistic therapists (53%) and cognitive–behavioral therapists (55%), and especially broad-spectrum integrative–eclectic therapists (66%), experienced therapeutic work as Effective Practice. However, those orientations are probably confounded with profession, being generally more common among psychologists and "other" therapists, and with experience level, because theoretical breadth tends to increase with seniority. On the other hand, rates of Effective Practice were significantly lower among analytic–psychodynamic therapists (43%), and especially among therapists with no salient theoretical orientation (34%)—but those results, too, may reflect confounds with profession and experience level, as more of our medically trained therapists were dynamically oriented, and lack of strong theoretical allegiance was most common among inexperienced therapists.

These same confounds limit the interpretability of the findings with respect to Distressing Practice, which is more frequent among therapists with no salient orientation (21%) and among analytic–psychodynamic therapists (13%) and rarest among humanistic and broad-spectrum therapists (9% and 3%, respectively). The difference between analytic and humanistic orientations may simply reflect different adherence to those approaches by medically and psychologically trained therapists, and the good showing of broad-spectrum therapists may to some extent be linked to a high experience level—although theoretical breadth was actually a strong predictor of Healing Involvement in the controlled analyses. The significantly elevated levels of Disengaged Practice for therapists with no salient orientation (25%) and analytic–psychodynamic therapists (24%), as compared with humanistic, systemic, and broad-spectrum therapists (15%, 14%, and 4%, respectively), are probably due to a combination of factors associated with profession and experience level in addition to orientation.

It is interesting that there were few significant differences in rates of Challenging Practice by theoretical orientation, and none by profession, experience level, or experience level within profession. It seems that good therapists of every background and career level, whose work is mostly successful, nevertheless encounter patients with problems that can be quite taxing and personal qualities that can be rather vexing, that are too difficult to be easily treated. Metaphorically speaking, when it rains it rains on all alike, for therapists in their work as for other folk.

Demographic Characteristics

Differences in practice patterns among therapists by their personal and demographic characteristics are shown in Table 6.3.

Gender

Although the differences were not great, therapeutic work was significantly more likely to be experienced as Effective Practice and less likely to be experienced as Disengaged Practice or Distressing Practice by female therapists than by male therapists—but women were more likely to be psychologists or in "other" professions (e.g., social work, nursing, counseling), and a greater proportion of medically trained therapists were men. However, in our statistically controlled (MRA) analyses, gender was a significant, if minor, predictor of Healing Involvement, as was profession (see Appendix C, Tables C.14 and C.15), so perhaps factors associated with both are influential here.

Age

The therapists' age, of course, is highly correlated with their experience level, although less than perfectly because therapists of different professions require differing amounts of preliminary academic work and begin to practice at different stages of their professional training. Still, the correlation is strong enough ($r = .75$ in our sample) to make the relationship between practice patterns and age look much like that with practice duration. Effective Practice was significantly lower for therapists under age 35 (41%) than for those 50 or older (59%), and Distressing Practice was more frequent in the youngest group than in the oldest group (17% vs. 6%). Disengaged Practice was also higher for therapists under 35 years of age.

Analysis of the combined effects of age and gender clearly shows that younger male therapists are at greatest risk for Distressing Practice, a fact that should be noted by supervisors (see chap. 12). In fact, even men between 35 and 50 show a rate of Distressing Practice as high as that for women

TABLE 6.3
Practice Patterns in Western Therapist Samples:
Demographic Characteristics

Characteristic	n	Effective Practice	Challenging Practice	Disengaged Practice	Distressing Practice
Total sample	3,629	49.7	22.6	17.3	10.4
Gender[a]					
Female	1,997	**53.4**	22.5	**16.0**	**8.1**
Male	1,594	**44.7**	23.0	**19.1**	**13.2**
Age[b]					
< 35 years	780	**40.5**	21.9	**21.0**	**16.5**
35 to < 50 years	2,048	49.1	23.5	17.5	10.0
50 to 70 years	701	**59.3**	21.5	**13.6**	**5.6**
Gender × Age[c]					
Female					
< 35 years	521	**44.5**	22.3	18.8	**14.4**
35 to < 50 years	1,105	**53.6**	23.8	15.8	**6.8**
50 to 70 years	342	**64.3**	19.6	**12.6**	**3.5**
Male					
< 35 years	256	**32.0**	21.5	**25.4**	**21.1**
35 to < 50 years	937	**43.9**	23.1	19.4	**13.7**
50 to 70 years	355	**54.1**	23.7	14.6	7.6
Marital status[d]					
Single	577	**38.8**	25.3	**21.3**	**14.6**
Living with partner	664	**42.2**	23.9	**20.2**	**13.7**
Married	1.848	**54.0**	23.1	**14.6**	8.3
Separated, divorced	319	**64.3**	**18.2**	**11.3**	6.3
Widowed	34	55.9	26.5	14.7	2.9
Gender × Single[e]					
Female					
Single	397	**42.6**	24.2	20.9	12.3
Not single	1,594	**56.1**	22.1	**14.8**	**7.0**
Male					
Single	202	**31.7**	26.7	21.8	**19.8**
Not single	1,383	**46.5**	22.4	18.8	**12.3**
Minority[f]					
No	2,850	48.8	22.0	**18.2**	11.0
Yes	365	51.5	25.8	**13.7**	9.0
Native born[g]					
No	2,582	47.2	21.5	19.4	11.9
Yes	363	50.7	21.8	18.2	9.4

Note. Unless otherwise noted, all table values are percentages. Numbers in boldface type indicate an adjusted standardized residual ≥ 2.
[a]$\chi^2(3, N = 3{,}591) = 41.3, p < .0000.$ [b]$\chi^2(6, N = 3{,}529) = 83.3, p < .0000.$ [c]$\chi^2(15, N = 3{,}516) = 143.9, p < .0000.$ [d]$\chi^2(12, N = 3{,}442) = 100.9, p < .0000.$ [e]$\chi^2(9, N = 3{,}576) = 89.1, p < .0000.$ [f]$\chi^2(3, N = 3{,}215) = 7.4, ns.$ [g]$\chi^2(3, N = 2{,}945) = 2.8, ns.$

under 35 (14% for both). Overall, female therapists between 50 and 70 had the highest incidence of Effective Practice (64%) and the lowest incidence of Distressing Practice (4%), whereas the opposite was true for male therapists under 35, who had the lowest incidence of Effective Practice (32%) and the highest incidence of Distressing Practice (21%)—somewhat reminiscent of earlier findings on therapist gender and age and patient outcome (Orlinsky & Howard, 1976, 1980). The balance between Effective Practice and Distressing Practice was progressively more favorable for successively older groups of both male and female therapists, but the oldest group of men only attained the frequency of Effective Practice already experienced by women between 35 and 50 (54% for both).

Marital Status

Marital status is also correlated with age, a fact probably reflected in the results shown in Table 6.3. Unmarried therapists, including singles and those with live-in partners, had the lowest rates of Effective Practice (39% and 42%, respectively) and the highest rates of Distressing Practice (15% and 14%, respectively). Married and formerly married (i.e., divorced or separated and widowed) therapists, contrariwise, had the highest rates of Effective Practice and the lowest rates of Distressing Practice. A combined analysis of single status and gender also shows the same interaction noted for age and gender: the most favorable balance of practice patterns for women who are not single, the worst for men who are single, with single women and nonsingle men at the same level.

Social Status

By contrast, neither of the social demographic variables included in Table 6.3 were significantly associated with practice patterns, and this is clearly not for lack of statistical power. Whether therapists felt identified as a minority group members in the country where they live,[8] and whether they were native born or immigrants, had no apparent influence on how they experienced their psychotherapeutic work.

Practice Conditions

Finally, the data in Table 6.4 show the incidence of practice experience patterns across different practice conditions: where, in what form, and with whom treatment was conducted.

---

[8]This was assessed by their response to the following question: "In the country where you live, would you be considered a member of a social, cultural, or ethnic minority?"

TABLE 6.4
Practice Patterns in Western Therapist Samples: Practice Characteristics

Characteristic	n	Effective Practice 49.7	Challenging Practice 22.6	Disengaged Practice 17.3	Distressing Practice 10.4
	3,629				
Treatment setting[a]					
Independent practice only	970	**56.1**	20.2	16.5	**7.2**
Outpatient institution only	813	**45.1**	**26.0**	17.0	11.9
Outpatient and independent practice	451	**58.3**	**17.7**	17.1	**6.9**
Inpatient institution only	455	**34.1**	**27.0**	19.8	**19.1**
Inpatient and independent practice	211	55.0	21.8	16.6	6.6
Inpatient and outpatient institutions	226	46.0	18.1	**23.9**	11.9
Inpatient, outpatient, and independent	112	51.8	22.3	17.9	8.0
Treatment modalities[b]					
Individual only	1,015	47.8	**18.8**	**21.3**	**12.1**
Individual and group	557	**44.5**	20.8	19.0	**15.6**
Individual and couple	386	52.8	24.6	15.8	**6.7**
Individual and family	225	47.1	25.8	20.9	**6.2**
Individual and other modality	115	52.2	27.8	12.2	7.8
Individual, couple, family	370	**57.8**	23.8	**11.4**	**7.0**
Individual, couple, group	192	53.6	**29.2**	**9.9**	7.3
Individual, family, group	106	44.3	25.5	19.8	10.4
Individual, couple, family, group	176	54.5	24.4	**10.2**	10.8

(continued)

TABLE 6.4 (Continued)

Characteristic	n	Effective Practice	Challenging Practice	Disengaged Practice	Distressing Practice
	3,629	49.7	22.6	17.3	10.4
Client age groups[c]					
Adult (20–64 years)	1,358	**46.4**	22.2	**19.4**	**12.1**
Adolescent (13–19 years) and adult	592	50.5	21.6	18.6	9.3
Adolescent, adult, senior (≥ 65 years)	212	47.6	28.3	**11.8**	12.3
Adult and senior	304	46.1	**28.9**	13.5	11.5
Child (≤ 12 years), adolescent, adult	492	**56.3**	21.7	14.6	**7.3**
Child and adolescent	129	49.6	27.1	14.0	9.3
Child and adult	122	48.4	25.4	16.4	9.8
Child, adolescent, adult, senior	148	**62.8**	16.9	12.2	8.1
Client impairment levels[d]					
Mild impairment	859	50.1	23.7	15.9	10.2
Moderate to serious impairment	1,415	48.9	23.0	18.5	9.6
Severe impairment	308	47.1	21.8	18.8	12.3
Mixed impairment focus	291	52.2	20.6	18.9	8.2

Note. Unless otherwise noted, all table values are percentages. Numbers in boldface type indicate an adjusted standardized residual ≥ 2. [a]$\chi^2(18, N = 3,238) = 121.3, p < 0000.$ [b]$\chi^2(24, N = 3,142) = 92.7, p < 0000.$ [c]$\chi^2(21, N = 3,357) = 51.9, p < .001.$ [d]$\chi^2(9, N = 2,873) = 7.4, ns.$

Treatment Settings

The key to frequently experienced Effective Practice seems to be having either a full-time independent private practice (56%) or a part-time independent practice combined with work in outpatient or inpatient institutional settings (58% and 55%, respectively). These therapists also rarely experience their work as a Distressing Practice (all less than the samplewide 10% average).

Considering the relative incidence of practice patterns, the most burdened therapists are those who conducted therapy only at inpatient institutions, who reported experiencing a rate of Distressing Practice that is twice the norm (19%), the lowest rate of Effective Practice (34%), and the most frequent occurrence of Challenging Practice (27%). Therapists who conduct therapy only in outpatient institutions fare surprisingly little better, and the combination of outpatient and inpatient institutional practice does not seem to improve the quality of therapeutic work experience. Yet combining any or all of those with some degree of independent private practice seems to transform the quality of therapists' work experience, as if adding leaven to the mix.

Treatment Modalities

By far the largest proportion of therapists conduct only individual psychotherapy, yet they do not have the happiest work experience. Fewer than half (48%) showed evidence of having an Effective Practice, and one third had either a Distressing Practice or a Disengaged Practice (12% and 21%, respectively). By contrast, therapists who used a combination of individual psychotherapy with both couple and family therapy most typically experience their work as an Effective Practice (58%) and only rarely as a Distressing Practice (7%). For the most part, use of other treatment modality combinations was associated with favorable distributions of practice patterns, although the least favorable of all variations is a combination of individual and group therapy (45% Effective Practice and 16% Distressing Practice)—a combination commonly found in institutional settings. The observed effects of variations in treatment modality are probably associated with profession, experience level, and treatment setting. Nevertheless, readers would do well to remember that breadth and depth of case experience across multiple treatment modalities was a stronger predictor of Healing Involvement than the any of other variables noted here (see chap. 5).

Client Age Groups

Breadth of case experience with respect to contrasting client age groups was also related to the quality of therapists' work experience. Therapists who treat adult patients only were by far the most numerous but had about the least favorable incidence of practice patterns, whereas therapists with the versatility to treat every age group had the most favorable distribution. Thus, 46% of the adults-only group, but 63% of the all-ages group, experienced therapeutic work as an Effective Practice, whereas 12% of the former group, but only 8% of the latter group, showed signs of having a Distressing Practice. Contrast appears to be a key factor in this, as therapists with child–adolescent–adult clienteles fare better than those with either adult–senior, child–adolescent, or combined adolescent–adult–senior clienteles. These findings may also be partly due to caseload size, as therapists with larger practices tend to treat a wider range of age groups ($r = .54$).

Client Impairment Levels

One might surmise that therapists who mainly treat clients who have relatively mild symptoms or functional impairments would most likely experience their work as an Effective Practice and that therapists who mainly treat clients who have extreme symptoms and severe functional impairments would more likely experience their work as a Distressing Practice. That, however, does not seem to be the case, at least for our sample of therapists.

Impairment levels among therapists' clients were surveyed in the DPCCQ by adapting the Global Assessment of Functioning scale that constitutes Axis V of the *Diagnostic and Statistical Manual of Mental Disorders* diagnostic system (American Psychiatric Association, 1994). Using the definitions provided in the Global Assessment of Functioning scale, respondents were asked to give a profile of their current clientele by indicating how many clients they were currently treating at each level.

To use that data, we constructed broader impairment categories by grouping Levels 1 through 3 as "mild impairment," Levels 4 and 5 as "moderate to serious impairment," and Levels 6 through 8 as "severe impairment" (Roberts, 2001). Therapists were considered to specialize in treating one of these groups if at least 50% of their current clients were in one of them. We were surprised to find that 90% of our therapists specialized in treating one or another of the three impairment-level groups, with about half (49%) mostly having clients who were moderately to seriously impaired. We also were surprised to find that there were *no statistically significant differences* between impairment-level specialties in the incidence of practice patterns, despite the large number of therapists in each specialty category. Therapists who mainly treated severely impaired patients were only slightly more likely to experience their work as Distressing Practice than those who mainly treated mildly symptomatic clients and were just slightly less likely to experience it as Effective Practice. In fact, the best (although not statistically different) distribution of practice patterns occurred for the 10% of our therapists whose clients spanned two or more of the broad impairment-level groups.

CONCLUDING COMMENT

In this chapter, we have seen how the many threads derived from the specific facets of therapeutic work (chap. 4), and the few broad strands of therapeutic involvement formed from them (chap. 5), were woven into four patterns of practice experience. Thus, we have moved inductively, in a step-by-step manner, from the actual responses of clinicians to questions posed in the DPCCQ, to construct a holistic view of the therapy from the psychotherapists' perspective.

The predominant pattern is clearly one of Effective Practice, experienced by fully half the therapists in our large and diverse sample. In this pattern, therapists experience much Healing Involvement and little Stressful Involvement when working with patients. The second most common pattern was Challenging Practice, in which high levels of Healing Involvement are present but are combined with more than a little Stressful Involvement. Taken together, approximately three of every four therapists felt generally successful in accomplishing the goals of treatment, although for some the work clearly was arduous.

The work experience of a minority of therapists revealed two less favorable patterns of practice. About one in six found themselves in what may be described as a *Disengaged Practice*, in which they experienced little Stressful Involvement but also not much Healing Involvement in their work (although it must be said on their behalf that the level of Healing Involvement exceeded that of Stressful Involvement).

More worrisome was the 1 of every 10 therapists in our sample for whom therapeutic work was a Distressing Practice. These troubled colleagues experienced more than a little Stressful Involvement and not much Healing Involvement when treating patients. Whether they are actually harmful to patients, or whether therapists who experience work as Effective Practice or Challenging Practice are actually helpful to patients, is a question that still needs to be addressed. However, unless there is no relation at all between the psychotherapists' perspective on therapy and that of others—something hard to imagine—therapists who are in a Distressing Practice must be viewed as a great concern to the profession.

Identification of the therapists with different patterns of practice experience was undertaken analytically but indirectly in chapter 5 through MRA to sort through the multiple predictors of involvement dimensions, and also descriptively, but with some caution, through direct comparisons in this chapter.

In terms of professional characteristics, seniority in clinical experience seemed an important factor, both overall and separately among therapists trained initially in psychology, medicine, or other professions. Beginners (those with less than 5 years in practice) were consistently more likely to find therapeutic work a Distressing Practice, and seasoned and senior therapists (those with more than 15 years in practice) were consistently more likely to find therapeutic work an Effective Practice. Those trained in medicine were likely to experience therapeutic work as a Distressing Practice and less likely to find it an Effective Practice at all career levels than those with different professional backgrounds. Therapists with broad theoretical approaches also were consistently more likely to find therapeutic work an Effective Practice, whereas those without any strong theoretical commitment were consistently more likely to experience therapeutic work as a Distressing Practice.

In terms of demographic and personal characteristics, it was not surprising that age—obviously highly correlated with clinical seniority—was a differentiating characteristic, both by itself and within each gender. However, female therapists in all age groups were consistently more likely than their male counterparts to experience therapeutic work an Effective Practice and consistently less likely to find it a Distressing Practice. Young men, especially single young men, seemed most vulnerable to distress and most in need of supervisory support.

Last, in terms of practice conditions, the groups of therapists with the least favorable practice distributions were those who conducted therapy only in institutional settings (inpatient, outpatient, or both), who used only individual or individual and group treatment modalities, and who mainly treated adults (or adults and seniors). By contrast, therapists with the most favorable pattern distributions were those who had some amount of independent practice (even if combined with institutional work), who used a broad range of treatment modalities, and whose clients belonged to a broad range of contrasting age groups. It was surprising that level of client impairment had little impact on the overall quality of therapists' work experience.

These descriptive findings need to be interpreted carefully in light of the results of the statistically controlled MRAs previously reported. Two key elements in those also were therapist breadth (both in theoretical outlook and across treatment modalities) and situational support (reflected in Professional Autonomy as well as Work Setting Support and Satisfaction). The variations in therapist traits that were described above—in career level and profession, in age and gender, in work setting and clientele—should be viewed as reflecting the less tangible qualities of breadth and support that are associated with them in often quite complex ways. Nevertheless, those descriptive indices may be useful, if properly understood, as guideposts for supervisory attention or therapist selection.

Our findings regarding seniority and age, as well as breadth and support, lead naturally to questions about professional growth and beyond that to questions about the interrelatedness of therapeutic work and professional development. In the next section of this book we focus on those questions.

III

PROFESSIONAL DEVELOPMENT

7

ASPECTS OF PROFESSIONAL DEVELOPMENT

DAVID E. ORLINSKY AND MICHAEL HELGE RØNNESTAD

The project described in this book started from a shared desire to study the development of psychotherapists, based on a sense (confirmed by informal observation) that the experience of professional development is very meaningful for psychotherapists and should have implications for their art and science as well. Because the ultimate aim of development is the improvement of practice, we focused in Part I on the experience of therapeutic work as a principal context of professional development. In the chapters that comprise this part of the book, we come to grips directly with the meanings and meaningfulness of professional development and probe its relation to the processes of therapeutic work.

IMPORTANCE OF DEVELOPMENT

Our sense that development is a topic of importance to therapists has been reinforced by the large number of colleagues internationally who volunteered their time, talents, and resources to participate in the Society for Psychotherapy Research Collaborative Research Network, and even more so by the thousands of others who donated some hours of their valuable time to do what therapists normally hate to do: respond to a questionnaire, and a lengthy one at that.

Yet this constitutes only anecdotal evidence. To check our impression systematically, the Development of Psychotherapists Common Core Questionnaire (DPCCQ) asks therapists "How important to you is your further development as a psychotherapist?" The responses to this question, given by more than 4,700 therapists, are presented in Appendix D (Table D.1). Replying on a 6-point scale (0 = *not at all*, 5 = *very*), 65% of the therapists gave it the highest possible rating, and another 21% gave it the next highest rating. Thus, 86% of the total sample appears highly motivated to pursue further professional development.

The consistency and generality of this endorsement of development as a goal are also illustrated in Appendix D (Table D.1), in which we analyze therapists' responses by professional background, theoretical orientation, career level, gender, and nationality. Almost uniformly, 80% to 90% or more of the therapists rated development as highly important (a 4 or 5 on the 0–5 scale).[1]

These figures may overestimate the actual importance of professional development to psychotherapists at large, because the words *development of psychotherapists* are prominently displayed in the title of our lengthy questionnaire. Among the many who were asked to complete the questionnaire but did not, there may well have been a disproportionate number who had relatively little interest in their professional development. Nevertheless, a very large number of highly diverse psychotherapists responded to the questionnaire, and development was a topic of extraordinary importance to them.

PERSPECTIVES ON DEVELOPMENT

This leads naturally to the question of what meaning (or meanings) the term *development* has for psychotherapists. Moreover, given our commitment to approach the topic empirically, what observational methods can be used to assess the extent and direction of development? In deliberating on this, the original Collaborative Research Network team (see chap. 2) found that four empirical approaches are available, each of which has some advantages and some limitations.

---

[1] The smallest majorities were found among therapists who had no salient theoretical orientation (52%), possibly because they are uncommitted to therapy as a vocation and, among our Korean therapists (58%), probably because so many had no salient theoretical commitment. However, even in these groups more than half the therapists rated development as highly important.

The approach generally viewed as methodologically most sound in the study of development relies on *longitudinal* analysis. This requires sequential measures of the same individual (or set of individuals) taken at successive points in their careers so that one can observe how, and how much, they change over time. However, although sound, this approach was not well suited to our immediate aim, which was to study development over the full span of a therapist's career—given that a therapist's career can extend over four or more decades.[2]

Another approach often used in studying development is the *cross-sectional* comparison of groups of individuals (cohorts) who are at different points in their lives or careers. This solves the practical problem of taking measures over an extended duration but suffers from an inability to distinguish between differences that reflect genuinely developmental transformations and those that reflect changing historical circumstances of the several cohorts. Certainly in the United States, and in many other countries too, the conditions and patterns of professional practice in psychotherapy have changed considerably over the past 3 decades (e.g., the advent of managed care), as have emphases in professional training (e.g., heightened sensitivity to multicultural issues). This same problem arises in longitudinal studies that cover extended spans of time.

A further complication of the longitudinal and cross-sectional approaches stems from the fact that researchers must focus their measures on the phenomena that are essential to development when examining individuals over time or comparing groups at different career levels. However, there is little consensus regarding the essential phenomena of therapeutic development (or, indeed, about the essential phenomena of therapeutic practice) and thus no consistent theoretical guidance for researchers concerning what to measure. The theories of therapist and counselor development that do exist mainly focus on the early stages of a therapist's career, and generally little has been done to operationalize them. Our research team's initial work had to focus as much on conceptual issues (as outlined below and in chap. 4) as on instrument design.

Thus, left to our own devices, we also considered two other approaches one can take to study the development of psychotherapists (or anyone else), which involve asking the subjects themselves about their own experiences of development. This *phenomenological* approach partly solves the problem of defining the essential features of therapeutic functioning by tapping the subjects' real, if normally tacit, practice-based knowledge (Polanyi, 1966).

---

[2] We did, however, design a form of the DPCCQ for use as a repeated measure and started to collect longitudinal data over more manageable intervals (e.g., 9–12 months), which we will report at a future date.

This is a particular advantage when the essential phenomena of the domain being studied are not clearly known or theorized.

One approach focuses on the therapist's overall experience of development to date, from his or her first days of therapeutic work to the present time. This can be called *cumulative career development*. Direct retrospective assessments of cumulative career development are based on asking therapists whether, how much, and in what directions they feel they have developed overall, from the start of their careers to the present. To supplement this, an indirect assessment of cumulative career development can be made by examining the differences between therapists' ratings of various clinical skills when they first began treating patients and their independent ratings of those same skills in their current practice.

The second phenomenological approach focuses on the therapist's current experience of change, whether that be development or decline, growth or impairment; we call this *currently experienced development*. The meaning that therapists attach to this aspect of development can be assessed directly by asking them whether, how much, and in what directions they currently feel themselves to be changing; for example, they experience themselves as learning, growing, improving (or the opposite).

In both cases, therapists can be asked directly for their conscious estimates and judgments about their development, and they can be questioned indirectly as well by exploring aspects of their experience that may be viewed as evidence of development. The main limitation of the two phenomenological approaches is their susceptibility to subjective bias, especially when direct ratings are involved. Social desirability or self-esteem issues may tempt therapists to exaggerate or to discount their experiences, although the impact of the former is mitigated by making the ratings anonymous (as they are in this study).

Another problem derives from the contexts in which therapists experience and judge themselves. In the case of cumulative career development, their recollection of how they were at the start constitutes a standard of comparison in terms of which they will always feel they have changed a great deal, even if they only started to practice a year ago. Looking back, one is always older—and, for most therapists, perhaps better—than one has ever been before. In the case of currently experienced development, by contrast, there is a foreshortened horizon of judgment such that therapists are likely to be influenced by what they have experienced most recently.

In any event, it can be safe to use evidence collected by these methods if they are not regarded as objective assessments of change over time (assessed by longitudinal and cross-sectional analyses) but rather as the psychotherapists' perspective on development. Such phenomenological data, focused concurrently or retrospectively, are intriguing in their own right and constitute types of evidence best treated as complementary to data drawn from

TABLE 7.1
Methodological Perspectives on Development

Observational standpoint	Temporal frame	
	Contemporaneous (synchronic)	Extended (diachronic)
Reflexive (own experience as data source)	Currently experienced development (direct and indirect measures)	Cumulative career development (direct and indirect measures)
Objective (other's behavior as data source)	Comparative cohort development (cross-sectional analysis)	Sequential individual development (longitudinal analysis)

other perspectives. By combining them with data from other approaches, cumulative career development and currently experienced development can be anchored to therapists' objective characteristics, for example, their professional backgrounds, work settings, or life circumstances.

The combination of data from different empirical perspectives on development is facilitated by a systematic understanding of their interrelations, as illustrated in Table 7.1. Each of the four approaches is defined by an intersection of two conceptual distinctions with respect to observational standpoint and timeframe. The distinction in observational standpoint hinges on whether one's own experience or another person's behavior is the target; that is, whether reflexive observation or objective observation is the source of data.[3] The distinction with respect to timeframe hinges on whether the scope of observation is contemporaneous (synchronic) or temporally extended (diachronic).

Currently experienced development is self-directed (reflexive) in focus and contemporaneous (synchronic) in scope. *Cumulative career development* is similarly reflexive in focus but is temporally extended (diachronic) in scope. In *comparative cohort development*—the cross-sectional approach, the focus and scope are other-directed (objective) and contemporaneous (synchronic). In *sequential individual development*—the longitudinal approach—the focus is other-directed (objective) and the scope is temporally extended (diachronic).

Explicit recognition of these four perspectives enables one to appreciate the potential complexity of determining how much development has occurred. For example, it is conceivable that therapists may change greatly over

---

[3] The term *objective* as used here carries no implication of greater validity or weightier ontological status but refers in a purely descriptive way to observation focused on others. Readers are referred to Lakoff and Johnson (1980), especially chapters 25 through 30, for an incisive discussion of these issues.

time but that they change so gradually that they do not *feel* they are changing very much at any particular point in time. An example of this that may be familiar to therapists comes from patients in long-term treatment who may feel that they are not changing much but, when asked to compare how they are now with how they were at the same time the previous year, are able to see a positive difference.

It may similarly happen that therapists feel they are growing continuously while no major changes in their functioning are observed over time. This may indicate a kind of illusory, or simply mislabeled, experience that is needed in order to sustain their morale, or else perhaps a sophisticated way of saying that they are enjoying their work. On the other hand, it may reflect the fact that continuous growth may be necessary to offset the constant stresses and abrasions of therapeutic work (so that, like Alice in the Red Queen's race, they have to move forward swiftly simply in order to stay in the same position).

We also note that changes that are noticeable from the researchers' perspective may not be so from the therapist's perspective, and vice versa. For example, the therapists' manner in relating to patients (which is clearly observable externally) may remain basically unchanged, whereas the way that therapists process clinical information (e.g., as described by Caspar, 1995) may develop considerably, although less noticeably to an external observer than to the therapists themselves.

For all these reasons, the surest way to study the development of psychotherapists in the long run is to use all of these perspectives and to look closely at convergences and differences among them. With the data at our disposal, we can analyze currently experienced development, experienced career development, and aspects of comparative cohort development.

CURRENTLY EXPERIENCED DEVELOPMENT

Development implies an ongoing process of change, even though the results of this process may take time to unfold. *Currently experienced development* refers to the psychotherapist's present, ongoing experience of transformation—either improvement or impairment—in contrast to a stable, basically unvarying sense of therapeutic functioning.

Therapists' experiences of their current development initially were assessed directly in the DPCCQ with four questions: "In your recent psychotherapeutic work . . . (a) How much do you feel you are changing as a therapist? (b) How much does this change feel like progress or improvement? (c) How much does this change feel like decline or impairment? (d) How much do you feel you are overcoming past limitations as a therapist?" After pilot testing, six additional questions were included (see Appendix D, Table D.2, for items and item statistics).

Therapists were generally positive in rating their current development, although to varying degrees. Distributions on the 0–5 scales for these items were divided as follows: 0 or 1 = *little*, 2 or 3 = *some*, and 4 or 5 = *much*. Almost all of our therapists (93%) felt they were currently "changing as a therapist"—43% much, and 51% to some degree. Similarly, almost all (95%) felt the direction of change was "progress or improvement"—66% strongly so, and 29% more moderately. Almost all (92%) also felt they were "overcoming past limitations," but just 42% felt it was much, whereas 50% said moderately. The specific aspects of change that were most strongly endorsed were gaining a "deepening . . . understanding of therapy" (67% indicated much) and "becoming more skillful in practicing therapy" (62% indicated much).

Because it is usually harder to rate oneself negatively, the distributions on the 0–5 scales for those items were divided as follows: 0 = *not at all*, 1 or 2 = *some*, and 3 to 5 = *a lot*. By this standard, as many as 31% of our therapists reported they experienced current change as "decline or impairment," although most of those who did (26% of the sample) felt just a small decline. Even more (44%) of our therapists complained that they were losing their "capacity to respond empathically"—but again, most of those who did so (33% of the total) reported only a small loss. However, clear majorities (about 60%) felt they were becoming at least a little "disillusioned about therapy" and at least a little routinized in its performance. Indeed, about one in six therapists reported experiencing more than a little disillusionment and routinization.

The therapists in our sample can hardly be accused of viewing themselves and their work through rose-tinted glasses. They paint a balanced and believable self-portrait. They claim to experience much ongoing change in their work as therapists, mostly of a positive or growthful nature, but their responses also indicate that the work is hard and wearing. Indeed, approximately one in five therapists reported experiencing more than a little disillusionment, and about one in six reported more than a little routinization. Thus, although therapists generally thrive in their work, they also pay a personal price for doing therapy.

To clarify the variable domain representing currently experienced development, we conducted a factor analysis that included the 10 direct questions about overall development, and two factors were identified (Table 7.2). Computations of Cronbach's alpha indicate that each dimension can be made into a reliable multi-item scale.[4]

---

[4] We also computed alphas for each of our main national subsamples, to test the generality of these findings, with the following results: United States, Growth = .86, Depletion = .76; Norway,

TABLE 7.2
Dimensions of Currently Experienced Development

Dimension	Factor	
	I	II
I. Currently Experienced Growth		
Becoming more skillful	.82	
Deepening understanding of therapy	.79	
Overcoming limitations as a therapist	**.77**	
Current change as progress/improvement	**.76**	
Currently changing as a therapist	**.72**	
Experience sense of enthusiasm	.65	
II. Currently Experienced Depletion		
Performance becoming routine		**.75**
Losing capacity to respond empathically		**.75**
Becoming disillusioned about therapy		**.72**
Sense of current decline/impairment		**.62**
Cronbach's α	.86/.76	.69
Correlation with years in practice (r)	.04	.02

Note. Loadings in boldface type are items included in factor scales. Some items were omitted to maximize the number of available respondents (reflected in second α).

As expected, the first factor was defined by all six directly rated positive questions. It presents a picture of vigorous progress in understanding and we named it *Currently Experienced Growth*. A second factor was defined by the four directly rated negative questions, and (after discussions with a focus group of working therapists) we named it *Currently Experienced Depletion*. Whereas the first factor suggested a process of heightened keenness, this second factor reflects a dulling and erosion of responsiveness that, if unchecked, might lead to a state of burnout (Maslach, Schaufeli, & Leiter, 2000; Pines & Maslach, 1978; Raquepaw & Miller, 1989).

Although contrasting in content, the dimensions had only a modest negative correlation ($r = -.20$), which suggests that therapists can experience either or both to varying degrees. In the next chapter, we analyze therapists' profiles on these dimensions to construct a typology of currently experienced development. At this point, we only note that the correlations of both dimensions with the number of years that therapists had been in practice was essentially null ($rs = .04$ and .02), indicating that Currently Experienced Growth and Currently Experienced Depletion are experienced with basically similar frequencies at all career levels.

Growth = .80, Depletion = .70; Germany, Growth = .86, Depletion = .70; Korea, Growth = .91, Depletion = .70; and "other" countries, Growth = .86, Depletion = .63. These figures attest to the reliability (internal consistency) and applicability of the scales for Currently Experienced Growth and Currently Experienced Depletion across five independent subsamples.

CUMULATIVE CAREER DEVELOPMENT

Cumulative career development refers to the therapists' overall experience of development, spanning the time from their first contact with patients in psychotherapy until the present. One direct measure of this overall, cumulative experience was obtained by asking therapists to judge retrospectively whether, how much, and in what directions they had developed since the start of their careers. We also made an indirect assessment of cumulative career development by computing the mean difference between therapists' ratings of their skills (on a set of specific clinical skills) as they were when they first began treating patients and as they are now, in their current practice. A third method of judging their experienced career development was to assess their level of attained proficiency as a therapist.[5]

Measures of Career Development

Direct Ratings

Four questions on the DPCCQ asked therapists directly about their cumulative development: "Since you began working as a therapist ... (a) How much have you changed overall as a therapist? (b) How much do you regard this overall change as progress or improvement? (c) How much do you regard this overall change as decline or impairment? (d) How much have you succeeded in overcoming past limitations as a therapist?"

The item distributions for these are shown in Appendix D (Table D.3). Three fifths (62%) of the therapists reported they had changed much, and four fifths (81%) described the change they experienced as much improvement. Respondents were more conservative in estimating how much they had overcome their past limitations as therapists. Only two fifths (42%) felt they had done so to a large degree, although one half (51%) said they had done so to some extent. Most (93%) said that little or none of the change they experienced had been for the worse, but a few said that it had been—6% to some extent, but only 1% to a considerable extent. Of those who reported negative change, three fourths also reported that much of the change they had experienced had also been positive, in effect reporting

---

[5] These measures aim to assess the therapist's experience of cumulative career development from somewhat different angles, but in one way or another are all derived from the psychotherapist's perspective. They are clearly not the same as judgments made from other observers' perspectives (e.g., those of teachers or supervisors). The degree of relationship between observational perspectives remains to be determined empirically, as are the conditions that influence the degree of their convergence.

both gains and losses. Although relatively minor, these reservations show that the therapists were not uncritical in their self-assessments.

Skill "Change"

We assessed career development indirectly by comparing how therapists rated themselves on 11 therapeutic skills, once as they had been "when you first began your training as a therapist" and later as they are "at the present time" (for information on the latter, see chap. 4 and Appendix C, Table C.2). The differences between initial and present ratings for skills are shown in Appendix D (Table D.4). None of the differences was negative, indicating that therapists experienced improvement on all the skills surveyed, although improvement in some skills was slight (less than 1 scale point). In fact, those were the basic relational skills that therapists felt they already possessed when they began to work with patients,[6] before they had much training or clinical experience: an ability to form an alliance with patients, to understand their problems, to empathize with those who were different, and to communicate their concern and understanding. In effect, these represent the natural talent for helping others that therapists bring to their profession (Orlinsky, Botermans, & Rønnestad, 1998).

By contrast, therapists showed the greatest improvement with respect to their technical skills (e.g., mastery of the therapeutic techniques and strategies, moment-by-moment understanding of therapeutic process) and advanced relational skills (e.g., ability to detect and deal with patients' emotional reactions to them, to make constructive use of their personal reactions to patients). Thus, the dividend that training and experience add to natural talent is precisely the development experienced by therapists in the course of their careers, and the ways that therapists find themselves most improved, when looking back to the start of their careers, define the endpoint of experienced development.

Attained Proficiency

Cumulative career development can also be viewed as culminating in a high level of therapeutic proficiency in technical expertise and advanced relational skills, as represented in the DPCCQ items assessing therapists' current clinical skills (chap. 4). These include mastery of techniques and strategies, moment-by-moment understanding of process, and the ability to deal effectively with the subtle psychological and emotional undercurrents of involvement between patient and therapist. Another DPCCQ item focused

---

[6]These skills change the least partly because they were highly rated at the outset.

specifically on the issue of mastery: "How much precision, subtlety, and finesse have you attained in your therapeutic work?" Overall, fewer than half (47%) of our therapists felt they had achieved a high measure of mastery, even though most reported that they had improved in their felt command of therapeutic techniques and understanding of therapeutic process. Direct assessments on the felt-mastery item were strongly related to length of time in practice but not at so high a level as to be redundant ($r = .41$). As we discuss in chapter 10, almost all senior therapists saw themselves as having attained a high level (78%) or at least a moderate level (20%) of proficiency. Far fewer novice therapists saw themselves as having attained a high level of proficiency (16%), although a surprisingly large number (72%) felt they had attained a moderate level. It seems plausible to suppose that the judgments of our most junior therapists are overly optimistic in this regard, as they have no direct experience of how they will perform at later stages of their career with which to compare their current expertise.

Dimensions of Career Development

To clarify the variable domain representing cumulative career development, we conducted a factor analysis that included the four direct questions about overall development, the difference scores for initial to current skill levels, scores for a selection of the current skills that changed most, and two other items from the DPCCQ that clearly reflect the therapist's sense of therapeutic mastery: "How much precision, subtlety and finesse have you attained in your therapeutic work?" and "How confident do you feel in your role as a therapist?" The results of this analysis are shown in Table 7.3.

Four factors were identified by the standard criterion (eigenvalue ≥ 1), but only three were retained and labeled, because the fourth was defined by a single item (sense of "overall change as decline or impairment"). The three retained factors were called *Retrospected Career Development*, *Felt Therapeutic Mastery*, and *Skill Change*. The alphas shown in Table 7.3 indicate that dimensional scales with satisfactory internal consistency can be constructed for each;[7] however, their fairly high positive correlation with each other suggests that, for many purposes, they are best viewed as aspects of a broader second-order dimension of *Overall Career Development*. This interpretation is supported by the relatively high positive correlations of the three scales with the number of years that therapists have practiced psychotherapy.

---

[7] Again, to test the generality of dimensions across national subsamples, we computed Cronbach's alphas separately for each, with the following results: United States, Retrospected = .81, Mastery = .93, Skill Change = .89; Norway, Retrospected = .68, Mastery = .82, Skill Change = .72; Germany, Retrospected = .76, Mastery = .85, Skill Change = .74; Korea, Retrospected = .83, Mastery = .91, Skill Change = .86; and "other" countries, Retrospected = .69, Mastery = .81, Skill Change = .75.

TABLE 7.3
Dimensions of Cumulative Career Development

Dimension	Factor[a]		
	I	II	III
I. Retrospected Career Development[b]			
Overall change as progress/improvement	**.80**		
Overall change as a therapist	**.76**		
Overcame past limitations as a therapist	**.61**	.48	
II. Felt Therapeutic Mastery			
Constructive use of personal reaction to patients		.80	
Detect and deal with patients' reactions to you		.80	
Understanding of moment-by-moment process		.75	
Mastery of techniques and strategies		.73	
Precision, subtlety, and finesse in therapeutic work		.72	
III. Skill Change			
Use own reactions to patients constructively			.69
Detect/deal with patients' reactions to you			.69
Confidence in role of therapist			**.68**
Understand process moment by moment			**.66**
Get patients to play their part in therapy			.65
Grasp essence of patients' problems			.65
Effective in communicating concern to patients			.64
Feel natural/authentic with patients			**.63**
Mastery of therapeutic techniques			**.60**
Engage patients in working alliance			**.58**
Empathic in relating to patients			.56
General theoretical understanding			**.55**
Cronbach's α	.77	.85/.83	.86/.77
Correlation with years in practice (r)	.45	.38	.28

Note. Loadings in boldface type are items included in factor scales. Some items were omitted to maximize the number of available respondents (reflected in second α).
[a]Factors positively intercorrelated as follows: I × II, r = .55; II × III, r = .44; I × III, r = .41. [b]For the therapists' sense of "overall change as decline or impairment," M = 0.37 and SD = 0.75 on a 0–5 scale (n = 4,798), and in the factor analysis this had a loading of .66 as a separate single-item factor.

COMPARATIVE COHORT DEVELOPMENT

The main challenge in assessing comparative cohort development was the conceptual definition of clinically meaningful categories from a continuous measure of practice duration. We conceive of these career cohorts as developmental levels rather than stages to avoid implicit assumptions of a universal, invariant ordering of changes involving a hierarchical, sequential ordering of qualitatively different structures and functions. Whether those properties obtain is an empirical question rather than something to be assumed. The less restrictive concept of developmental *level* denotes a less precisely bounded temporal distinction and is more consistent with the

TABLE 7.4
Definition of Career Cohorts

Career level	n	Boundaries		Years in practice		Therapist age	
		Lower	Upper	M	SD	M	SD
Novice	534	1 month	< 1.5 years	0.7	0.4	32.9	8.3
Apprentice	549	1.5 years	< 3.5 years	2.4	0.6	34.7	7.3
Graduate	774	3.5 years	< 7.0 years	5.0	0.9	37.2	7.2
Established	1,429	7.0 years	< 15 years	10.4	2.1	42.6	6.9
Seasoned	1,074	15 years	< 25 years	18.7	2.8	49.1	6.5
Senior	373	25 years	< 55 years	31.3	6.6	60.8	8.4

progressive accumulation of many gradual changes that occur in therapists' professional lives over time.[8]

Our formulation of cohorts based on the duration of clinical practice involved a dialectical process between examining the distribution of data and our clinical judgment, informed by our experiences as practicing therapists and supervisors and our knowledge of theoretical models in the literature (cf. Skovholt & Rønnestad, 1995, chap. 1). Because the precise boundaries between these groups had to be arbitrary, we tried to define them in a way that made each cohort large enough to support statistical analyses. However, the cohort categories are internally heterogeneous and fairly broad, with the result that each includes some therapists near the boundaries of the cohort whose practice duration is more similar to some therapists in the adjacent cohort than to others near the opposite boundary of their own cohort. This inevitable consequence of defining cohort boundaries lends a fuzziness to comparative statistical analyses of cohorts but, on the other hand, it means that contrasts between cohorts that do emerge clearly have done so against a background of intracohort variability and are thus more likely to represent relatively substantial effects.

This process resulted in a set of six sequential cohorts whose chronological parameters are shown in Table 7.4. First, we reasoned that regardless of their professional background, therapists in their 1st year or so of working with patients would just be learning how to apply the most basic clinical skills and could well be called *novices*. The criterion for novice therapists was having had less than 18 months of clinical experience. Novices numbered more than 500 in our sample, averaged just over half a year in practice, and had a mean age of 33.

---

[8] The Latin root of stage is *stare* ("to stand"), indicating a position within some structure, for example, a status, station, or a standing place. The root of level in classical Latin is *libella* (diminutive libra), meaning "balance" (Oxford English Dictionary, 1992).

For the next couple of years after this initial period, therapists of most professional backgrounds would still be participating in some training program and would most likely still be receiving extensive supervision, and so the term *apprentice* would be an apt description for them. Apprentice therapists, who were defined as having from 1.5 to less than 3.5 years of experience, also numbered more than 500 in our sample, averaged just over 2 years in practice, and had a mean age of 35.

The foregoing are groups of young therapists relatively new to their craft. After about 3 or 4 years of clinical experience, most would probably have completed their basic professional training and could be classified as *graduate* therapists, ready to practice independently. There were nearly 800 therapists in our sample at this more advanced level. These graduate therapists were defined as having had at least 3.5 years but less than 7 years of experience, averaged 5 years in practice, and had a mean age of 37.

The next three cohorts were defined progressively more broadly and contained correspondingly larger numbers of older therapists. Most in the next cohort, given another few years of continued work with patients, would have settled into some type of *established* practice. There were more than 1,400 established therapists, defined as having from 7 to less than 15 years of experience, in our sample. They averaged 10 years in practice and had a mean age of 43.

Then, as the years of practice accumulate, therapists may be said to become *seasoned* clinicians who have "had a serious commitment to being a practitioner for at least a decade" (Goldberg, 1992, p. 2, footnote). Our sample includes more than 1,000 highly experienced, seasoned therapists, defined as having from 15 to less than 25 years of experience. They averaged 19 years in practice and had a mean age of 49.

Finally, we recognized as *senior* therapists a group of nearly 400 in our sample who had been in practice for 25 years or more and who could look back across a lengthy career. These senior therapists, defined as having from 25 to 53 years of experience, averaged over 31 years in practice and had a mean age of 61.

Our analysis of comparative cohort development in chapter 10 involves comparisons of these six groups with respect to therapeutic work experience, current development, and career development. First, however, to gain a better understanding of those aspects of professional development, we examine the correlates of currently experienced development (in chap. 8) and cumulative career development (in chap. 9).

8

CURRENT DEVELOPMENT: GROWTH AND DEPLETION

DAVID E. ORLINSKY AND MICHAEL HELGE RØNNESTAD

In analyzing therapists' reports about their experiences of ongoing change and development in chapter 7, we identified independent dimensions that reflect a sense of continuing improvement or advance and a sense of incipient impairment or decline. We labeled the former *Currently Experienced Growth* and the latter *Currently Experienced Depletion*.

PATTERNS OF CURRENTLY EXPERIENCED DEVELOPMENT

Although contrasting in content, the two dimensions are largely independent of one another statistically. This means that therapists can have high or low scores on one dimension without that unduly influencing scores on the other dimension.[1] It appears that current development for most therapists is actually a mixed experience, balancing a certain amount of Currently Experienced Growth with some degree of Currently Experienced Depletion.

---

[1] The small negative correlation ($r = -.20$) between the two dimensions implies that an extreme score on one dimension does somewhat moderate the therapist's standing on the other.

TABLE 8.1
Patterns of Currently Experienced Development

Currently	Currently Experienced Depletion[b]	
Experienced Growth[a]	Little	More than a little
Much	Progress (*n* = 2,044, 52.9%)	Flux (*n* = 543, 14.1%)
Not much	Stasis (*n* = 852, 22.0%)	Regress (*n* = 425, 11.0%)

Note. *N* = 3,864. Ratings were made on scales that ranged from 0 to 5.
[a]*Much* ≥ 3.33, *Not much* < 3.33. [b]*Little* ≤ 1.25, *More than a little* > 1.25.

The independence of these dimensions also means that broader patterns of Currently Experienced Development can be identified by creating profiles for therapists based on the two dimension scores. As in deriving patterns of work experience practice (chap. 6), we first divided each continuous dimension into categories and then combined the categories into a 2 × 2 table. Examination of the distributions of therapists on each dimension led to a division between those reporting "much" or "not much" Currently Experienced Growth and between those reporting "little" or "more than a little" Currently Experienced Depletion. The resulting patterns and their relative incidence are shown in Table 8.1.

A majority (53%) of therapists from Western countries[2] experienced much growth and little depletion, which seems reasonable to denote as a sense of *progress*. These therapists experience themselves as thriving in their work, continually augmenting their understanding of therapy and further increasing their ability to engage constructively in it.

Next most common was a pattern that combined little Currently Experienced Depletion with not much Currently Experienced Growth. Called *stasis*, this steady state or constancy in professional skill was displayed by nearly one quarter (22%) of the therapists. They were neither advancing nor declining in proficiency.

In contrast to stasis was a pattern characterized by much Currently Experienced Growth as well as more than a little Currently Experienced

[2]Korean therapists were excluded from this analysis because of their distinctly different distribution of current experience patterns (40% felt stasis, 26% felt regress, 10% felt struggle, and only 25% felt progress). This contrasts with our therapists from Western countries, for example, the United States (16% felt stasis, 10% felt regress, 19% felt struggle, and 55% felt progress), Norway (16% felt stasis, 11% felt regress, 19% felt struggle, and 55% felt progress), Germany (26% felt stasis, 13% felt regress, 14% felt struggle, and 48% felt progress), and Switzerland (26% felt stasis, 5% felt regress, 15% felt struggle, and 55% felt progress). These differences seemed to warrant a separate investigation.

Depletion, a contrariety of impressions reflecting a sense of *flux*. Approximately one in seven therapists (14%) displayed this mixed pattern.

The fourth profile unfortunately showed more than a little Currently Experienced Depletion and not much Currently Experienced Growth. This sense of *regress* was experienced by approximately 1 in 10 therapists (11%). Thus, a small but numerically significant minority of therapists appear to be at risk and probably need some supportive intervention themselves in order to be helpful to their patients.

CURRENT GROWTH PATTERNS AND THERAPIST CHARACTERISTICS

Before we turn to separate controlled statistical analyses of Currently Experienced Growth and Currently Experienced Depletion, it would be interesting to look briefly at the therapist and practice characteristics associated with each current growth pattern in our present sample. These are shown in Appendix D (Tables D.5–D.7).[3]

Demographic Characteristics

With regard to other demographic characteristics, therapists' gender and age were both significantly associated with current growth patterns—an association that was made clearer when age and sex were combined (see Table D.5). Progress was generally somewhat more characteristic of female therapists, and regress was generally somewhat less so, and the most notable differences were between younger women (< 35 years old) and older men (50–70 years). Felt progress was most evident among the former and least evident among the latter. Of the different Age × Gender groups, younger women were also least likely to experience regress or stasis. As might be expected, stasis was more common among older therapists of both sexes, but to keep this in context it should be noted that progress was still the most common pattern in all age groups. No significant associations of growth pattern with therapists' marital status were observed.

Professional Characteristics

Profession and Experience

Regarding therapists' professional characteristics, both professional background and experience level were also associated with current growth

---

[3] Because the therapists in our Korean subsample differed substantially from other countries in the distribution of growth patterns (Table D.5), we excluded them from the remaining analyses, as we did in the descriptive analyses of practice patterns in chapter 6.

patterns (see Table D.6). In general, the therapists in our sample who had medical training were more likely than others to show signs of felt stasis and less likely than others to show progress, although the latter was experienced by a majority (52%). Therapists from professional backgrounds other than medicine or psychology were comparatively more likely than others to show signs of felt progress and less likely than others to show regress.

As might be expected, less experienced therapists (< 5 years in practice) were somewhat more likely to experience progress than were highly experienced therapists who had been in practice from 15 to 50 years, but fully half of the latter group still showed evidence of felt progress. Despite this, highly experienced therapists were also somewhat more likely than their juniors to experience regress.

These findings are clarified when profession and experience level are considered jointly. The highest proportion of therapists showing progress were relatively inexperienced psychologists and both inexperienced and moderately experienced therapists in "other" professions; the lowest proportion was found for highly experienced therapists with a medical background. Those highly experienced medically trained therapists also showed the highest incidence of stasis. The potentially high-risk category of felt regress was found more frequently not only among moderately and highly experienced medical therapists but also among inexperienced psychologists. Those inexperienced psychologists might still have supervisors who could intervene supportively, but the more experienced medical practitioners would be less likely to have such resources available even though their need might be as great.

Theoretical Orientation

Some striking descriptive differences were also found when theoretical orientation groups were compared. Therapists who were theoretically uncommitted, having claimed no salient orientation, were by far the least likely to show signs of progress or flux and had the highest incidences of felt stasis and regress. Lower levels of progress and more frequent signs of flux and regress were also observed among mainly cognitive–behavioral therapists.

By contrast, broad-spectrum integrative–eclectic practitioners were the "most growing" therapists, being much more likely than most others to experience progress and least likely to show stasis. This may reflect a link between theoretical breadth and a tendency to experiment in practice. The experience of felt progress also characterized a majority of the mainly humanistic therapists, perhaps reflecting the emphasis of their orientation on openness to experience.

Personal Therapy

We also found an interesting association with current growth patterns with respect to therapists' personal therapy. Clinicians with no experience of personal therapy showed the lowest rate of felt progress and the highest rates of regress and stasis. By contrast, practitioners who were currently in therapy showed the highest rate of progress and the lowest rates of stasis. This influence of the therapists' personal therapy may be added to a number of others that have been recently documented (Orlinsky, Norcross, Rønnestad, & Wiseman, 2005), although the effect on current growth seems to fade when therapy had been experienced only some time in the past. It also reminds one again of Freud's (1937/1964) recommendation that practitioners should resume their personal therapy about every 5 years, and it tallies well with the fact that 3 in 10 of our Western therapists—including 1 in 6 of the most experienced therapists—actually were in personal treatment when they participated in the study.

Practice Conditions

Descriptive differences in current growth patterns were also associated with certain conditions of practice, such as setting, types of clientele, and patterns of work experience quality. These findings are presented in Appendix D (Table D.7).

Setting

Practitioners who conduct therapy only in inpatient settings had the lowest rates of felt progress and the highest rates of regress and stasis. Regardless of why this may occur, the finding should be a warning to supervisors and administrators in those settings. However, combining inpatient practice with work in some other settings (e.g., independent practice or outpatient institutional practice) appears to offset much of the disadvantage. By contrast, therapists who do have some independent private practice show high rates of progress and comparatively low rates of regress.

Client Age Groups

Some slight variations in current growth patterns were associated with treatment of different client age groups, with clinicians who conducted therapy with contrasting groups (children, adolescents, and adults) having the highest rate of felt progress and the lowest rate of regress. The complexity of other findings makes them difficult to interpret and suggests that factors other than client ages have more impact on therapists' experiences of current development.

Client Impairment Levels

We were surprised to note that our therapists' tendency to focus their practice on clients at different impairment levels was not significantly associated with current growth patterns. In fact, therapists whose caseloads included 50% or more of severely impaired clients evidenced slightly higher rates of progress and very slightly lower rates of regress. Thus, if therapists who treat patients only at inpatient institutions seem to be disadvantaged, it appears not to be due to the fact that their clients are more severely impaired—suggesting that contextual or institutional aspects of their work situation are the source of difficulty.

Practice Patterns

The quality of therapeutic work experience reflected in different practice patterns showed a very strong association with therapists' current growth patterns. For example, therapists experiencing an Effective Practice were more than twice as likely to experience current progress and six times less likely to show regress than therapists in a Distressing Practice. In fact, a substantially higher proportion of those having an Effective Practice experienced progress than therapists in any other group. As if to underline the association, therapists having a Challenging Practice were more likely than others to experience flux, those in a Disengaged Practice were more likely than others to experience stasis, and those with a Distressing Practice were more likely than others to experience regress.

OBJECTIVE PREDICTORS OF CURRENT DEVELOPMENT

To examine the influence of these diverse factors on current development more precisely, we turn next to separate controlled statistical analyses of Currently Experienced Growth and Currently Experienced Depletion. To assess possible predictors, we computed bivariate correlations between each dimension and a range of therapist and practice characteristics, as shown in Appendix D (Table D.8). Variables found to have correlations exceeding .10 were retained for use in hierarchical multiple regression analyses (MRAs), with a first block to control for the influence of nationality.

Currently Experienced Growth

The strongest bivariate correlate of Currently Experienced Growth shown in Table D.8 was the experience of therapeutic work as a Healing Involvement ($r = .52$), a finding clearly implied by the descriptive analyses of current growth patterns. Other notable bivariate correlates of Currently

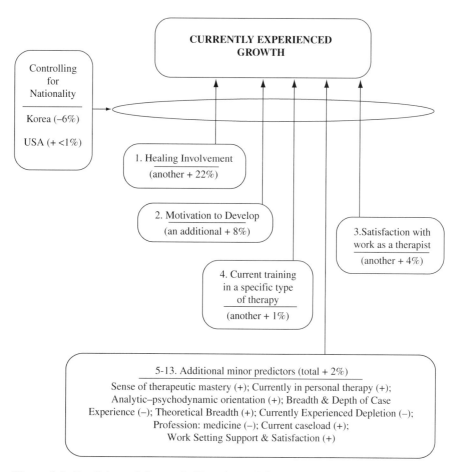

Figure 8.1. Predictors of Currently Experienced Growth.

Experienced Growth included Development of Psychotherapists Common Core Questionnaire (DPCCQ) scales assessing the Importance of Further Development ($r = .46$), Satisfaction With Therapeutic Work ($r = .40$), Work Setting Support and Satisfaction ($r = .30$), and the career development dimension of Felt Therapeutic Mastery ($r = .35$). There was also a notable negative correlation with being Korean ($r = -.25$), reflecting the fact that scores for that national subsample were clearly atypical.

The results of the MRA for the total sample are summarized in Figure 8.1 (see also Table D.9 in Appendix D). With variations due to nationality controlled, 13 variables jointly predicted more than one third (37%) of the remaining variance. Of that, three fifths was due to the influence of Healing Involvement alone. Beyond that, commitment to the Importance of Further Development was another strong predictor. Smaller but statistically significant additional contributions to Currently Experienced Growth were made by therapists' satisfaction with therapeutic work and their active use of various professional development resources such as current specialty training and personal therapy.

It is worth noting that some of the therapist and practice characteristics that appeared to be significantly associated with current growth patterns in our descriptive analyses failed to survive the statistical controls imposed in the MRA. Therapists' profession and experience level did not significantly predict Currently Experienced Growth; neither did their age and gender. Currently Experienced Growth was mainly influenced by therapists' experiences of therapeutic work, their motivation for continued development, and their use of resources to enhance professional development.

The generality of these predictors for therapists from different countries, despite their different mean levels of Currently Experienced Growth, is shown by the separate MRAs presented in Appendix D (Table D.10). Large amounts of the variance in Currently Experienced Growth were predicted in each case, and in each case most of the variance was predicted by the same two or three variables. Experiencing therapeutic work as a Healing Involvement was the leading predictor of Currently Experienced Growth among German therapists, Korean therapists, and therapists from "other" countries, and it was the second leading predictor for American and Norwegian therapists. Importance of Further Development was the leading predictor of Currently Experienced Growth for American therapists, the second leading predictor for therapists from Germany and "other" countries, and the third predictor for Norwegian and Korean therapists. Satisfaction With Therapeutic Work was the leading predictor of Currently Experienced Growth among Norwegian therapists; the second leading predictor among Korean therapists; and the third predictor for American, German and "other" therapists. These analyses consistently demonstrated the importance of therapists' work quality and motivation as elements in their positive experience of current development.

Currently Experienced Depletion

We used a parallel set of analyses to evaluate potential predictors of Currently Experienced Depletion. Table D.8 in Appendix D shows that the strongest bivariate correlates of Currently Experienced Depletion were therapists' tendency to experience therapeutic work as a Stressful Involvement and to feel Dissatisfaction With Therapeutic Work, especially if they had no concurrent compensatory experiences of satisfaction with their work as a therapist or of social support and satisfaction in their main work setting.

Results of the MRA of Currently Experienced Depletion for the total sample are summarized in Figure 8.2 (see also Table D.11 in Appendix D). With no significant variance due to nationality, nine variables jointly pre-

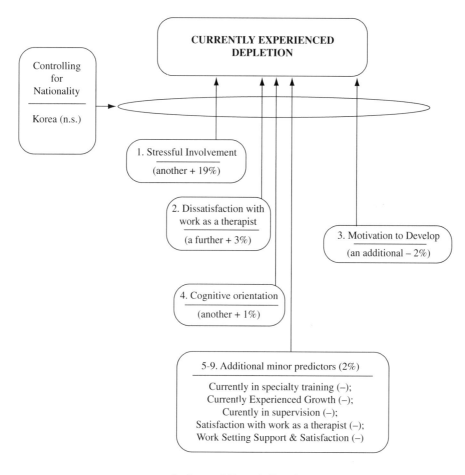

CURRENTLY EXPERIENCED
DEPLETION

Controlling
for
Nationality

Korea (n.s.)

1. Stressful Involvement

(another + 19%)

2. Dissatisfaction with
work as a therapist

(a further + 3%)

3. Motivation to Develop

(an additional – 2%)

4. Cognitive orientation

(another + 1%)

5-9. Additional minor predictors (2%)

Currently in specialty training (–);
Currently Experienced Growth (–);
Curently in supervision (–);
Satisfaction with work as a therapist (–);
Work Setting Support & Satisfaction (–)

Predictors of Currently Experienced Depletion
(total sample MRA)

Figure 8.2. Predictors of Currently Experienced Depletion.

dicted 28% of the variance. As anticipated, therapists' experiences of therapeutic work as a Stressful Involvement was by far the most important
predictor, accounting for more than three quarters of the amount predicted.
Dissatisfaction with work as a therapist added insult to injury.

However, some variables can also be viewed as mitigating the harmful
impact of Stressful Involvement, because they were negatively predictive
of Currently Experienced Depletion. Even when therapeutic practice was
stressful, Currently Experienced Depletion was less likely to be experienced
by therapists who were committed to their professional development, were
currently in specialty training or supervision, experienced some Currently
Experienced Growth and satisfaction with their therapeutic work, and had

social support and satisfaction in their main work setting. (These findings have practical implications that we discuss further in chap. 12.)

Again, it is worth noting that some therapist and practice characteristics implicated in the descriptive analyses of current growth patterns failed to survive the statistical controls imposed by the MRAs. These include therapists' profession, experience level, and practice setting, as well as their gender and nationality.

The MRAs that were computed separately for the main national subgroups to test the generality of these findings across countries are presented in Appendix D (Table D.12). In every subgroup, therapists' experiences of work with patients as a Stressful Involvement was the leading predictor of Currently Experienced Depletion, by itself accounting for 32% of the variance for Koreans, 23% for Norwegians, 22% for Germans, and 18% for Americans.

In Sum

These objective analyses reinforce the impression that therapists' experiences of current development are influenced mainly by the quality of their experiences in treating patients. The sense of ongoing growth as a therapist arises most strongly in a context of Healing Involvement with patients and satisfaction with one's work as a therapist, especially when accompanied by a commitment to further one's professional development. Correspondingly, a sense of decline or impairment as a therapist arises most strongly in a context of Stressful Involvement in working with patients and a felt lack of motivation for professional development.

These impressions are based on objective analyses that we, as researchers, have made of the dimensions underlying the information reported in the DPCCQ. We compare these next with the therapists' own perceptions of the positive and negative influences on their current development.

INFLUENCES ON CURRENT DEVELOPMENT
AS VIEWED BY THERAPISTS

One set of questions included in the DPCCQ asked practitioners directly about the impact of various influences on their current development. A list of 13 potential sources of influence was presented following the question "How much influence (positive and/or negative) do you feel each of the following is having on your current development as a therapist?" Each possible source of influence was rated on a 7-point scale ranging from +3 (*very positive*) to −3 (*very negative*), with a midpoint of 0. The instruction to respondents said "You may circle *both* a positive and a negative response."

TABLE 8.2
Perceived Sources of Influence on Currently Experienced Growth

Source of influence	n	Positive			Negative		
		M	SD	% High	M	SD	% Any
Experience in therapy with patients	4,643	2.4	0.8	84	0.1	0.3	5
Personal therapy, analysis, or counseling[a]	1,187	2.3	0.9	80	> 0.1	0.2	2
Getting supervision or consultation[b]	1,983	2.2	0.9	79	> 0.1	0.3	2
Taking courses or seminars[c]	1,357	1.8	0.9	63	> 0.1	0.2	2
Experiences in personal life	4,639	1.8	1.0	60	0.1	0.4	5
Informal case discussion with colleagues	4,637	1.6	1.0	55	> 0.1	0.2	2
Reading relevant books or journals	4,643	1.6	0.9	50	> 0.1	0.2	1
Working with cotherapists	4,108	1.1	1.0	36	0.1	0.3	4
Teaching courses or seminars	4,603	0.9	1.0	29	> 0.1	0.3	2
Institutional conditions of one's practice	4,637	0.9	1.0	27	0.4	0.8	24
Observing other therapists	4,111	0.9	1.0	26	> 0.1	0.3	2
Doing research	4,066	0.6	0.9	18	0.1	0.4	3
Other	4,121	0.1	0.5	5	> 0.1	0.2	1

Note. Ratings were made on a scale that ranged from 0 *(none)* to 3 *(very)*. Ratings of 2 or 3 were categorized as "high"; ratings of 1 to 3 were categorized as "any."
[a]Computed for therapists currently in personal therapy; for those who are not currently in therapy but have been in the past (*n* = 3,618), *M* = 1.5 and *SD* = 1.3 as a positive influence, *M* = > 0.1 and *SD* = 0.3 as a negative influence. [b]Computed for therapists currently in supervision; for those who are not currently in supervision but have been in the past (*n* = 2,445), *M* = 1.5 and *SD* = 1.0 as a positive influence, *M* = > 0.1 and *SD* = 0.2 as a negative influence. [c]Computed for therapists currently taking courses or seminars; for those who are not currently in supervision but have been in the past (*n* = 4,636), *M* = 1.6 and *SD* = 1.0 as a positive influence, *M* = > 0.1 and *SD* = 0.2 as a negative influence.

Our therapists' perceptions concerning positive and the negative influences on their current development are presented in Table 8.2.[4]

The first point worth noting is that therapists cited many more positive than negative influences on development. The strongest and most widely endorsed positive influence was "experiences in therapy with patients." Very nearly all (97%) of our therapists said this, with 84% rating the influence as "high." It is interesting to note that some 5% also rated "experiences in therapy with patients" as a negative influence, making it the second leading negative influence on current development (after "institutional conditions,"

---

[4]Each response was coded twice, once for positive and once for negative influence, on a 4-point (0–3) scale. (Thus, positive values were given for both poles if both sides of the bipolar 7-point scale were checked; if only side was checked, the other was scored as 0.) Where it could be determined from other items of the DPCCQ whether therapists had actually had a particular experience (e.g., personal therapy, or supervising others), results were computed just for those who had (and, separately, who were currently having) that experience (e.g., ever had personal therapy, were currently having personal therapy).

and tied with "experiences in personal life"). This illustrates the double-edged impact of therapeutic work, as does the fact that most (87%) of those who rated therapeutic work as a negative influence also rated it as a positive influence (with the positive intensity typically outweighing the negative).

Close behind direct experience with patients were the most widely endorsed positive influences on current development: "getting personal therapy, analysis or counseling" (rated highly by 80% of those currently in personal therapy) and "getting formal supervision or consultation" (rated highly by 79% of those currently receiving some form of regular supervision). Of those currently training in a specific type of therapy, 63% rated "taking courses or seminars" as a strong positive influence.

"Experiences in personal life" was rated as a strong positive influence on their current professional development by a large majority (60%) of our therapists, but 5% of the sample also rated their personal lives as a source of negative influence. It is clear that the therapists feel that other than professional factors have a real impact on professional development.[5]

Indications of negative influence on current development were basically quite rare, with one exception: As many as one in four therapists indicated that "the institutional conditions in which [they] work" were having a negative influence on their current development. Of these nearly 1,100 therapists, 19% rated that influence as very negative, and another 29% rated the influence of institutional conditions on them as moderately negative. Which particular aspects of institutional conditions were most deleterious was not specified, but some idea about that can be gained from the objective correlates of current development presented in Table D.8, which showed that Currently Experienced Depletion was significantly correlated with an absence of Work Setting Support and Satisfaction ($r = -.37$) and a lack of Professional Autonomy ($r = -.23$).

CONCLUDING COMMENT

Therapists' own perceptions of the influence on their current development appear to agree well with the results of our objective analyses. Practitioners rated "experiences in therapy with patients" as the most important positive and as one of the few negative influences on their current development. Controlled statistical analyses showed that experiencing therapeutic

---

[5] Four of the five sources of influence rated as most impactful (i.e. clients, supervision, personal therapy, and personal life) are all basically interpersonal in nature. These findings converge in some respects with the work of Rønnestad and Skovholt (2003), who formulated 1 of the 14 themes of professional development found in their data as follows: "Interpersonal sources of influence propel professional development more than 'impersonal' sources of influence" (p. 35).

work as a Healing Involvement was the leading predictor of Currently Experienced Growth and that finding therapeutic work to be a Stressful Involvement was the leading predictor of Currently Experienced Depletion.

Activities designed to enhance professional development—training, supervision, and personal therapy—were also highly rated as positive influence by therapists and were found among the significant predictors of Currently Experienced Growth. The institutional conditions in which therapists work were the only widely felt negative influence on current development, and work situation deficiencies were found among the significant predictors of Currently Experienced Depletion.

The salience of therapists' expressed motivation for further development, and their feeling of satisfaction and dissatisfaction with therapeutic work, as predictors of Currently Experienced Growth and Currently Experienced Depletion, suggest that positive current development is closely associated with the therapist's work morale, whereas a sense of current impairment seems to reflect a state of demoralization.

The high rates of commitment to continued development reported by therapists at all career levels, and the high degree of Currently Experienced Growth manifested by therapists at all career levels, point to the conclusion that much of this current growth serves to refresh the therapists' constantly challenged work morale and to regenerate their constantly eroded capacity to engage constructively with patients (Orlinsky, Rønnestad, et al., 1999). However, some part of current growth also constitutes a gradual enhancement and expansion of therapeutic skill and capacity through new learning. Some portion of currently experienced development must carry forward and incrementally accrue as a source of the therapist's Cumulative Career Development. We discuss in chapter 9 how that may happen.

9

CAREER DEVELOPMENT: CORRELATES OF EVOLVING EXPERTISE

DAVID E. ORLINSKY AND MICHAEL HELGE RØNNESTAD

Therapists' cumulative career development begins with the start of their first therapy case and extends to their most recent experiences in practice. We assessed this aspect of development in three ways using information collected with the Development of Psychotherapists Common Core Questionnaire. First and most directly, we sought a retrospective appraisal of career development from therapists by asking how much they had changed, improved, declined, and overcome past limitations since they began to work as therapists. In another approach, we examined the current level of therapeutic mastery that therapists felt they had attained at the present point in their careers, presumably as a result of their cumulative development, in contrast to the previous focus on the change they had experienced. Finally, as an indirect measure, we constructed a "skill change index" for therapists by computing the difference between estimates of their initial levels on a set of clinical skills and ratings of their current levels on those same skills (see Appendix D, Table D.4). The three measures proved to be sufficiently distinct in a factor analysis (reported in chap. 7) and were positively intercorrelated, as expected. This warranted their combination into a scale of Overall Career Development to form a more robust measure of the therapists' evolving expertise.[1]

In this chapter, we examine the correlates and predictors of Overall Career Development to understand how psychotherapists' accumulated expertise may evolve from therapeutic work with patients and then influence it in turn.

CORRELATES OF OVERALL CAREER DEVELOPMENT

Our first step in exploring the sources of Overall Career Development was to determine its bivariate correlations with therapists' demographic, professional, and practice characteristics. These are shown in Appendix D (Table D.13), both as direct correlations and as partial correlations controlling for the effect of practice duration. To better detect the relations of other therapist and practice characteristics with Overall Career Development, independent of longevity, we computed partial correlations that controlled the effect of practice duration.

Professional Characteristics

Career development (unlike current development) was strongly and positively correlated with practice duration. However, even with practice duration controlled there was still a fairly substantial correlation (r_p = .30) between Overall Career Development and therapists' Breadth and Depth of Case Experience. At every career level, therapists who have used a variety of treatment modalities tend to experience higher levels of development. This demonstrates that Overall Career Development reflects more than a mere passage of years.

In terms of professional background, therapists who were trained in psychology tended to have somewhat higher scores on Overall Career Development than those trained initially in medicine or social work, but the correlations were small and could reflect unrelated sampling differences between those groups.

Regarding theoretical orientation, the most striking finding was between Overall Career Development and Theoretical Breadth, in a way that was unaffected by practice duration (r = .25, r_p = .24). Therapists at every career level who combined several theoretical perspectives in their practice tended to evince greater amounts of career development. By comparison, the

---

[1] This broader measure also showed adequate internal consistency, as indicated by an alpha of .71. Comparable alphas for the three component measures are shown in Table 7.3.

differences in development among therapists espousing different orientations were actually rather slight.

The relevance of preparatory experience was best reflected in modest but meaningful correlations between Overall Career Development, specialized therapeutic training, and personal therapy. Controlling for practice duration showed, at each point in the career span, that higher levels of development were found among therapists who had previously trained in a specific type of therapy and who had previously experienced personal therapy. By contrast, there was curiously little evidence of a relation between Overall Career Development and the amount of didactic or academic training therapists received, or (when the effect of practice duration was controlled) with the overall amount of their supervision. These professional resources appear to contribute more to current development than to career development, but their impact on long-term development may well be mediated through the relation of Currently Experienced Growth to Overall Career Development that we note below.

Demographic Characteristics

Although older therapists, on average, experienced higher levels of career development, the association with age disappeared when practice duration was controlled; neither was therapists' gender related to Overall Career Development.

Differences between therapists of various countries also were minimal, with the exception of the Korean therapists, who tended to have lower scores on average. Although a large part of the negative correlation of career development was due to the relative inexperience of many therapists in that sample, a significant difference persisted when practice duration was controlled. How much that reflects therapists' distinctive culture or other sampling contingencies remains to be determined.

Practice Characteristics

At every career level, therapists who felt more support and more autonomy in their work settings also tended to experience higher levels of Overall Career Development. In a possible reflection of this, there was also a small positive association between career development and having some independent private practice, whereas those who practice in inpatient institutional settings seemed to have a slight disadvantage in this respect. Because the medically trained therapists in our sample were somewhat more likely to do inpatient therapy ($r = .26$), the association of these professional and practice characteristics with career development may have a common source.

Therapists' Work Experience

Of all the variables surveyed, Overall Career Development was most strikingly correlated with aspects of the therapists' work experience. At every career level, therapists who showed signs of greater development also experienced more Healing Involvement in their therapeutic work, felt higher levels of Satisfaction With Therapeutic Work, and exhibited more Currently Experienced Growth. The reverse is true as well: At all career levels, therapists who evinced *less* Overall Career Development also experienced working with patients as a Stressful Involvement and tended to show signs of Currently Experienced Depletion.

PREDICTORS OF OVERALL CAREER DEVELOPMENT

In the analyses of career development reported thus far, we controlled for practice duration but not for the overlapping effects of therapist and practice characteristics. The combined predictive effect of those variables, together with practice duration, can be gauged through the use of multiple regression analysis (MRA), which imposes controls for their simultaneous influences. As before, we used a two-stage hierarchical MRA model, allowing stepwise entry within each block of variables, with the first block controlling for notable differences in level among national subgroups. The second block included all the other demographic, professional, and practice characteristics that correlated .10 or higher with Overall Career Development, including practice duration.[2]

The results of this analysis for the total sample are summarized in Figure 9.1 (see also Appendix D, Table D.14). Controlling for national differences, a group of 11 variables together predicted 40% of the variance in therapists' Overall Career Development. Two of these variables predicted the lion's share: therapists' Breadth and Depth of Case Experience (17%) and their level of Currently Experienced Growth (11%). The first indicates that work in a variety of treatment modalities—group, couple, and family, along with individual therapy—acts as an accelerant to therapists' sense of career development. (This has implications for training programs that we discuss more fully in chap. 12.) The fact that Currently Experienced Growth

---

[2] For conceptual reasons, the variables reflecting current therapeutic work—Healing Involvement, Stressful Involvement, Satisfaction With Therapeutic Work, and a lack of Satisfaction With Therapeutic Work—were not included as predictors despite their high correlations with Overall Career Development. It seems more plausible to view these as effects rather than causes of the therapist's cumulatively acquired expertise, although they may also be indirect or mediated causes of career development in an extended network of dynamic influences (for a further discussion of this, see chap. 11).

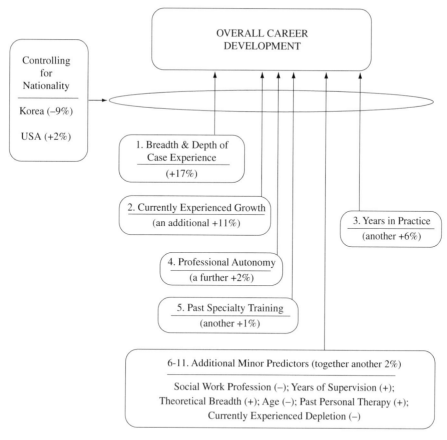

Figure 9.1. Predictors of Cumulative Career Development.

was a major additional predictor of Overall Career Development implies that current growth involves actual cumulative learning and not just an ongoing restoration of therapists' opennness, sensitivity, and morale.

Beyond those, an additional 6% of the variance in career development was predicted by practice duration. Thus, number of years of service does make some independent contribution to Overall Career Development, but that effect is secondary to the more important contributions made by broad-ranging experience and ongoing professional growth.

Smaller additional positive contributions in predicting Overall Career Development were made by the therapists' sense of control over their work conditions, their having received training in a specific form of therapy, and their having had longer supervision.

To test the generality of these findings, we computed separate MRAs for each of the main national subsamples. The results, shown in Appendix D (Table D.15), indicate that Breadth and Depth of Case Experience was the leading predictor of Overall Career Development among our therapists from the United States, Germany, and "other" countries and was the third leading predictor for Norway. In Norway and South Korea, on the other hand, Currently Experienced Growth was the leading predictor of Overall Career Development and was the second leading predictor among American, German, and "other" therapists. This consistency of principal predictors, as replicated across our main national samples, indicates their general importance as factors in the career development of psychotherapists.[3]

INFLUENCES ON CAREER DEVELOPMENT
AS VIEWED BY THERAPISTS

Therapists were asked in the Development of Psychotherapists Common Core Questionnaire to rate the positive and negative influences on their career development, using the same items they used with respect to their current development. This allows us to again compare therapists' perceptions with the objective analyses of career development predictors reported above. The therapists' ratings are shown in Table 9.1.

As with the similar ratings of influences on current development, the positive influences here far outweighed the negative. Once again, direct experience in therapy with patients was most frequently endorsed as a strong positive influence. This corresponds well with the finding that Breadth and Depth of Case Experience was the leading objective predictor of Overall Career Development.

The common high positive ratings given to supervision and personal therapy (among therapists who reported having had those experiences) further agree with their appearance as significant additional predictors of Overall Career Development. They complement direct clinical experience, helping therapists learn the lessons to be had from their work with patients. Together, these three constitute what may be described as the major triad

---

[3]There was also consistency across nationality groups, with some variation in salience, among other predictors. Thus, practice duration was the second leading predictor of Overall Career Development for Norwegian and Korean therapists and the third leading predictor for therapists in Germany and "other" countries. Professional Autonomy was the fourth leading predictor of career development among therapists from the United States, Germany, and "other" countries. Past specialty training was the third leading predictor for Korean therapists, the fifth for therapists from Norway and "other" countries, and the sixth among therapists in the United States and Germany. We checked the possibility that the relatively small contribution of practice duration to career development in the American sample might have been due to the inclusion of a large group of relatively inexperienced social workers by recomputing the MRA without including the latter as a variable, but practice duration still ranked low among the seven predictors ($R = .748$, adjusted $R^2 = .549$), which emerged in the following order: Breadth and Depth of Case Experience, 32.5%; Professional Autonomy, 7.0%; Currently Experienced Growth, 6.9%; Work Setting Support and Satisfaction, 4.1%; professional identification as a psychologist, 2.78%; past specialty training, 1.1%; and years in practice, 0.6%.

TABLE 9.1
Perceived Sources of Influence on Career Development

Source of influence	n	Positive influence			Negative influence		
		M	SD	% High	M	SD	% Any
Experience with patients	4,516	2.5	0.7	89	0.1	0.3	3
Getting formal supervision[a]	3,966	2.3	0.9	80	< 0.1	0.3	2
Getting personal therapy[a]	3,570	2.2	1.0	77	< 0.1	0.2	2
Experiences in personal life	4,129	1.9	1.0	66	0.1	0.3	4
Informal case discussions	4,506	1.8	0.9	63	< 0.1	0.3	2
Taking courses or seminars	4,514	1.8	0.9	61	< 0.1	0.2	3
Reading books or journals	4,515	1.7	0.9	55	< 0.1	0.2	2
Giving formal supervision[a]	2,382	1.6	1.0	53	< 0.1	0.2	1
Working with cotherapists	4,496	1.4	1.1	45	0.1	0.4	5
Observing other therapists	3,859	1.3	1.0	39	0.1	0.3	3
Institutional work conditions	4,507	1.0	1.0	32	0.4	0.8	26
Teaching courses/seminars	4,540	1.0	1.0	31	< 0.1	0.3	2
Doing research	4,506	0.7	1.0	19	0.1	0.4	4
Other	4,120	0.2	0.7	6	< 0.1	0.2	1

Note. Items were rated on a scale that ranged from 0 (none) to 3 (very). High = 2 or 3; Any = 1–3.
[a]Computed, respectively, for therapists who indicated that they received supervision, had received personal therapy, or had given supervision.

of positive influences on therapists' career development (Orlinsky, Botermans, & Rønnestad, 2001), and they are as well the same factors that therapists rated as having the most positive influences on their current development.

In contrast to these professional factors, experiences in personal life are the next most salient among the influences to which most therapists attribute their development—ranking ahead of academic resources, such as taking courses or reading books and journals. Many also feel that their career development has been facilitated by personal contacts with colleagues in the context of informal case discussions. From this and other sources (e.g., Rønnestad & Skovholt, 2003; Skovholt & Rønnestad, 1995), it appears that therapists tend to place greater emphasis on the interpersonal influences, in professional and in private life, than on more purely intellectual influences, important as the latter clearly are.

The only notable negative influence on career development was attributed by therapists to the institutional conditions in which they practiced, which they did as well with respect to current experienced development.

THERAPEUTIC WORK AND PROFESSIONAL DEVELOPMENT

In our analyses thus far, we have explored the relationship between therapeutic work experience and professional development in only one direction, finding (in chap. 8) that Healing Involvement with patients was by far the strongest and most consistent predictor of therapists' Currently Experienced Growth and, similarly, that Stressful Involvement was the strongest and most consistent predictor of Currently Experienced Depletion. Successful and satisfying experiences of actively helping their patients seem to fill therapists with a glow of positive, morale-sustaining energy, enabling them to return to their work with enthusiasm and freshness. Frustrating and threatening experiences with patients whom they are unable to help seem, on the other hand, to undermine therapists' morale and drain or divert their energy from further involvement.

In this chapter, we have discussed how Currently Experienced Growth, in its turn, contributes substantially to therapists' career development. Together with Breadth and Depth of Case Experience, it is consistently among the leading predictors of Overall Career Development, exceeding the ripening, mellowing impact that is due mainly to an increasing number of years in practice. We interpreted this as meaning that a portion of Currently Experienced Growth does involve incremental learning, resulting in a deepening of therapists' understanding and a broadening and refining of their skills—even if a greater portion of Currently Experienced Growth seems to result in regeneration or repair rather than new growth.

In our analyses thus far we have chosen not to explore the contribution that varying levels of current and career development may make to the character and quality of therapists' work experience. We made this decision partly on conceptual grounds (i.e., the plausibility of viewing variables as potential causes or effects) and partly to establish a logical order of presentation. Now, having looked progressively at therapeutic work experience, current development, and career development, we can examine more effectively how much those aspects of professional development contribute to Healing Involvement and Stressful Involvement, the dimensions that underlie and organize therapists' varying experiences of therapeutic work.

Professional Development and Healing Involvement

To explore the impact of professional development on Healing Involvement, we recomputed the MRA previously reported in chapter 5, this time including in the equation the newly constructed development dimensions. As a first step, we again computed bivariate correlations for Healing Involvement and a series of therapist and practice characteristics, and then we included variables with $r \geq .10$ as potential predictors in a hierarchical MRA, in which the first block controlled for national differences (see Appendix D, Tables D.16 and D.17). The addition of development dimensions extended the amount of variance in Healing Involvement that was

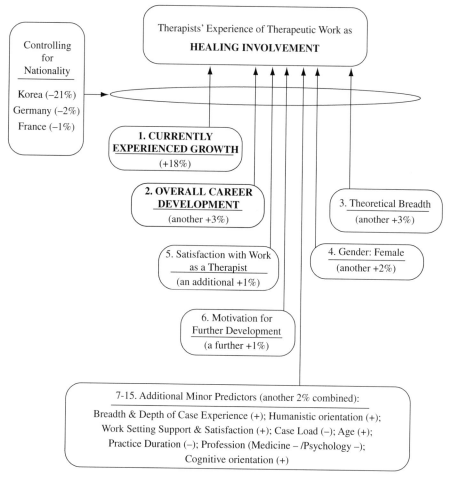

Figure 9.2. Predictors of Healing Involvement including current and career development.

predicted after controlling for nationality from 18% (see Appendix C, Table C.14) to 29%.

The order of the new predictors for Healing Involvement is summarized in Figure 9.2. Currently Experienced Growth was clearly the leading predictor of Healing Involvement, accounting for 18% after national differences were removed. Overall Career Development was the second leading predictor, accounting for an additional 3%. Thus, three quarters of the predicted variance in Healing Involvement remaining after controlling for nationality was accounted for by the therapists' status on the two development dimensions.

It is worth emphasizing that Theoretical Breadth, the most salient predictor in the previous MRA, was the third leading predictor in this analysis. Equating for both nationality and developmental status, Theoretical Breadth still contributed significantly to therapists' experience of their work as a Healing Involvement. At all levels of development, therapists who bring a broader array of conceptual perspectives to their treatment of patients are more likely to experience their clinical work as successful and inherently rewarding.

As in the previous analysis, therapist gender and work satisfaction also accounted for small amounts of additional variance in Healing Involvement. Thus, with the factors of nationality, current and career development, and theoretical breadth equalized, female therapists were somewhat more likely than men to experience Healing Involvement and, with gender also equalized, satisfaction with one's work as a therapist also contributed to Healing Involvement.

The basic consistency of these findings is demonstrated by the reanalyses of Healing Involvement we conducted separately for the main national subsamples (see Appendix D, Table D.18). Currently Experienced Growth was the leading predictor of Healing Involvement in all national subgroups, and Overall Career Development was the second or third leading predictor for Americans, Germans, Koreans, and therapists from "other" countries. Other consistently significant predictors included satisfaction with one's work as a therapist, Theoretical Breadth, Breadth and Depth of Case Experience, and therapist gender.

Professional Development and Stressful Involvement

We followed the same procedures in recomputing the analysis of predictors for Stressful Involvement (see Appendix D, Tables D.16 and D.19). After controlling for nationality, therapist and practice variables accounted for a total of 25% of the variance in Stressful Involvement, compared with 5% previously predicted (in Table C.16). The results of the new MRA, summarized in Figure 9.3, show that this fivefold increase in predictive power was due mainly to the therapists' level of Currently Experienced Depletion. The therapists' sense of dissatisfaction with work as a therapist was an aggravating factor, adding to the demoralizing impact. By contrast, higher concomitant levels of Overall Career Development and Currently Experienced Growth helped to counteract the effect of therapists' demoralization on their therapeutic work with patients.

Currently Experienced Depletion was consistently the leading predictor of Stressful Involvement when MRAs were recomputed separately for therapists from the United States, Norway, Germany, South Korea, and "other"

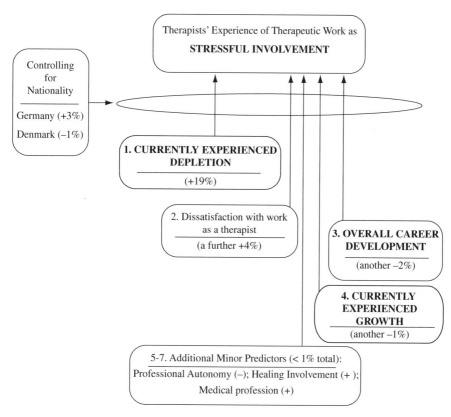

Figure 9.3. Predictors of Stressful Involvement including current and career development.

countries (see Appendix D, Table D.20). Limited career development was the second leading predictor of Stressful Involvement among therapists in the United States, South Korea, and "other" countries and ranked third among our Norwegian and German therapists. Dissatisfaction with work as a therapist was the second leading predictor for the Norwegian and German therapists and was the third leading predictor for American, Korean, and "other" therapists.

An Apparent Circularity

These new results leave us confronting an apparent circularity, with respect to both Healing Involvement and Stressful Involvement. The cross-influences of therapeutic work experience and professional development are reflected in the fact that Healing Involvement in therapeutic work, Currently Experienced Growth, and Overall Career Development are strongly and positively intercorrelated (rs = .54, .52, and .44)[4] and were moderately and negatively correlated (rs ranged from −.11 to −.22) with Stressful Involvement and Currently Experienced Depletion, which themselves are strongly and positively intercorrelated (r = .44).

Our interpretation of these correlations is that the *circularities* they appear to suggest are due to an absence of temporal perspective. Given a temporally extended framework, as required by the concept of development, those apparent circularities are viewed as interlocking *spirals* of reciprocal influence.

In the positive spiral, Healing Involvement is the leading predictor of Currently Experienced Growth (see Figure 8.1). In turn, Currently Experienced Growth is one of the main predictors of Overall Career Development (see Figure 9.1). Finally, both Currently Experienced Growth and Overall Career Development are leading predictors of Healing Involvement (see Figure 9.2). In this aspect of the cycle, Overall Career Development may be seen as a source of therapeutic mastery that contributes to Healing Involvement, and Currently Experienced Growth may be seen as a source of renewed enthusiasm and optimism that sustain the therapists' motivation for therapeutic work.

In the negative spiral, Stressful Involvement is the strongest predictor of Currently Experienced Depletion (see Figure 8.2). In its turn, Currently Experienced Depletion is the strongest predictor of therapists' experiencing therapeutic work as a Stressful Involvement (see Figure 9.3). This aspect of development describes a self-reinforcing cycle of stress and demoralization that is detrimental for therapists at all levels, but is mitigated somewhat at higher levels of career development.

We present in chapter 11 a conceptual model of the two spirals of reciprocal influence linking therapeutic work with professional development, and in chapter 12 we explore some practical implications of the model. First, to complete our report on the aspects of professional development, in the next chapter we compare cohorts of therapists who are at distinctly different stages of their therapeutic careers.

---

[4]Indeed, there is sufficient internal consistency among these three variables to support their combination into a single comprehensive dimension having a very general name like "being a therapist the right way," but doing so would offer little conceptual leverage on the phenomena that we seek to understand.

10

COMPARATIVE COHORT DEVELOPMENT: NOVICE TO SENIOR THERAPISTS

MICHAEL HELGE RØNNESTAD AND DAVID E. ORLINSKY

Some psychotherapists may experience sudden changes in their development that are associated with life-transforming events (Rønnestad & Skovholt, 2001) or with critical incidents in their professional work (Flanagan, 1954; Skovholt & McCarthy, 1988), whereas others experience a more orderly process of change. But even though individuals experience development in various ways and for different reasons, there are bound to be similarities among therapists in certain types of change that occur through their careers. These will reflect differences between neophyte therapists who have just begun to practice under the watchful eye of a supervisor, those same therapists as they may appear after 10 or 15 years of clinical experience, and those same therapists again after a further 20 or 25 years, in the final phase of practice before retirement.

As we noted in chapter 7, the usual approach to studying career changes involves cross-sectional or longitudinal research designs. As originally conceived, our study emphasized the cross-sectional approach (with plans for limited longitudinal studies) because a therapist's career span may well last 50 years. To implement cross-sectional comparison, we delineated six career cohorts that seemed reasonable in terms of our knowledge of theoretical models in the literature (cf. Skovholt & Rønnestad, 1995, chap. 1) and the distribution of therapists in our database (see descriptions in chap. 7 and Table 7.4).

Novice therapists were defined as having had less than 18 months of experience and averaged just over 6 months in practice. *Apprentice* therapists were defined as having from 1.5 to less than 3.5 years of experience and averaged close to 2.5 years in practice. At a more advanced but still early career level, *graduate* therapists had at least 3.5 but less than 7 years of experience and, in our sample, averaged 5 years in practice.

The next three cohorts consisted of relatively mature therapists, and the boundaries defined for these cohorts were broader. *Established* therapists had at least 7 but less than 15 years of experience and averaged 10 years in practice. *Seasoned* psychotherapists were defined as having at least 15 but less than 25 years of experience (averaging 19 years in practice), and *senior* therapists had from 25 to 55 years of experience (averaging 31 years in practice).

COMPARISON OF CAREER COHORTS

When comparing cohorts in a cross-sectional analysis, it is important to view the observed differences as a source of hypotheses about the paths and processes of development for several reasons, some common to all cross-sectional analyses and others specific to this study. In all cross-sectional studies, the differences observed may be due to selective attrition or dropout of cohort members over time (e.g., the respecialization of some therapists into other professional activities), or it may be attributable to historical changes that impinged on the careers being studied (e.g., the advent of managed care in mental health service delivery systems). Moreover, the mere fact that each cohort contains different individuals means that, although they all share some common qualities—here, as professional psychotherapists—they are also bound to differ from one another in other respects that remain unknown.

Complicating the situation in our study is that fact our database is composed of various samples that differ in their constitution (see Appendix B). To check on potential confounds, we have generally replicated analyses in separate subgroups based on nationality or other therapist characteristics—a strategy that is satisfactory when searching for *commonalities* and general effects because observed differences can be set aside pending further study. However, when the research interest focuses on between-group *differences*, as it does with respect to career cohorts, that strategy is less effective precisely because there are many potential sources of difference. Our strategy in that case has been to exclude known sources of extraneous difference (e.g., the Korean therapists), by comparing only cohorts of therapists from Western countries (predominantly the United States, Norway, and Germany), or by comparing cohorts of therapists of the same profession. We also sought to provide detailed descriptions of sample characteristics so that readers can form their own estimates of potential biases.[1]

Cumulative Career Development

Career cohorts have been defined in chronological terms and thus ought to be strongly related to therapists' experiences of cumulative career development. We found that to be the case in chapter 9 ($r = .47$ for practice duration and Overall Career Development, as shown in Appendix D, Table D.13), but we also know from the controlled multiple regression analyses (see Appendix D, Tables D.14 and D.15) that Overall Career Development is more powerfully predicted by Breadth and Depth of Case Experience across treatment modalities, and by Currently Experienced Growth, than by a count of the number of years one has practiced. Nevertheless, it is logical and potentially instructive to start our descriptive analysis by comparing the distribution of cumulatively experienced development across career cohorts.

The percentages of Western therapists with high, moderate, and low scores on Retrospected Career Development and Felt Therapeutic Mastery (two of the three dimensions of cumulative development we presented in chap. 7) are shown in Table 10.1. The overall impression—implied in the results of previous analyses—is that of an orderly progression *across cohorts*, with a significant differential between aspects of experienced development, and yet significant variation *between individuals* within cohorts regarding the extent of career development actually experienced.

First, we note a steady linear progression from lower to higher levels of Retrospected Career Development and Felt Therapeutic Mastery. Within this progression there clearly is also a tendency for therapists to vary in the extent to which they have experienced development, as shown by the fact that some therapists in each cohort are to be found at each level of experienced development. The third trend worth noting is a consistent modesty among therapists with respect to their sense of attained mastery relative to their experienced sense of cumulative change and improvement.

---

[1] A correct interpretation of results requires noting the presence and potential influence of other types of heterogeneity across cohorts, such as the presence of more or fewer therapists from a particular country, of a particular profession or theoretical orientation, or of a particular gender. By the same token, when similarities or regularities across cohorts are observed, they may be regarded as robust because they emerged despite the extraneous differences in cohort composition that would generally mask them through the influence of developmentally irrelevant variability.

TABLE 10.1
Cumulative Career Development as Experienced in Successive Career Cohorts of Western Therapists

Career cohort	Retrospected Career Development[a]				Felt Therapeutic Mastery[b]			
	n	Low	Moderate	High	n	Low	Moderate	High
Novice	467	**35.9**	38.7	25.3	472	**61.0**	36.5	**2.5**
Apprentice	512	**18.2**	**48.2**	33.6	213	**34.0**	62.1	**3.8**
Graduate	715	8.3	**46.7**	45.0	737	17.3	**72.6**	**10.2**
Established	1,299	6.3	36.0	57.6	1,379	7.3	69.5	23.2
Seasoned	937	5.3	26.9	67.7	1,039	**4.6**	58.2	**37.2**
Senior	300	**4.1**	**19.6**	**76.2**	362	**4.7**	45.7	**49.6**

Note. Unless otherwise noted, all table values are percentages. Numbers in boldface type indicate adjusted standardized residuals ≥ 2.
[a] $\chi^2(10, N = 4,083) = 574.5$, $p < .00000$. [b] $\chi^2(10, N = 4,169) = 1,210.4$, $p < .00000$.

The percentage of novices who, looking back, feel they have already developed is 25%, but only one tenth that number (2.5%) subjectively sense a high level of mastery. The same differential between retrospected improvement and actual mastery is characteristic of each successive cohort, even among seniors, who have practiced therapy for 25 to more than 50 years. As might be expected, looking back over their time in practice, three quarters of the senior therapists experienced much Retrospected Career Development, but only one half felt that they had attained a high level of therapeutic mastery. Most of the remaining senior therapists were in the moderate range of mastery, with only 5% revealing a low level (in contrast to 61% of novices and 34% of apprentices, who experienced low levels of therapeutic mastery).[2]

These results indicate that, on average, therapists in different cohorts do indeed experience different degrees of "therapeutic maturity," as Goldberg (1992) suggested and as reported in Skovholt and Rønnestad's (1995) qualitative study of therapist development. The fact that successive cohorts differ in terms of cumulative career development sets the context for what is observed next when cohorts are compared with regard to their experiences of therapeutic work.

Work Practice Patterns

The extent to which psychotherapists in successive career cohorts differ in their experience of therapeutic work is an interesting issue. The percentages of therapists in an Effective Practice, a Challenging Practice, a Disengaged Practice, and a Distressing Practice, at each career level, are shown in Table 10.2. To estimate the extent of variation due to sample differences among cohorts, we conducted separate analyses for therapists of all professions from Western countries and for therapists of all countries who have in common the fact that they were trained in psychology.[3]

There is a clear and rather substantial trend for the incidence of Effective Practice to increase across successive cohorts, from approximately 38% or 39% to a high of 60% among Western therapists and from between 41% and 46% to a high of 65% among psychologist–psychotherapists. This was complemented by a clear and rather substantial trend for the incidence

---

[2] The "deviant cases" comprising the 5% of senior therapists having a low sense of therapeutic mastery and the 2% to 4% of novices and apprentices having a high sense of mastery both constitute important targets for further analysis.
[3] The difference in demographic and professional characteristics between the Western therapists and the psychologically trained therapists (shown in Appendix D, Table D.21) are greater among novices and apprentices than among seasoned and senior therapists, due to the fact that a disproportionately high percentage of psychologists in our sample were highly experienced therapists.

TABLE 10.2
Career Cohort and Practice Experience Patterns Among Western Therapists and Psychologists

Career cohort	n	Effective Practice	Challenging Practice	Disengaged Practice	Distressing Practice
Western therapists[a]					
Novice	330	**39.4**	21.8	19.4	**19.4**
Apprentice	372	**38.2**	22.8	**22.8**	**16.1**
Graduate	627	**43.7**	23.0	19.6	**13.7**
Established	1,149	**52.9**	22.5	16.9	**7.7**
Seasoned	849	**54.7**	24.1	**14.3**	**6.9**
Senior	237	**60.3**	20.7	**12.7**	**6.3**
Psychologists[b]					
Novice	136	**45.6**	16.9	18.4	**19.1**
Apprentice	177	**41.2**	21.5	**24.9**	**12.4**
Graduate	354	49.2	22.0	17.8	**11.0**
Established	727	55.8	22.1	16.8	**5.2**
Seasoned	598	56.4	24.9	**12.4**	6.4
Senior	181	**65.2**	21.0	**10.5**	**3.3**

Note. Unless otherwise noted, all table values are percentages. Numbers in boldface type indicate adjusted standardized residuals ≥ 2.
[a]$\chi^2(15, N = 3,564) = 117.6, p < .0000.$ [b]$\chi^2(15, N = 2,173) = 80.7, p < .00000.$

of Distressing Practice to decrease, from 19% to a low of 6% among Western therapists and from 19% to a low of 3% among psychologists.

It is curious that in both analyses novices were slightly more likely than apprentices to experience an Effective Practice, although in both analyses apprentices were less likely than novices to have a Distressing Practice. In something of a turnabout, the rates of Disengaged Practice in both analyses reached a peak (23%–25%) among apprentices and then declined steadily across successive cohorts to a low among senior therapists (11%–13%). This suggests that some apprentice therapists, at least, took shelter from the stressfulness of therapeutic work by personally distancing themselves from the work experience—a need that evidently diminished among the therapists who remained in practice to populate our more experienced cohorts.

In contrast to these trends, the percentage of Western therapists who experienced a Challenging Practice was fairly constant across cohorts (ranging from 21% to 24%) and was fairly constant across cohorts for psychological therapists (from 17% to 25%). This may reflect the fact that therapists at all career levels are about equally likely to encounter clients who are not readily helped by therapy, whether because they lack the personal resources to do so or because their life situations undermine the positive impact that therapy can have.[4]

Dimensions of Therapeutic Work Experience

A comparison of the career cohorts of Western therapists with respect to the specific dimensions of work experience is presented in Appendix D (Table D.23). The results can be summarized as follows.

---

[4] A more highly controlled but statistically less powerful assessment of these findings is presented in Appendix D (Table D.22), in which we report the results of separate analyses we computed for American psychologists, Norwegian psychologists, and German psychologists. To preserve minimally adequate cell sizes, the six career cohorts were collapsed into three broader career levels. The analyses compared therapists in practice for less than 5 years with those having 5 to 15 years of practice and others who had been in practice from 15 to 50 years. Overall, the results show a basic similarity in the pattern across successive career levels. In each country, the most experienced psychologists were most likely to experience an Effective Practice, although the range of percentages was smallest in the Norwegians and greatest among the German psychologists. The likelihood of experiencing a Distressing Practice declined most greatly among German therapists (from 29% to 9%) and among Americans (from 17% to 2%) but was consistently low for Norwegian psychologists at all three career levels. Disengaged Practice also declined more dramatically among German psychologists (from 29% to 17%) and American psychologists (11% to 3%) but was basically the same (13% to 15%) at all levels for the Norwegian therapists. The most striking difference in practice patterns among our psychologists from the three countries was in the incidence of Challenging Practices, which declined over successive career levels for the Norwegians but appeared to double from the least to most experienced therapists among American and German psychologists. Because the sample sizes involved in these analyses are considerably reduced by disaggregation, the results should be viewed as tentative findings requiring replication (or correction) in future analyses.

Treatment Goals

A broad similarity characterizes the typical treatment goals endorsed by different career cohorts. In every cohort, the three leading goals were to help patients gain "a strong sense of self-worth and identity"; "improve the quality of their relationships"; and "understand their feelings, motives, and behavior." Another goal frequently endorsed by therapists in all cohorts was to help patients "develop the courage to approach new or previously avoided situations." The only statistically significant difference among cohorts for a leading treatment goal was the extent to which the top four goals selected included helping patients to "integrate excluded or segregated aspects of experience." This typically psychodynamic and humanistic goal was least common among novices, who were less inclined to those orientations, and relatively more prominent among graduate, established, and seasoned therapists, for whom those orientations had more appeal (see Table D.21).

Current Therapeutic Skills

Differences among career cohorts in therapists' ratings of current therapeutic skills were noted earlier (chap. 4), but we review them again here. In Appendix D, Table D.23 shows progressive and statistically significant increases across successive cohorts in the mean levels of Technical Expertise, Basic Relational Skills, and Advanced Relational Skills. The most significant differences typically were between the three least experienced and the three most experienced career levels, but descriptively there appear to be notable improvements in skills even between the novice and apprentice therapist cohorts.[5]

Difficulties in Practice

One would also hope to find significant decreases in the frequency of difficulties in successive career cohorts, and the data (in Table D.23) bear that out. There were modest but significant differences in each of the three types of difficulty, although descriptively the most notable decline is in

---

[5] In addition, the dimensionality of this domain was clarified only when factor analyses were computed separately for each career cohort, as the dimensions became progressively more differentiated the longer therapists had practiced. Novice therapists experienced only a single general dimension of current therapeutic skill. On the other hand, the analysis of current skill ratings of apprentice therapists effectively distinguished between relational and technical skills, and this same distinction was observed in separate analyses of graduate and established therapists. In more experienced cohorts, a subset of the skills that less experienced therapists defined as Technical Expertise was seen by seasoned therapists as part of Basic Relational Skills and then was distinguished by senior therapists as Advanced Relational Skills, distinct from but complementary to Basic Relational Skills and Technical Expertise. The skills in question were those concerned with effectively managing the subtler aspects of the therapeutic relationship, such as transference and countertransference reactions.

Professional Self-Doubt, which is the dimension that reflects therapists' professional qualities more than patient characteristics (Frustrating Treatment Case) or a mix of patient and therapist characteristics (Negative Personal Reaction). Difficulties of all types were not very frequent but were least commonly experienced by senior therapists.

Coping Strategies

Senior therapists were understandably less likely to Seek Consultation as a way of coping than were novices and apprentices, who typically have supervisors readily available for that purpose (Table D.23). However, senior and seasoned therapists were more often inclined to Problem Solve With a Patient or to exercise reflective control when confronted with a difficulty in practice. There were no significant differences among cohorts in tendency toward Reframing the Helping Contract, which is probably considered only as a last resort. Neither were there significant differences in the tendency to Avoid Therapeutic Engagement as a means of coping with difficulties, which may be related more to therapist personality and stressful life quality than to career status.

Relational Agency

Therapists at all career levels experienced themselves as highly Invested in relating to patients, with all cohorts averaging above 2 on a 0–3 scale (see Table D.23). Moreover, this high level of personal investment was maintained, and even slightly increased, in successive cohorts and was highest of all among senior therapists, who might plausibly be thought to have become less Invested. A slight but statistically significant increase in feeling Efficacious was observed across cohorts, which is reassuring if expectable. More noteworthy, perhaps, is the fact that therapists' sense of being Invested in relating to patients was at a higher level than feeling Efficacious with patients over the whole career spectrum, suggesting a characteristic but perhaps productive gap between aspiration and performance.

Relational Manner

In their manner of relating to patients, therapists in different cohorts did not experience themselves differently with respect to being either Dominant or Accommodating (see Table D.23). However, although therapists in all cohorts perceived themselves as very Affirming and only slightly Reserved with patients, therapists in successively more experienced cohorts became even more Affirming and less Reserved. These high levels of being Affirming parallel the high levels of being Invested and reflect the energy therapists expended in generating a stimulating and supportive relational environment for patients (Orlinsky, 1998; Orlinsky et al., 1996), energy that is routinely depleted and in need of being replenished (Orlinsky, Rønnestad, et al., 1999).

In-Session Feelings

The high levels of Flow experienced by therapists at all career levels (averaging 2.4 on a 0–3 scale) suggest that the emotional–motivational energy for engaging in therapeutic work is in fact replenished for most therapists, most of the time. Differences among cohorts were nonsignificant and were found only in the hundredths place of the decimal. However, it is clear that some meaningful differences do exist between therapists in the affective quality of sessions with patients. We were not surprised to replicate the finding that novices definitely experience Anxiety during therapy sessions more frequently than others (Skovholt & Rønnestad, 2003). Also, as expected, established, seasoned, and especially senior therapists are less likely to feel anxious than their juniors. A slight but statistically significant trend shows that novices (and apprentices), perhaps in compensation, are somewhat less likely than their elders to experience Boredom during sessions. Nevertheless, both Boredom and Anxiety are relatively rare experiences, especially when compared with the feelings of being stimulated, engrossed, and inspired that define the Flow dimension.

Healing and Stressful Involvement

All the specific aspects of therapeutic work just reviewed were found (in chap. 4) to be reflected, at a higher level of analysis, in two broad dimensions of work experience called *Healing Involvement* and *Stressful Involvement*.[6] We used these to profile the practice patterns that we reused in comparing career cohorts (see Table 10.2). At the level of constituent dimensions, Table D.23 documents further what Table 10.2 implies: a progressive, statistically significant increase in Healing Involvement and decrease in Stressful Involvement over successive cohorts. Table D.23 also shows, reassuringly, that at every career level Healing Involvement is at least twice as high as Stressful Involvement. This suggests that, from the psychotherapist's perspective, clinicians in all cohorts can have a favorable impact on their patients.[7]

---

[6] A third broad dimension, Controlling Involvement, was defined descriptively but did not have adequate internal consistency to be used in further analyses as a psychometrically reliable measure.
[7] However, as "a word to the wise," it seems that prospective patients might be well advised to seek treatment from highly experienced therapists, or at least from those who already have had a minimum of 5 to 7 or even 10 years in clinical practice.

Current Growth Patterns

One would expect that successive career cohorts will experience patterns of current growth in different degrees, and the data in Table 10.3 show that this was indeed the case. Apprentice therapists manifested the highest rate of Felt Progress and the lowest rate of Felt Stasis in the analyses of both Western therapists and psychologists. This contrasted with the comparatively lower rates of Felt Progress and relatively higher rates of Felt Stasis among seasoned and senior therapist cohorts (although Felt Progress was still high, and Felt Stasis low, among the latter).[8]

Examination of cohort means for Currently Experienced Growth and Currently Experienced Depletion shows that the differences in current growth patterns was due to a slightly increasing tendency of the more senior cohorts to experience depletion, rather than to a decline in growth. Currently Experienced Growth remained at a consistently high level at all career levels. On the one hand, this reinforces our interpretation of Currently Experienced Growth as a process of regeneration primarily and new learning secondarily; however, the findings suggest a heightened vulnerability to depletion among highly experienced therapists that may deserve specific remedial attention.[9]

Influences on Therapists' Current Development

Finally, one may ask whether the same things influence therapists' current growth at different career levels or whether the factors that stimulate growth are different at different periods in the therapists' career. The analysis presented in Table 10.4 shows the mean level and relative rank of each perceived influence on current development for successive cohorts.

We have found that differences emerge only as nuances within a broad context of similarity. For example, "experiences in therapy with patients"

---

[8] Slightly contradictory results were found when we analyzed the data separately for psychologists in the United States, Norway, and Germany (Appendix D, Table D.24), but those results are less stable because of the relatively small samples and, related to that, the fact that only three broadly defined career levels could be compared. For example, Felt Progress was at a peak (73%) for the few Americans with less than 5 years in practice in our sample and at a high plateau (50%) for the larger number who had been in practice for 5 to 15 or 15 to 50 years. By contrast, Felt Progress was about the same (52%–56%) for Norwegian psychologists at all three career levels, and for German psychologists Felt Progress was at a peak (53%) in the middle years but declined to a low point (33%) among those in practice for 15 to 50 years. Thus, although the main finding remains clear—that Felt Progress is the dominant pattern in all groups—clarity about trends and patterns in specific national professional groups will require much more extensive data.

[9] Another unexpected finding is that about one fourth of the novice therapists manifested felt stasis (both among Westerners and psychologists). This high level contrasted with the low level of Felt Stasis among apprentices, suggesting an initial latency of responsiveness among some beginners that is followed by a second period of vigorous development.

TABLE 10.3
Current Development Patterns Across Career Cohorts Among Western Therapists and Psychologists

Career cohort	n	Felt Progress (%)	Felt Flux (%)	Felt Stasis (%)	Felt Regress (%)	Currently Experienced Growth[c] (M)	Currently Experienced Depletion[d] (M)
Western therapists[a]							
Novice	322	57.8	**10.6**	24.2	7.5	3.5	0.7
Apprentice	333	**64.6**	12.0	**14.1**	9.3	3.6	0.8
Graduate	547	56.9	14.4	18.5	10.2	3.6	0.9
Established	1,085	57.0	15.5	20.1	**7.5**	3.6	0.8
Seasoned	850	**52.2**	15.2	21.8	10.8	3.5	0.9
Senior	278	**48.9**	17.3	22.3	11.5	3.5	0.9
Psychologists[b]							
Novice	153	59.5	**7.2**	23.5	9.8	3.5	0.8
Apprentice	199	**64.3**	11.1	**13.6**	11.1	3.6	0.8
Graduate	362	56.9	14.6	17.7	10.8	3.6	0.9
Established	773	56.8	**17.2**	18.9	**7.1**	3.6	0.9
Seasoned	657	52.8	14.8	20.9	11.6	3.5	1.0
Senior	235	**48.1**	17.4	21.3	13.2	3.5	0.9

Note. Values in the central block of 4 columns are cohort percentages of high Progress, Flux, Stasis, and Regress; chi-square statistics comparing frequencies across cohorts were computed, and percentages in boldface type indicated adjusted standardized residuals ≥ 2. Values in the right-hand block of 2 columns are cohort means based on scales for Currently Experienced Growth and Currently Experienced Depletion that ranged from 0 to 5; one-way analyses of variance were computed comparing means across cohorts, with between-cohort differences ($p < .05$ by Scheffé test) indicated in parenthesis (cohorts indicated by numerals: 1 = novices, 2 = apprentices, 3 = graduates, 4 = established therapists, 5 = seasoned therapists, 6 = seniors).

[a]$\chi^2(15, N = 3,415) = 37.1, p < .01.$ [b]$\chi^2(15, N = 2,379) = 36.1, p < .01.$ [c]$F(5, N = 3,420) = 1.8, p = ns.$ [d]$F(5, N = 3,544) = 4.4, p < .000$ (5, 3 > 1). $F(5, N = 2,387) = 1.3, p = ns.$ $F(5, N = 2,508) = 1.7, p = ns.$

TABLE 10.4
Leading Positive Influences on Current Development by Career Cohort for Western Therapists

Influence	Novice (< 1.5 yrs)		Apprentice (1.5–3.5 yrs)		Graduate (3.5–7 yrs)		Established (7–15 yrs)		Seasoned (15–25 yrs)		Senior (25–45 yrs)	
	Rank	M	Rank	M	Rank	M	Rank	M	Rank	M	Rank	M
Experience in therapy with patients[a]	2	2.3	1	2.4	1	2.4	1.5	2.4	1	2.4	1	2.5
Getting personal therapy, analysis, or counseling[b]	3	2.2	2.5	2.3	2	2.3	1.5	2.4	2	2.3	2	2.1
Getting formal supervision or consultation[c]	1	2.4	2.5	2.3	3	2.2	3	2.2	3.5	2.0	4.5	1.8
Taking courses or seminars[d]	5	1.8	4	1.8	4	1.8	4	1.9	3.5	2.0	3	1.9
Experiences in personal life outside therapy[e]	5	1.8	5.5	1.7	5	1.7	5	1.8	5	1.8	4.5	1.8
Informal case discussion with colleagues[f]	5	1.8	5.5	1.7	6	1.6	6.5	1.6	7	1.6	8	1.5
Reading books or journals relevant to your practice[g]	7	1.6	7	1.6	7	1.5	6.5	1.6	7	1.6	7	1.6
Giving formal supervision or consultation[h]	8	1.2	8	1.2	8	1.3	8	1.4	7	1.6	6	1.7

Note. Cohort means on scales for influence on current development ranged from 0 to 3; one-way analyses of variance were computed comparing means across cohorts, with between-cohort differences ($p < .05$ by Scheffé test) indicated in parentheses (cohorts indicated by numerals: 1 = novices, 2 = apprentices, 3 = graduates, 4 = established therapists, 5 = seasoned therapists, 6 = seniors). Within-cohort ranks of the influence are specified when the cohort mean for that influence was rated ≥ 1.5.

[a]F (5, N <equal) 4,152) = 1.6, *ns*. [b]Computed only for those currently in personal therapy ($n = 1,155$: 143 novices, 167 apprentices, 263 graduates, 357 established therapists, 194 seasoned therapists, and 31 senior therapists); F (5, $N = 1,149$) = 0.7, $p = ns$. [c]Computed only for those currently in formal supervision ($n = 1,828$: 251 novices, 234 apprentices, 376 graduates, 595 established therapists, 326 seasoned therapists, and 46 senior therapists); F (5, $N = 1,822$) = 5.7, $p < .0000$ (1 > 5, 6). [d]Computed for those currently in specialty therapy training ($n = 1,239$: 169 novices, 204 apprentices, 298 graduates, 384 established therapists, 159 seasoned therapists, and 25 senior therapists); F (5, $N = 1,233$) = 1.7, $p = ns$. [e]F (5, $N = 4,149$) = 0.6, $p = ns$. [f]F (5, $N = 4,146$) = 3.3, $p < .01$ (1 > 6). [g]F (5, $N = 4,154$) = 1.0, $p = ns$. [h]Computed for respondents who have supervised other therapists ($n = 2,390$: 90 novices, 129 apprentices, 242 graduates, 776 established therapists, 823 seasoned therapists, and 330 senior therapists); F (5, $N = 2,384$) = 10.4, $p < .0000$ (6 > 4, 3 ,2 ; 1; 5 > 4, 3 , 2).

is almost always the leading source to which therapists attribute their current growth, followed by their experiences in "personal therapy, analysis or counseling" and "formal supervision or consultation." These form a dominant triad of positive influences at virtually every level of career development.

Less salient but still meaningful sources of current development include "taking courses or seminars" (especially if the therapist is currently in a specialty program), "experiences in personal life outside of therapy," "informal case discussion with colleagues," and "reading books or journals relevant to [one's] practice." These also are much the same influences to which therapists attribute their overall career development (see Table 9.1, and Orlinsky, Botermans, & Rønnestad, 2001).

It is noteworthy that for novice therapists formal supervision was more salient as a positive influence than was direct clinical experience with patients, which in other cohorts always ranked first. Discussing cases informally with colleagues was also more salient for novices than for members of other career cohorts. By contrast, taking courses or seminars was viewed as relatively less important by novices—although (or possibly because) that is a more common experience for novices.

Apprentice, graduate, and established therapists resemble each other in their ranking of influences on their current development. Seasoned therapists follow the same pattern, with the addition of "giving formal supervision or consultation" to the list of leading influences.

It is interesting that a shift in priorities appears to take place among senior therapists. Direct clinical experience with patients is more than ever the leading influence to which they attribute their professional growth—and, if they are currently in personal therapy, that ranks second—whereas taking courses or seminars (if they are doing so) ranks third, and getting supervision and seeking consultation tie for fourth. However, relatively few senior therapists are in personal therapy (9%) or in formal supervision (16%) or in a specialty training (10%), and for the majority who were not so engaged, the second leading influence on current professional growth was "experiences in personal life outside of therapy." Indeed, personal life was a more salient influence on current development even for senior therapists who were involved in those other professional activities.

SUMMARY

Comparisons of therapists' career cohorts reveal both differences and continuities in their experiences of therapeutic work and professional development. Although time in practice, as a separate variable, was not the strongest predictor of Overall Career Development (as noted in chap. 9), it nevertheless formed a meaningful basis for descriptive cross-sectional analysis.

Imposing a moderate degree of control by comparing only Western therapists first, and then only professional psychologists with one another, made it possible to see that therapists in successive career cohorts have a greater sense of cumulative improvement, a stronger sense of therapeutic mastery, and a more effective experience in therapeutic practice. Beginning therapists felt less Anxiety and Professional Self-Doubt as apprentices than as novices, but they experienced significantly higher levels of both than did senior therapists.

By contrast, therapists in all career cohorts experienced themselves as strongly Invested and Affirming in relating to patients and felt a consistently high level of Flow during therapy sessions. Similarly high levels of Currently Experienced Growth were also observed for therapists at all career levels, even among those who had been in practice for many years, supporting the interpretation of this experience as a process of renewal and regeneration.

Regarding current influences on development, therapists at all career levels gave prominence to the same dominant triad of influences: learning by working with patients, being in personal therapy, and taking supervision, although formal supervision was the most salient influence for novices, and personal life events were comparatively more salient as a source of influence for senior therapists.

In the final chapters of this book, we offer a theoretical synthesis of our findings, explore their implications for clinical training and practice, and discuss the questions they raise for future research.

IV

INTEGRATION AND IMPLICATIONS

11

THEORETICAL INTEGRATION: CYCLES OF WORK AND DEVELOPMENT

DAVID E. ORLINSKY AND MICHAEL HELGE RØNNESTAD

The time has come to take stock and make a reckoning: to review the main findings reported in this book, and to reflect on what they show about the nature of therapeutic work and professional development.

We start this process, first, by summarizing our key findings about therapists' experiences of therapeutic work. Then, we revisit the main points of our findings regarding therapists' experiences of professional development. Finally in this section, we review the relationships between the varied aspects of therapeutic work and professional growth, before offering a theoretical interpretation of the findings later in the chapter.

THE MAIN FINDINGS

Work Experience

Modes of Involvement

Analyses of many specific aspects of therapeutic work, described by a large and diverse group of therapists, resulted in the depiction of two inclusive modes of participation identified as Healing Involvement and Stressful Involvement. *Healing Involvement* reflects a mode of participation in which therapists experience themselves as personally committed and affirming in relating to patients, engaging at a high level of basic empathic and communication skills, conscious of Flow-type feelings during sessions, having a sense of efficacy in general, and dealing constructively with difficulties encountered if problems in treatment arose. By contrast, *Stressful Involvement* is a pattern of therapist experience characterized by frequent difficulties in practice, unconstructive efforts to deal with those difficulties by avoiding therapeutic engagement, and feelings of boredom and anxiety during sessions.

Although it would be hard to experience both modes of involvement at the same time with the same patient, Healing Involvement and Stressful Involvement are not mutually exclusive when viewed in terms of a therapist's overall practice, because one mode (e.g., Healing Involvement) may be the norm with some or most of a therapist's patients while the alternate mode (e.g., Stressful Involvement) predominates with just one or a few. It is also conceivable that both modes of involvement may be experienced at different times in a single treatment case—as, for example, a case that starts out well but subsequently becomes problematic for the therapist.

Practice Patterns

The statistical independence of Healing Involvement and Stressful Involvement at the level of the therapist's practice led to the delineation of four practice patterns based on the relative salience of the two modes in the therapist's overall work experience. An *Effective Practice* is characterized by the presence of much Healing Involvement and little Stressful Involvement. A *Challenging Practice* for the therapist is characterized by the presence of much Healing Involvement but also more than a little Stressful Involvement. By contrast, a *Distressing Practice* signifies the presence of more than a little Stressful Involvement along with not much Healing Involvement. Finally, a *Disengaged Practice* for the therapist reflects a situation defined by little Stressful Involvement combined with not much Healing Involvement.

Half of the Western therapists in our study experienced an Effective Practice by our criteria, and one quarter of the sample fit the Challenging Practice pattern—with both patterns reflecting high levels of Healing Involvement. In both cases, the therapists clearly were engaged personally in their work with patients. This included therapists of every theoretical orientation, nationality, and career level.

Thus, from the perspective of a large majority of therapists, psychotherapy is a matter not only of procedure (what the therapist does) but also of manner (how it is done) and presence (who does it). They experienced themselves not as detached technicians dispassionately administering treatment procedures but, rather, as healers working with heart as well as mind.

The traditional image of the psychotherapist as a neutral, detached, impersonal presence is clearly at odds with how most therapists experience themselves and appears to be typical only of a minority who, by comparison, experience themselves as relatively ineffective. Only 1 in 6 of the therapists in our study experienced themselves in a Disengaged Practice, in which they saw themselves as neutral, distant, impassive practitioners—and as less empathic, affirming, skillful, and efficacious. There were also 1 in 10 therapists for whom therapeutic work was actually a Distressing Practice. (In the next chapter, we offer some recommendations, derived from our findings, about how to help both these minorities improve in their experience of therapeutic work.)

Professional Development

Four concepts of development and four corresponding research strategies were considered in this study's design, of which three were included. *Currently Experienced Development* represents therapists' ongoing experiences of growth and depletion as they engage in psychotherapeutic work. *Cumulative Career Development* reflects therapists' experiences of improvement and decline over the time since they began to practice their profession. *Comparative Cohort Development* involves cross-sectional analyses to detect similarities and differences between groups of therapists at successive positions in the professional career, from novices to seniors. These three concepts and research strategies were included in the design. A fourth concept, *Sequential Individual Development*, would have required long-term longitudinal analysis and was not viewed as a practical approach for this study (although a foundation for later work of this sort was prepared).

Current Development

Analyses of therapists' reports resulted in identification of two dimensions of current development: *Currently Experienced Growth* and *Currently Experienced Depletion*. Currently Experienced Growth reflects an enthusiastic sense of ongoing improvement in therapists' understanding of and ability to do therapeutic work and a sense of gradually overcoming past limitations. Because high levels of Currently Experienced Growth were observed at all career stages, we interpreted the experience as having two aspects: one consisting of new learning that accumulates over time as a main source of career development and another consisting of positive work morale resulting in the recurrent refreshment of therapists' personal openness and motivation for therapeutic work. By contrast, *Currently Experienced Depletion* reveals a sense of increased routinization in conducting therapy, disillusion about its effectiveness, and a decline in empathic responsiveness to patients. We interpreted this as reflecting the abrasive aspects of therapeutic work and a demoralization that, if unchecked, could result in burnout.

Currently Experienced Growth and Currently Experienced Depletion were statistically independent at the level of overall practice, indicating that current development is best represented by a profile of therapists' scores on the two dimensions. Thus, we constructed four profile categories to reflect patterns of current development. Current *progress* is an experience of much Growth and little Depletion, which typified about half of our therapists. Current *flux* reveals a pattern of much Growth combined with more than a little Depletion. Current *stasis* reflects a steady state involving little Depletion and not much Growth. Current *regress* reflects a sad state of more than a little Depletion and not much Growth, which was the situation of about 1 in 10 of our therapists.

Career Development

Three different aspects of Cumulative Career Development were assessed by the Development of Psychotherapists Common Core Questionnaire, resulting in the derivation of multi-item scales for *Retrospected Career Development*, *Felt Therapeutic Mastery*, and a *Skill Change Index*. Retrospected Career Development includes therapists' estimates of their overall change, improvement, and transcendence of limitations since starting in practice. By contrast, Felt Therapeutic Mastery reflects the therapists' current sense of professional adeptness and expertise, including mastery of therapeutic strategies and techniques, moment-by-moment understanding of the therapeutic process, ability to deal constructively with their patients' and their own emotional reactions, and a general sense of artistry in the therapeutic craft. Finally, the Skill Change Index represents the mean difference between therapists' ratings of their initial and current levels on 12 distinct clinical skills. As expected, these three aspects of career development were substantially and positively intercorrelated (although not to the point of being redundant), and we combined them into a comprehensive scale called *Cumulative Career Development*. Although this measure is positively correlated with the number of years in practice, as one would hope, diversity and depth of experience rather than mere duration of practice proved to be the main predictor of Cumulative Career Development.

Cohort Development

The length of time in practice of therapists in our sample ranged from a few months to more than 50 years. Having an ample number of therapists at every career level let us divide the sample into six career cohorts:

(a) *novices*, who had less than 1.5 years of experience; (b) *apprentices*, with 1.5 to 3.5 years of practice; (c) *graduates*, who had done therapy for 3.5 to 7 years; (d) *established* therapists, who had been in practice for 7 to 15 years; (e) *seasoned* therapists, with 15 to 25 years of experience; and (f) *senior* therapists, who had been in the profession for 25 years or more. We compared these groups, which represent successive periods in a psychotherapist's career, on a series of dimensions reflecting their experiences of therapeutic work and professional development.

Although they clearly differed in Cumulative Career Development, therapists in all career cohorts value their continuing development highly and, more surprising, therapists at all levels (including seasoned and senior therapists) showed high levels of Currently Experienced Growth. Therapists at all career levels further agreed that direct experience in therapy with patients, personal therapy, and formal case supervision were the leading influences on their career development and on their current development. However, therapists in successive cohorts exhibited progressively increasing levels of Healing Involvement and decreasing levels of Stressful Involvement, with the result that the incidence of Effective Practice grew from about 40% to 45% among novices to 60% to 65% among senior therapists, the incidence of Disengaged Practice diminished to half its earlier level (from 23%–25% to 11%–13%), and the incidence of Distressing Practice dropped from about 20% to a low of 3% to 6%.

Interrelations of Work and Development

Analyses of the factors that predict therapists' levels on the main work involvement dimensions and the dimensions of current and career development revealed two notable findings (shown in Table 11.1). First, an impressive amount of the variance in each of those dimensions was successfully predicted after controlling for differences between countries: 29% for Healing Involvement, 25% for Stressful Involvement, 37% for Currently Experienced Growth, 28% for Currently Experienced Depletion, and 40% for Cumulative Career Development. In each case, just a few variables accounted for a substantial majority of added variance.

Second, an apparent circularity emerged in the relations between work involvement and development dimensions. Healing Involvement was the leading predictor of Currently Experienced Growth, Currently Experienced Growth was one of the main predictors of Cumulative Career Development, and both current and Cumulative Career Development accounted for most of the variance in Healing Involvement. The positive correlations between these dimensions were high but far short of redundant (see Appendix D, Table D.25). In effect, therapists at the highest levels of career development and current growth showed the highest levels of Healing Involvement,

TABLE 11.1

Leading Predictors of Work and Development Dimensions: Total Sample

Criterion variable	Leading predictors	Δ Variance[a]
	Positive developmental cycle	
Currently Experienced Growth (37% variance predicted)	Healing Involvement	+22%
	Importance of Further Development	+8%
	Satisfaction with work as therapist	+4%
Cumulative Career Development (40% variance predicted)	Breadth and Depth of Case Experience	+17%
	Currently Experienced Growth	+11%
	Practice duration	+6%
Healing Involvement (29% variance predicted)	Currently Experienced Growth	+18%
	Cumulative Career Development	+3%
	Theoretical Breadth	+3%
	Negative developmental cycle	
Currently Experienced Depletion (27% variance predicted)	Stressful Involvement	+20%
	Dissatisfaction with work as a therapist	+3%
	Importance of Further Development	−2%
Stressful Involvement (25% variance predicted)	Currently Experienced Depletion	+19%
	Dissatisfaction with work as therapist	+4%
	Cumulative Career Development	−2%

[a]Percentages of added variance controlling for differences associated with nationality.

therapists with the highest levels of Healing Involvement experienced the highest current growth levels, and therapists who experienced the highest current growth levels were among those who advanced most in career development.

Similarly, a substantial positive correlation was found between Stressful Involvement and Currently Experienced Depletion. Practitioners whose therapeutic work was most stressful were the ones most likely to feel depleted, and at the same time the therapists who felt most depleted were the ones most likely to experience therapeutic work as stressful. This vicious cycle was exacerbated if the practitioners felt generally dissatisfied with their work as therapists, but it was attenuated if they were committed to their further development as therapists and if they had attained a higher level of Cumulative Career Development.

A CYCLICAL–SEQUENTIAL MODEL OF PSYCHOTHERAPEUTIC DEVELOPMENT

We suggested earlier that these apparent circularities, if viewed as temporally extended, actually reflect developmental cycles. Metaphorically, the circles—stretched by the forward thrust of time's arrow—should be visualized as *spirals*. There are two such spirals operating concurrently, one representing a cycle of positive development and the other a cycle of negative development. The actual course of a therapist's development is determined by the balance between these two interrelated and partially interpenetrating cycles—although, for the sake of clarity, we begin by discussing each separately.

Positive Developmental Cycle

The positive cycle of events is represented in Figure 11.1 as a pattern of interlocking loops—a short interior loop and a long exterior loop—each with some independent (external) influences.

First, a *short interior* loop (in the lower left quadrant of Figure 11.1) reflects the close connection between therapeutic work experienced as Healing Involvement and the therapists' sense of Currently Experienced Growth, both directly and indirectly through the effect of each on the therapists' work satisfaction. First, experiencing therapy as a Healing Involvement generates a sense of Currently Experienced Growth and work satisfaction in therapists. In return, Currently Experienced Growth and satisfaction with therapeutic work both contribute to the practitioners' positive work morale, which enables them to bring a sense of engagement, optimism, and openness to their ongoing work with patients. Last, therapists' continually renewed sense of engagement, optimism, and openness in turn increases the likelihood that their participation in therapy will be experienced as a Healing Involvement.

In addition, a *long exterior* loop (extending from the lower left quadrant to the upper right quadrant and back in Figure 11.1) reflects the less immediate but cumulative connection between Healing Involvement and Cumulative Career Development. Experiencing therapy as a Healing Involvement generates a sense of Currently Experienced Growth, part of which does consist of an expanding mastery of therapeutic skills. This expanded mastery, as part of the therapists' Cumulative Career Development, results in a greater sense of assurance, resourcefulness, and flexibility in approaching their work with patients, which independently increases the likelihood that that their participation in therapy will be experienced as a Healing Involvement. (As noted in Table 11.1 and as seen in Figure 11.2, the expansion of therapists' Cumulative Career Development also decreases the likelihood that therapeutic work will be experienced as a Stressful Involvement.)

Therapeutic Work as a Healing Involvement

The experience of Healing Involvement is indicative of having therapeutically effective, personally absorbing, and strongly affirming relationships

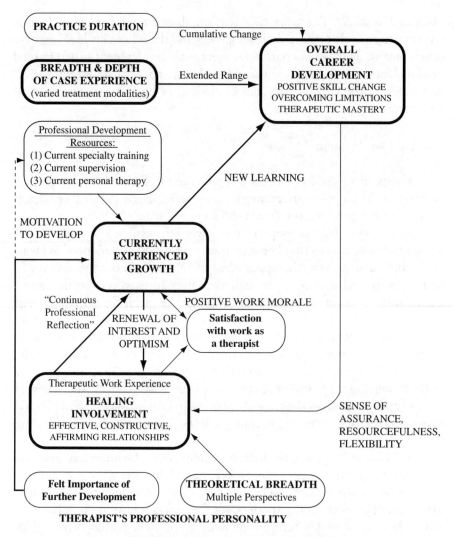

Figure 11.1. Positive developmental cycle linking therapeutic work to professional development.

with patients and, on the basis of our findings, Healing Involvement has three main independent sources.

One source is the level of therapists' Cumulative Career Development, reflecting improvement in clinical skills, increasing therapeutic mastery, and a gradual surpassing of past limitations as a therapist (part of the long developmental cycle depicted in Figure 11.1). Accumulating career development enables therapists to approach therapeutic work with a sense of assurance, resourcefulness, and flexibility—factors that should increase

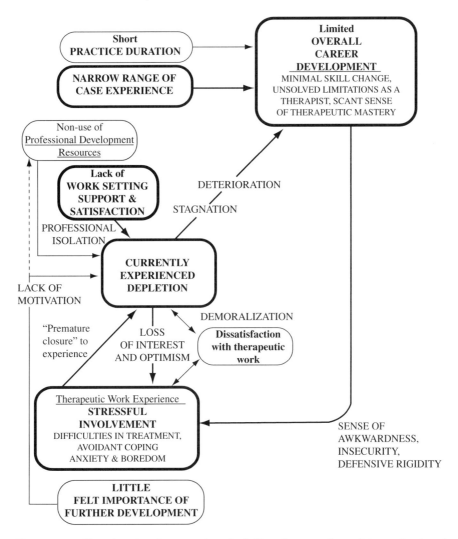

Figure 11.2. Negative developmental cycle linking therapeutic work to professional development.

the likelihood of their work with patients being experienced as a Healing Involvement.

The therapists' theoretical breadth is another positive influence on Healing Involvement (shown at the bottom of Figure 11.1). Breadth of perspective enables therapists to view patients from different angles, and in a multiplicity of conceptual contexts, rather than fitting all patients to a single theoretical template. Theoretical breadth enhances the therapists' adaptive flexibility in responding to the varying challenges that patients present and enriches the process of "continual professional reflection" (Rønnestad & Skovholt, 1991; Skovholt & Rønnestad, 1995) through which therapists learn the lessons imparted by clinical experience.

The third and most powerful influence on Healing Involvement, however, is the therapists' sense of Currently Experienced Growth, which remains at a high level in all career cohorts. The positive work morale derived from this sense of current growth energizes therapists to apply their skills and understanding on behalf of their patients. The genuine interest, investment, and optimism that therapists of all orientations actually convey to patients must be a major part of the common factors that so much research identifies as a key source of treatment outcome.

Currently Experienced Growth

The findings of our study have led us to interpret Currently Experienced Growth as having two aspects. One aspect is positive work morale, which has a direct feedback link to therapists' experience of their therapeutic work. We view this as a process of remoralization in which the tiring and taxing nature of therapeutic work is counteracted and the therapist's openness to and zest for encountering patients are continuously restored and refreshed (Orlinsky, Rønnestad, et al., 1999)—a process that is comparable, with respect to the therapist's participation in treatment, to the remoralization that so positively influences the patient's well-being (Frank, 1974; Howard, Lueger, Maling, & Martinovich, 1993). This remoralization process helps repair the abrasions and stresses of therapeutic work that inevitably accrue through a relatively slight but widespread tendency toward routinization, disillusionment, and loss of empathic responsiveness. Two main sources of the remoralization process are, primarily, the intrinsic satisfaction of therapeutic work itself, reflected in the therapists' sense of efficacy and feelings of Flow, which are part of Healing Involvement, and secondarily, the more general sense of worthiness and satisfaction that therapists derive from being treatment providers.

The second aspect of Currently Experienced Growth is a process of contemporary learning from clinical experience through continuous professional reflection. This aspect feeds forward to Cumulative Career Development (see upper right quadrant of Figure 11.1) in the form of new learning. Both the feedforward and feedback aspects of current growth are probably stimulated by therapists' experiences of Healing Involvement, accounting for the strength of the statistical relationship. By contrast, the new learning aspect of Currently Experienced Growth is probably supported especially by therapists' motivation for continued improvement. This motivation, seen in the importance that therapists attach to further professional development, prompts them to seek and use development-related resources such as supervision, personal therapy, and specialty training courses but, perhaps more importantly, fosters a process of continuous professional reflection. Through this process therapists respond (consciously or preconsciously) to the complexities and challenges of therapeutic work, learning to adapt through the complementary actions of assimilation and accommodation (Piaget, 1950, 1981) and enabling them cumulatively to become—through ongoing cognitive, affective, and interpersonal learning (Jennings & Skovholt, 1999; Skovholt & Jennings, 2004)—ever more adept as reflective practitioners.

Cumulative Career Development

For psychotherapists, Cumulative Career Development, as distinct from mere length of time in practice, consists of having improved in therapeutic skills, overcome past limitations in therapeutic ability, and attained a higher level of therapeutic mastery. Through this progressive enrichment therapists develop a fund of clinical wisdom and expertise on which they draw in their work with patients and that serves as a foundation for the sense of assurance, resourcefulness, and flexibility that (along with theoretical breadth) allows them to tailor treatment to the individual needs of their patients.

Our findings indicate three main independent sources of Cumulative Career Development, two of which are represented in Figure 11.1 as external influences. The dominant source is breadth and depth of case experience across treatment modalities. This variety evidently creates heightened clinical contrasts and reveals parallels among treatment modalities that provide a challenge and stimulus to professional growth in therapists. Currently Experienced Growth functions as another potent source of Cumulative Career Development, providing a fertile ground for new learning. Thus, although breadth and depth of clinical experience are an impetus to career development, the readiness and ability of therapists to benefit from varied experience also is crucial. Cognitive and affective intelligence, personal openness, tolerance for complexity, and an ability to manage anxiety are undoubtedly essential for learning. Finally, time for the maturation process to unfold is also a contributing factor in career development. Therapists are like good wines, able to deliver an immediate and satisfying impact even when young but capable of displaying a still more valuable refinement and finesse as they mature.

Negative Developmental Cycle

The negative spiral of influences between therapeutic work and professional development is generally, but not entirely, the obverse of the positive spiral, because some different variables are included in it. Figure 11.2 shows a similar structure of two interconnected loops, together with some external influences. The *short inner* loop (lower left quadrant) represents a relationship of reciprocal influence between Stressful Involvement in therapeutic work and Currently Experienced Depletion. The *long outer* loop includes the therapists' Cumulative Career Development as well.

Therapeutic Work as a Stressful Involvement

The experience of Stressful Involvement is indicative of therapists' having fairly frequent difficulties in practice, an inclination to escape from difficulties by avoidance of therapeutic engagement, and a propensity to feel anxious or bored during sessions. Stressful Involvement has two main sources.

One source of Stressful Involvement is a low level of Cumulative Career Development. Therapists who have experienced little Cumulative Career Development—typically because they are beginners—are more likely to be relatively awkward, insecure, and somewhat rigid in their approach to patients. Therapists who present themselves and interact with patients in this way are more likely to evoke negative responses from patients and to have less success, and both of those results are likely to make the therapists' participation more stressful.

However, therapists at all levels of career development are especially likely to experience Stressful Involvement when they have become demoralized in their work through a combination of Currently Experienced Depletion and general dissatisfaction with therapeutic work. This demoralization, more than anything else, is likely to convey a dispirited and dispiriting lack of interest or investment or hopefulness to patients, further aggravating rather than counteracting the demoralization that patients who come for therapy are prone to feel (Frank, 1974; Frank & Frank, 1991).

Currently Experienced Depletion

Stressful Involvement in therapeutic work is the main source of Currently Experienced Depletion and acts in two ways. The primary source is difficulties with patients that are not constructively managed; such difficulties arouse in the therapist feelings of anxiety, boredom, or both. As these threaten to become overwhelming, they engender a reaction that Rønnestad and Skovholt (1991) defined as *premature closure*. Skovholt and Rønnestad (1995) noted that "Premature closure means interrupting the reflection process before the assimilation/accommodation work is completed. It is an unconscious, predominantly defensively motivated, distorting process that sets in when the challenge is too great" (p. 135).

Stressful Involvement in therapy also leads to a sense of dissatisfaction with therapeutic work that contributes to Currently Experienced Depletion and thereby augments the therapist's demoralization. Demoralization and premature closure in the therapist foster a loss of interest in working with patients and a decline in optimism about the outcome of that work, which in turn increase the likelihood that therapy will be a Stressful Involvement for the therapist and, quite likely, for his or her patients as well. Therapists who feel dispirited and disillusioned, who convey a subtle sense of cynicism or pessimism to their patients, are even more likely to experience difficulties in treatment and to cope poorly with them. Because of the therapists' premature closure to experience, this may be coupled with a rigid adherence to an inappropriate therapeutic frame or a dogmatic insistence on particular interpretations that can produce harmful results for patients (e.g., Henry, Schacht, & Strupp, 1990).

An additional independent source of Currently Experienced Depletion is the therapists' lack of motivation for further professional development and, convergent with that, a lack of work setting support. Fortunately, these lacks imply that practitioners who are strongly motivated to develop as therapists, and who do feel supported in their work setting, will be less prone to Currently Experienced Depletion even when therapeutic work becomes a Stressful Involvement for them. To some extent, Currently Experienced Depletion can also be mitigated by the therapists' use of professional development resources such as formal supervision, advanced training, or personal therapy. Of course, those who do so are most likely to be therapists who are strongly motivated to extend their professional development.

Cumulative Career Development

In addition to its immediate negative impact on therapeutic work, Currently Experienced Depletion also has a long-term negative impact on Cumulative Career Development. At the least, Currently Experienced Depletion may foster a state of stagnation in which the therapist changes little over time. In the worst case, a protracted period of Currently Experienced Depletion can induce a process of deterioration that may undo any progress in career development the therapist had made previously, ending either in an actual exit from therapeutic work or a virtual withdrawal through burnout.

The feedback loop from Currently Experienced Depletion through limited Cumulative Career Development is completed by the impact of the latter on the quality of the therapist's work experience. Limited or deteriorated career development clearly increases the likelihood of therapy being a Stressful Involvement rather than a Healing Involvement for the therapist. Other things being equal, lack of adequate career development will be reflected in a sense of awkwardness and insecurity in the therapist's approach to patients and in a tendency toward defensive rigidity under pressure.

Two additional influences on Cumulative Career Development are relevant to the long exterior loop in the negative developmental cycle.

Having been in practice only a short time, and having treated relatively few case in only one treatment modality, both independently limit the therapist's Cumulative Career Development. However, a high level of Cumulative Career Development moderates the effect of the negative developmental cycle by minimizing the long-term impact of Currently Experienced Depletion on the therapist's ability for positive involvement in therapeutic work. This mitigating effect, unfortunately, is not available to therapists at an early stage in their careers, such as novice, apprentice, and even graduate therapists. For those young practitioners, large doses of support—in their work setting and through supervision, training, or personal therapy—are clearly in order when therapeutic work becomes a Stressful Involvement.

Temporal Sequence

The positive and negative developmental cycles described above must be viewed as operating concurrently. Every therapist's experience of practice reflects varying levels or degrees of Healing Involvement and Stressful Involvement, whose balance relative to each other approximates one or another of the practice patterns delineated in chapter 6 (Effective Practice, Challenging Practice, Disengaged Practice, or Distressing Practice). The balance between Healing Involvement and Stressful Involvement may shift over time as the levels of each change in response to varying conditions, such as the addition or departure of difficult patients from therapists' caseloads, the acquisition or loss of a supportive supervisor, or a gradual increase in therapeutic mastery as the therapist matures.

Similarly, every therapist sustains varying levels or degrees of Currently Experienced Growth and Currently Experienced Depletion, whose balance relative to each other approximates one or another of the current development patterns delineated in chapter 8 (progress, flux, stasis, or regress). The balance between Growth and Depletion also may shift over time as the levels of each change, largely but not exclusively in response to variations in therapists' experiences of Healing Involvement and Stressful Involvement.

The changes that inevitably occur over time in work experience and in current development point to another important feature of the model. As the positive and negative developmental cycles operate concurrently, linking work experience and developmental states to one another, a sequential unfolding takes place (as illustrated in Figure 11.3). The concurrent levels of Healing Involvement and Stressful Involvement existing at Time 1 largely determine parallel states of Currently Experienced Growth and Depletion. These, in turn, exert a strong influence on levels of Healing Involvement and Stressful Involvement at Time 2 (and, at the same time, contribute to therapists' Cumulative Career Development).

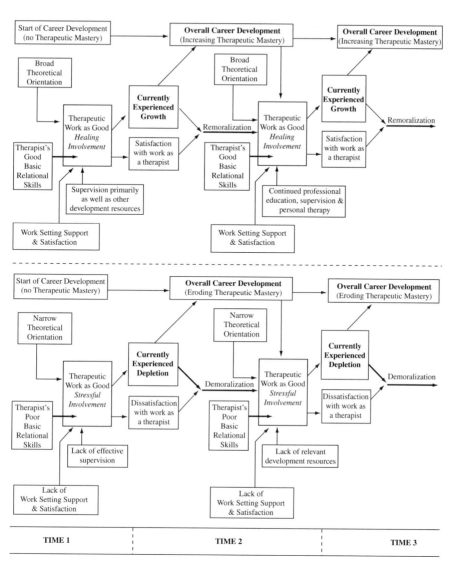

Figure 11.3. Temporal sequence of therapeutic work and positive and negative developmental cycles.

With the further passage of time, changing or stable levels of Healing Involvement and Stressful Involvement at Time 2 influence the extent of current Growth and Depletion then experienced by the therapist; in turn, those parallel states of Currently Experienced Growth and Depletion contribute to shaping the therapist's practice experience (and Cumulative Career Development) at Time 3.

As this sequential unfolding proceeds—from Time 3 to Time 4, and so forth—the pattern of the therapist's practice may fluctuate, from a distressing one to an effective one (or vice versa); correspondingly, the therapist's experience of current development may alter from progress to flux to regress and eventual burnout (or the reverse). Yet despite, and through, these fluctuations time also brings an increasing level of Cumulative Career Development for most therapists—that is, some cumulative improvement in therapeutic skills, a gradual surpassing of past limitations, and a progressive rise in current level of therapeutic mastery. This steady upward trend also must be reckoned as an important factor as the complex linkages between therapeutic work and professional development evolve.[1]

This last feature of the cyclical–sequential model raises an interesting question regarding clinical students who are about to start their therapeutic practice. Theoretically, at this point, both career development and current development would be set at zero. How do the positive and negative cycles linking work and development begin? How can a beginning therapist, with little or no clinical experience, engage patients in a way that generates an experience of Healing Involvement? How can a beginning therapist, with little or no clinical experience, limit the extent to which therapeutic work becomes a Stressful Involvement and avert the danger of demoralization? Once started, the developmental cycles in the model operate concurrently and unfold sequentially over time, but how are they started—and how can a therapist start "on the right foot," with Healing Involvement and Currently Experienced Growth predominant in the balance of cycles?

In anticipation of this question, the diagram shown in Figure 11.3 extracts for special emphasis one key aspect of Healing Involvement: the therapist's Basic Relational Skills. These basic relational skills include the ability to engage others in a helping alliance, the capacity to empathize with others who differ from oneself, an aptitude for being natural in personal encounters, and a knack for communicating understanding and concern to persons in distress. Practitioners at all career levels report possessing high levels of these skills when they first began their training as a therapist, and thus these are the skills that appear to change the least. Although an integral part of Healing Involvement, these Basic Relational Skills reflect the "natural talent" (Orlinsky, Botermans, & Rønnestad, 1998) that therapists bring with them when they enter professional training. As illustrated on the

---

[1] As we noted in chapter 7, the actual course and extent of sequential individual development among therapists, and the proportions of therapists who change in one way or another over time, can be determined only through longitudinal analysis of data collected over extended periods. Nevertheless, the cross-sectional findings for successive career cohorts (see chap. 10) and the conceptual model presented here permit a plausible extrapolation to increasing levels of Cumulative Career Development for most therapists, especially for those who continue to practice beyond the initial career levels.

left-hand side of Figure 11.3, beginning therapists who possess good Basic Relational Skills will infuse these skills into their therapeutic work and will experience the application of those skills in practice as a central element of Healing Involvement. If they have *also* acquired a theoretical orientation that is sufficiently broad to fit the range of patients they encounter, and *also* receive adequate supervision, and *also* work in a supportive clinical milieu, then they most likely will *also* experience the sense of Efficacy in practice and feelings of Flow during sessions through which Healing Involvement engenders Currently Experienced Growth. To the extent that these conditions are not met, of course, the opposite result is likely to ensue, with a dominant position taken by the negative developmental cycle.

OUR STUDY IN THE CONTEXT OF OTHER PSYCHOTHERAPY RESEARCH

The study we have pursued in our project and reported in this book is in some major respects tangential to the mainstream of psychotherapy research as that has been practiced over the past 50 years (Freedheim, 1992; Hill & Corbett, 1993; Orlinsky, Rønnestad, & Willutzki, 2004; Orlinsky & Russell, 1994; Strupp & Howard, 1992).[2] Yet, despite the differences, there are points of contact.

First, our project thus far has focused on therapeutic process at a broader, more macroscopic level than most other studies, which have examined sessions or segments of sessions in microscopic detail. We have focused on therapeutic process at the level of a therapist's practice overall, summing over all current patients rather than on ratings of a specific response to a particular patient in a single session.[3] A line of work already begun (Willutzki, Hernandez Bark, Davis, & Orlinsky, 1997; Willutzki & Orlinsky, 2002) traces the connections between these disparate levels of analysis.[4]

---

[2] In the volume edited by Freedheim (1992), we make special reference to chapter 12 (pp. 391–450), which is a diversely authored description of historically significant programs of psychotherapy research, written in several parts by Frank (1992), Luborsky (1992), Wallerstein (1992), Howard and Orlinsky (1992), Bergin (1992), Lewinsohn (1992), Horowitz (1992), Sloane and Staples (1992), Barlow (1992), Sampson and Weiss (1992), Henry and Strupp (1992), and Parloff and Elkin (1992). A similar compendium of international scope describing major research programs was published by Beutler and Crago (1991).

[3] Descriptive levels in the analysis of therapeutic process and outcome were discussed by Orlinsky et al. (1994, pp. 275–276). In terms of the schematic table (Orlinsky et al., 1994, Table 8.1, p. 276), our focus is largely at Level 6, whereas most studies of therapy process have focused on Levels 2 and 3.

[4] Willutzki et al. (1997) adapted the Development of Psychotherapists Common Core Questionnaire scales rating therapists' difficulties in practice and coping strategies for use by therapists (and, potentially, others) in assessing their experience at specific points of time in individual treatment cases.

Second, our project differs in that we chose to view the therapeutic process just from the psychotherapist's perspective, at least initially, whereas most other studies have viewed the process either alternatively or additionally from the observational perspectives of patients and objective (i.e., nonparticipant) raters. Our choice was based on practical considerations and constitutes a limitation of the present study, although plans and some initial steps (noted in chap. 13) have already been made to broaden the base of observational perspectives.[5]

Finally, to our knowledge, the only empirical studies of psychotherapist development that span the entire professional career are the Collaborative Research Network program reported here and the long-term qualitative project conducted by Skovholt and Rønnestad (e.g., Rønnestad & Skovholt, 2003; Skovholt & Rønnestad, 1995). Also, with a few notable exceptions (e.g., Bernard & Goodyear, 2004; Holloway, 1995; Neufeldt, 1999), psychotherapy researchers have paid little attention to the supervisory and training implications of empirical research on the development of psychotherapists. For nearly 2 decades, no chapter has been devoted to "research on the teaching and learning of therapeutic skills" (Matarazzo & Patterson, 1986) in the definitive *Handbook of Psychotherapy and Behavior Change* (Bergin & Garfield, 1994; Lambert, 2004), which is widely consulted as a comprehensive guide to research on psychotherapy.[6] We hope that our work will help reverse this trend by showing how extensively therapists' current and career development influences the quality of their experiences of therapeutic work.

Despite these differences in focus and method, there is nevertheless a clear convergence between the findings of this study and the established body of psychotherapy research in one key respect. There is, in fact, a striking similarity between the depiction of effective therapeutic process based on 50 years of process–outcome research and the therapeutic work dimension of Healing Involvement. On the basis of our most recent review of process–outcome research (Orlinsky, Rønnestad, & Willutzki, 2004) as well as preceding reviews of that literature (Orlinsky, Grawe, & Parks, 1994; Orlinsky & Howard, 1978, 1986a), two broad conclusions can be drawn about the nature of effective therapy. First, therapeutic process and outcomes are largely determined by what patients bring to treatment by way of deficits and resources and by how patients experience and utilize their therapists' help. The second conclusion is that the quality of the therapeutic bond or

---

[5] Data presented by Willutzki and her colleagues (Willutzki et al., 1997; Willutzki & Orlinsky, 2002) indicate that patients whose therapists rated themselves as having more Frequent Difficulties (a key component of Stressful Involvement) had significantly poorer treatment outcomes, as assessed from diverse observational perspectives.

[6] To illustrate this neglect, the topic of supervision is not included in the indexes of either the fourth or fifth editions, and the index of the latter refers to 8 pages in the text (of a total exceeding 800) on which training is mentioned.

alliance between patient and therapist exerts a highly consistent and often powerful influence on therapeutic outcomes.

Regarding the first conclusion, the accumulated research clearly demonstrates the importance of patients' responsiveness to therapist interventions. The patient's cooperativeness with and openness to the therapist's interventions are crucial mediators of their effectiveness. No matter how potent an intervention may be in general, patients who are highly resistant and defensive will gain little from them. The relevance of this point to the present study is indirect because patient characteristics were not directly assessed; however, it serves as a reminder that the composition of a therapist's caseload is likely to be a major influence on the relative levels of Healing Involvement and Stressful Involvement experienced in practice.

The second point, focusing more on the therapist's contribution, is also more directly relevant to our study. Positive therapeutic outcomes are robustly predicted when therapists are experienced as being personally engaged rather detached, collaborative rather than directive, empathic, and warmly affirming. This is especially true when these therapist attributes are experienced from the patients' perspective, but it also is true when process and outcome are observed and evaluated by outside observers or by therapists themselves. *This pattern of relating to patients is the same that therapists experience in Healing Involvement.* The positive responsiveness of patients to the empathic, personally affirming relationship offered by therapists helps account for the sense of efficacy that is incorporated in the experience of therapeutic work as a Healing Involvement.

Because our study focused on the therapist's experience, we can cite no data (yet) as to how closely the therapists' experience of Healing Involvement corresponds to their patients' experiences of a supportive, enabling therapeutic relationship. We cannot (yet) demonstrate the extent to which Healing Involvement, seen from the psychotherapist's perspective, actually enters and is experienced as such in the patient's perspective on therapy, or would be seen from the external perspective of nonparticipant observers. However, on the basis of the close similarity of Healing Involvement to the portrait of effective psychotherapy that has emerged through decades of process–outcome research, we feel justified in proposing this as a highly plausible hypothesis—one that will guide the future direction of our research program.

We hope that another convergence of our findings with some slight but intriguing findings from traditional psychotherapy research will stimulate more work in the latter area. On the basis of our study, we refer to therapists' experiences of Stressful Involvement in their therapeutic work, especially insofar as these experiences lead therapists to project a demoralized attitude during therapy sessions. On the basis of traditional psychotherapy research, we refer to the suggestive findings of W. P. Henry et al. (1990) concerning the apparently deleterious impact on patients of subtle signs of ambivalence and negativity from therapists.

Our findings about Stressful Involvement and Currently Experienced Depletion also converge with the cumulative body of research on job burnout recently summarized by Maslach, Schaufeli, and Leiter (2000). The cascading tendency of Stressful Involvement and Currently Experienced Depletion to reciprocally amplify each other, unless deterred and counteracted, seems like a sure prescription for eventual therapist burnout.

More generally, our findings point to an unexpectedly strong influence of therapists' current work morale, both positive and negative, on their experience in therapeutic practice. The apparently vital importance of this variable has not been recognized yet in the psychotherapy research literature, and on the strength of our findings we believe that it should receive serious attention. It may well be one source of the problematic intragroup variability typically found in studies that seek to compare alternative treatments (Howard, Krause, & Vessey, 1994; Rogers, Howard, & Vessey, 1993).

Convergences between other areas and modes of psychotherapy research and our findings on therapeutic work and professional growth, seen from the psychotherapist's perspective, suggest that the latter are truly grounded in clinical reality. We believe that the cyclical–sequential model of work and development, based on our findings, is likewise reflective of clinical reality and has three specific virtues to recommend it. First, it includes the main findings reported in the book and links them together in a coherent way. Second, the model relies on explanations using common-sense concepts that are widely shared, although sometimes known by different names, in various theoretical orientations. Third, the model allows one to draw a series of empirically grounded proposals for optimizing the development of therapists and minimizing the damage that may occur to them (and, through them, to their patients) when adverse conditions prevail. In the next chapter, we present and discuss these practical implications.

12

CLINICAL IMPLICATIONS: TRAINING, SUPERVISION, AND PRACTICE

MICHAEL HELGE RØNNESTAD AND DAVID E. ORLINSKY

At various points throughout this book, we have commented on potential implications for clinical training and practice. In this chapter, we attempt to draw together the practical implications of our findings and those of other researchers to make explicit recommendations concerning the design of training programs, the practice of clinical supervision, and the ongoing conduct of psychotherapeutic work. Our recommendations are grounded mainly on the results reported in the preceding chapters, supplemented by findings reported in the literature by other researchers and by our long experience as clinical trainers, supervisors, and practitioners. Readers should remember, of course, that practical recommendations are extrapolations extending beyond the available data. As general principles, they can guide but should not replace sound judgment based on specific knowledge of local training and practice conditions. Trusting in the reader's good sense, then, we offer the following proposals.

IMPLICATIONS FOR CLINICAL EDUCATION

We focus first on implications that can help those responsible for clinical training increase the likelihood that students will experience therapeutic work in ways that facilitate their professional development. The students of main concern here are relative beginners, that is, novice and apprentice therapists in their first months and early years of clinical experience. On the basis of our findings, we recommend the following for training programs:

1. Candidates selected for training should have, and experience themselves as having, already well-developed basic interpersonal skills and a warm manner in their close personal relationships.
2. Direct clinical work with patients should start early in students' training, once they have been given a basic initial orientation to theory and technique that is relevant to the patients they will treat.
3. The initial theoretical and technical orientation given to students should be offered in a pragmatic rather than ideological or dogmatic spirit, to maximize flexibility of application and openness to further learning and the eventual cultivation of theoretical breadth.
4. Case selection for beginners should ensure the best possible match between students' skill levels and the clinical challenges that patients present to maximize the likelihood that students will experience therapeutic work as a Healing Involvement, will minimize the experience of Stressful Involvement, and also should include cases in multiple treatment modalities (group, couple, and family as well as individual therapy) to extract the maximum Cumulative Career Development from the time devoted to initial practice.
5. Continual supportive supervision by well-experienced therapists should accompany the early clinical work of novices and apprentices, and ample social support should be available in the students' clinical work setting, to limit the extent to which Stressful Involvement evolves into Currently Experienced Depletion and thereby impedes or diminishes their Cumulative Career Development.
6. Training programs should enlist students in collaborative methods of monitoring their experiences of therapeutic work, to ensure that Healing Involvement is present in a majority of cases and that Stressful Involvement is kept to a minimum and to

assess the quality of their current and Cumulative Career Development (see Appendixes E and F for related material).

Basic Interpersonal Skills

The recommendation to select candidates for clinical training who possess well-developed interpersonal skills as an essential quality is hardly new, but it deserves renewed emphasis. These basic interpersonal skills reflect a high level of social maturity rather than mere gregariousness or sociability—as, for example, having a composed, responsive personal presence; a capacity for empathizing with a broad range of human experiences; and an ability to feel and communicate genuine concern for others. This recommendation is based partly on the finding that practicing therapists report having experienced high levels of these when they first began training, before they acquired technical skills, and partly on the basis of the cyclical–sequential model of development, which focuses on basic interpersonal skills as a key element in novice therapists' experiences of Healing Involvement.

Another key ingredient of Healing Involvement is the therapists' experience of feeling *Affirming*—acceptance, friendliness, tolerance, and warmth—in relating to patients. The propensity for relating affirmatively in therapy can be gauged in large part by assessing how potential candidates for clinical training experience themselves in close personal relationships. In an analysis of data on therapists' personal lives (Orlinsky & Rønnestad, 2003), we found a highly positive correlation ($r = .57$) between feeling Affirming toward patients in therapeutic relationships and the extent of warmth (acceptance, friendliness, tolerance, and warmth) experienced with intimates.

In many countries, the emphasis on basic interpersonal skill and maturity as essential selection criteria will tend to favor female over male candidates, but readers should recall that (whether for cultural or other reasons) men generally are slower to develop and can eventually reach levels comparable to those of their female colleagues. They do, however, appear to need greater supervisory and other forms of support in their clinical work as novice and apprentice therapists. Because men often bring other qualities to therapeutic work that may be desirable for some clients (e.g., Orlinsky & Howard, 1980), our emphasis on initial basic interpersonal skills should not lead to the exclusion or serious underrepresentation of men in the therapeutic professions but should focus instead on at least adequate levels of these skills in young men and on their capacity to develop further in this regard.

In addition to strong interpersonal skills, other highly desirable qualities would certainly include intellectual strength, curiosity, and flexibility; openness to new experiences (Dlugos & Friedlander, 2001); a reflective temperament (Rønnestad & Skovholt, 1991; Skovholt & Rønnestad, 1995); and freedom from serious personal psychopathology (Beutler et al., 2004).

Early Clinical Practice

Our research has documented that therapists—regardless of experience level, theoretical preference, profession, and gender—are remarkably consistent in their views concerning influences on current development.[1] Practical–experiential learning through direct clinical work with patients is consistently endorsed as the most influential experience, with the sole exception of supervision for novices (for whom direct clinical work ranked a close second).

Accordingly, we recommend that students start to do real therapeutic work relatively early in training, before traditional coursework is completed. However, it is essential that early direct clinical experience is provided only if students have been given an initial theoretical orientation relevant to the clients they are given and only if they are concurrently receiving close supervision and are participating in didactic training. Our recommendation needs to be balanced against the ethical concern to provide competent treatment to clients and an educational concern to provide students with frequent experiences of Healing Involvement and prevent them from experiencing more than a little Stressful Involvement.

Students necessarily have only limited Cumulative Career Development and thus are more likely to experience Stressful Involvement with clients, which in turn promotes a potentially harmful state of Currently Experienced Depletion. Our findings indicate that this can be mitigated to some extent by supportive supervision and by working in a socially supportive and satisfying setting. However, given the potent relationship of Stressful Involvement to Currently Experienced Depletion, it is clearly best to avoid assigning students to clients who may be too difficult for their current skill level.

Our experiences as teachers and supervisors of psychotherapy have demonstrated how detrimental it can be for students if they do not experience support and satisfaction in their clinical work and do not feel they are succeeding in their practicum or internship program. Students and interns who experience failure (e.g., clients failing to show up for appointments or dropping out of therapy; clients not improving or deteriorating) may easily experience accelerating doubts about themselves as therapists. Moreover, therapists' dysfunctional emotional reactions and nonconstructive coping responses may not only negatively influence their interactions with a particu-

---

[1]The findings with respect to career development were presented in an earlier publication (Orlinsky, Botermans, & Rønnestad, 2001).

lar client but also may transfer to their work with other clients, making the novice therapist even more vulnerable to experiencing a Distressing Practice.

Students are also more likely to feel anxious and overwhelmed during therapy sessions (Skovholt & Rønnestad, 2003), and excessive student anxiety may have detrimental effects on the client–therapist interchange by its contribution to the experience of Stressful Involvement and, through that, to Currently Experienced Depletion. Educators need to recognize this and structure the learning situation so that anxiety-related emotions can be kept to a level where they can be mastered.

The dynamics described above combine to suggest that students be continually provided with ample support in their work and study environment and be provided with an optimal opportunity to experience therapeutic work as effective and satisfying. This requires that students encounter work challenges that are well suited to their current skill levels. Training programs should therefore create learning environments that are supportive and where the challenge for the student can be regulated. We cannot emphasize enough how important it is that *training programs ensure that novice and apprentice therapists be given every opportunity to experience therapeutic work as a Healing Involvement and not as a Stressful Involvement.*

Initial Theoretical Orientation

Another recommendation stems directly from the core principle that students and interns should only be assigned cases that they have been given adequate theoretical guidance and technical skills to treat effectively. This principle of matching challenge and level of competence is of course not unique to learning therapeutic skills but is assigned particular importance because of the special nature of therapeutic work. The fact that many or most students are testing whether they are personally suited to be a therapist constitutes a demanding background for assessing their own clinical competence. The consequences of a poor match between challenge and skill can therefore be unduly taxing for students, in terms of an immediate negative impact both on their ongoing work and for their current and long-term professional development.

The question of which theoretical orientation is most relevant for beginning students clearly depends on the treatment setting in which they will be working and the types of client they will treat. Because we strongly recommend that students gain experience in several treatment modalities, it would be well to first introduce a theoretical perspective that can be used in the various modalities available at the training clinic. For example, if psychodynamic theory is the institutionally preferred orientation, then analytic group theory and dynamic family theory might accompany a traditional focus on intrapsychic processes; if a cognitive–behavioral perspective is the institutionally preferred orientation, then congruent theories of group process (e.g., Transactional Analysis) might also be taught; if a systems–theoretic model is the institutionally preferred orientation, then the impact of participation in family systems on the self-concept and motivations of individuals should be considered.

Whichever orientation is taught first, we urge that it be taught in a manner that does not foreclose the student's later acquisition of theoretical breadth by critically disparaging alternative orientations—because theoretical breadth enhances the likelihood of experiencing therapeutic work as a Healing Involvement. The emphasis should be on what students can learn from the special insights and interventions offered by each orientation. Students should be motivated and made ready to learn, for example, how to carefully attend to, and constructively reflect, a client's ongoing experience during sessions; how to understand and interpret recurrent motivational patterns in the patient's life; how to recognize and constructively manage the subtle effects of those patterns on the therapeutic relationship; how to apply or devise practical interventions that mobilize the clients' own resources and focus directly on problematic client behaviors to provide morale-enhancing experiences of efficacy; and how to appreciate and constructively moderate the influence of clients' relational or family environments on their personal functioning and role contributions to those environments.

Students should be provided models of how to open-mindedly explore and integrate the concepts and methods of various treatment models. Although learning more than one theoretical orientation initially may be confusing to students, they should be taught their initial orientation in a way that enables them eventually to "learn from many masters" (Orlinsky, 1994). Educators can facilitate this by placing the specific clinical theory being taught into a research-based metatheoretical framework such as the Generic Model of Psychotherapy (Orlinsky & Howard, 1986a, 1987, 1994), the Transtheoretical Model of Prochaska and his colleagues (Prochaska & DiClemente, 1982; Prochaska & Norcross, 1999), or Grawe's (2004) General Psychotherapeutic Model. These broad frameworks provide students with a context for understanding and integrating a variety of clinical orientations.

Although there are limits to what can be learned at any one time, and it is likely that mastery and competence are best facilitated by focused learning of specific methods, training programs need to balance in-depth focused learning over time with broader perspectives. As noted, initial theoretical approaches should support applications in various treatment modalities. Therapeutic approaches that do not support application in various treatment modalities should be taught at a later stage. Over the course of graduate training, however, students should be exposed to and have experience with varied work modalities and theoretical orientations taught in nondogmatic ways. A pedagogy can thus be created that facilitates both acquisition of skills and a sense of mastery and that promotes the openness to experience that appears necessary for optimal professional development.

Multiple Treatment Modalities

More than anything else, more than even the number of years in practice, Cumulative Career Development was predicted by the breadth and depth of a therapist's experience across treatment modalities. Thus, although students necessarily lack length of time in practice, it is still possible for them to accumulate experiences that strongly promote their career development. Training programs would best serve their students by providing them with a number of cases in several treatment modalities—groups and couples or families as well as individual therapy cases. If this clinical diversity is not available in one training setting—as it might not be in a departmental clinic—then program faculty might collaborate with external clinics that can provide varied work experience for students and interns. We emphasize again that this is likely to be a positive experience for students only if they are adequately prepared for, and supervised in, the various modalities to which they are assigned.

Supervisory and Work Setting Support

Unlike more experienced therapists, for whom direct experience with patients was viewed as the most positive influence on their development, supervision ranked as the most positive influence on the development of novice therapists. Accordingly, we recommend that programs for novices continually strengthen and expand the supervision component of training. It likely takes considerable supervisory skill to assist novice therapists in processing the challenges of therapeutic work and overcoming the potential effects of Stressful Involvement. If supervisors are highly competent as therapists as well as skilled supervisors, students not only are assisted in overcoming immediate obstacles but also are provided with effective models to guide their future practice. Furthermore, a personal identification with a competent and respected senior is likely to facilitate identification with their new professional role.

Support for novices especially—and indeed, for therapists at all levels—can also be provided in treatment settings by regular participation in peer group interactions of various sorts, such as case seminars, topical workshops, and informal collegial discussions, all of which stimulate therapists' motivation to further their development and facilitate the process of continuous professional reflection that Skovholt and Rønnestad (1995) found to be the essential factor in therapist development. If possible, such groups should meet continually over several semesters. They should be small enough to facilitate and encourage active involvement among participants yet large enough to ensure varied stimulation and input.

Beyond the novice level, our findings indicated that case supervision and therapists' personal therapy alternated as the second and third most highly ranked influence on development, whereas experiences in personal life typically ranked as fourth most influential. These results echo and amplify the previous findings of Morrow-Bradley and Elliott (1986) and Rachelson and Clance (1980) and are largely consistent with work by Skovholt and Rønnestad (1992), who found that interpersonal experiences (e.g., clients, personal therapists, supervisors, professional elders, and one's personal life) were found to be more important than more impersonal sources of data such as seminars, coursework, and theories. These latter were viewed not as unimportant but as secondary in importance to direct interpersonal influences.

Collaborative Monitoring of Experience

The empirical findings on which our prior recommendations are based stem either directly or indirectly from the reported experiences of psychotherapists, rather than from an external observer's perspective. Therefore, educators and supervisors cannot rely solely, or even primarily, on their own perceptions of how students and supervisees are faring in their training programs. Over and above its many specific findings, our study should serve to establish the importance of having psychotherapists' own perspectives on their therapeutic work and professional development. With regard to student therapists, this translates to a recommendation that the students' experiences be accorded the same respect for training purposes that the patients' experiences are accorded in the context of therapy. In Appendixes E and F, we offer a selection of key items from the Development of Therapists Common Core Questionnaire that may serve this purpose.

IMPLICATIONS FOR SUPERVISION

As noted above, practitioners at all experience levels, theoretical orientations, professions, and nationalities report that supervised client experience is highly important for their current and career development[2] as therapists. Moreover, supervision is clearly a standard aspect of professional practice, as witnessed by the fact that approximately two thirds of therapists at the novice, apprentice, and graduate career levels—as well as a majority of

---

[2] The findings with respect to career development were presented in an earlier publication (Orlinsky, Botermans, & Rønnestad, 2001).

established therapists—were currently receiving some form of supervision for at least some treatment cases.[3]

In this section, we first consider a potentially harmful supervisory process that both students and supervisors should strive to avoid—a process that, if allowed to emerge, most likely will undermine the therapeutic development of the supervisee. Following that, we note a number of general concerns regarding the effectiveness of supervision.

Double Traumatization

Our study has sensitized us to the dynamic relationship between involvement styles and current and cumulative career development. Knowledge of the negative cycle leading to the experience of depletion of skills and to dissatisfaction with work as a therapist constitutes a disconcerting background against which supervision can be viewed. A growing body of research has recently indicated considerable discontent and conflict in supervision (i.e., Gray, Ladany, Walker, & Ancis, 2001; Ladany, Hill, Corbett, & Nutt, 1996; Nelson & Friedlander, 2001). What may be called *double traumatization* refers to a process in which the supervisee is simultaneously experiencing therapeutic work as Stressful Involvement and experiencing a conflict with his or her supervisor (Ladany, Friedlander, & Nelson, in press). We briefly summarize some of the research on conflictual supervision and draw some additional implications for supervision that emerge from the combination of perspectives generated from the research on conflictual supervision and our own project. We use the term *negative supervision* to refer to supervision characterized by conflict, dissatisfaction, and defensiveness.

Moskowitz and Rupert (1983) surprised the field 20 years ago when they reported that almost 40% of master's and doctoral degree candidates had experienced a substantial conflict with their supervisor, a conflict that interfered in significant ways with supervision. They differentiated among conflicts arising from differences in theoretical orientation, dissatisfaction with supervisory style (typically, disagreement regarding directiveness and support in supervision), and a personality clash between student and supervisor.

This line of research was pursued by Ladany, Hill, Corbett, and Nutt (1996), who documented that most candidates did not disclose important material to their supervisors (e.g., negative and positive reactions to supervisor and client, personal themes, clinical errors, client observations, client–therapist attraction themes). A similar study was published by Yourman and

[3] More surprising is that two fifths (39%) of seasoned therapists in our sample (with 15–25 years in practice) also reported having some current supervision, as did 16% of the senior therapists (with 25+ years of practice).

Farber (1996), who reported that 40% of a sample of doctoral students had distorted reports of what occurred in therapist–patient interaction sometimes or often. Yourman and Farber's study also documented that many candidates (approximately one third) did not correct the supervisor when he or she was wrong, and a majority felt uncomfortable in revealing negative reactions to the supervisor.

Ladany's group has followed up their research by studying negative and counterproductive events in supervision (Gray et al., 2001). Trainees typically attributed these events to the supervisor dismissing their thoughts and feelings. Counterproductive events were typically not discussed and were seen as negatively affecting their client work and the supervisory alliance. A study of impasses in supervision (Nigam, Cameron, & Leverette, 1997) explored the phenomenology of supervisory impasses that had lasted for at least 3 or 4 weeks. Approximately 40% of the participants reported such impasses, which varied in content; for example, dismissal of material seen by the supervisee as being important, disagreements regarding case management, and the supervisor insisting on being present in the family therapy conducted by the supervisee.

Reichelt and Skjerve's (2002) study also focused on what contributed negatively to the supervisory relationship. A majority of their respondents complained of one or more of the following: dual-role relationship, personal characteristics of the supervisor, supervisor's lack of professional competence, and supervisor's lack of openness. Almost half reported experiences that were perceived as particularly disturbing, such as the supervisor talking too much and not listening enough, the supervisor being professionally unengaged, and the supervisor not showing up for supervision.

In a review of selected research on conflictual and dissatisfying aspects of supervision, which include the studies above, published before 2000, we noted that the majority of reports of and perspectives on negative supervision could be conceptualized as limitations and insufficiencies in the interpersonal bond aspect of supervision (Rønnestad & Orlinsky, 2000). Overall, subsequent studies of negative supervision indicate that negative supervision erodes the candidates' professional self-confidence, increases the candidates' self-doubt, encourages negative personal reactions, and invites negative countertransference reactions to patients in the therapist (e.g., Gray et al., 2001; Ladany, 2004; Ladany, Hill, Corbett, & Nutt, 1996; Moskowitz & Rupert, 1983; Nelson & Friedlander, 2001; Nigam et al., 1997; Reichelt & Skjerve, 2002; Rønnestad & Orlinsky, 2001). Negative supervision increases the candidates' performance anxiety and exaggerates the candidates' self-criticism. Negative supervision does not facilitate the acquisition of therapeutic skills and attitudes and precludes the supervisor from being viewed as a positive role model.

If, as we suspect, the above negative consequences combine to influence the supervisee's experience of therapeutic work, even a competent student can become doubly traumatized if the supervisor is perceived as being critical rather than supportive. We cannot demonstrate an empirical relationship between the bond aspect of supervision and the quality of therapist involvement styles from our data; however, it seems plausible to suppose that therapists who have a Stressful Involvement with their clients may be more likely to have experienced conflictual supervision, and vice versa, that supervisees who experience conflict in supervision are more likely to have a Stressful Involvement with their clients.

Within the supervision literature the development of a reciprocal relationship between the therapeutic relationship and the supervisory relationship is formulated as the concept of *parallel process*. Extending the conceptual work of Searles (1955), who described how therapists' identification with patients could "transport" therapy processes into the supervision relationship, Doehrman (1976) demonstrated empirically how the "traffic of influence" could also go the other way (i.e., unresolved conflicts in supervision could unconsciously transfer to therapy). The concept of parallel process thus provides a conceptual tool to understand the reciprocal dynamics between experiences of the qualities of therapists' work involvement in therapy and their supervision.

Given the general interrelatedness of therapy and supervision, and the risk of double traumatization for the supervisee in particular, our initial recommendation that supervisors be sure to provide adequate support seems amply warranted. Supervisors should be continually aware both of Stressful Involvement experienced by supervisees in their work with patients and of supervisory conflicts with them that may be experienced but not overtly expressed by supervisees. Supervisors should make a planned and strategic effort to optimize learning among candidates.

There is no doubt that the main source of conflictual feeling that is virtually built into supervision—especially into the supervision of novices and apprentices—is the need imposed on supervisors to evaluate the supervisee (Rønnestad & Orlinsky, 2000). This stems in part—but only in part—from the supervisor's ethical obligation to ensure that the supervisee's clients receive competent professional treatment. That obligation is necessary and desirable. However, the need to rate the supervisee's therapeutic performance also is due in large part to training programs' habitual practice of grading students. When there is in addition a mutual evaluation required by the supervisor and supervisee of one another, a reality is created that turns "both partners into threatening judges of each other, both being potential sources of embarrassing exposure and rejection" (Berman, 2000, p. 277).

Whether it is structured unilaterally or reciprocally, the practice of supervisory evaluation inevitably makes the relationship between supervisor and supervisee adversarial. Where the power to evaluate is vested in the supervisor, a temptation is created for the supervisor to become judgmental, if not overtly critical, and for the supervisee to become circumspect, if not openly defensive. If this adversarial process develops in the supervisory relationship and cannot be reversed, it is likely to engender a state of double traumatization for the supervisee.

A good working alliance based on mutual trust is as crucial in supervision as it is in therapy. To ensure that such a working alliance is established, supervisors must recognize the inherent structural ambivalence of the supervisory relationship when evaluation is required. On the one hand, the supervisor represents potential guidance and support to the supervisee; on the other hand, the supervisor represents scrutiny and potential reprimand. Because our findings clearly imply that supervisory support (and work setting support) are important in limiting the emergence of Currently Experienced Depletion from Stressful Involvement, a major challenge that supervisors confront is how to optimize the supportive aspect of supervision in relation to its evaluative aspect.

Supervisors may find help in meeting this challenge by calling to mind their own feelings as students in supervision and using this as a source of empathy with their supervisees. It may also help to regard their supervisees as a talented sculptor might regard a block of fine marble, searching to perceive within it the nascent shape already there waiting to be drawn out, for unless the candidate selection process has wholly failed there should be present in the supervisee a potentially competent, if not talented, therapist. If therapists can find something to like or respect in most patients,[4] then supervisors—who, one would hope, are well-experienced therapists—should be able to do this even more readily with their young colleagues.

Effective Supervision

As a background to understanding the challenges of supervision, especially for novice and apprentice therapists, we recall our finding that these junior cohorts are less likely than experienced practitioners to experience therapeutic work as a Healing Involvement. Thus, when they experience more than a little Stressful Involvement, they are correspondingly more likely to find themselves enmeshed in a Distressing Practice. The emergence of significant Stressful Involvement, if unchecked, will lead to an experience

---

[4]The least frequently reported of 20 difficulties encountered by therapists was being "unable to find something to like or respect in a patient."

of depletion and an erosion of skillfulness, adding in the short term to the likelihood of more Stressful Involvement and, over time, negatively influencing the career development process. The prime task and responsibility of the supervisor are detection and reversal of this negative cycle of events and the encouragement of a positive cycle based on experiences of Healing Involvement.[5]

Although it may not always be possible to identify the origin of processes in an interchange as complex as supervision, the client, the student therapist, and the supervisor each may exacerbate the processes prompting the therapist's Stressful Involvement. The client may be poorly motivated for therapy and may lack the capacity to engage in a therapeutic relationship and carry out the activities stipulated by the particular treatment offered. The student therapist may lack the capacity to create an effective working alliance, even if the client is motivated to change and has the personal resources to engage successfully in therapy. Finally, the supervisor may not have the skills necessary to create an optimal learning environment for the student therapist, or the supervisor may act in ways that undermine the student's efforts.

In cases where Stressful Involvement arises from the client being insufficiently motivated for therapy, or not having the ability to do what is prescribed by the treatment model, supervisors should help the student realistically assess the client's limitations and resources. This should help student therapists discern the boundary on their responsibility and prevent their development of excessive self-doubt or dysfunctional self-attributions. Concurrently, the supervisor should help the therapist explore whether the treatment model being used can be adapted, or an alternative model can be found, to beneficially engage the client's actual level of skill and motivation.

In cases where the therapist's lack of professional skills is the primary cause of Stressful Involvement, the challenge for both supervisor and student is of course much more difficult. The supervisor has the responsibility to ensure that the treatment provided meets professional standards as well as to assist candidates in their development as therapists. The potential for double traumatization is substantial in such cases. Although a discussion of the ethical dilemma arising in such situations is beyond the scope of this chapter, we can make one strategic recommendation: As the student therapist's limitations become clear, the supervisor must focus first on what the client needs. After a careful assessment of those needs, the scene is set for making the therapeutic implications explicit. In situations like this, the

---

[5] Despite the natural emphasis on problems in a discussion of supervision, it is worth remembering that most student therapists do experience their work as a Healing Involvement, find satisfaction in their work as therapists, and are engaged in a positive developmental cycle of Currently Experienced Growth and Cumulative Career Development.

supervisor's objectives that are not shared with the student may disrupt the supervisory alliance (Reichelt & Skjerve, 2002). It is our experience that if this occurs, candidates generally appreciate supervisors being concrete and specific in their communication. Clear conceptual formulations of therapist skills, such as those outlined by Bernard (1979)—process skills, conceptualization skills, and personalization skills—may help the student and the supervisor keep a shared focus for discussion in supervision. Also, structured therapist skill training programs, such as Microtraining (Ivey & Authier, 1978) and Interpersonal Process Recall (Kagan & Kagan, 1997), can be used to supplement supervision and may prevent the student from experiencing double traumatization.

Supervisory Qualifications

The question of who should supervise can be answered only indirectly from our study, on the basis of therapists' judgments of their ability to guide the development of colleagues. One of the questions that clinicians were asked in the Development of Psychotherapists Common Core Questionnaire was "How capable do you feel to guide the development of other psychotherapists?" Therapists rated themselves on a 6-point scale from *not at all* to *very capable* and, when we subjected those ratings to a stepwise multiple regression analysis, we found that 43% of the variance was predicted by three variables. The first, and by far the strongest, predictor was our combined measure of Cumulative Career Development (33%). Additional, though smaller, amounts beyond that were accounted for by the number of other therapists one had supervised (9%) and the number of years one had practiced therapy (1%). This strongly suggests that assessed career development, and not simply time in practice, should be a leading criterion for selecting supervisors. Cumulative Career Development includes the practitioner's sense of therapeutic mastery and general increments in skill level as well as retrospected estimates such as the degree to which one has overcome past limitations.

Of course, this does not mean that clinicians necessarily become objectively more expert as supervisors as they gain more supervisory and therapeutic experience (Worthington, 1987); however, it seems unlikely that inexperienced therapists would be effective supervisors, although in fact some therapists are thrust into a supervisory role quite early in their careers (Rønnestad, Orlinsky, Parks, et al., 1997). Our current data show that one fourth (24%) of novice therapists reported having done supervision, although only half that number (12%) were highly confident of their ability guide the development of other therapists. Similarly, one third (33%) of the apprentices had done some supervision, although only 15% felt well able to do so.

The doubts of relatively inexperienced therapists about their capacity as supervisors are reinforced by the fact that novice and apprentice therapists are significantly less likely themselves to experience therapeutic work as a Healing Involvement and significantly more likely to experience it as a Stressful Involvement. Despite the fact that North American training institutions not uncommonly have doctoral students supervise master's-level students in psychotherapy practica, it seems unlikely that neophyte supervisors—who may experience "role shock" in shifting from the role of therapist to supervisor (Watkins, 1994)—will provide the confidence and expertise necessary to facilitate optimal skill acquisition and professional development in other student therapists.

The perspectives presented above converge in a recommendation to the field that the bulk of the supervision of student therapists should be provided by experienced therapists who have demonstrated a high level of therapeutic and supervisory skillfulness. This means that practitioners should establish a solid experience base as therapists before they start to supervise. As such, they are more likely to facilitate the current growth and career development of young therapists who are already experiencing much Healing Involvement and are more likely to mitigate the impact of Stressful Involvement before the negative developmental cycle of depletion and deterioration proceeds too far.

Given the likelihood that Stressful Involvement may be exacerbated by inadequate supervisory skills, as well as the incidence of supervisory conflict and dissatisfaction among trainees reported in previous studies, our proposal regarding a minimal level of formal training in supervisory skills seems reasonable. We know of no research to show that supervisors who have had formal supervisory training become better supervisors, but we nevertheless recommend that those who undertake or are assigned that responsibility receive such training and strive to continually upgrade their supervisory competence.[6]

IMPLICATIONS FOR PRACTICING THERAPISTS

The satisfactions, rewards, hazards, and strains of being a psychotherapist have been competently explored by many of our colleagues who have also given valuable recommendations to practicing psychotherapists (Coster & Schwebel, 1997; Dlugos & Friedlander, 2001; Farber, 1983; Farber & Heifetz, 1981; Kramen-Kahn & Hansen, 1998; Mahoney, 1997; Maslach, Schaufeli, & Leiter, 2000; Murtagh & Wollersheim, 1997; Norcross, 2000;

---

[6]Our personal experience is that supervisors who seek collegial consultation or who seek "supervision of supervision" typically report this to be helpful.

Radeke & Mahoney, 2000; Schwebel & Coster, 1998). Our own research has further sensitized us to the critical importance of therapists' positive and negative work morale—Currently Experienced Growth and Currently Experienced Depletion—in the cyclical relationship between therapeutic practice and development. Of the many variables we assessed, Currently Experienced Growth was by far the strongest predictor of Healing Involvement; similarly, Currently Experienced Depletion was by far the strongest predictor of Stressful Involvement.

We believe it is safe to assume that therapeutic improvement in their patients is the highest priority of almost all psychotherapists.[7] In addition, the findings of our study, and the theoretical formulations drawn from them, lead us to hypothesize that Healing Involvement reflects the psychotherapists' experience of effective therapeutic process, whereas Stressful Involvement reflects their experience of problematic and probably ineffective interaction with patients. On this basis, we strongly recommend that practitioners of all professions, career levels, and theoretical orientations give careful and serious attention to their current work morale as reflected in their ongoing sense of development as psychotherapists.

If therapists honestly find that they are experiencing much Healing Involvement in their current practice, and feel a positive balance of Currently Experienced Growth over Currently Experienced Depletion in their current development, then most likely they are working well and should continue on as they are. This appeared to be the case with somewhat over half the therapists in our study. On the other hand, if they recognize a lack of those positive experiences, then responsible therapists should take some action to avert potential harm to themselves and to their patients. Our remaining recommendations consider possible corrective actions that therapists may take in that circumstance.

Therapists in Stasis

One group of the therapists who should be concerned are those who report little Currently Experienced Depletion but also not much Currently Experienced Growth. These were described as being in *stasis* and comprised a considerable number (22%) of those surveyed. Their lack of positive work morale (low Currently Experienced Growth) limits the extent to which their therapeutic work is likely to be experienced as a Healing Involvement, and thus (according to our hypothesis) limits the extent to which their

---

[7] We recognize that in some theoretical orientations (e.g., Lacanian analysis) a philosophical emphasis on self-knowledge through understanding of unconscious processes may have a higher value than the pragmatic goal of healing and as well that some (very few, we hope) therapists practice their profession merely as a source of livelihood.

patients are likely to benefit from treatment. This would be offset to some extent if the therapists had much Cumulative Career Development and considerable theoretical breadth but on the other hand would be especially likely if they had experienced little career development and were committed to a single theoretical perspective.

For this group of therapists, we recommend seeking greater variety or diversification in therapeutic work. Our study has shown that participating in multiple treatment modalities instead of just one facilitates Cumulative Career Development. Norcross's (2000) recommendation to "Diversify, diversify, diversify" (p. 712) highlights an important principle in therapists' self-care, a principle that likely can be generalized:

> The diversity is grounded in conducting multiple forms of therapy (e.g., individual, couples/family, group therapy), engaging in multiple activities (e.g., psychotherapy, assessment, research, teaching, supervision, consultation), working with multiple types of patients and problems (e.g., age, ethnicity, disorders), and balancing professional responsibilities with personal needs. (p. 712)

A parallel recommendation can also be expressed as openness to different theoretical perspectives. Our finding in this study that theoretical breadth contributes significantly to experiencing therapy as a Healing Involvement converges with Skovholt and Rønnestad's (1995) qualitative finding regarding the importance of active engagement in theory and openness to different theoretical perspectives. We suggest to therapists in stasis that they see what they can learn from other theoretical perspectives that might be applicable in their practice. They can do this through continuing education seminars and courses or by attending professional conferences that feature programs of diverse interest.

Supervision is another form of professional development activity that therapists at all career levels rated highly as a positive influence on current development, and this would very likely be beneficial to therapists experiencing stasis. Although we previously noted research showing dissatisfaction with supervision, that applied mainly to student therapists who were subject to evaluation by their supervisors. In our data, only 2% of therapists reported any negative impact of supervision, whereas 95% of those currently in supervision rated it as beneficial (and 79% rated it as highly beneficial) to their current development. In fact, our therapists on average reported having had regular supervision for about 5 years, indicating that therapists seek supervision well beyond what is formally required for training and licensure. As previously noted, large numbers of experienced therapists—53% of established therapists (7–15 years of practice) and 39% of seasoned therapists (15–25 years of practice)—reported that they were in some form of regular supervision. With greater experience, therapists have more freedom to choose their supervisors, evaluation of supervisees typically is not a concern, and supervision that is not perceived as helpful can be discontinued without negative consequences. Peer groups also can serve an important function for therapists (Coster & Schwebel, 1997), and peer supervision is highly appreciated by many experienced practitioners as a means of continued professional development.

Therapists in Distress

Approximately one quarter of the therapists were experiencing more than a little Currently Experienced Depletion at the time of our study. For many, this was balanced by concurrently experiencing much growth, so that their state was described as one of *flux*. Most therapists in this group found themselves in either an Effective Practice (40%) or a Challenging Practice (37%), and they appeared to be functioning well overall. Less numerous (11% in our sample) but of greater concern are therapists who experience a negative balance of Currently Experienced Depletion over Currently Experienced Growth (or *regress*) in their current development.[8] Of these, 40% found themselves in a Distressing Practice. Practitioners in this state (about 1 in 20) are at risk of being harmed by their practice and of being potentially harmful to their patients.

It is particularly important that therapists recognize the potential negative dynamics that can ensue from engaging in therapeutic work. Hazard recognition implies specifically that therapists be sensitive to their own emotional reactions in sessions and detect dysfunctional emotionality (e.g., anxiety and boredom) or relatedness (e.g., avoidant coping with difficulties) when they occur. Recognizing the hazards of psychological practice also tops the list of recommendations for practitioner-tested and research-informed self-care recommendations provided by Norcross (2000).

The most immediate way to counteract Stressful Involvement is to alter the composition of the therapist's caseload by reducing the number of patients whose needs or characteristics are too difficult for the therapist, but this may not be a practical or an ethically responsible option. Our findings suggest that when it is not possible or desirable to do this, the best alternative for counteracting Stressful Involvement and limiting its exacerbating impact on Currently Experienced Depletion is to provide support for the therapist. Therapists can do this by seeking formal supervision

---

[8] Another 14% were in a state of flux with respect to current development, experiencing jointly elevated levels of Currently Experienced Growth and Currently Experienced Depletion. Should the balance between those tip toward the negative, they and their patients might also be in some jeopardy, so it would seem wise for practitioners whose current development is in flux to undertake some depletion-reducing activities.

or by participating in supportive professional peer groups, as suggested above, either within or outside the work setting. The support afforded should be professional and social, imparting ideas that may help the beleaguered therapist cope more effectively with difficulties in practice and provide a sense of community with other therapists to help overcome feelings of helplessness and isolation.

In examining the levels of work setting satisfaction and support in different treatment milieus, we have found that therapists working in inpatient institutions, either exclusively or in combination with some other work setting, experience significantly less support and satisfaction than therapists in outpatient and independent practice settings. They also feel less satisfaction and more dissatisfaction with their work as therapists. The inpatient settings where psychotherapists typically find the least support and satisfaction are medical or psychiatric institutions. Luhrmann (2000) provided a detailed ethnographic description and analysis of the paradigmatic struggle in American psychiatry between pharmacological and psychotherapeutic treatment models that may help understand our finding. Given the emphasis on pharmacological treatment in current psychiatric culture, it is easy to believe that individuals practicing psychotherapies in such institutional contexts receive less backing and feel more marginal, although we recognize that institutions can vary considerably in regard to the support they provide for their therapists.

Our data suggest that therapists who practice mainly at inpatient institutions can improve their sense of satisfaction and support to some degree by including practice in other settings as well. We are hesitant to recommend explicitly that therapists who experience Stressful Involvement, little work setting support, and scant work satisfaction seek other types of setting for their therapeutic work; however, it seems that the frustration and disillusionment that can follow prolonged dissatisfaction (for whatever reason) may warrant considering a change in work setting or change in professional role. We certainly recommend that therapists thoroughly explore the resources and limitations within themselves and in the work setting before such decisions are made.

In this connection (and more broadly), we recommend that therapists in distress seriously consider seeking personal therapy as a corrective means of restoring and enhancing professional growth. At every career level, personal therapy ranked as one of the most important sources of positive influence on therapists' current development. Moreover, personal and professional growth was cited by our therapists as the leading reason for seeking therapy, ahead of personal problems and training (Orlinsky, Rønnestad, Willutzki, Wiseman, & Botermans, 2005; Wiseman & Shefler, 2001). Therapists in general clearly are well aware of the benefits that personal therapy offers: Four fifths of those in our study had at least one course of therapy (over half had had more than one), and its use also extends to related professions (e.g., Brady, Guy, & Norcross, 1995; Wiseman & Egozi, 2002). A thorough examination of personal therapy from a variety of theoretical perspectives—drawing on personal narratives, clinical experience, and quantitative research—is available for practitioners who wish to explore the issues involved more deeply, both as potential patients and as therapists' therapists (Geller, Norcross, & Orlinsky, 2005).[9]

Self-Reflection

Within the psychotherapy field, self-awareness is viewed not only as a strategy for development but also as prerequisite for therapists' professional conduct. It is deeply embedded in conceptions of high-level therapeutic functioning as one of the key characteristics of master therapists (Skovholt, Jennings, & Mullenbach, 2004). Therapists, regardless of career levels, would be wise to continually assess the quality of their therapeutic work experience and their current professional growth. As a final recommendation, then, we restate how important it is that practitioners of all professions and theoretical orientations *consistently monitor and carefully attend to their sense of current professional development and their level of satisfaction with therapeutic work.*

To assist in this assessment, we offer practicing therapists two brief self-rating forms based on the Development of Psychotherapists Common Core Questionnaire that may be used at regular intervals and compared both with the therapist's own previous levels and with the average levels attained by nearly 5,000 therapists in our current database.[10] The *Therapeutic Work Involvement Scales* contains a selection of questions that can serve as markers of Healing Involvement and Stressful Involvement (see Appendix E). The *Current and Career Development Scales* contains most of the questions that serve as markers of Currently Experienced Growth, Currently Experienced Depletion, and Cumulative Career Development

---

[9] Surprisingly few studies to date have investigated the impact of personal therapy (or training therapy) on client outcome (Macran & Shapiro, 1998), and the results are inconclusive. For example, Sandell et al. (2002) found a positive association among the psychoanalysis cases but a negative association between length of personal therapy and patient outcome among the psychotherapy cases. It is obvious that many factors other than therapists' personal therapy influence their patients' outcomes—most notably the patient's own resources and limitations and the practitioner's natural therapeutic talent (e.g., basic interpersonal skills)—so that empirically demonstrating a relatively indirect connection such as the one between patient outcome and the therapist's therapy (or training, or supervision) may be extremely difficult.

[10] This information does not have the status of psychometric norms but merely provides information about central tendency and variation in the heterogeneous samples that constitute our database. To be circumspect, therapists should refer to our description of samples in chapter 3 and Appendix B and judge for themselves how closely they resemble our respondents both personally and professionally.

(see Appendix F). Both sets of scales are accompanied by scoring keys as well as norms for the therapists in our current sample to be used as a basis for self-comparison.

These forms can be used separately or in combination by therapists as a convenient, empirically grounded framework and a guide for systematic self-reflection. Student therapists, for instance, might use them privately to monitor their own clinical functioning and development or share them as a basis for discussion with supervisors. Supervisors might use the forms in a parallel fashion to record their impressions of supervisees' work experiences and professional progress. Experienced practitioners might use the forms to monitor their own work morale and establish benchmarks for detecting signs of stagnation or decline. Thus, by taking as its data the experiences of many varied kinds of psychotherapists, our study is finally able to contribute something of practical value in return for the contributions that so many psychotherapists have made to us.

13

RESEARCH IMPLICATIONS: ONGOING AND FUTURE STUDIES

DAVID E. ORLINSKY AND MICHAEL HELGE RØNNESTAD

Scientific research is a kind of "never-ending story" in which answers, or even attempts to find answers, inevitably lead to further questions. No report of a study is therefore complete unless it ends with some further questions and plans for future research to answer them, and so we end this lengthy report with a brief description of work currently in progress and of projects planned to extend what we have learned and presented here.

DATA COLLECTION

After 15 years, colleagues in the Society for Psychotherapy Research Collaborative Research Network (CRN) continue to use, with some enthusiasm, advanced versions of the Development of Psychotherapists Common Core Questionnaire (DPCCQ) in several languages. Major data collections have recently been completed among counselors and psychotherapists in the United Kingdom (T. Schröder) and New Zealand (N. Kazantzis) and among psychologists and psychiatrists in Canada (L. Z. Hakim, S. Touk-manian). These add further breadth to new data collected from therapists in Austria (A. Laireiter), Brazil (J. de Abreu), Finland (P. Lehtovuori, R. Erkolahti), Greece (G. Lampropoulos, J. Nestoros), Norway (M. H. Rønnestad and colleagues), and South Africa (I. Michalopoulos, S. Solheim). Although received too late for inclusion in the present study, these data will soon be integrated and ready for use in further studies conducted with the international CRN database.

Of special value are data from non-Western countries, where cultural differences in psychotherapy are most dramatic and may be most fruitfully studied (Draguns, 2004). Data have recently been collected, or are currently being collected, in China (X. Y. Chen, Z. X. Dhong), Egypt (L. Kassem), Malaysia (W.-S. Ng), and Turkey (G. Guneri), using items about therapists' typical treatment goals collaboratively designed with Korean and Indian colleagues (K. Kim, C. Shamasundar) to better reflect the traditional socio-centric values of many Asian (and other) societies, in contrast to the individualistic goals of therapy valued in Western societies.

In addition to data on therapists from other countries, an important gap to be filled in our current knowledge concerns therapists in professions that have not yet been extensively sampled in countries already studied. These include, most prominently, social workers, psychiatrists, and pastoral psychotherapists in the United States; psychiatrists in Norway; and psychologists and counselors in South Korea. Data from those professions should provide a more balanced view of the main groups of therapists in our current database. Similarly, collection of data from family therapists is being undertaken (L. Knobloch-Fedders, J. Lebow, M. Tarragona) to clarify their distinctive characteristics and contributions.

PARALLEL AND CONTRASTING PROFESSIONS

Our study has yielded some interesting information about characteristics that appear to be common to most psychotherapists (e.g., high levels of acceptance and tolerance in relating to others). However, these common characteristics may be typical of other professions, too. To find what is distinctive as well as what is typical of psychotherapists, studies of parallel and contrasting professions will need to be done. One such study has already been conducted. In it, an adaptation of the DPCCQ was used to study Roman Catholic pastoral workers in Germany (J. Meyerberg). Studies of similar human service professions (e.g., teachers, physicians) as well as contrasting professions (e.g., engineers, accountants) should ultimately yield valuable understanding of the social and psychological characteristics distinctive of each.

SEQUENTIAL INDIVIDUAL DEVELOPMENT

Our initial conceptualization of ways to analyze development included four types of data (see Table 7.1), only three of which have been addressed in this book. The first three—Currently Experienced Development, Experienced Career Development, and Comparative Cohort Development—are amenable to study with data collected at a single time point. The fourth, Sequential Individual Development, requires analysis of data collected repeatedly at meaningful intervals from the same individuals. This prospective, longitudinal mode of analysis is traditionally viewed as the gold standard in developmental research, although such research requires, by its nature, considerable time.

The longitudinal analysis of repeated-measures data to study Sequential Individual Development was an original goal of the CRN program, and a version of the DPCCQ was designed specifically for use in recurrent administrations. At present, samples of repeated-measurement data have been collected with this instrument in Bochum, Germany (U. Willutzki), and Lisbon, Portugal (A. Vasco). Another repeated-measures data set is being collected from a group of 55 therapists as part of the Norwegian Multicenter Project for the Study of Process and Outcome of Psychotherapy (O. Havik, P. Høglend, A. von der Lippe, G. Lyngstad, J. Monsen, T. Stiles, M. Svartberg). A principal goal of further research will be the analysis and comparison of these and other data sets that may be collected in future.

ADDITIONAL VARIABLES

A sequel to the present report will focus on therapists' lives and personalities and relate those to the currently reported findings on therapeutic work and professional development. Large amounts of data on the therapists' self-concepts and life quality already collected are being supplemented by new questions exploring the extent to which therapists think about patients outside of therapy sessions, therapists' early life quality and family experiences, and therapists' religious backgrounds and religious/spiritual experiences. Analyses of those data will significantly extend our knowledge of therapists' personal characteristics and their impact on therapeutic and developmental processes.

ADDITIONAL OBSERVATIONAL PERSPECTIVES
AND PROCESS LEVELS

At present, the DPCCQ focuses on the total practice of individual clinicians, providing an overview of the therapist's experience. However, many sections of the DPCCQ would lend themselves readily to adaptations to other perspectives and levels of process analysis. These might include focusing the questions on a particular treatment case, which, for example, would permit a study comparing the therapist's experiences in an effective case and a difficult case for each of several therapists. Some sections of the DPCCQ could also be used to study particular treatment sessions, in a manner complementing the original Therapy Session Report questionnaire (Orlinsky & Howard, 1975, 1986b). Other perspectives could include that of the clinical supervisor and that of the patient, especially when focused at the case or session level. Adaptations of specific DPCCQ sections such as those on difficulties in practice and coping strategies have already been successfully used in studies by Willutzki and her colleagues (Willutzki, Hernandez Bark, Davis, & Orlinsky, 1997; Willutzki & Orlinsky, 2002). Another adaptation for use by patients in rating their therapists has been made of items describing the therapist's manner of relating (J. Meyerberg). These could have applications in training and supervision as well as research.

THE GRAND HYPOTHESIS: CONVERGENCE OF
OBSERVATIONAL PERSPECTIVES

Perhaps the most pressing task for future research is testing the hypothesis that therapists' experiences of Healing Involvement actually converge with effective therapeutic process assessed from other observational perspectives. This will require comparison of work experience dimensions derived from the DPCCQ with measures of therapeutic process and outcome that tap the perspectives of independent raters, clinical judges, and patients. In pursuit of this aim, researchers associated with the Norwegian Multicenter Project for the Study of Process and Outcome of Psychotherapy (M. H. Rønnestad, A. von der Lippe) will be collaboratively analyzing data that have been gathered on treatments conducted by therapists of diverse orientations. Similarly, U. Willutzki and her colleagues will be extending their study of patients and therapists at the university clinic at Ruhr-University Bochum who participated in cognitive–behavioral treatments.

The strong form of the hypothesis is that psychotherapists' perspectives on effective therapeutic process will essentially resemble the perspectives of patients, supervisors, and "objective" raters. A more moderate version of the hypothesis is that psychotherapists' perspectives will be systematically and meaningfully, if obliquely, related to those other perspectives. It may be that psychotherapists live in a world of their own, one that has little relation to the world perceived by others and, if that is the case, a number of our interpretations and recommendations will prove to be wrong. Yet it is hard to believe that this is so—that the therapists, whose expert views on our personal lives and problems we seek when we are troubled, are in fact myopic and unable to see very far beyond their own noses. However it may turn out, our work goes on with a belief that the facts, being always friendly, will yield further insights worth having and future challenges worth meeting.

APPENDIX A

Origins of the Society for Psychotherapy Research Collaborative Research Network Study

DAVID E. ORLINSKY

Most of us learned in school, and have since taught our own students, that a research project should start from a set of specific questions or hypotheses, grounded either in theory or in previous research—or, preferably, in both. Then one should write a proposal, get a grant to fund the project, and hire a group of qualified people to assist with the work. We don't doubt that it is often done this way, particularly by people who find it convenient and are able to plan and program their lives by setting regular goals for the future.

There is also another, less publicized way research projects get started. They can begin from the desire to collaborate with particular colleagues and seem to evolve as an answer to the question "What would be interesting and feasible for us to do together?" Of course, this is not as blind or atheoretical a method of proceeding as it might first appear, since one is likely to be attracted in the first place to colleagues who share a strong interest and theoretical perspective. When all goes well, one becomes involved in quite a meaningful dialogue when jointly seeking the answer to that question. The dialogue leads progressively from an open exploration of shared interests to a set of concrete possibilities and from there to consideration of available or obtainable resources; and on to agreement about a particular topic in which all want to invest themselves; and thence to the discussion of specific questions, hypotheses, methods, and responsibilities. Following this procedure requires a measure of trust in the creativity of preconscious processes and the intellectually stimulating influence of dialogue, but personal experience attests to the viability and value of this alternative path to research (despite its lack of mention in treatises on research methods).

A PERSONAL TALE

Here's how it happened in our case. I had been invited to a meeting of the UK chapter of the Society for Psychotherapy Research in 1986, and there I met John and Marcia Davis. Subsequently, en route to visiting friends in Paris, I contacted Winfred Huber in Brussels, Belgium, to see if he could arrange an invitation to meet therapy research colleagues in France, in particular the team of Paul Gerin and Alice Dazord in Lyon. (To be completely honest, I was also on my usual quest to find a very good meal and knew that Lyon was the place to go.) Gerin and Dazord were kind enough to invite me to Lyon, and this led to a series of mutually interesting and increasingly friendly contacts. Prior to going to Bern, Switzerland, for the European chapter meeting of the Society for Psychotherapy Research in September 1989, Gerin and Dazord invited me to visit them in Lyon and arranged a meeting with colleagues at the University of Geneva department of psychiatry in Switzerland (Antonio Andreoli and Nicoletta Aapro) who were involved with them in a collaborative study. A fantasy about the desirability of a Lyon–Geneva–Chicago research collaboration was already hatching. After presenting a talk at departmental grand rounds, I met with Gerin, Dazord, Aapro, and Andreoli in Andreoli's office, and there the question was posed: "What would be interesting and possible for us to do together?"

Having done most of my previous work studying patients' and therapists' experiences of therapy, and the relation of therapeutic processes to clinical outcomes, I invited my Lyon and Geneva colleagues to use a research protocol to match data that Kenneth Howard and I were then collecting at Northwestern University in Chicago. Others felt that this would not be possible because of the protective attitude toward "the transference relationship" of this psychoanalytically oriented institution; that is, any direct study of patients and therapists in treatment would be regarded as a disruptive intrusion. An alternative proposal by the Genevans suggested that, since theirs was a major training center, we could focus on trainees and residents instead of patients and therapists. The meeting adjourned inconclusively as Gerin, Dazord, and I continued on our journey to the conference in Bern, where Andreoli and Aapro would join us the following day.

The drive from Geneva to Bern allowed a couple of hours for us three voyagers to debate the topic. None of our research or practical work involved the training of therapists, and so the potential interest of studying the training process did not seem strong. Another objection stemmed from a reluctance, on ethical grounds, to make research subjects of students who were dependent on the power of their supervisors. We then overrode the ethical objection to the possible exploitation of students by broadening the study to include teachers and supervisors—in fact, to include therapists at all career stages. The study might be conceived of as a collaborative, collective self-study of senior therapists in which therapists at all levels of experience would be invited to join. This egalitarian and communal spirit was in accord with our values and opened a broader intellectual perspective on the topic. If we were to study therapists at all career levels, our research focus would shift from the training of student therapists to the development of psychotherapists. The concept of development in general—sometimes known as "the idea of progress"—is a very potent and densely meaningful theme that lies close to the core of modern culture. The concept of development also lies at the foundation of much 20th-century psychology (Freud, Piaget, Vygotsky, et al.). Although I am mainly a psychotherapy researcher (as well as a psychotherapist), I was and am a faculty member of the Committee on Human Development at the University of Chicago, which is an interdisciplinary department devoted to research on the cultural, social, biological, and psychological aspects of development. By the time we arrived in Bern, the potential interest of a study on the development of psychotherapists seemed very clear.

How widespread that interest was became clear the following day. A brief announcement was made inviting interested attendees at the Bern conference to an impromptu session to discuss the possibility of a collaborative study on the development of psychotherapists, and to our surprise the designated room filled to overflowing. Paul Gerin, Alice Dazord, John and Marcia Davis, Hanruedi Ambühl, Ulrike Willutzki, Nicoletta Aapro, myself, and others were active participants. After a lively hour, a listing was made of those wanting further involvement and a decision was made that they would continue to communicate, by fax, with the aim of producing an initial research design by March 1990, when there would be a chance for more sustained conversation at the UK chapter meeting of the Society for Psychotherapy Research (SPR), at which time Jean-François Botermans and Thomas Schröder joined the group. Thus began the SPR Collaborative Research Network, which eventually expanded to include several dozen colleagues around the world and which is still active more than a decade later. In 1993, M. H. Rønnestad joined the group and brought to it experiences from his prior involvement in a major qualitative study of psychotherapist and counselor development (e.g., Rønnestad & Skovholt, 1991; Skovholt & Rønnestad, 1995).

THE COLLABORATIVE RESEARCH NETWORK

The SPR Collaborative Research Network operates as a self-supporting research co-op, combining the resources of researchers who share a strong interest in the development and practices of psychotherapists but whose individual resources for research are too limited to permit doing so independently. Like other cooperative societies, the SPR Collaborative Research Network gives researchers who combine their resources an opportunity to participate in a major undertaking (a study that no one individually could afford to do) and access to the result of their combined efforts (a rich and extensive database). Oversight of operations is vested in a steering committee composed of the most active members, and administrative responsibility is vested in American and European coordinators who consult frequently in order to work as a team. (Gerin, Ambühl, and Rønnestad have served successively as European coordinators, and I have served as coordinator for the Americas and elsewhere.)

Operating without external financial support or paid staff, the SPR Collaborative Research Network provides an alternative to the customary entrepreneurial model of research organization. In the typical entrepreneurial situation, a principal investigator acquires funding for a project from an agency or foundation and then hires research assistants to help collect and analyze data (Orlinsky, 1987). The alternative cooperative model is bound to be less efficient than a bureaucratically organized research team of paid assistants, because it depends on the time and skills of voluntary workers who always have other, generally more pressing responsibilities to meet before they are free to devote themselves to the project. But the cooperative model has other values. It empowers researchers to study what interests them rather than what they can interest sponsors to support and, as our case demonstrates, doesn't necessarily limit them to small-scale projects. Another value of the cooperative model is that it has an egalitarian–collaborative structure, in which initiative and responsibility are shared in equal measure, rather than a hierarchical-command organizational structure. A third advantage is that the project is not limited to the term of a research grant but can continue for as long as interest is sustained by those involved and by new colleagues who are attracted to join.

AN INVITATION

To psychotherapy researchers and psychotherapists who are interested in research, I would like to say that the SPR Collaborative Research Network, which started in 1989, is still a thriving enterprise. During the past 15 years, data have been gathered from thousands of psychotherapists by scores of colleagues in many countries and have been analyzed, published, and reported at numerous conferences—all without a grant! We know that major research in an area that is unlikely to gain major grant support can be done, because it *has* been done. It was done because those who participated cared enough to contribute some of their time, skills, and institutional resources (and, now and then, small out-of-pocket funds). No one was hired and paid to do this study, so of course it has progressed slowly, as a project to be worked on after the obligations of job, family, and daily life have been met. This has created a special bond among participants, with collaboration often blossoming into friendship. To pursue a study simply out of a deep and abiding interest in a topic, working according to one's own creative standards, confers a rare and exhilarating sense of intellectual freedom. To share that interest and creative effort with others conveys a wonderful sense of intellectual community. It may be true, as we have often joked among ourselves, that as a group we have enjoyed more fine dinners together over the years than we have had publications—but that is a metaphoric as well as a literal truth. Interested colleagues are always welcome at this table and are invited to help create and enjoy an ongoing feast.

APPENDIX B
Sample Characteristics

DAVID E. ORLINSKY AND MICHAEL HELGE RØNNESTAD

TABLE B.1
Percentages of Therapists by Country: Professional Characteristics

Characteristics	USA	Norway	Germany	South Korea	Total
n	844	804	1,059	538	4,923
Profession					
Psychology	67.5	92.2	36.6	13.0	57.3
Medicine	5.5	4.9	54.4	64.3	28.1
Social work	19.0	0.9	1.5	5.9	5.7
Counseling	2.3	0.0	0.9	6.9	2.0
Nursing	1.8	2.0	0.1	7.1	1.9
Lay therapist[a]	2.7	0.0	3.0	1.1	3.0
Other	1.3	0.1	3.5	1.7	2.2
Career cohort[b]					
Novice	15.9	9.4	11.3	26.5	11.3
Apprentice	7.0	10.4	14.3	26.7	11.6
Graduate	6.4	17.1	24.0	17.4	16.4
Established	14.2	30.8	30.7	19.2	30.2
Seasoned	30.6	24.7	17.2	9.3	22.7
Senior	26.0	7.3	2.5	0.9	7.9
Orientation[c]					
Analytic–dynamic	48.6	64.9	68.1	38.6	57.6
Behavioral	23.5	6.3	13.4	14.6	14.2
Cognitive	40.2	32.9	14.4	20.9	23.9
Cognitive–behavioral[d]	20.5	5.2	8.1	9.8	10.7
Humanistic	33.2	31.9	30.7	36.1	31.2
Systemic	28.6	24.4	16.6	6.9	20.9
Other	14.8	17.4	11.4	4.6	13.4
None salient	10.1	5.8	5.1	34.5	9.4
2+ salient	54.4	53.8	42.6	34.9	45.5
Years in practice					
M	16.9	11.5	9.1	5.6	11.2
SD	12.5	8.2	7.0	5.9	8.9

[a]Includes therapists who listed no core profession other than psychotherapist or psychoanalyst. [b]Novice = < 1.5 years of experience, apprentice = 1.5 to < 3.5 years of experience, graduate = 3.5 to < 7 years of experience, established = 7 to < 15 years of experience, seasoned = 15 to < 25 years of experience, senior = 25 to 53 years of experience. [c]An orientation was considered salient if it was rated 4 or 5 on a 0–5 scale of influence on therapeutic practice. [d]A subset of saliently behavioral or cognitive therapists who rated both orientations as salient.

TABLE B.2
Percentages of Therapists by Country: Practice Characteristics

Characteristics	USA	Norway	Germany	South Korea	Total
Practice setting					
Any inpatient practice	14.2	22.6	40.2	52.4	28.4
Any outpatient practice	32.0	58.5	29.8	48.7	43.1
Any independent practice	44.8	42.5	38.5	9.5	44.0
Only independent practice	35.0	20.6	24.3	5.6	25.1
> 1 setting	37.1	37.6	33.2	47.0	44.2
Client age groups[a]					
Children	33.5	24.6	15.9	13.0	25.1
Adolescents	50.7	50.9	31.6	42.9	45.7
Adults	89.6	86.3	92.1	91.2	87.1
Older adults	64.1	56.4	59.6	37.3	55.0
Seniors	33.7	15.0	19.3	12.4	19.0
> 1 age group	67.1	79.4	73.0	60.3	72.3
Impairment levels					
Minimal	16.6	19.7	16.8	23.7	19.2
Mild, transient symptoms	39.5	44.1	30.2	43.2	39.9
Mild, enduring symptoms	61.6	66.8	54.4	70.7	63.5
Moderate symptoms	63.5	70.5	62.9	74.7	69.1
Serious symptoms	62.3	70.2	65.9	70.1	68.6
Significantly impaired	41.1	41.3	44.3	48.6	44.6
Seriously impaired	23.1	22.7	29.2	30.0	26.9
Danger to self/other	19.7	20.6	20.0	24.8	21.3
Treatment modality					
Individual	92.2	94.6	92.4	90.1	93.3
Couple	49.5	34.8	27.7	16.8	34.1
Family	36.3	31.4	17.7	20.3	27.9
Group	32.4	22.4	46.6	36.9	34.1
Other	5.7	10.3	12.4	1.5	9.2
Only individual therapy	19.2	31.1	28.9	43.8	30.5
> 1 modality	74.7	63.6	64.3	46.7	63.8
Caseload[b]					
M	19.3	18.2	14.3	9.1	16.5
SD	17.3	12.6	12.0	12.9	14.5

[a]Children = age ≤ 12, adolescents = ages 13–19, adults = ages 20–49, older adults = ages 50–64, seniors = age 65+. [b]Total number of cases across treatment modalities.

TABLE B.3
Percentages of Therapists by Country: Demographic Characteristics

Characteristics	USA	Norway	Germany	South Korea	Total
Age					
M	47.6	43.7	41.7	33.8	42.4
SD	14.0	8.7	8.9	8.0	10.6
Gender					
Female	49.0	53.3	57.0	34.9	53.0
Male	51.0	46.7	43.0	65.1	47.0
Marital status					
Single	16.9	11.2	23.0	32.6	17.9
Live-in partner	7.2	17.5	35.8	2.3	16.7
Married	63.5	60.4	35.3	64.2	56.0
Separated/divorced	10.6	10.0	5.4	0.8	8.5
Widowed	1.8	0.9	0.5	0.2	0.9
Social status					
Non-native	8.8	13.1	11.0	0.9	10.9
Minority	27.7	3.9	4.0	1.7	10.5

TABLE B.4
Percentages of Therapists by Profession: Professional Characteristics

Characteristics	Psychology	Medicine	Other[a]	Total
n	2,810	1,378	728	4,923
Years in practice				
M	13.1	8.8	8.1	11.2
SD	9.2	7.8	7.2	8.9
Career level[b]				
Novice	6.6	15.9	21.8	11.3
Apprentice	8.0	17.7	14.6	11.6
Graduate	15.0	19.3	16.0	16.4
Established	31.9	27.0	29.6	30.2
Seasoned	27.5	15.9	16.0	22.7
Senior	11.0	4.2	2.1	7.9
Salient orientation[c]				
Analytic–dynamic	53.6	67.2	55.6	57.6
Behavioral	16.8	9.4	13.4	14.2
Cognitive	32.0	10.5	17.4	23.9
Cognitive–behavioral[d]	13.9	5.1	9.0	10.7
Humanistic	35.7	20.5	34.1	31.2
Systemic	23.8	12.5	24.7	20.9
Other	16.4	7.8	14.2	13.4
None salient	3.9	16.6	10.7	8.4
2+ salient	52.2	31.7	45.0	45.5

[a]Includes social work (n = 280), counseling (n = 97), nursing (n = 91), lay therapists (n = 145), and other therapists (n = 107). [b]Novice = < 1.5 years of experience, apprentice = 1.5 to < 3.5 years of experience, graduate = 3.5 to < 7 years of experience, established = 7 to < 15 years of experience, seasoned = 15 to < 25 years of experience, senior = 25 to 53 years of experience. [c]An orientation was considered salient if it was rated 4 or 5 on a 0–5 scale of influence on therapeutic practice. [d]A subset of saliently behavioral or cognitive therapists who rated both orientations as salient.

TABLE B.5
Percentages of Therapists by Profession: Practice Characteristics

Characteristics	Psychology	Medicine	Other[a]	Total
Practice setting				
Any inpatient practice	21.5	47.2	20.1	28.4
Any outpatient practice	44.2	41.1	42.9	43.1
Any independent practice	50.0	37.0	33.7	44.0
Only independent practice	28.4	20.9	20.1	25.1
Works in > 1 setting	45.8	46.4	34.3	44.2
Client age groups[b]				
Children	30.9	14.0	27.6	25.1
Adolescents	52.3	37.4	40.8	45.7
Adults	91.1	96.4	84.2	87.1
Older adults	57.1	58.4	45.7	55.0
Seniors	18.4	22.9	17.9	19.0
Treats > 1 age group	74.4	70.0	68.3	72.3
Impairment levels				
Minimal	17.6	20.1	22.2	19.2
Mild, transient symptoms	41.3	35.6	41.8	39.9
Mild, enduring symptoms	65.3	59.4	63.3	63.5
Moderate symptoms	72.1	67.9	59.2	69.1
Serious symptoms	71.9	67.0	59.1	68.6
Significant impairment	44.6	49.4	35.5	44.6
Serious impairment	25.4	32.6	19.9	26.9
Danger to self or others	20.6	23.5	18.4	21.3
Treatment modality				
Individual	95.1	92.7	87.7	93.3
Couple	39.8	26.9	25.7	34.1
Family	32.3	19.4	27.0	27.9
Group	28.6	36.9	49.3	34.1
Other	10.4	7.6	7.8	9.2
Only individual therapy	28.3	37.6	25.7	30.5
Uses > 1 modality	67.5	53.0	63.8	63.8
Caseload[c]				
Mdn	15.0	10.0	10.0	12.0
M	18.1	14.7	13.6	16.5
SD	14.3	15.1	13.4	14.5

[a]Includes social work ($n = 280$), counseling ($n = 97$), nursing ($n = 91$), lay therapists ($n = 145$), and other therapists ($n = 107$). [b]Children = age ≤ 12, adolescents = age 13–19, adults = age 20–49, older adults = age 50–64, seniors = age 65+. [c]Total number of cases across treatment modalities.

TABLE B.6
Percentages of Therapists by Profession: Demographic Characteristics

Characteristics	Psychology	Medicine	Other[a]	Total
Age				
M	44.0	40.3	40.6	42.4
SD	10.5	9.8	11.1	10.6
Gender				
Female	55.8	36.0	74.0	53.0
Male	44.2	64.0	26.0	47.0
Marital status				
Single	14.6	20.5	26.2	17.9
Living with partner	14.2	22.8	15.5	16.7
Married	61.1	52.4	42.8	56.0
Separated/divorced	9.1	3.9	14.0	8.5
Widowed	1.0	0.3	1.6	0.9
Social status				
Non-native	13.3	8.5	9.0	10.9
Minority	11.4	6.1	16.0	10.5
Nation				
USA	20.3	3.4	31.7	17.3
Germany	13.8	42.6	13.3	21.7
Switzerland	7.7	1.8	2.8	5.4
Norway	26.4	2.9	3.3	16.5
Denmark	5.0	0.3	2.1	3.2
Sweden	1.4	0.7	9.3	2.4
Portugal	4.4	3.9	1.7	3.8
Spain	4.8	2.2	2.4	3.7
Belgium	3.5	0.1	4.4	2.7
France	0.7	7.1	0.3	2.4
Russia	2.3	2.3	1.9	2.3
Israel	2.6	0.5	2.8	2.0
South Korea	2.5	25.6	16.9	11.0
Other	4.6	6.4	7.3	5.6

[a]Includes social work (n = 280), counseling (n = 97), nursing (n = 91), lay therapists (n = 145), and other therapists (n = 107).

TABLE B.7
Percentages of Therapists by Career Level: Professional Characteristics

Characteristics	Novice	Apprentice	Graduate	Established	Seasoned	Senior	Total
n	534	549	774	1,429	1,074	373	4,923
Years in practice							
M	0.7	2.4	5.0	10.4	18.8	31.3	11.2
SD	0.4	0.6	0.9	2.1	2.8	6.6	8.9
Profession							
Psychology	34.0	40.5	53.7	61.7	70.9	81.9	57.3
Medicine	38.3	41.8	32.2	24.3	19.2	14.6	28.1
Social work	20.9	6.6	3.6	4.1	3.1	0.5	5.7
Counseling	2.4	3.7	2.8	1.7	1.2	0.5	2.0
Nursing	0.8	2.0	2.3	2.0	0.6	0.5	1.9
Lay therapist	0.8	3.1	2.7	3.9	3.7	0.8	3.0
Other	2.8	2.4	2.6	2.3	1.3	1.1	2.2
Salient orientation[a]							
Analytic–dynamic	42.7	54.9	62.4	61.7	59.3	59.3	57.6
Behavioral	14.9	15.1	12.7	13.3	14.7	17.1	14.2
Cognitive	21.5	20.1	22.7	22.6	27.7	33.4	23.9
Cognitive–behavioral[b]	10.5	9.6	9.8	10.2	11.7	15.8	10.7
Humanistic	22.7	26.2	32.2	33.4	33.8	34.2	31.2
Systemic	19.9	19.0	18.0	22.3	23.6	20.3	20.9
Other	25.6	9.9	13.0	16.4	15.2	15.7	13.4
None salient	52.2	12.7	6.0	4.6	3.9	1.1	8.4
2+ salient	40.4	38.7	45.2	47.6	50.0	48.2	45.5

Note. Novice = < 1.5 years of experience, apprentice = 1.5 to < 3.5 years of experience, graduate = 3.5 to < 7 years of experience, established = 7 to < 15 years of experience, seasoned = 15 to < 25 years of experience, senior = 25 to 53 years of experience. [a]An orientation was identified as salient if it was rated 4 or 5 on a 0–5 scale of influence on therapeutic practice. [b]A subset of saliently behavioral or cognitive therapists who rated both orientations as salient.

TABLE B.8
Percentages of Therapists by Career Level: Practice Characteristics

Characteristics	Novice	Apprentice	Graduate	Established	Seasoned	Senior	Total
Practice setting							
Any inpatient practice	35.4	40.3	36.2	27.3	20.3	12.1	28.4
Any outpatient practice	43.1	51.0	50.1	46.3	39.9	24.1	43.1
Any independent practice	10.9	22.0	33.9	53.3	61.6	66.2	44.0
Only independent practice	6.9	11.5	16.9	26.9	37.0	50.4	25.1
> 1 setting	24.2	36.2	40.7	51.5	49.9	44.8	44.2
Client age groups[a]							
Children	19.8	21.4	23.3	27.1	29.7	22.5	25.1
Adolescents	35.6	39.5	42.4	49.8	51.7	47.1	45.7
Adults	78.9	83.4	89.2	87.7	89.8	90.8	87.1
Older adults	36.4	41.4	47.7	58.2	68.0	73.4	55.0
Seniors	14.0	12.2	15.4	18.3	24.8	33.9	19.0
> 1 age group	58.7	63.7	71.1	78.5	78.3	67.8	72.3
Treatment modality							
Individual	85.5	89.5	94.6	95.4	95.3	95.9	93.3
Couple	16.1	18.1	26.0	38.5	48.4	51.0	34.1
Family	23.6	24.4	24.1	29.0	34.2	28.8	27.9
Group	34.4	36.8	37.3	36.2	31.1	22.3	34.1
Other	5.8	5.3	9.9	10.9	11.2	6.8	9.2
> 1 modality	50.9	55.7	61.6	67.3	72.6	67.5	63.8
Only individual therapy	35.7	35.3	34.2	28.8	23.7	28.2	30.5
Caseload[b]							
M	8.0	9.5	14.1	18.6	22.1	21.5	16.5
SD	8.2	8.8	12.6	14.5	16.0	16.5	14.5

Note. Novice = < 1.5 years of experience, apprentice = 1.5 to < 3.5 years of experience, graduate = 3.5 to < 7 years of experience, established = 7 to < 15 years of experience, seasoned = 15 to < 25 years of experience, senior = 25 to 53 years of experience.
[a]Children = age ≤12, adolescents = age 13–19, adults = age 20–49, older adults = age 50–64, seniors = age 65+. [b]Total number of cases across treatment modalities.

TABLE B.9
Percentages of Therapists by Career Level: Demographic Characteristics

Characteristics	Novice	Apprentice	Graduate	Established	Seasoned	Senior	Total
Age							
M	32.9	34.7	37.2	42.6	49.1	60.8	42.4
SD	8.3	7.3	7.2	6.9	6.5	8.4	10.6
Gender							
Female	57.5	58.6	62.7	55.3	46.2	29.6	53.0
Male	42.5	41.4	37.3	44.7	53.8	70.4	47.0
Marital status							
Single	43.0	32.1	22.9	11.6	5.4	3.9	17.9
Live-in partner	17.1	18.7	23.0	18.3	13.9	6.1	16.7
Married	34.1	42.5	47.1	60.4	68.4	76.0	56.0
Separated/divorced	5.4	6.4	6.4	9.0	11.2	10.3	8.5
Widowed	0.4	0.2	0.5	0.7	1.2	3.6	0.9
Social status							
Non-native	6.3	10.4	9.7	11.7	13.5	18.4	10.9
Minority	12.8	7.9	7.4	9.2	11.5	21.9	10.5
Nation							
USA	25.0	10.7	6.9	8.3	23.8	58.1	17.3
Germany	21.9	27.1	32.1	22.2	16.5	7.0	21.7
Switzerland	2.1	1.5	3.3	8.6	7.9	3.5	5.4
Norway	14.0	15.1	17.6	17.1	18.2	15.9	16.5
Denmark	1.7	2.8	3.3	4.9	3.0	1.6	3.2
Sweden	1.3	1.5	2.0	2.9	3.6	0.5	2.4
Portugal	1.1	2.0	5.0	1.1	2.3	1.6	3.8
Spain	1.9	1.8	3.0	5.1	5.2	2.2	3.7
Belgium	1.5	4.6	3.3	2.7	2.7	0.8	2.7
France	0.2	1.3	2.1	3.0	3.3	1.6	2.4
Russia	3.0	4.8	3.5	2.4	0.7	3.0	2.3
Israel	0.2	0.9	3.5	2.9	1.8	0.2	2.0
South Korea	22.7	22.3	10.3	6.1	3.9	1.6	11.0
Other	3.4	3.5	4.3	7.2	7.1	4.6	5.6

Note. Novice = < 1.5 years of experience, apprentice = 1.5 to < 3.5 years of experience, graduate = 3.5 to < 7 years of experience, established = 7 to < 15 years of experience, seasoned = 15 to < 25 years of experience, senior = 25 to 53 years of experience.

TABLE B.10
Percentages of Practice Patterns for Different Career Cohorts by Profession

Profession	Novice	Apprentice	Graduate	Established	Seasoned	Senior	n	%
Psychology								
Effective Practice	45.6	41.2	49.2	55.8	56.4	65.2	1,170	53.8
Challenging Practice	16.9	21.5	22.0	22.1	24.9	21.0	487	22.4
Disengaged Practice	18.4	24.9	17.8	16.8	12.4	10.5	347	6.0
Distressing Practice	19.1	12.4	11.0	5.2	6.4	3.3	169	7.8
n	136	177	354	727	598	181	2,173	
%	6.3	8.1	16.3	33.5	27.5	8.3		100
Medicine								
Effective Practice	10.7	23.4	28.7	35.9	40.0	37.0	327	29.2
Challenging Practice	12.6	15.6	21.7	19.4	20.0	15.2	203	18.1
Disengaged Practice	34.0	31.7	29.1	27.6	28.0	23.9	330	29.5
Distressing Practice	42.8	29.3	20.4	17.1	12.0	23.9	259	23.1
n	159	205	230	304	175	46	1,119	
%	14.2	18.3	20.6	27.2	15.6	4.1		100
Other professions								
Effective Practice	41.5	38.9	42.0	58.1	65.6	58.3	289	50.7
Challenging Practice	25.4	23.6	19.3	23.3	22.9	33.3	133	23.3
Disengaged Practice	18.5	19.4	19.3	14.0	8.3	8.3	88	15.4
Distressing Practice	14.6	18.1	19.3	4.7	3.1	0.0	60	10.5
n	130	72	88	172	96	12	570	
%	22.8	12.6	15.4	30.2	16.8	2.1		100

Note. Novice = < 1.5 years of experience, apprentice = 1.5 to < 3.5 years of experience, graduate = 3.5 to < 7 years of experience, established = 7 to < 15 years of experience, seasoned = 15 to < 25 years of experience, senior = 25 to 53 years of experience. The chi-square for each profession was significant at $p < .0000$. *Medicine* includes psychiatry and medical psychotherapy/psychosomatics (in Germany); "other" professions include social work, nursing, counseling, and lay therapy.

TABLE B.11
Percentages of Therapists by Theoretical Orientation: Professional Characteristics

Characteristics	Analytic–dynamic	Behavioral	Cognitive	Humanistic	Systemic	None salient	Total
n	2,784	688	1,154	1,507	1,008	403	4,923
Years in practice							
M	11.5	11.5	12.4	12.0	11.6	5.9	11.2
SD	8.8	8.9	9.1	8.9	8.1	6.6	8.9
Career cohort[a]							
Novice	7.9	11.3	9.6	7.8	10.2	36.4	11.3
Apprentice	11.0	12.4	9.7	9.7	10.5	19.5	11.6
Graduate	17.5	14.6	15.3	16.8	13.9	13.0	16.4
Established	32.2	28.5	28.3	32.4	32.1	18.4	30.2
Seasoned	23.3	23.7	26.2	24.7	25.6	11.6	22.7
Senior	8.1	9.5	10.9	8.6	7.6	1.1	7.9
Profession							
Psychology	53.8	68.0	77.2	65.9	66.2	26.3	57.3
Medicine	32.4	18.3	12.2	18.2	16.7	55.1	28.1
Social work	5.7	5.2	3.6	5.2	10.0	7.2	5.7
Counseling	1.1	2.9	2.7	3.9	1.9	2.5	2.0
Nursing	1.6	1.7	1.6	1.4	0.8	5.0	1.9
Lay therapist[b]	3.7	1.7	1.3	3.2	2.4	0.7	3.0
Other	1.6	2.0	1.3	2.2	2.1	3.2	2.2

[a]Novice = < 1.5 years of experience, apprentice = 1.5 to < 3.5 years of experience, graduate = 3.5 to < 7 years of experience, established = 7 to < 15 years of experience, seasoned = 15 to < 25 year of experience, senior = 25 to 53 years of experience. [b]Includes therapists who listed no profession other than psychotherapist or psychoanalyst.

TABLE B.12

Percentages of Therapists by Theoretical Orientation: Practice Characteristics

Characteristics	Analytic–dynamic	Behavioral	Cognitive	Humanistic	Systemic	None salient	Total
Client age group[a]							
Children	23.1	28.3	28.7	26.0	40.4	19.6	25.1
Adolescents	43.9	50.6	54.8	48.7	59.4	39.2	45.7
Adults	89.5	85.5	87.0	90.3	84.0	85.2	87.1
Older adults	57.0	58.6	60.2	58.3	54.8	43.0	55.0
Seniors	18.0	24.1	23.8	19.7	19.6	18.5	19.0
> 1 age group	73.9	72.7	75.8	75.8	78.8	63.6	72.3
Impairment level							
Minimal	19.0	15.2	18.0	20.1	17.4	22.6	19.2
Mild, transient	38.3	37.8	41.3	40.8	39.7	41.5	39.9
Mild, enduring	61.0	64.7	64.1	65.0	61.1	69.2	63.5
Moderate symptoms	67.1	68.7	69.4	70.6	66.4	74.0	69.1
Serious symptoms	67.6	69.6	67.4	68.3	66.0	72.1	68.6
Significant impairment	43.7	47.1	43.2	44.6	43.4	47.6	44.6
Serious impairment	26.4	27.5	25.2	27.3	25.6	29.3	26.9
Danger to self/other	20.6	19.8	19.7	22.3	19.9	25.6	21.3
Treatment modality							
Individual	95.7	93.3	93.9	94.0	92.5	88.5	93.3
Couple	31.9	40.0	43.4	41.7	53.7	19.9	34.1
Family	24.1	34.3	34.3	32.1	58.5	20.8	27.9
Group	33.4	39.4	34.1	40.9	36.6	27.8	34.1
Other	9.6	7.0	8.0	9.2	11.2	7.0	9.2
Only individual therapy	34.0	23.2	24.5	23.4	10.6	41.1	30.5
> 1 modality	62.4	70.9	70.0	71.6	83.5	48.6	63.8
Caseload[b]							
M	16.6	17.6	19.2	18.2	18.5	10.4	16.5
SD	13.6	16.2	16.7	15.3	14.5	12.4	14.5

[a]Children = age ≤ 12, adolescents = age 13–19, adults = age 20–49, older adults = age 50–64, seniors = age 65+. [b]Total number of cases across treatment modalities.

TABLE B.13
Percentages of Therapists by Theoretical Orientation: Demographic Characteristics

Characteristics	Analytic–dynamic	Behavioral	Cognitive	Humanistic	Systemic	None salient	Total
Age							
M	43.4	42.0	43.0	43.2	42.3	35.9	42.4
SD	10.3	10.7	10.5	10.5	9.5	9.0	10.6
Gender							
Female	54.4	47.3	49.5	54.3	55.5	48.2	53.0
Male	45.6	52.7	50.5	45.7	44.5	51.8	47.0
Marital status							
Single	17.3	17.0	14.8	16.6	17.8	25.9	17.9
Live-in partner	19.7	11.8	13.2	15.9	15.8	10.2	16.7
Married	53.8	62.8	63.6	56.9	55.8	57.9	56.0
Separated/divorced	8.3	7.3	7.2	9.6	9.8	5.2	8.5
Widowed	0.9	1.0	1.2	1.0	0.8	0.8	0.9
Social status							
Non-native	11.7	10.2	10.8	10.9	13.3	5.3	10.9
Minority	10.0	10.1	11.2	12.4	14.1	7.3	10.5
Nation							
USA	14.7	28.7	29.1	18.4	23.9	8.2	17.3
Germany	25.3	20.1	12.8	20.9	17.0	13.0	21.7
Switzerland	4.6	8.9	6.2	6.7	8.2	2.7	5.4
Norway	18.7	7.3	22.8	16.8	19.4	11.5	16.5
Denmark	4.5	0.7	1.3	3.3	2.8	2.2	3.2
Sweden	3.2	0.7	0.3	0.7	0.8	2.5	2.4
Portugal	2.6	7.5	5.5	2.7	4.8	1.5	3.8
Spain	3.7	3.1	3.4	2.2	4.1	1.5	3.7
Belgium	2.2	3.2	1.9	3.1	3.7	1.7	2.7
France	3.2	0.6	0.3	2.1	1.2	3.2	2.4
Russia	1.6	2.3	0.8	3.4	1.8	3.0	2.3
Israel	2.9	0.9	1.1	1.8	2.3	0.2	2.0
South Korea	7.3	11.1	9.5	12.5	3.6	44.9	11.0
Other	5.5	4.7	5.0	5.5	6.5	3.7	5.6

APPENDIX C
Analyses of Therapeutic Work Experience

DAVID E. ORLINSKY AND MICHAEL HELGE RØNNESTAD

TABLE C.1
Treatment Goals

How important do you think it is for most of your patients to realize the following goals? (Check the 4 that you judge generally most important)	%	Rank
Have a strong sense of self-worth and identity.	60.1	1
Improve the quality of their relationships.	43.8	2
Understand their feelings, motives and/or behavior.	41.2	3
Integrate excluded or segregated aspects of experience.	31.7	4
Experience a decrease in their symptoms.	29.6	5
Develop courage to approach new or previously avoided situations.	28.5	6
Allow themselves to experience feelings fully.	26.7	7
Identify and pursue their own goals.	24.8	8
Learn to behave effectively in problematic situations.	21.9	9
Modify or control problematic patterns of behavior.	18.8	10
Think realistically about the meaning of events in their lives.	17.6	11
Evaluate themselves realistically.	16.8	12
Moderate their excessive or irrational emotional reactions.	12.6	13
Resolve emotional conflicts in relation to you as their therapist.	9.4	14
Reason validly about the probable consequences of their behavior.	6.4	15

TABLE C.2
Current Therapeutic Skill: Single-Factor and Three-Factor Solutions

Dimension and items	M	SD	% High[a]	Factors I	II	III
Single factor: Currently Skillful (total scale)	3.61	0.65				
I. Technical Expertise	3.49	0.80				
How good is your general theoretical understanding of therapy?	3.66	0.91	62.1	**.78**		
How much mastery do you have of the techniques and strategies involved in practicing therapy?	3.49	0.93	53.2	**.77**		.32
How much precision, subtlety and finesse have you attained in your therapeutic work?	3.35	1.02	46.8	**.79**		.31
How well do you understand what happens moment-by-moment during therapy sessions?	3.47	0.92	52.5	**.72**		.37
II. Basic Relational Skills	3.83	0.66				
How empathic are you in relating to patients with whom you have relatively little in common?	3.57	0.86	57.6		**.77**	
How "natural" (authentically personal) do you feel while working with patients?	4.07	0.83	80.5	.34	**.67**	
How effective are you at engaging patients in a working alliance?	3.92	0.82	77.4	.40	**.65**	
How effective are you in communicating your understanding and concern to your patients?	3.86	0.86	72.7	.60	**.60**	.47
How good are you at grasping the essence of your patients' problems?	3.75	0.87	67.6	.42	.47	.37
III. Advanced Relational Skills	3.54	0.76				
How well are you able to detect and deal with your patients' emotional reactions to you?	3.61	0.88	60.0			**.76**
How good are you at making constructive use of your personal reactions to patients?	3.60	0.91	59.0	.30		**.75**
How skillful are you at getting your patients to play their part in therapy?	3.45	0.97	52.6	.31		**.64**
Cronbach's alpha				.86	.79	.78

Note. Items were rated on a scale that ranged from 0 (*not at all*) to 5 (*very*). Factor loadings in boldface type indicate items scored for factor dimension scale. For the Currently Skillful dimension, Cronbach's alpha = .90.

[a]High = rating of 4 or 5.

TABLE C.3
Difficulties in Practice

Currently, how often do you feel . . .	M	SD	% > Rarely[a]	Factors I	II	III
I. Professional Self-Doubt	1.72	0.77				
Lacking in confidence that you can have a beneficial effect on a patient.	1.87	1.05	58.0	**.75**		
Unsure how best to deal effectively with a patient.	2.35	1.11	76.4	**.74**		
Demoralized by your inability to find ways to help a patient.	1.48	1.07	42.8	**.57**	.49	
Afraid that you are doing more harm than good in treating a patient.	0.86	0.85	17.2	**.50**		
Unable to comprehend the essence of a patient's problems.	1.36	0.95	37.5	.50		.45
Unable to generate sufficient momentum to move therapy with a patient in a constructive direction.	1.55	1.05	46.6	**.48**	.38	.49
In danger of losing control of the therapeutic situation to a patient.	1.15	0.94	29.2	.45		.45
II. Frustrating Treatment Case	1.48	0.80				
Angered by factors in a patient's life that make a beneficial outcome impossible.	1.36	1.15	37.9		**.70**	.30
Distressed by your powerlessness to affect a patient's tragic life situation.	1.96	1.26	59.3		**.63**	.42
Conflicted about how to reconcile obligations to a patient and equivalent obligations to others.	1.20	1.18	31.6	.42	**.62**	
Bogged down with a patient in a relationship that seems to go nowhere.	1.41	1.04	41.2		**.51**	
Irritated with a patient who is actively blocking your efforts.	1.56	1.05	46.5		.48	.42
Troubled by moral or ethical issues that have arisen in your work with a patient.	1.14	1.01	29.2		.45	.35
III. Negative Personal Reaction	1.07	0.69				
Unable to find something to like or respect in a patient.	0.78	0.83	15.1			**.70**
Unable to have much real empathy for a patient's experiences.	1.19	0.91	29.0			**.65**
Unable to withstand a patient's emotional neediness.	1.22	0.97	32.1		.31	**.60**
Uneasy that personal values make it difficult to maintain an appropriate attitude.	1.08	0.96	25.0			**.60**
Frustrated with a patient for wasting time.	1.03	1.01	25.9			.49
Disturbed that circumstances in your personal life are interfering in your work with a patient.	1.25	1.13	32.3			.40
Guilty about having mishandled a critical situation with a patient.	1.22	0.96	30.9	.37	.35	.39
Cronbach's alpha				.77	.67	.74

Note. Items were rated on a scale that ranged from 0 (*never*) to 5 (*very often*). Factor loadings in boldface type indicate items scored for factor dimension scales.
[a] > Rarely ≥ 1.

TABLE C.4
Coping Strategies

Dimension and items	M	SD	% Often[a]	I	II	III	IV	V	VI
I. Exercise Reflective Control	3.10	0.73				.35		−.32	
Review privately with yourself how the problem arose.[b]	3.53	1.26	57.9	.57					
Attempt to contain your troublesome feelings.	2.79	1.32	33.2	.57					
Try to see the problem from a different perspective.[b]	3.49	1.05	53.6	.52					
Interpret the patient's resistant or troublesome behavior.	2.79	1.38	31.2	.48					
Set limits to hold a patient to an appropriate therapeutic frame.	2.87	1.38	36.4	.48					
II. Seek Consultation	2.79	0.96							
Consult about the case with a more experienced therapist.[b]	3.30	1.43	53.1		.78				
Discuss the problem with a colleague.[a]	3.44	1.29	55.7		.71				
Involve another professional or agency in the case.[b]	2.41	1.47	26.7		.65				
Consult relevant articles or books.[b]	2.90	1.34	36.1		.59				
Sign up for a conference or workshop on the problem.[b]	1.89	1.48	16.9		.52				
III. Problem-Solve With Patient	3.00	0.87							
See whether you and your patient can deal with the difficulty.[b]	3.08	1.29	41.8			.68			
Share your experience of the difficulty with your patient.	2.10	1.37	17.3			.67			
Give self permission to experience difficult/disturbing feelings.[b]	3.28	1.27	48.7	.44		.52			
IV. Reframe the Helping Contract	1.71	0.84							
Invite collaboration from a patient's friends or relatives.	1.48	1.42	11.4				.65		
Make changes in your therapeutic contract with a patient.	1.68	1.17	7.1				.64		
Postpone therapy to care for a patient's immediate needs.	1.71	1.32	10.4				.63		
Step out of the therapist role to take action on a patient's behalf.	1.22	1.15	4.9				.60		
Modify your therapeutic stance or approach with a patient.[b]	2.45	1.22	19.4				.56		

V. Seek Alternative Satisfactions

	M	SD	%	I	II	III	IV	V	VI
Seek some form of alternative satisfaction away from therapy.	2.20	1.63	26.3					.61	
Express your upset feelings to somebody close to you.	2.60	1.55	33.8					.46	
VI. Avoid Therapeutic Engagement	1.22	0.65							
Avoid dealing with the problem for the present.	1.45	1.13	4.2						**.63**
Criticize a patient for causing you trouble.	0.51	0.79	0.6			.31			**.62**
Seriously consider terminating therapy.	1.25	1.09	4.2			−.34			**.59**
Simply hope that things will improve eventually.	1.46	1.23	6.8				.40		**.57**
Show your frustration to the patient.	1.14	1.04	2.7			.41			**.55**
Explore possibility of referring the patient to another therapist.	1.52	1.17	6.1			−.33			**.42**
Cronbach's alpha				.59	.71	.60	.69	.46	.64

Note. Items were rated on a scale that ranged from 0 (*never*) to 5 (*very often*). Factor loadings in boldface type indicate items scored for factor dimension scales.
[a]Often = items rated 4 or 5.

TABLE C.5
Relational Agency

Dimension and items	M	SD	% High[a]	Factors I	II	III
I. Invested	2.20	0.57				
Involved	2.22	0.77	84.2	**.78**		
Committed	2.27	0.75	85.9	**.67**		
Intuitive	2.12	0.77	80.0	**.57**		
(not) Neutral[b]	1.31	0.88	58.2[c]	−.45	.41	
II. Efficacious	1.66	0.53				
Skillful	1.83	0.73	71.6		**.69**	
Organized	1.63	0.81	56.4		**.67**	
Effective	1.84	0.73	72.3		**.67**	
Subtle	1.32	0.92	43.6		**.54**	
Pragmatic[c]	1.70	0.84	61.3		.47	
Determined	1.67	0.78	59.5	.40	.42	
III. Baffled						
Confused	0.50	.63	6.3			.76
Unhelpful	0.58	.69	9.3			.75
Cronbach's alpha				.67	.59	.38

Note. Items were rated on a scale that ranged from 0 (*not at all*) to 3 (*very much*). Factor loadings in bold-face type indicate items scored for factor dimension scale. (Factor III was unscored because of a low alpha).
[a]High = rating of 2 or 3. [b]Percentage who rated item as low, corresponding to "not neutral." [c]Not included in scale because of a lowered or inadequate alpha.

TABLE C.6
Relational Manner

Dimension and items	M	SD	% High[a]	I	II	III	IV
I. Affirming	2.36	0.47					
Warm	2.29	0.68	89.3	**.76**			
Friendly	2.32	0.70	89.2	**.70**			
Accepting	2.53	0.58	96.6	**.63**			
Tolerant	2.31	0.66	91.1	**.62**			
II. Accommodating	1.70	0.55					
Permissive	1.58	0.87	56.3		**.70**		
Receptive	2.00	0.90	72.5		**.52**		
Nurturant	1.82	0.79	68.2		**.51**		
Protective	1.46	0.77	47.3	.40	**.47**		
III. Dominant	1.11	0.49					
Directive	1.18	0.76	32.0			**.68**	
Demanding	1.06	0.80	26.8			**.61**	
Authoritative	1.17	0.79	32.0			**.60**	
Challenging	1.25	0.86	38.7			**.55**	
Critical	0.92	0.79	21.2	−.34		**.50**	.45
IV. Reserved	0.82	0.53					
Guarded	1.20	0.90	36.5				**.73**
Reserved	1.20	0.78	32.4				**.67**
Detached	0.69	0.76	14.5				**.67**
Cold	0.34	0.59	5.1	−.40			**.57**
Cronbach's alpha				.69	.56	.59	.65

Note. Items were rated on a scale that ranged from 0 (*not at all*) to 3 (*very much*). Factor loadings in bold-face type indicate items scored for factor dimension scale.
[a]High = rating of 2 or 3.

TABLE C.7
In-Session Feelings

Dimension and items	M	SD	% Often[a]	Factors I	II	III
I. Flow	2.00	0.62				
Inspired	1.99	0.78	79.3	**.79**		
Stimulated	1.97	0.82	76.6	**.73**		
Engrossed	2.05	0.86	79.6	**.67**		
Challenged	1.85	0.88	69.7	**.47**		.30
II. Anxiety	0.91	0.61				
Pressured	1.03	0.80	25.5		**.77**	
Overwhelmed	0.87	0.80	19.1		**.70**	
Anxious	0.80	0.70	13.8		**.68**	
Trapped	0.77	0.70	11.9		**.56**	.33
III. Boredom	0.84	0.53				
Absent	0.77	0.64	9.4			**.75**
Bored	0.88	0.69	15.4			**.74**
Inattentive	0.80	0.61	8.8			**.74**
Drowsy	0.84	0.72	14.2			**.73**
Cronbach's alpha				.62	.66	.74

Note. Items were rated on a scale that ranged from 0 (*not at all*) to 3 (*very much*). Factor loadings in bold-face type indicate items scored for factor dimension scale.
[a]Often = rating of 2 or 3.

TABLE C.8
Dimensions of Work Involvement by Profession

Dimension and items	Professional background				
n	Psychology 2,810	Medicine 1,378	Social work 280	Nursing 91	Lay therapy[a] 214
Healing Involvement					
Invested	I	I	I	I	I
Affirming	I	I	I	I	I
Flow	I	I	I	I	I [II]
Constructive Coping	I	I	I [III]	I	I
Accommodating	I	III	I	III	I [III]
Basic Relational Skill	III [I, −II]	I [−II]	III	I [−II]	−II [I]
Stressful Involvement					
Frequent Difficulties	II	II	II	II	II
Anxiety	II	II	−III	II	II
Avoiding Therapeutic Engagement	II	II [III]	II	II	II
Boredom	II	II	II	II	II
Controlling Involvement					
Dominant	III	III	II	III [II]	II
Reserved	III [II, −I]	III	II	III [II]	II
Efficacious	III [I]	III [I]	I [III]	III [I]	−II [I]
Cronbach's alpha					
Healing Involvement	.69	.73	.74	.79	.71
Stressful Involvement	.67	.65	.61	.71	.63

Note. A three-factor solution is shown; loadings above .30 are noted, with secondary loadings bracketed.
[a]Includes "psychotherapists," "psychoanalysts," or "counselors" who listed no other profession.

TABLE C.9
Dimensions of Work Involvement by Theoretical Orientation

Dimension and items	Theoretical orientation					
	Salient Analytic–dynamic	Mainly Cognitive–behavioral	Mainly humanistic	Mainly systemic	Broad-spectrum eclectic	No salient orientation
n	1,508	528	744	393	241	545
Healing Involvement						
Invested	–	–	–	–	–	–
Affirming	–	–	–	–	–	–
Flow	–	–	–	–	–	–
Constructive Coping	–	–	–	–	–	–
Accommodating	–	–	–	–	–	≡
Basic Relational Skill	III [– II]	I [III, – II]	≡	≡	– II [I]	–
Stressful Involvement						
Frequent Difficulties	=	=	=	II [– III]	=	=
Anxiety	=	=	II [– III]	–III [II, I]	III [III]	=
Avoiding Therapeutic Engagement	=	=	=	=	III [III]	=
Boredom	=	=	=	=	=	=
Controlling Involvement						
Dominant	III [II]	III	II [III]	II [III]	=	=
Reserved	III [III]	II [III]	=	=	=	=
Efficacious	III [I]	III [I]	≡	≡	I [III]	I [III]
Cronbach's alpha						
Healing Involvement	.66	.73	.73	.68	.62	.81
Stressful Involvement	.65	.69	.65	.66	.62	.67

Note. A three-factor solution is shown; loadings > .30 are noted, with secondary loadings bracketed.

TABLE C.10
Dimensions of Work Involvement by Career Level

Dimension and items	Career cohort[a]					
	Novice	Apprentice	Graduate	Established	Seasoned	Senior
n	534	549	774	1,429	1,074	375
Healing Involvement						
Invested	—	—	—	—	—	—
Affirming	—	—	—	—	—	—
Flow	—	—	—	—	—	—
Constructive Coping	—	—	—	—	—	—
Accommodating	—	—	—	—	—	—
Basic Relational Skill	III [− II]	I [III, −II]	III	III	− II [I]	III
Stressful Involvement						
Frequent Difficulties	II	II	II	II [− III]	II	II
Anxiety	II	II	II [− III]	−III [II, I]	II	II
Avoiding Therapeutic Engagement	II	II	II	II	III [II]	II
Boredom	II	II	II	II	II	II
Controlling Involvement						
Dominant	III [II]	III	II [III]	II [III]	III	III
Reserved	III [II]	II [III]	II	II	III	III
Efficacious	III [I]	III [I]	III	III	I [III]	I [III]
Cronbach's alpha						
Healing Involvement	.66	.73	.73	.68	.62	.81
Stressful Involvement	.65	.69	.65	.66	.62	.67

Note. A three-factor solution is shown; loadings above .30 are noted, with secondary loadings bracketed.
[a]Novice = < 1.5 years of experience, apprentice = 1.5 to < 3.5 years of experience, graduate = 3.5 to < 7 years of experience, established = 7 to < 15 years of experience, seasoned = 15 to < 25 years of experience, senior = 25 or more years of experience.

TABLE C.11
Dimensions of Work Involvement by Therapist Gender

Dimension and items	Gender	
	Female	Male
n	2,580	2,288
Healing Involvement		
Invested	I	I
Affirming	I	I
Flow	I	I
Constructive Coping	I	I [II]
Accommodating	I	I
Basic Relational Skill	– II [I, III]	I [– II]
Stressful Involvement		
Frequent Difficulties	II	II
Anxiety	II	II
Avoiding Therapeutic Engagement	II	II [III]
Boredom	II	II
Controlling Involvement		
Dominant	III	III
Reserved	III	III
Efficacious	III [I, – II]	I [III]
Cronbach's alpha		
Healing Involvement	.71	.76
Stressful Involvement	.65	.68

Note. A three-factor solution is shown; loadings above .30 are noted, with secondary loadings bracketed.

TABLE C.12
Dimensions of Work Involvement by Country

Dimension and items n	Country			
	USA 844	Germany 1,059	Norway 804	South Korea 538
Healing Involvement				
Invested	I	I	I	I
Affirming	I	I	I	I
Flow	I	I	I [–II]	I
Constructive Coping	I	I [III]	I	I
Accommodating	I	I [II]	I	I
Basic Relational Skill	III	–II [I, III]	–II [I, III]	I
Stressful Involvement				
Frequent Difficulties	II	II	II	II
Anxiety	–III [II]	II	II	II
Avoiding Therapeutic Engagement	II	II	II	II
Boredom	II	II	II	II
Controlling Involvement				
Dominant	II [III]	III	III	II [I]
Reserved	II	II	III [II]	I
Efficacious	III [I]	III	III	I
Cronbach's alpha				
Healing Involvement	.73	.64	.65	.79
Stressful Involvement	.68	.66	.67	.71

Note. A three-factor solution is shown; loadings above .30 are noted, with secondary loadings bracketed. A two-factor solution shown for South Korea because the three-factor solution was not clearly interpretable. Alphas for Healing Involvement and Stressful Involvement, respectively, for other countries, were as follows: Switzerland = .61 and .60, omitting "Bored"; Portugal = .74 and .69; Spain = .68 and .65; Denmark = .71 and .62; Belgium = .63 and .67; Sweden = .64 and .68; France = .60, omitting Basic Relational Skill, and .46, omitting "Bored"; Russia = .77 and .56; Israel = .67 and .52; other countries = .75 and .66.

TABLE C.13
Bivariate Correlates of Therapist Work Involvement Dimensions

Correlates	Healing Involvement	Stressful Involvement	Dominant Manner[a]
Profession and experience			
Profession			
Medicine	−.32	.12	−.00
Psychology	.23	−.10	.02
Practice duration	.17	−.10	−.02
Breadth and depth of case experience	.36	−.06	.13
Training experiences			
Years of academic instruction	.17	−.07	−.05
Years of formal supervision	.20	−.05	−.01
Current supervision	.10	.05	.00
Current personal therapy	.04	.09	−.06
Previous personal therapy	.25	−.05	−.05
Theoretical orientation			
Analytic–dynamic	.06	.04	−.14
Behavioral	.04	.03	.23
Cognitive	.12	−.01	.19
Humanistic	.15	.00	.05
Systemic	.20	.01	.13
Theoretical breadth	.34	−.04	.13
Practice conditions			
Current caseload	.15	−.02	.05
Any inpatient practice	−.15	.08	.09
Any outpatient practice	.02	−.00	−.02
Any independent practice	.17	−.14	−.06
Professional autonomy	.26	−.18	−.04
Work setting support and satisfaction	.33	−.18	.02
Personal status			
Age	.22	−.12	−.06
Gender: Female	.20	−.06	−.10
Marital status: Married	−.01	−.02	.01
Nation			
Korea	−.45	.05	.04
USA	.11	−.02	−.04
Germany	−.03	.16	.13
Norway	.14	−.01	−.08
Denmark	.09	−.10	.04
Sweden	.08	.02	−.03
Portugal	.08	−.10	.04
Switzerland	.07	−.04	.07
France	−.10	−.03	−.09
Belgium	−.04	−.08	−.04

Note. $p < .01$ for correlations exceeding $r = \pm .04$.
[a]The first-level factor scale of Dominant relational manner was used as a proxy for the unscaled second-level factor Controlling Involvement.

TABLE C.14
Healing Involvement Predictors: Total Sample

Predictor	Step	± Beta	ΔR^2 (% variance)
Block 1: Nation[a]			
Korea	1	–	20.6
France	2	–	1.4
Block 2: Therapist and Practice Characteristics[b]			
Theoretical Breadth	1	+	8.0
Work Setting Support and Satisfaction	2	+	3.4
Gender: Female	3	+	2.0
Breadth and Depth of Case Experience	4	+	1.7
Professional Autonomy	5	+	0.6
Profession: Medicine	6	–	0.4
Profession: Psychology	7	–	0.6
Humanistic orientation	8	+	0.3
Current supervision	9	+	0.2
Previous personal therapy	10	+	0.2
Stressful Involvement	11	–	0.2
Cognitive orientation	12	+	0.1
Age	13	+	0.1
Practice duration	14	–	0.1

Note. Multiple R = .633, total adjusted R^2 = .397. The following variables did not enter significantly ($p \geq .05$) into the equation: nationality (USA, Norway), current caseload, years of academic training, years of supervision, inpatient practice, systemic orientation.
[a]Variance due to nationality = 22.0%. [b]Additional variance due to therapist and practice = 17.9%.

TABLE C.15
Healing Involvement Predictors: Main National Subsamples

Predictor	USA ±	USA (Step)	USA %	Norway ±	Norway (Step)	Norway %	Germany ±	Germany (Step)	Germany %	South Korea ±	South Korea (Step)	South Korea %	Other countries ±	Other countries (Step)	Other countries %
Theoretical Breadth	+	(3)	4.3	+	(1)	8.1	+	(1)	6.8	+	(1)	22.7	+	(1)	7.1
Work setting support and satisfaction	+	(2)	5.2	+	(3)	3.5	+	(2)	4.7	+	(2)	3.3	+	(2)	5.0
Breadth and Depth of Case Experience	+	(1)	9.0	+	(8)	0.5	+	(4)	1.7				+	(3)	2.9
Gender: Female	+	(5)	2.2	+	(2)	5.0	+	(5)	1.7				+	(4)	3.4
Years of formal supervision	+	(4)	2.7												
Independent practice							+	(3)	2.2						
Cognitive orientation				+	(5)	1.3				+	(3)	1.4			
Stressful Involvement				–	(6)	1.2				+	(5)	1.8			
Some independent practice	+	(6)	1.4												
Current supervision	+	(7)	1.6												
Practice duration	+	(8)	1.6	–	(9)	0.7				+	(4)	1.7			

Systemic orientation		+ (9) 1.0			
Profession: Psychology	− (7) 0.4			+ (7) 0.9	− (10) 0.9
Profession: Medicine	− (6) 0.6				− (11) 1.0
Years of academic instruction				+ (4) 1.8	+ (12) 1.0
Humanistic orientation			+ (7) 0.5		+ (13) 0.9
Professional autonomy	+ (5) 0.8				
Previous personal therapy			+ (6) 0.7	+ (10) 0.6	
Caseload					+ (14) 0.8
R	.454	.573	.442	.501	.612
Total adjusted R^2	.201	.309	.184	.236	.343

Note. The list of variables entered was identical to that in Table C.14; those not listed were not significant predictors in any of the national multiple regression analyses.
± = sign of Beta; % = increment in variance.

TABLE C.16
Stressful Involvement Predictors: Total Sample

Predictor	Step	± Beta	ΔR^2 (% variance)
Block 1: Nation[a]			
Germany	1	+	2.5
Portugal	2	–	0.7
Denmark	3	–	0.7
Block 2: Therapist and Practice Characteristics[b]			
Work Setting Support and Satisfaction	1	–	3.2
Some independent practice	2	–	1.1
Professional Autonomy	3	–	0.4
Age	4	–	0.1

Note. $R = .297$, total adjusted $R^2 = .087$. The following variables did not enter significantly ($p \geq .05$) into the equation: profession (medicine, psychology) and practice duration.
[a]Variance due to nationality = 3.9%. [b]Additional variance due to therapist and practice = 4.8%.

TABLE C.17
Stressful Involvement Predictors: Main National Subsamples

Predictor	USA ±	(Step)	%	Germany ±	(Step)	%	Norway ±	(Step)	%	South Korea ±	(Step)	%	Other countries ±	(Step)	%
Work Setting Support and Satisfaction	–	(1)	3.0	–	(1)	0.8	–	(1)	4.5	–	(2)	1.0	–	(3)	0.5
Professional Autonomy				–	(2)	1.7							–	(1)	2.0
Age				–	(3)	0.8	–	(2)	1.7						
Practice duration										–	(1)	2.2			
Some independent practice													–	(2)	0.8
Profession: Psychology													–	(4)	0.4
Profession: Medicine				+	(4)	0.5									
R	.184			.283			.254			.203			.198		
Total adjusted R^2	.030			.076			.062			.032			.036		

Note. The list of variables entered was identical to that in Table C.16; those not listed were not significant predictors in any of the national multiple regression analyses.
± = sign of Beta; % = increment in variance.

TABLE C.18
Dominant Manner Predictors: Total Sample

Predictor	Step	± Beta	ΔR^2 (% variance)
Block 1: Nation[a]			
Germany	1	+	1.7
Russia	2	−	0.9
Block 2: Therapist and Practice Characteristics[b]			
Dominant in personal relations	1	+	18.8
Behavioral orientation	2	+	4.9
Breadth and Depth of Case Experience	3	+	0.9
Gender: Male	4	+	0.6
Analytic–dynamic orientation	5	−	0.6
Cognitive orientation	6	+	0.2
Systemic orientation	7	+	0.1

$R = .537$
Total adjusted $R^2 = .287$

Note. The following variables did not enter significantly ($p \geq .05$) into the equation: Theoretical Breadth.
[a]Variance due to country = 2.6%. [b]Additional variance due to therapist and practice = 26.1%.

TABLE C.19
Dominant Manner Predictors: Main National Subsamples

Predictor	USA ±	(Step)	%	Norway ±	(Step)	%	Germany ±	(Step)	%	South Korea ±	(Step)	%	Other countries ±	(Step)	%
Dominant in personal relations	+	(1)	14.0	+	(1)	16.5	+	(1)	20.2	+	(1)	21.0	+	(1)	24.8
Cognitive orientation	+	(2)	8.0				+	(2)	2.2	+	(2)	1.1			
Behavioral orientation				+	(2)	1.7							+	(2)	6.4
Analytic–dynamic orientation										−	(3)	0.9	−	(4)	1.1
Systemic orientation													+	(6)	0.5
Breadth and Depth of Case Experience	+	(3)	2.5	+	(5)	0.4							+	(3)	2.0
Gender: Male	+	(4)	1.2	+	(3)	1.0							+	(7)	0.3
Reliance on diagnosis				+	(4)	0.7				+	(4)	0.7	+	(5)	0.7
Dissatisfaction in work as a therapist													+	(8)	0.2
R	.517			.456			.476			.495			.602		
Total adjusted R^2	.258			.203			.224			.238			.359		

Note. The list of variables entered was identical to that in Table C.18; those not listed were not significant predictors in any of the national multiple regression analyses.
± = sign of Beta; % = increment in variance.

TABLE C.20
Practice Experience Pattern Parameters

Descriptive statistics	Effective Practice	Challenging Practice	Disengaged Practice	Distressing Practice
Healing Involvement				
M	11.18	10.91	8.29	8.30
SD	1.04	0.96	1.17	1.07
Max	14.48	14.79	9.55	9.54
Mdn	11.05	10.74	8.61	8.64
Min	9.55	9.55	1.39	3.83
Stressful Involvement				
M	3.18	5.89	3.26	6.02
SD	1.03	1.03	0.99	1.07
Max	4.71	11.04	4.71	11.54
Mdn	3.33	5.58	3.42	5.83
Min	0.00	4.75	0.04	4.75

Note. Max = maximum; min = minimum.

TABLE C.21
Percentage of Practice Patterns for Main National Subgroups

Group	n	Effective Practice (%)	Challenging Practice (%)	Disengaged Practice (%)	Distressing Practice (%)	Healing Involvement (Mdn)	Stressful Involvement (Mdn)
Total	3,991	45.9	20.9	20.0	13.1	10.29	4.04
USA	603	59.7	26.2	8.3	5.8	11.33	3.92
Germany	963	34.7	27.0	20.6	17.8	9.93	4.50
Norway	596	53.9	24.8	13.9	7.4	10.63	4.00
South Korea	362	8.0	4.1	47.2	40.6	7.72	4.40
Other	1,441	54.0	17.5	20.1	8.4	10.40	3.63

TABLE C.22
Percentages of Practice Patterns for Different Career Cohorts by Profession

Profession	Novice	Apprentice	Graduate	Established	Seasoned	Senior	n	%
Psychology								
Effective Practice	45.6	41.2	49.2	55.8	56.4	65.2	1,170	53.8
Challenging Practice	16.9	21.5	22.0	22.1	24.9	21.0	487	22.4
Disengaged Practice	18.4	24.9	17.8	16.8	12.4	10.5	347	6.0
Distressing Practice	19.1	12.4	11.0	5.2	6.4	3.3	169	7.8
n	136	177	354	727	598	181	2,173	
%	6.3	8.1	16.3	33.5	27.5	8.3	100	
Medicine								
Effective Practice	10.7	23.4	28.7	35.9	40.0	37.0	327	29.2
Challenging Practice	12.6	15.6	21.7	19.4	20.0	15.2	203	18.1
Disengaged Practice	34.0	31.7	29.1	27.6	28.0	23.9	330	29.5
Distressing Practice	42.8	29.3	20.4	17.1	12.0	23.9	259	23.1
n	159	205	230	304	175	46	1,119	
%	14.2	18.3	20.6	27.2	15.6	4.1	100	
Other professions								
Effective Practice	41.5	38.9	42.0	58.1	65.6	58.3	289	50.7
Challenging Practice	25.4	23.6	19.3	23.3	22.9	33.3	133	23.3
Disengaged Practice	18.5	19.4	19.3	14.0	8.3	8.3	88	15.4
Distressing Practice	14.6	18.1	19.3	4.7	3.1	0.0	60	10.5
n	130	72	88	172	96	12	570	
%	22.8	12.6	15.4	30.2	16.8	2.1	100	

Note. Novice = < 1.5 years of experience, apprentice = 1.5 to < 3.5 years of experience, graduate = 3.5 to < 7 years of experience, established = 7 to < 15 years of experience, seasoned = 15 to < 25 years of experience, senior = 25 to 53 years of experience. The chi-square for each profession was significant at $p < .0000$. *Medicine* includes psychiatry and medical psychotherapy/psychosomatics (in Germany); "other" professions include social work, nursing, counseling, and lay therapy.

APPENDIX D
Analyses of Professional Development

DAVID E. ORLINSKY AND MICHAEL HELGE RØNNESTAD

TABLE D.1
Importance of Professional Development to Psychotherapists

Characteristics	n	% High[a]
Profession		
Psychology	2,733	88.0
Psychiatry/psychosomatics	1,306	80.3
Social work	282	91.2
Lay therapy[b]	177	94.9
Other	121	89.3
Theoretical orientation		
Salient analytic–dynamic	1,482	89.4
Mainly cognitive–behavioral	504	80.7
Mainly humanistic	698	87.4
Mainly systemic	387	92.7
Broad spectrum	232	91.8
No salient orientation	469	52.2
Career level		
Novice	482	83.1
Apprentice	517	87.8
Graduate	740	90.9
Established	1,390	91.5
Seasoned	1,053	84.7
Senior	370	73.5
Gender		
Female	2,460	90.4
Male	2,199	81.4
Nation		
USA	832	79.4
Germany	1,022	91.0
Norway	798	93.9
South Korea	408	57.6
Switzerland	259	88.0
Portugal	186	85.5
Spain	179	94.9
Denmark	156	95.5
Belgium	129	83.0
Sweden	115	93.0
France	114	72.8
Russia	110	93.6
Israel	99	92.9
Other countries	267	93.7

Note. Novice = < 1.5 years of experience, apprentice = 1.5 to < 3.5 years of experience, graduate = 3.5 to < 7 years of experience, established = 7 to < 15 years of experience, seasoned = 15 to < 25 years of experience, senior = 25 to 53 years of experience.
[a]High = a rating of 4 or 5 on a 0–5 scale.
[b]Self-identification as a therapist, analyst, or counselor with no other profession specified.

TABLE D.2
Currently Experienced Development: Positive and Negative Items

Items	n	M	SD	% Little	% Some	% Much
Positive						
How much do you feel you are changing as a therapist?	4,650	3.28	1.04	5.7	51.1	43.2
How much does this change feel like progress or improvement?	4,636	3.73	1.10	4.5	29.3	66.2
How much do you feel you are overcoming past limitations as a therapist?	4,640	3.19	1.10	7.6	50.2	42.2
How much do you feel you are becoming more skillful in practicing therapy?	3,904	3.61	1.00	3.8	34.6	61.7
How much do you feel you are deepening your understanding of therapy?	3,911	3.74	1.01	3.3	29.9	66.8
How much do you feel a growing sense of enthusiasm about doing therapy?	3,909	3.27	1.25	9.7	43.2	47.1

Negative	n	M	SD	% None	% Some	% A lot
How much does this change feel like decline or impairment?	4,632	0.5	0.9	69.1	26.1	4.9
How much do you feel you are becoming disillusioned about therapy?	4,030	1.2	1.3	39.8	41.7	18.6
How much do you feel you are losing your capacity to respond empathically?	4,038	0.8	1.2	56.1	32.6	11.2
How much do you feel your performance is becoming mainly routine?	4,037	1.1	1.2	40.5	43.1	16.3

Note. Items were rated on a scale that ranged from 0 (*not at all*) to 5 (*very much*). For positive items, Little = 0–1, Some = 2–3, Much = 4–5; for negative items, None = 0, Some = 1–2, A lot = 3–5.

TABLE D.3
Cumulative Career Development: Direct Assessment and Sense of Current Proficiency

Since you began working as a therapist. . .	n	M	SD	% Little	% Some	% Much
How much have you changed overall as a therapist?	4,801	3.7	1.0	2.7	35.3	61.9
How much do you regard this overall change as progress or improvement?	4,795	4.2	1.0	2.2	16.6	81.2
How much do you regard this overall change as decline or impairment?	4,798	0.4	0.8	93.1	6.0	0.9
How much have you succeeded in overcoming past limitations as a therapist?	4,783	3.2	1.1	6.4	51.2	42.4
Overall, at the present time. . .						
How much precision, subtlety, and finesse have you attained in your therapeutic work?	4,679	3.3	1.0	4.5	48.7	46.8

Note. Items were rated on a scale that ranged from 0 (*not at all*) to 5 (*very much*). Little = 0–1, Some = 2–3, Much = 4–5.

TABLE D.4
Skill Change Index: Indirect Assessment of
Cumulative Career Development

Item	n	Skill change M	SD
How much mastery do you have of the techniques and strategies involved in practicing therapy?	4,659	1.28	1.08
How well do you understand what happens moment-by-moment during therapy sessions?	4,658	1.26	1.06
How "natural" (authentically personal) do you feel while working with patients?	4,673	1.18	1.19
How good are you at making constructive use of your personal reactions to patients?	4,233	1.17	1.14
How good is your general theoretical understanding of therapy?	4,674	1.13	1.08
How well are you able to detect and deal with your patients' emotional reactions to you?	4,232	1.11	1.09
How good are you at grasping the essence of your patients' problems?	4,153	0.93	1.00
How effective are you at engaging patients in a working alliance?	4,664	0.91	1.03
How skillful are you at getting your patients to play their part in therapy?	4,143	0.90	1.04
How effective are you in communicating your understanding and concern to your patients?	4,189	0.79	1.00
How empathic are you in relating to patients with whom you have relatively little in common?	4,195	0.69	0.96

Note. Difference scores (current skills − initial skills) potentially range from +5 to −5.

TABLE D.5
Current Development Patterns by Demographic Characteristics:
Western Therapists

Subsample	n	% Progress	% Flux	% Stasis	% Regress
Nationality[a]					
USA	675	55.1	**19.0**	**16.1**	9.8
Norway	774	54.8	**18.5**	**15.8**	11.0
Germany	565	**47.8**	13.5	**25.5**	13.3
South Korea	385	**24.7**	**9.6**	**39.5**	**26.2**
Other countries	1,446	**60.3**	**10.9**	22.2	**6.6**
Gender[b]					
Women	1,959	**58.9**	13.9	19.0	**8.2**
Men	1,493	**52.4**	15.5	21.2	**10.9**
Age[c]					
< 35 years	745	58.5	14.6	17.3	9.5
35 to < 50 years	1,922	55.8	14.5	20.1	9.6
50 to 70 years	722	53.2	15.1	**22.7**	9.0
Gender × Age[d]					
Female					
< 35 years	504	**60.7**	14.7	**15.9**	8.7
35 to < 50 years	1,072	57.9	14.1	19.2	8.8
50 to 70 years	354	57.9	13.0	22.9	**6.2**
Male					
< 35 years	238	54.2	14.7	19.7	11.3
35 to < 50 years	847	53.0	15.0	21.3	10.7
50 to 70 years	363	**48.2**	17.4	22.6	11.8
Marital status[e]					
Single	626	51.3	12.9	23.0	12.8
Living with partner	432	53.5	13.9	21.3	11.3
Married	2,240	52.3	14.4	22.4	10.9
Separated, divorced	416	54.3	14.4	22.1	9.1
Widowed	52	65.4	5.8	23.1	5.8

Note. Numbers in boldface type indicate adjusted standardized residuals ≥ 2. Korean therapists were included in the cross-national comparison only.
[a]$\chi^2(12, N = 3,845) = 305.7$, $p < .0000$. [b]$\chi^2 (3, N = 3,452) = 16.2$, $p < .01$. [c]$\chi^2 (6, N = 3,389) = 7.6$, *ns.* [d]$\chi^2 (15, N = 3,378) = 28.4$, $p < .05$. [e]$\chi^2 (12, N = 3,766) = 11.1$, *ns.*

TABLE D.6
Current Development Patterns by Professional Characteristics:
Western Therapists

Subsample	n	% Progress	% Flux	% Stasis	% Regress
Profession[a]					
Psychology	2,398	56.0	14.9	**19.1**	10.0
Medicine	537	**52.0**	12.3	**25.0**	10.8
Other	540	**60.4**	15.2	19.4	**5.0**
Experience level[b]					
< 5 years	885	**60.3**	12.7	18.2	8.8
5 to < 15 years	1,542	56.5	15.3	20.1	**8.1**
15 to < 50 years	986	**51.0**	15.2	22.3	**11.5**
Experience level × Profession[c]					
Psychology					
< 5 years	503	**61.6**	**11.7**	**15.9**	10.7
5 to < 15 years	1,082	56.4	**16.5**	19.4	**7.8**
15 to < 50 years	775	**51.4**	15.1	21.0	**3.5**
Medicine					
< 5 years	165	54.5	13.9	24.2	7.3
5 to < 15 years	241	52.3	11.2	24.1	12.4
15 to < 50 years	119	**47.1**	10.9	**30.3**	11.8
Other professions					
< 5 years	217	61.8	13.8	18.9	**5.5**
5 to < 15 years	218	61.5	14.2	19.3	**5.0**
15 to < 50 years	90	53.3	**22.2**	22.2	**2.2**
Theoretical orientation[d]					
Salient analytic–dynamic	1,049	56.8	12.7	22.0	8.5
Mainly cognitive–behavioral	404	**48.5**	**16.1**	22.5	**12.9**
Mainly humanistic	528	**60.2**	12.1	19.7	8.0
Mainly systemic	323	59.8	13.9	19.8	**6.5**
Broad spectrum integrative–eclectic	178	**65.7**	16.3	**9.0**	9.0
No salient orientation	240	**39.6**	**7.5**	**34.2**	**18.8**
Personal therapy[e]					
None	569	**49.6**	13.7	**24.4**	**12.3**
Current only	167	**67.1**	11.4	16.2	5.4
Past and current	826	**62.0**	14.9	**15.1**	8.0
Past only	1,884	**54.4**	14.9	**21.3**	9.3

Note. Numbers in boldface type indicate adjusted standardized residuals ≥ 2.
[a]χ^2 (6, N = 3,475) = 26.3, p < .001. [b]χ^2 (6, N = 3,413) = 22.0, p < .01. [c]χ^2 (24, N = 3,410) = 66.8, p < .0000.
[d]χ^2 (15, N = 2,722) = 95.3, p < .0000. [e]χ^2 (9, N = 3,446) = 43.6, p < .0000.

TABLE D.7

Current Development Patterns by Practice Characteristics:
Western Therapists

Subsample	n	% Progress	% Flux	% Stasis	% Regress
Practice setting[a]					
Inpatient only	356	**43.3**	13.8	**25.3**	**17.7**
Outpatient only	820	54.6	16.2	20.2	8.9
Independent practice only	932	**59.5**	**12.2**	20.4	7.8
Inpatient and outpatient	194	60.8	13.4	16.5	9.3
Inpatient and independent	187	53.5	17.6	21.9	7.0
Outpatient and independent	479	**61.6**	13.4	18.2	**6.9**
Inpatient, outpatient, and independent	107	60.7	17.8	13.1	8.4
Client age groups[b]					
Adult (20–64 years)	1,186	56.6	**12.2**	21.8	9.4
Adolescent (13–19 years) and adult	598	53.3	16.9	20.7	9.0
Adolescent, adult, senior					
(≥ 65 years)	202	55.4	18.8	**13.9**	11.9
Adult and senior	267	51.3	16.9	21.3	10.5
Child (≤ 12 years), adolescent, adult	479	**63.0**	12.5	19.2	**5.2**
Child and adolescent	134	57.5	13.4	19.4	9.7
Child and adult	121	51.2	16.5	19.8	12.4
Child, adolescent, adult, senior	128	53.9	20.3	**13.3**	12.5
Client impairment level focus[c]					
Mild impairment	835	54.0	**16.6**	19.0	10.3
Moderate to serious impairment	1,382	57.2	**12.4**	21.7	8.7
Severe impairment	255	58.8	14.1	18.4	8.6
Mixed impairment levels	281	55.5	15.7	19.2	9.6
Work practice pattern[d]					
Effective Practice	1,635	**66.7**	**11.4**	**16.9**	**5.0**
Challenging Practice	693	**49.9**	**24.7**	**13.6**	**11.8**
Disengaged Practice	449	**42.8**	**8.7**	**38.8**	9.8
Distressing Practice	268	**26.9**	16.8	**25.7**	**30.6**

[a]χ^2 (18, N = 3,075) = 68.1, p < .0000. [b]χ^2(21, N = 3,115) = 43.9, p < .01. [c]χ^2 (9, N = 2,753) = 12.4, *ns.*
[d]χ^2 (9, N = 3,045) = 434.7, p < .0000.

TABLE D.8
Bivariate Correlates of Currently Experienced Growth
and Currently Experienced Depletion

Correlates	Growth	Depletion
Demographic characteristics		
Gender: Female	.11	−.07
American	.10	.02
South Korean	−.25	.10
Professional characteristics		
Practice duration	.04	.02
Profession: Medicine	−.19	.02
Profession: Psychology	.11	.02
Currently in specialty training	.14	−.10
Years of formal supervision	.11	−.02
Currently in supervision	.14	−.10
Currently in personal therapy	.14	−.04
Previous personal therapy	.16	−.04
Breadth and Depth of Case Experience	.13	.06
Theoretical Breadth	.25	.00
Analytic–psychodynamic orientation	.13	−.02
Behavioral orientation	.00	.11
Cognitive orientation	.06	.11
Humanistic orientation	.10	.05
Systemic orientation	.13	.04
Practice setting		
(Any) independent practice	.13	−.11
(Any) inpatient practice	−.12	.09
Current caseload	.12	.01
Professional Autonomy	.19	−.11
Work Setting Support and Satisfaction	.30	−.23
Work experience		
Healing Involvement	.54	−.16
Stressful Involvement	−.11	.44
Felt Therapeutic Mastery	.35	−.08
Satisfaction with therapeutic work	.40	−.23
Dissatisfaction with therapeutic work	−.20	.29
Motivation for further development	.46	−.19
Currently Experienced Growth	—	−.20
Currently Experienced Depletion	−.20	—

Note. Ns range from 3,467 to 4,001; for $r \geq .04$, $p = .01$.

TABLE D.9
Predictors of Currently Experienced Growth: Total Sample

Predictor	Step	± Beta	ΔR^2 (% variance)
Block 1: Nation[a]			
South Korea	1	−	6.2
USA	2	+	0.3
Block 2: Therapist and practice characteristics[b]			
Healing Involvement	1	+	22.3
Importance of development	2	+	7.9
Satisfaction with work as a therapist	3	+	3.8
Current specialty training	4	+	1.0
Felt Therapeutic Mastery	5	+	0.6
Currently in personal therapy	6	+	0.6
Analytic–psychodynamic orientation	7	+	0.3
Breadth and Depth of Case Experience	8	−	0.2
Theoretical Breadth	9	+	0.2
Currently Experienced Depletion	10	−	0.2
Profession: Medicine	11	−	0.1
Current caseload	12	+	0.1
Work Setting Support and Satisfaction	13	+	0.1

Note. Multiple R = .663, total adjusted R^2 = .437. The following variables were entered but not significant predictors: profession (psychologist), inpatient practice, independent practice, Professional Autonomy, humanistic orientation, systemic orientation, Stressful Involvement, dissatisfaction with work as a therapist, gender.

[a]Variance due to nationality = 6.5%. [b]Additional variance due to therapist and practice = 37.2%.

TABLE D.10
Predictors of Currently Experienced Growth: Main National Subsamples

Predictor	USA			Norway			Germany			South Korea			Other countries		
	±	(Step)	%	±	(Step)	%	±	(Step)	%	±	(Step)	%	±	(Step)	%
Healing Involvement	+	(2)	8.7	+	(2)	8.7	+	(1)	23.1	+	(1)	34.2	+	(1)	21.1
Importance of further development	+	(1)	30.9	+	(3)	3.6	+	(2)	9.0	+	(3)	4.3	+	(2)	6.5
Satisfaction with work as a therapist	+	(3)	0.9	+	(1)	23.8	+	(3)	4.0	+	(2)	10.9	+	(3)	3.2
Currently in specialty training							+	(4)	3.0				+	(7)	0.7
Work Setting Support and Satisfaction							+	(5)	1.3						
Felt Therapeutic Mastery				+	(4)	1.7	+	(8)	0.4				+	(6)	0.5
Analytic–dynamic orientation										+	(6)	0.8	+	(8)	0.4
Years of supervision													−	(9)	0.3
Currently in supervision				+	(5)	2.0							+	(10)	0.4
Currently Experienced Depletion													−	(5)	0.6

Dissatisfaction with work as a therapist				+ (4) 2.4	– (11) 0.3
Currently in personal therapy					+ (4) 1.7
Breadth and Depth of Case Experience		– (6) 0.7	– (6) 0.9		
Theoretical Breadth			+ (7) 0.6		
Systemic orientation				+ (5) 1.5	
R	.640	.641	.657	.743	.602
Total adjusted R²	.405	.404	.423	.541	.357

Note. The list of variables entered was identical to that in Table D.9; those not listed were not significant predictors in any of the national multiple regression analyses.
± = sign of Beta; % = increment in variance predicted.

TABLE D.11
Predictors of Currently Experienced Depletion: Total Sample

Predictor	Step	± Beta	ΔR^2 (% variance)
Block 1: Nation			
South Korea	*ns*	+	0.1
Block 2: Therapist and Practice Characteristics[a]			
Stressful Involvement	1	+	19.0
Dissatisfaction with work as a therapist	2	+	2.7
Importance of further development	3	−	2.0
Cognitive orientation	4	+	1.2
Currently in specialty training	5	−	0.9
Currently Experienced Growth	6	−	0.4
Currently in supervision	7	−	0.3
Satisfaction with work as a therapist	8	−	0.2
Work Setting Support and Satisfaction	9	−	0.1

Note. Multiple R = .529, total adjusted R^2 = .277. The following variables were entered but not significant predictors: profession (psychiatrist, psychologist), inpatient practice, independent practice, professional autonomy, orientation (humanistic, systemic), current caseload, number of treatment modalities, Healing Involvement, gender.
[a]Additional variance due to therapist and practice = 27.7%.

TABLE D.12
Predictors of Currently Experienced Depletion: Main National Subsamples

Predictors	USA			Norway			Germany			South Korea			Other countries		
	±	(Step)	%	±	(Step)	%	±	(Step)	%	±	(Step)	%	±	(Step)	%
Stressful Involvement	+	(1)	17.8	+	(1)	22.9	+	(1)	22.4	+	(1)	31.5	+	(1)	12.1
Importance of further development	−	(3)	3.5	−	(3)	2.1	−	(5)	1.4				−	(5)	0.4
Dissatisfaction with work as a therapist	+	(2)	8.9	+	(4)	1.5	+	(4)	1.4				+	(3)	1.0
Satisfaction with work as a therapist	−	(5)	1.3	−	(2)	5.4	−	(2)	3.8						
Currently in specialty training							−	(3)	1.9	−	(3)	0.9	−	(4)	0.6
Currently in supervision	−	(4)	1.6	−	(5)	1.3									
Healing Involvement	+	(6)	1.4	+	(6)	0.7				+	(2)	0.7			
Cognitive orientation	+	(7)	0.9												
Currently Experienced Growth				−	(7)	0.4							−	(2)	2.4
Behavioral orientation													+	(6)	0.4
Work Setting Support and Satisfaction													−	(7)	0.3
R		.608			.592			.562			.581			.411	
Total adjusted R^2		.354			.343			.309			.331			.166	

Note. The list of variables entered was identical to that in Table D.11; those not listed were not significant predictors in any of the national multiple regression analyses.

TABLE D.13
Correlates of Overall Career Development

Correlates	Overall career development	Controlling years in practice
Professional characteristics		
Years in practice	.47	
Breadth and Depth of Case Experience	.48	.30
Profession		
Psychology	.27	.17
Medicine	−.22	−.17
Social work	−.14	−.09
Orientation		
Analytic–psychodynamic	.07	.06
Behavioral	.02	.03
Cognitive	.09	.07
Humanistic	.12	.11
Systemic	.12	.13
Theoretical Breadth	.25	.24
Training		
Years of academic training	.08	−.01
Years of supervision	.17	.03
Past specialty training	.34	.23
Past personal therapy	.27	.20
Demographic characteristics		
Age	.37	.01
Gender: Female	−.03	.06
Nation		
South Korea	−.30	−.23
United States	.18	.05
Germany	−.07	−.02
Norway	−.01	−.02
Practice setting		
(Any) independent practice	.28	.16
(Any) inpatient practice	−.16	−.09
Professional Autonomy	.39	.27
Work Setting Support and Satisfaction	.25	.20
Experience of therapeutic work		
Healing Involvement	.54	.48
Stressful Involvement	−.22	−.20
Currently Experienced Growth	.44	.48
Currently Experienced Depletion	−.11	−.14
Satisfaction with work as therapist	.37	.29
Dissatisfaction with work as a therapist	−.15	−.09

Note. Ns range from 3,736 to 4,550; for $r \geq .04$, $p = .01$.
[a]r_p controlling for years in practice.

TABLE D.14
Predictors of Overall Career Development: Total Sample

Predictors	Step	± Beta	ΔR^2 (% variance)
Block 1: Nation[a]			
South Korea	1	–	8.8
USA	2	+	1.8
Block 2: Therapist and Practice Characteristics[b]			
Breadth and Depth of Case Experience	1	+	17.1
Currently Experienced Growth	2	+	11.3
Practice duration	3	+	6.0
Professional Autonomy	4	+	1.9
Past specialty training	5	+	1.4
Profession: Social work	6	–	0.7
Years of supervision	7	+	0.6
Theoretical Breadth	8	+	0.2
Age	9	–	0.1
Past personal therapy	10	+	0.1
Currently Experienced Depletion	11	–	0.1

Note. R = .710, total adjusted R^2 = .502. Stepwise entry was used within blocks. The following variables were entered but not significant predictors: profession (psychologist, medicine), treatment setting (inpatient, independent), theoretical orientation (humanistic, systemic).
[a]Variance due to country = 10.6%. [b]Additional variance due to therapist and practice = 39.5%.

TABLE D.15
Predictors of Overall Career Development: Main National Subsamples

Predictors	USA ±	USA (Step)	USA %	Norway ±	Norway (Step)	Norway %	Germany ±	Germany (Step)	Germany %	South Korea ±	South Korea (Step)	South Korea %	Other countries ±	Other countries (Step)	Other countries %
Breadth and Depth of Case Experience	+	(1)	32.5	+	(3)	0.8	+	(1)	17.4				+	(1)	15.2
Currently Experienced Growth	+	(3)	8.1	+	(1)	20.9	+	(2)	15.9	+	(1)	30.7	+	(2)	11.5
Practice duration	+	(7)	0.7	+	(2)	11.4	+	(3)	2.5	+	(2)	15.9	+	(3)	5.4
Professional Autonomy	+	(4)	2.8				+	(4)	2.0				+	(4)	2.3
Profession: Social work	–	(2)	7.7							+	(8)	0.2			
Past specialty training	+	(6)	1.0	+	(5)	1.1	+	(6)	0.5	+	(3)	1.6	+	(5)	0.8
Satisfaction with work as a therapist				–	(4)	0.7	+	(8)	0.4	+	(4)	1.1			
Years of supervision							+	(5)	1.0	–	(6)	0.8	–	(6)	0.4
Work Setting Support and Satisfaction	+	(5)	3.1												
Dissatisfaction with work as a therapist										–	(5)	1.0			

Past personal therapy	+ (6) 0.4	+ (6) 0.4			
Age		+ (6) 0.4	+ (7) 0.4		
Some inpatient practice				− (7) 1.3	
Currently Experienced Depletion					+ (7) 0.3
Theoretical Breadth					− (8) 0.7
R	.755	.601	.650	.747	.603
Total adjusted R^2	.559	.355	.416	.545	.360

Note. The list of variables entered was identical to that in Table D.14; those not listed were not significant predictors in any of the national multiple regression analyses.
± = sign of Beta; % = increment in variance predicted.

TABLE D.16
Bivariate Correlates of Therapist Work Involvement Dimensions

Correlates	Healing Involvement	Stressful Involvement
Professional characteristics		
Profession		
Medicine	−.34	.12
Psychology	.27	−.10
Practice duration	.28	−.10
Breadth and Depth of Case Experience	.36	−.06
Years of academic training	.17	−.07
Years of formal supervision	.24	−.05
Past specialty training	.18	−.10
Previous personal therapy	.27	−.05
Cognitive orientation	.17	−.01
Humanistic orientation	.17	.00
Systemic orientation	.22	.01
Theoretical Breadth	.35	−.04
Demographic characteristics		
Age	.30	−.12
Gender: Female	.14	−.06
Marital status: Single	−.14	.08
Nation		
South Korea	−.44	.05
USA	.24	−.02
Germany	−.08	.16
Norway	.10	−.01
Denmark	.08	−.10
France	−.10	−.03
Practice characteristics		
Current caseload	.21	−.02
Any inpatient practice	−.18	.08
Any independent practice	.20	−.14
Professional Autonomy	.30	−.18
Work Setting Support and Satisfaction	.34	−.18
Satisfaction with work as a therapist	.42	−.19
Dissatisfaction with work as a therapist	−.18	.29
Professional development		
Currently Experienced Growth	.52	−.11
Currently Experienced Depletion	−.14	.44
Overall Career Development	.54	−.22
Motivation for further development	.34	−.07

Note. $p < .01$ for correlations exceeding $r = \pm\ .04$. Other variables tested that had correlations <.10 include nationality (Belgium, Spain, Switzerland, Sweden), demographic status (native born, minority), marital status (married), profession (social work), current personal therapy, theoretical orientation (analytic–dynamic, behavioral), outpatient practice setting, current specialty training.

TABLE D.17
Predictors of Healing Involvement: Total Sample (Recomputed)

Predictors	Step	± Beta	ΔR^2 (% variance)
Block 1: Nation[a]			
South Korea	1	−	20.6
France	2	−	1.4
Germany	3	−	1.5
Block 2: Therapist and Practice Characteristics[b]			
Currently Experienced Growth	1	+	17.8
Overall Career Development	2	+	3.4
Theoretical Breadth	3	+	2.5
Gender: Female	4	+	1.7
Satisfaction with work as a therapist	5	+	0.8
Motivation for further development	6	+	0.7
Breadth and Depth of Case Experience	7	+	0.4
Humanistic orientation	8	+	0.2
Work Setting Support and Satisfaction	9	+	0.2
Caseload	10	−	0.1
Age	11	+	0.1
Practice duration	12	−	0.2
Profession: Medicine	13	−	0.1
Profession: Psychology	14	−	0.2
Cognitive orientation	15	+	0.1

Note. $R = .724$, total adjusted $R^2 = .521$. The following variables were entered but not significant predictors: nation (USA, Norway), years of supervision, years of academic training, past specialty training, past personal therapy, inpatient practice, independent practice, Professional Autonomy, systemic orientation, dissatisfaction with work as a therapist, Stressful Involvement, Currently Experienced Depletion.
[a]Variance due to country = 23.6%. [b]Additional variance due to therapist and practice = 28.5%.

TABLE D.18
Healing Involvement Predictors: Main National Subsamples (Recomputed)

Predictor	USA ±	(Step)	%	Norway ±	(Step)	%	Germany ±	(Step)	%	South Korea ±	(Step)	%	Other countries ±	(Step)	%
Currently Experienced Growth	+	(1)	24.8	+	(1)	21.5	+	(1)	23.1	+	(1)	34.1	+	(1)	21.1
Overall career development	+	(2)	11.4	+	(8)	0.6	+	(2)	7.5	+	(3)	3.4	+	(2)	5.2
Satisfaction with work as a therapist	+	(3)	5.5	+	(2)	3.5	+	(3)	2.2	+	(4)	1.0			
Gender: Female	+	(6)	1.8	+	(3)	3.6	+	(6)	0.6				+	(4)	2.4
Theoretical Breadth				+	(10)	0.4				+	(2)	6.3	+	(3)	2.7
Motivation for further development	+	(5)	2.7	+	(7)	0.9							+	(11)	0.2
Systemic orientation	+	(4)	4.0												
Breadth and Depth of Case Experience				+	(5)	1.5	+	(5)	0.6				+	(5)	1.3
Practice duration	+	(7)	3.0												
Profession: Psychology	−	(8)	1.4	+	(6)	0.9							−	(9)	0.7
Years of supervision	+	(9)	0.9												

Humanistic orientation	+ (10) 0.7		+ (4) 1.7		
Profession: Medicine					– (7) 0.4
Cognitive orientation		+ (4) 3.6			+ (10) 0.5
Work Setting Support and Satisfaction					+ (6) 1.0
Age					+ (8) 0.3
Stressful Involvement				+ (5) 1.0	
Currently Experienced Depletion		– (9) 0.5			
Professional Autonomy					+ (12) 0.2
R	.764	.620	.603	.686	.606
Total adjusted R^2	.567	.371	.350	.455	.361

Note. The list of variables entered was identical to that in Table D.17; those not listed were not significant predictors in any of the national multiple regression analyses.
± = sign of Beta; % = increment in variance predicted.

TABLE D.19
Predictors of Stressful Involvement: Total Sample (Recomputed)

Predictors	Step	± Beta	ΔR^2 (% variance)
Block 1: Nation[a]			
Germany	1	+	2.5
Denmark	2	−	0.6
Block 2: Therapist and Practice Characteristics[b]			
Currently Experienced Depletion	1	+	18.9
Dissatisfaction with work as a therapist	2	+	3.5
Overall Career Development	3	−	1.7
Currently Experienced Growth	4	−	0.6
Professional Autonomy	5	−	0.1
Healing Involvement	6	+	0.1
Medical profession	7	+	0.1

Note. R = .533, total adjusted R^2 = .282. Variables not entering equation significantly ($p > .05$) include: practice duration, profession (psychology), past specialty training, independent practice, work setting support and satisfaction, satisfaction with work as a therapist, age.
[a]Variance due to country = 3.1%. [b]Additional variance due to therapist and practice = 25.0%.

TABLE D.20
Stressful Involvement Predictors: Main National Subsamples (Recomputed)

Predictor	USA ±	(Step)	%	Norway ±	(Step)	%	Germany ±	(Step)	%	South Korea ±	(Step)	%	Other countries ±	(Step)	%
Currently Experienced Depletion	+	(1)	17.8	+	(1)	22.9	+	(1)	22.4	+	(1)	31.4	+	(1)	12.1
Overall Career Development	−	(2)	2.3	−	(3)	1.1	−	(3)	1.5	−	(2)	4.8	−	(2)	2.1
Dissatisfaction with work as a therapist	+	(3)	1.6	+	(2)	6.7	+	(2)	3.2	+	(3)	2.8	+	(3)	0.9
Currently Experienced Growth	+	(4)	0.9	+	(4)	0.4							+	(5)	0.4
Healing Involvement										+	(4)	2.0			
Profession: Psychology							−	(5)	0.8	−	(5)	0.7	−	(4)	0.6
Age							−	(4)	0.6						
Professional Autonomy													−	(6)	0.3
Practice duration													+	(7)	0.4
Some independent practice													−	(8)	0.3
R	.486			.562			.539			.653			.420		
Total adjusted R^2	.226			.310			.284			.417			.169		

Note. The list of variables entered was identical to that in Table D.19; those not listed were not significant predictors in any of the national multiple regression analyses.
± = sign of Beta; % = increment in variance predicted.

TABLE D.21
Composition of Career Cohort Samples Among Western Therapists and Psychologists

Characteristics	Novice	Apprentice	Graduate	Established	Seasoned	Senior
Western therapists n =	386	424	685	1,330	1,027	365
Demographic characteristics						
USA	32.3	13.8	7.7	8.9	24.7	58.7
Norway	18.1	19.5	19.6	18.2	19.0	16.0
Germany	28.4	34.9	35.8	23.6	17.1	7.1
Switzerland	2.7	1.9	3.6	9.2	8.2	3.5
Spain	2.4	2.4	3.3	5.5	5.4	2.2
Portugal	1.5	2.6	5.5	6.9	2.4	1.6
Other countries	14.7	24.9	24.4	27.7	23.2	10.9
Female	65.9	65.0	64.6	56.2	47.3	29.9
Male	34.1	35.0	35.4	43.8	52.7	70.1
Professional characteristics						
Psychology	41.6	49.2	57.3	64.4	72.3	82.6
Medicine	26.6	34.7	60.3	22.4	17.4	13.6
Other professions	31.7	16.2	12.4	13.3	10.4	3.8
Analytic–dynamic orientation	48.2	61.1	64.2	62.0	59.0	59.2
Behavioral orientation	16.3	16.3	11.7	12.9	14.8	17.3
Cognitive orientation	24.1	21.2	21.3	21.9	27.8	33.8
Humanistic orientation	21.5	22.6	31.5	32.6	32.9	34.3
Systemic orientation	24.6	22.4	18.8	23.3	24.1	20.5

Psychologists $n =$	180	219	413	879	759	304
Demographic characteristics						
USA	7.2	7.8	6.1	9.6	28.7	66.4
Norway	40.6	33.8	29.1	24.8	24.6	18.4
Germany	17.8	12.8	21.8	14.8	12.4	2.6
Switzerland	4.4	3.9	3.9	11.9	9.1	3.6
Spain	5.6	4.4	4.4	6.3	5.1	1.0
Portugal	3.2	3.2	6.5	7.2	1.4	1.0
South Korea	5.0	5.0	4.1	1.9	1.8	0.0
Other countries	16.1	30.6	24.2	23.5	16.7	6.9
Female	63.3	70.5	67.2	59.2	48.9	31.0
Male	36.7	29.5	32.8	40.8	51.1	69.0
Professional characteristics						
Analytic–dynamic orientation	37.9	49.8	54.1	58.1	52.5	55.5
Behavioral orientation	24.1	17.6	15.4	15.1	16.3	19.3
Cognitive orientation	40.8	32.6	29.0	28.4	33.4	38.0
Humanistic orientation	29.3	28.5	37.3	36.1	36.8	36.3
Systemic orientation	20.1	27.1	20.2	25.2	24.6	22.3

Note. Unless otherwise noted, all table values are percentages. Novice = < 1.5 years of experience, apprentice = 1.5 to < 3.5 years of experience, graduate = 3.5 to < 7 years of experience, established = 7 to < 15 years of experience, seasoned = 15 to < 25 years of experience, senior = 25 to 53 years of experience.

TABLE D.22
Career Levels and Practice Experience Patterns for
American, Norwegian, and German Psychologists

Nationality	n	Effective Practice	Challenging Practice	Disengaged Practice	Distressing Practice
American psychologists[a]					
< 5 years	35	54.3	17.1	**11.4**	**17.1**
5 to < 15 years	78	64.1	28.2	5.1	2.6
15 to 50 years	231	65.8	29.0	3.0	**2.2**
Norwegian psychologists[b]					
< 5 years	152	49.3	30.3	12.5	7.9
5 to < 15 years	226	54.5	26.5	12.8	6.2
15 to 50 years	169	58.0	**18.9**	14.8	8.3
German psychologists[c]					
< 5 years	86	**26.7**	**15.1**	**29.1**	**29.1**
5 to < 15 years	199	**44.7**	26.1	16.1	13.1
15 to 50 years	75	42.7	30.7	17.3	9.3

Note. Unless otherwise noted, all table values are percentages. Numbers in boldface type indicate adjusted standardized residuals ≥ 2.
[a]$\chi^2(6, N = 344) = 25.7, p < .001.$ [b]$\chi^2 (6, N = 547) = 6.5, ns.$ [c]$\chi^2 (6, N = 360) = 27.2, p < .001.$

TABLE D.23

Experiences of Therapeutic Work in Successive Career Cohorts of Western Therapists

Work experience facets and dimensions[a,b]	1 Novice	2 Apprentice	3 Graduate	4 Established	5 Seasoned	6 Senior
Treatment goals (% top 4)						
Enhance self-worth and identity[c]	60.5	60.6	63.5	61.7	56.9	58.0
Improve relationships[d]	43.2	42.1	43.1	48.5	46.1	43.7
Understand feelings, motives[e]	43.7	45.0	41.9	41.5	40.1	39.2
Face new and avoided situations[f]	30.3	31.7	30.5	30.1	31.1	**24.1**
Integrate excluded experiences[g]	**23.8**	32.0	35.8	**36.6**	34.6	29.4
Current skills (0–5)						
Technical skills[h]	2.6	3.1	3.3	3.7	3.9	4.0
Basic relational skills[i]	3.4	3.7	3.8	4.0	4.1	4.1
Advanced relational skills[j]	2.9	3.3	3.5	3.8	3.8	3.9
Difficulties (0–5)						
Professional self-doubt[k]	2.1	1.9	1.8	1.6	1.6	1.4
Frustrating treatment case[l]	1.6	1.6	1.5	1.4	1.4	1.3
Negative personal reaction[m]	1.1	1.1	1.1	1.0	0.9	0.9
Coping strategies (0–5)						
Exercise reflective control[n]	3.0	3.1	3.1	3.2	3.2	3.2
Problem-solve with patient[o]	2.9	3.0	3.0	3.1	3.2	3.3
Seek consultation[p]	3.1	3.1	2.9	2.8	2.7	2.4
Reframe helping contract[q]	1.8	1.7	1.7	1.7	1.7	1.7
Avoid therapeutic engagement[r]	1.2	1.3	1.2	1.2	1.2	1.2
Relational agency (0–3)						
Invested[s]	2.2	2.2	2.3	2.3	2.3	2.4
Efficacious[t]	1.5	1.5	1.6	1.7	1.8	1.9

(continued)

TABLE D.23 (Continued)

Work experience facets and dimensions[a,b]	1 Novice	2 Apprentice	3 Graduate	4 Established	5 Seasoned	6 Senior
Relational manner (0–3)						
Affirming[u]	2.4	2.3	2.4	2.4	2.4	2.5
Accommodating[v]	1.7	1.7	1.7	1.7	1.7	1.7
Dominant[w]	1.1	1.1	1.1	1.1	1.1	1.1
Reserved[x]	0.8	0.8	0.8	0.8	0.7	0.6
In-session feelings (0–3)						
Flow[y]	2.1	2.1	2.1	2.1	2.2	2.2
Boredom[z]	0.7	0.8	0.9	0.8	0.9	0.9
Anxiety[aa]	1.2	1.0	1.0	0.9	0.8	0.8
Work experience (0–15)						
Healing Involvement[bb]	9.3	9.6	10.0	10.4	10.7	11.0
Stressful Involvement[cc]	4.5	4.4	4.3	4.0	4.0	3.9

Note. Novice = < 1.5 years of experience, apprentice = 1.5 to < 3.5 years of experience, graduate = 3.5 to < 7 years of experience, established = 7 to < 15 years of experience, seasoned = 15 to < 25 years of experience, senior = 25 to 53 years of experience. (Cohorts indicated by numerals: 1 = novices, 2 = apprentices, 3 = graduates, 4 = established therapists, 5 = seasoned therapists, 6 = seniors).

[a]Cell values in the first horizontal block are percentages of therapists in each career cohort endorsing the item as one of the four leading treatment goals. Chi-square statistics were computed to compare cohorts, and numbers in boldface type indicate adjusted standardized residuals ≥ 2.

[b]All other cell values are cohort means based on dimension scales with ranges as specified for each of the subsequent horizontal blocks. One-way analyses of variance were computed comparing means across numbered cohorts, with between-cohort differences ($p < .05$ by Scheffé test) indicated parenthetically in footnotes.

[c]$\chi^2(5, N = 4010) = 9.3$, *ns.*
[d]$\chi^2(5, N = 4009) = 9.6$, *ns.*
[e]$\chi^2(5, N = 4009) = 4.3$, *ns.*
[f]$\chi^2(5, N = 4008) = 5.9$, *ns.*
[g]$\chi^2(5, N = 4009) = 26.5$, $p < .0001$.
[h]$F(5, 4166) = 297.9$, $p < .0000$ (6 > 5 > 4 > 3 > 2 > 1).
[i]$F(5, 3726) = 100.1$, $p < .0000$ (6, 5, 4 > 3, 2, 1; 3 > 2, 1; 2 > 1).
[j]$F(5, 3689) = 13.7$, $p < .0000$ (6, 5, 4 > 3, 2, 1; 3 > 2, 1; 2 > 1).
[k]$F(5, 3955) = 52.5$, $p < .0000$ (6, 5, 4 < 3, 2, 1; 3, 2 < 1).
[l]$F(5, 3954) = 10.9$, $p < .0000$ (6, 5, 4 < 2, 1; 6 < 3).
[m]$F(5, 3961) = 7.9$, $p < .0000$ (6 < 3, 2, 1; 5 < 3, 2).
[n]$F(5, 3567) = 5.3$, $p < .000$ (5, 4 > 1).
[o]$F(5, 3921) = 12.5$, $p < .0000$ (6, 5, 4 > 3, 1; 6 > 2).
[p]$F(5, 3933) = 29.7$, $p < .0000$ (6 < 5, 4, 3, 2, 1; 5 < 4, 3, 2, 1; 4 < 2, 1).
[q]$F(5, 3885) = 1.3$, *ns.*

[r]$F(5, 3915) = 1.5$, *ns.*
[s]$F(5, 3933) = 8.6$, $p < .0000$ (6 > 3; 6, 5 > 2, 1; 4 > 2).
[t]$F(5, 3884) = 46.6$, $p < .0000$ (6, 5, 4 > 3, 2, 1; 6, 5 > 4; 6 > 5).
[u]$F(5, 3934) = 8.9$, $p < .0000$ (6 > 5, 1, 4, 3, 2).
[v]$F(5, 3553) = 0.9$, *ns.*
[w]$F(5, 3932) = 1.5$, *ns.*
[x]$F(5, 3439) = 6.1$, $p < .0000$ (2, 1, 4, 3 > 6).
[y]$F(5, 3894) = 1.8$, *ns.*
[z]$F(5, 4078) = 6.2$, $p < .0000$ (6, 5, 4, 3 > 2, 1).
[aa]$F(5, 4133) = 21.1$, $p < .0000$ (6, 5, 4 < 3, 2, 1; 2 < 1).
[bb]$F(5, 3295) = 73.2$, $p < .0000$ (6, 5, 4 > 3, 2, 1; 6 > 4).
[cc]$F(5, 4072) = 12.7$, $p < .0000$ (6, 5, 4 < 2, 1; 5, 4 < 3).

TABLE D.24
Career Levels and Current Development Patterns for American, Norwegian, and German Psychologists

Nationality	n	% Progress	% Flux	% Stasis	% Regress
American psychologists[a]					
< 5 years	37	**73.0**	13.5	8.1	5.4
5 to < 15 years	91	49.5	**31.9**	12.1	6.6
15 to 50 years	275	50.9	**17.8**	17.1	**14.2**
Norwegian psychologists[b]					
< 5 years	208	56.3	15.4	14.9	13.5
5 to < 15 years	284	54.2	**22.9**	14.8	**8.1**
15 to 50 years	215	52.1	17.7	17.7	12.6
German psychologists[c]					
< 5 years	68	47.1	13.2	20.6	19.1
5 to < 15 years	135	**52.6**	12.6	25.2	**9.6**
15 to 50 years	75	**33.3**	13.3	32.0	21.3

Note. Numbers in boldface type indicate adjusted standardized residuals ≥ 2.
[a]χ^2 (6, N = 403) = 18.0, p < .0000. [b]χ^2 (6, N = 707) = 8.8, *ns.*
[c]χ^2 (6, N = 278) = 11.1, *ns.*

TABLE D.25
Intercorrelations of Work Experience, Current Development, and Career Development

Dimension	1	2	3	4	5
1. Healing Involvement	—				
2. Currently Experienced Growth	.54	—			
3. Overall Career Development	.47	.44	—		
4. Stressful Involvement	−.11	−.11	−.22	—	
5. Currently Experienced Depletion	−.16	−.20	−.11	.44	—

APPENDIX E
Work Involvement Self-Monitoring Scales

DAVID E. ORLINSKY AND MICHAEL HELGE RØNNESTAD

PSYCHOTHERAPISTS' WORK INVOLVEMENT SCALES

Identification Code: _____   Date: _____

[0 = None .... 5 = Total]

1. How much satisfaction do you currently find in your work as a therapist? 0 1 2 3 4 5
2. How much dissatisfaction do you currently feel in your work as a therapist? 0 1 2 3 4 5

Overall, at the present time ... **[0 = Not at all ... 5 = Very much]**

3. How effective are you at engaging patients in a working alliance? 0 1 2 3 4 5
4. How natural (authentically personal) do you feel while working with patients? 0 1 2 3 4 5
5. How empathic are you in relating to patients with whom you have relatively little in common? 0 1 2 3 4 5
6. How effective are you in communicating your understanding and concern to patients? 0 1 2 3 4 5

Currently, how would you describe yourself as a therapist—your actual style or manner with patients?

[0 = Not at all ... 3 = Very much]

7. Accepting	0	1	2	3
8. Committed	0	1	2	3
9. Detached	0	1	2	3
10. Effective	0	1	2	3
11. Friendly	0	1	2	3
12. Guarded	0	1	2	3
13. Intuitive	0	1	2	3

[0 = Not at all ... 3 = Very much]

14. Involved	0	1	2	3
15. Organized	0	1	2	3
16. Reserved	0	1	2	3
17. Skillful	0	1	2	3
18. Subtle	0	1	2	3
19. Tolerant	0	1	2	3
20. Warm	0	1	2	3

Currently, how *often* do you feel . . .

[0 = Never .... 5 = Very often]

Item	0	1	2	3	4	5
21. Unsure how best to deal effectively with a patient?	0	1	2	3	4	5
22. Lacking in confidence that you can have a beneficial effect on a patient?	0	1	2	3	4	5
23. Unable to have much real empathy for a patient's experiences?	0	1	2	3	4	5
24. Demoralized by your inability to find ways to help a patient?	0	1	2	3	4	5
25. Unable to withstand a patient's emotional neediness?	0	1	2	3	4	5
26. Distressed by your powerlessness to affect a patient's tragic life situation?	0	1	2	3	4	5
27. Unable to generate sufficient momentum to move therapy with a patient in a constructive direction?	0	1	2	3	4	5
28. Conflicted about how to reconcile obligations to a patient and equivalent obligations to others?	0	1	2	3	4	5

When encountering *difficulties* in therapy, how often do you . . . ?

[0 = Never .... 5 = Very often]

Item	0	1	2	3	4	5
29. Review privately with yourself how the problem has arisen.	0	1	2	3	4	5
30. Seek some form of alternative satisfaction away from therapy.	0	1	2	3	4	5
31. Try to see the problem from a different perspective.	0	1	2	3	4	5
32. Simply hope that things will improve eventually.	0	1	2	3	4	5
33. Consult about the case with a more experienced therapist.	0	1	2	3	4	5
34. Discuss the problem with a colleague.	0	1	2	3	4	5
35. See whether you and your patient can together deal with the difficulty.	0	1	2	3	4	5
36. Seriously consider terminating therapy.	0	1	2	3	4	5
37. Avoid dealing with the problem for the present.	0	1	2	3	4	5
38. Show your frustration to the patient.	0	1	2	3	4	5
39. Criticize a patient for causing you trouble.	0	1	2	3	4	5
40. Just give yourself permission to experience difficult or disturbing feelings.	0	1	2	3	4	5

Recently in sessions with patients, how often have you found yourself feeling . . .

	[0 = Not at all ... 3 = Very often]					[0 = Not at all ... 3 = Very often]		
41. Absent	0	1	2	3	47. Inattentive	0	1	2	3
42. Anxious	0	1	2	3	48. Inspired	0	1	2	3
43. Bored	0	1	2	3	49. Overwhelmed	0	1	2	3
44. Challenged	0	1	2	3	50. Pressured	0	1	2	3
45. Drowsy	0	1	2	3	51. Stimulated	0	1	2	3
46. Engrossed	0	1	2	3	52. Trapped	0	1	2	3

Scoring Key for Healing Involvement (HEAL: range 0 to 15)

HEAL = [[Items 7 + 8 + 10 + 11 + 13 + 14 + 15 + 17 + 18 + 19 + 20 + 44 + 46 + 48 + 51) × 5]
+ [(Items 3 + 4 + 5 + 6 + 29 + 31 + 33 + 34 + 35 + 40) × 3]] / 25.

Component Scales

Current Therapeutic Skills: **Basic Relational Skills** (Items 3, 4, 5, 6; α = .79)

Relational Agency: **Invested** (Items 8, 13, 14; α = .67)

Relational Agency: **Efficacy** (Items 10, 15, 17, 18; α = .59)

Relational Manner: **Affirming** (Items 7, 11, 19, 20; α = .69)

In-Session Feelings: **Flow** (Items 44, 46, 48, 51; α = .62)

Coping Strategies: **Constructive Coping** (Items 29, 31, 33, 34, 35, 40; α = .67)

Scoring Key for Stressful Involvement (STRESS: range 0 to 15)

STRESS = [[Items 41 + 42 + 43 + 45 + 47 + 49 + 50 + 52) × 5] + [(Items 21 + 22 + 23 + 24 + 25 + 26 + 27 + 28 + 30 + 32 + 36
+ 37 + 38 + 39) × 3]] / 22.

Component Scales

Difficulties in Practice: **Frequent Difficulties** (Items 21, 22, 23, 24, 25, 26, 27, 28; α = .81)

In-Session Feelings: **Boredom** (Items 41, 43, 45, 47; α = .66)

In-Session Feelings: **Anxiety** (Items 42, 49, 50, 52; α = .74)

Coping Strategies: **Avoidant Coping** (Items 30, 32, 36, 37, 38, 39; α = .64)

Scoring Key for Net Work Satisfaction–Dissatisfaction (WORKSAT: range +5 to −5)

WORKSAT = [Item 1 − Item 2].

TABLE E.1
Descriptive Statistics for Healing Involvement in Successive Career Cohorts

Career cohort	Healing Involvement				Range and percentile scores					
	n	M	Mdn	SD	Min	20th	40th	60th	80th	Max
Novice	427	9.3	9.5	1.9	3.4	7.7	9.0	10.0	10.9	14.0
Apprentice	465	9.6	9.6	1.6	1.4	8.4	9.3	10.0	11.0	13.6
Graduate	683	10.0	10.0	1.6	4.4	8.8	9.7	10.4	11.3	14.0
Established	1,222	10.4	10.4	1.5	4.1	9.2	10.1	10.8	11.7	14.0
Seasoned	889	10.7	10.8	1.5	3.8	9.4	10.3	11.2	12.0	14.8
Senior	245	11.0	11.1	1.6	5.6	9.5	10.8	11.5	12.5	14.5

Note. Items were rated on a 0–15 scale. Novice = < 1.5 years of experience, apprentice = 1.5 to < 3.5 years of experience, graduate = 3.5 to < 7 years of experience, established = 7 to < 15 years of experience, seasoned = 15 to < 25 years of experience, senior = 25 to 53 years of experience. Consult Appendix B, Table B.7, for data on composition of career cohorts. Min = minimum; max = maximum.

TABLE E.2
Descriptive Statistics for Stressful Involvement in Successive Career Cohorts

Career cohort	Stressful Involvement				Range and percentile scores					
	n	M	Mdn	SD	Min	20th	40th	60th	80th	Max
Novice	454	4.5	4.4	1.7	0.5	2.9	4.0	4.8	6.0	10.9
Apprentice	476	4.4	4.3	1.7	0.7	3.0	3.8	4.7	5.8	11.0
Graduate	691	4.3	4.3	1.6	0.2	2.3	3.8	4.6	5.6	11.5
Established	1,275	4.0	3.9	1.6	< 0.1	2.5	3.5	4.3	5.2	11.0
Seasoned	908	4.0	3.9	1.7	0.1	2.5	3.5	4.3	5.2	10.6
Senior	274	3.9	3.8	1.8	0.0	2.4	3.5	4.3	5.4	9.5

Note. Items were rated on a 0–15 scale. Novice = < 1.5 years of experience, apprentice = 1.5 to < 3.5 years of experience, graduate = 3.5 to < 7 years of experience, established = 7 to < 15 years of experience, seasoned = 15 to < 25 years of experience, senior = 25 to 53 years of experience. Consult Appendix B, Table B.7, for data on composition of career cohorts. Min = minimum; max = maximum.

TABLE E.3
Descriptive Statistics for Net Work Satisfaction–Dissatisfaction in Successive Career Cohorts

Career cohort	Net work satisfaction				Range and percentile scores					
	n	M	Mdn	SD	Min	20th	40th	60th	80th	Max
Novice	480	1.1	1.0	2.1	−5.0	0.0	1.0	2.0	3.0	5.0
Apprentice	523	1.1	1.0	2.0	−5.0	0.0	1.0	2.0	3.0	5.0
Graduate	752	1.3	2.0	1.8	−5.0	0.0	1.0	2.0	3.0	5.0
Established	1,390	1.8	2.0	1.9	−5.0	0.0	2.0	3.0	3.0	5.0
Seasoned	1,056	2.1	2.0	1.8	−5.0	1.0	2.0	3.0	3.0	5.0
Senior	353	2.4	3.0	1.8	−5.0	1.0	2.0	3.0	4.0	5.0

Note. Items were rated on a 0–5 scale. Novice = < 1.5 years of experience, apprentice = 1.5 to < 3.5 years of experience, graduate = 3.5 to < 7 years of experience, established = 7 to < 15 years of experience, seasoned = 15 to < 25 years of experience, senior = 25 to 53 years of experience. Consult Appendix B, Table B.7, for data on composition of career cohorts. Min = minimum; max = maximum.

APPENDIX F
Professional Development
Self-Monitoring Scales

DAVID E. ORLINSKY AND MICHAEL HELGE RØNNESTAD

PSYCHOTHERAPISTS' PROFESSIONAL DEVELOPMENT SCALES

Identification Code: _____   Date: _____

1. How long is it since you first began to practice psychotherapy? _____ years _____ months
   [Count practice during and after training but exclude periods when you did not practice.]

Since you began working as a therapist ...

[0 = Not at all ... 5 = Very much]

2. How much have you changed overall as a therapist?	0	1	2	3	4	5
3. How much do you regard this overall change as progress or improvement?	0	1	2	3	4	5
4. How much have you succeeded in overcoming past limitations as a therapist?	0	1	2	3	4	5
5. How much have you realized your full potential as a therapist?	0	1	2	3	4	5

Overall, at the *present time* ...

[0 = Not at all ... 5 = Very much]

6. How much mastery do you have of the techniques and strategies involved in practicing therapy?	0	1	2	3	4	5
7. How well do you understand what happens moment-by-moment during therapy sessions?	0	1	2	3	4	5
8. How well are you able to detect and deal with your patients' emotional reactions to you?	0	1	2	3	4	5
9. How good are you at making constructive use of your personal reactions to patients?	0	1	2	3	4	5
10. How much precision, subtlety and finesse have you attained in your therapeutic work?	0	1	2	3	4	5
11. How capable do you feel to guide the development of other therapists?	0	1	2	3	4	5

In your *recent* psychotherapeutic work, how much ...

[**0** = Not at all .... **5** = Very much]

12. Do you feel you are changing as a therapist?	0	1	2	3	4	5
13. Does this change feel like progress or improvement?	0	1	2	3	4	5
14. Does this change feel like decline or impairment?	0	1	2	3	4	5
15. Do you feel you are overcoming past limitations as a therapist?	0	1	2	3	4	5
16. Do you feel you are becoming more skillful in practicing therapy?	0	1	2	3	4	5
17. Do you feel you are deepening your understanding of therapy?	0	1	2	3	4	5
18. Do you feel a growing sense of enthusiasm about doing therapy?	0	1	2	3	4	5
19. Do you feel you are becoming disillusioned about therapy?	0	1	2	3	4	5
20. Do you feel you are losing your capacity to respond empathically?	0	1	2	3	4	5
21. Do you feel your performance is becoming mainly routine?	0	1	2	3	4	5
22. How important to you is your further development as a therapist?	0	1	2	3	4	5

SCORING KEYS:

Scoring Key for Overall Career Development (CARDEV: range 0 to 5)
CARDEV = (Items 2 + 3 + 4 + 5 + 6 + 7 + 8 + 9 + 10 + 11) / 10
α = .88

Scoring Key for Currently Experienced Growth (CEGAIN: range 0 to 5)
CEGAIN = (Items 12 + 13 + 15 + 16 + 17 + 18) / 6
α = .86

Currently Experienced Depletion (CELOSS: range 0 to 5)
CELOSS = (Items 14 + 19 + 20 + 21) / 4
α = .69

Motivation to Develop = Item 22 (range 0 to 5)

TABLE F.1
Descriptive Statistics for Cumulative Career Development in Successive Career Cohorts

Career cohort	Overall Career Development				Range and percentile scores					
	n	M	Mdn	SD	Min	20th	40th	60th	80th	Max
Novice	400	2.7	2.8	0.8	0.0	2.1	2.6	2.9	3.3	4.8
Apprentice	417	3.1	3.1	0.6	0.0	2.7	3.0	3.2	3.6	4.7
Graduate	573	3.4	3.4	0.5	1.7	3.0	3.3	3.6	3.9	4.7
Established	1,077	3.7	3.8	0.5	2.1	3.3	3.7	3.9	4.1	5.0
Seasoned	748	3.9	3.9	0.5	1.7	3.4	3.8	4.1	4.3	5.0
Senior	333	4.0	4.0	0.5	2.3	3.6	3.9	4.1	4.4	5.0

Note. Items were rated on a 0–5 scale. Novice = < 1.5 years of experience, apprentice = 1.5 to < 3.5 years of experience, graduate = 3.5 to < 7 years of experience, established = 7 to < 15 years of experience, seasoned = 15 to < 25 years of experience, senior = 25 to 53 years of experience. Consult Appendix B, Table B.7, for data on composition of career cohorts. Min = minimum; max = maximum.

TABLE F.2
Descriptive Statistics for Currently Experienced Growth in Successive Career Cohorts

Career cohort	Currently Experienced Growth				Range and percentile scores					
	n	M	Mdn	SD	Min	20th	40th	60th	80th	Max
Novice	422	3.3	3.3	1.0	0.0	2.7	3.2	3.7	4.2	5.0
Apprentice	422	3.5	3.5	0.8	0.0	2.8	3.3	3.7	4.2	5.0
Graduate	597	3.5	3.7	0.8	0.2	2.8	3.5	3.8	4.2	5.0
Established	1,146	3.6	3.7	0.8	0.2	3.0	3.5	3.8	4.2	5.0
Seasoned	876	3.5	3.7	0.8	0.2	3.0	3.3	3.8	4.2	5.0
Senior	282	3.5	3.7	0.9	1.0	2.8	3.5	3.8	4.2	5.0

Note. Items were rated on a 0–5 scale. Novice = < 1.5 years of experience, apprentice = 1.5 to < 3.5 years of experience, graduate = 3.5 to < 7 years of experience, established = 7 to < 15 years of experience, seasoned = 15 to < 25 years of experience, senior = 25 to 53 years of experience. Consult Appendix B, Table B.7, for data on composition of career cohorts. Min = minimum; max = maximum.

TABLE F.3
Descriptive Statistics for Currently Experienced Depletion in Successive Career Cohorts

Career cohort	Currently Experienced Depletion				Range and percentile scores					
	n	M	Mdn	SD	Min	20th	40th	60th	80th	Max
Novice	424	0.8	0.8	0.7	0.0	0.0	0.5	1.0	1.5	4.0
Apprentice	422	0.8	0.8	0.7	0.0	0.0	0.5	1.0	1.5	3.8
Graduate	596	0.9	0.8	0.8	0.0	0.3	0.5	1.0	1.5	3.5
Established	1,164	0.9	0.8	0.8	0.0	0.0	0.5	1.0	1.5	3.8
Seasoned	930	0.9	0.8	0.9	0.0	0.0	0.5	1.0	1.5	4.3
Senior	333	0.9	0.8	0.8	0.0	0.0	0.5	1.0	1.8	3.8

Note. Items were rated on a 0–5 scale. Novice = < 1.5 years of experience, apprentice = 1.5 to < 3.5 years of experience, graduate = 3.5 to < 7 years of experience, established = 7 to < 15 years of experience, seasoned = 15 to < 25 years of experience, senior = 25 to 53 years of experience. Consult Appendix B, Table B.7, for data on composition of career cohorts. Min = minimum; max = maximum.

TABLE F.4
Descriptive Statistics for Motivation to Develop in Successive Career Cohorts

Career cohort	Motivation to develop				Range and percentile scores					
	n	*M*	*Mdn*	*SD*	Min	20th	40th	60th	80th	Max
Novice	482	4.3	5.0	1.1	0.0	4.0	5.0	5.0	5.0	5.0
Apprentice	517	4.5	5.0	1.0	0.0	4.0	5.0	5.0	5.0	5.0
Graduate	740	4.6	5.0	0.8	0.0	4.0	5.0	5.0	5.0	5.0
Established	1,390	4.6	5.0	0.8	0.0	4.0	5.0	5.0	5.0	5.0
Seasoned	1,053	4.4	5.0	1.0	0.0	4.0	5.0	5.0	5.0	5.0
Senior	368	4.0	4.0	1.4	0.0	4.0	5.0	5.0	5.0	5.0

Note. Items were rated on a 0–5 scale. Novice = < 1.5 years of experience, apprentice = 1.5 to < 3.5 years of experience, graduate = 3.5 to < 7 years of experience, established = 7 to < 15 years of experience, seasoned = 15 to < 25 years of experience, senior = 25 to 53 years of experience. Consult Appendix B, Table B.7, for data on composition of career cohorts. Min = minimum; max = maximum.

REFERENCES

Abbott, A. (1988). *The system of professions: An essay on the division of expert labor.* Chicago: University of Chicago Press.

Albee, G. W. (1959). *Mental health manpower trends.* New York: Basic Books.

Ambühl, H., & Orlinsky, D. E. (1995). Changing patterns of theoretical orientation in the development of psychotherapists. In S.-H. Kang (Ed.), *Proceedings of the 16th International Congress of Psychotherapy: Psychotherapies East and West. Integration of psychotherapies* (rev. ed., pp. 56–69). Seoul, Korea: Korean Academy of Psychotherapists.

Ambühl, H., & Orlinsky, D. E. (1999). Therapieziele aus der Perspektive der PsychotherapeutInnen [Psychotherapists' perspectives on their therapeutic goals]. In H. Ambühl & B. Strauss (Eds.), *Therapieziele* (pp. 319–334). Göttingen, Germany: Hogrefe.

American Psychiatric Association. (1994). *Diagnostic and statistical manual of mental disorders* (4th ed.). Washington, DC: Author.

Anthony, N. A. (1967). A longitudinal analysis of the effect of experience on the therapeutic approach. *Journal of Clinical Psychology, 23,* 512–516.

Ariès, P. (1962). *Centuries of childhood: A social history of family life.* New York: Vintage Books.

Arthur, A. R. (2000). The personality and cognitive–epistemological traits of cognitive–behavioural and psychoanalytic psychotherapists. *British Journal of Medical Psychology, 73,* 243–257.

Auerbach, A. H., & Johnson, M. (1977). Research on the therapist's level of experience. In A. S. Gurman & A. M. Razin (Eds.), *Effective psychotherapy: A handbook of research* (pp. 84–102). New York: Pergamon.

Aveline, M., & Shapiro, D. A. (Eds.). (1995). *Research foundations for psychotherapy practice.* Chichester, England: Wiley.

Bae, S.-H., Joo, E., & Orlinsky, D. E. (2004). Psychotherapists in South Korea: Professional and practice characteristics. *Psychotherapy, 40,* 302–316.

Bae, S.-H., & Orlinsky, D. E. (2003, June). *Western theories of psychotherapy in collectivist cultures.* Paper presented at the 34th annual conference of the Society for Psychotherapy Research, Weimar, Germany.

Baltes, P. B., & Smith, J. (1994). Toward a psychology of wisdom and its ontogenesis. In R. E. Sternberg (Ed.), *Wisdom: Its origins and development* (pp. 87–120). Cambridge, England: Cambridge University Press.

Bandura, A. (1997). *Self-efficacy: The exercise of control.* New York: W. H. Freeman.

Barlow, D. (1992). The development of an anxiety research clinic. In D. K. Freedheim (Ed.), *History of psychotherapy: A century of change* (pp. 429–431). Washington, DC: American Psychological Association.

Becker, H. S., & Strauss, A. L. (1956). Careers, personality, and adult socialization. *American Journal of Sociology, 62*, 253–263.

Bellah, R. N., Madsen, R., Sullivan, W. M., Swidler, A., & Tipton, S. M. (1985). *Habits of the heart: Individualism and commitment in American life.* Berkeley: University of California Press.

Benjamin, L. S. (1974). Structural analysis of social behavior. *Psychological Review, 81*, 392–425.

Benjamin, L. S. (1996). *Interpersonal diagnosis and treatment.* New York: Guilford.

Berger, P., Berger, B., & Kellner, H. (1973). *The homeless mind: Modernization and consciousness.* New York: Vintage Books.

Bergin, A. E. (1992). Outcome research. In D. K. Freedheim (Ed.), *History of psychotherapy: A century of change* (pp. 413–416). Washington, DC: American Psychological Association.

Bergin, A. E., & Garfield, S. L. (Eds.). (1971). *Handbook of psychotherapy and behavior change* (1st ed.). New York: Wiley.

Bergin, A. E., & Garfield, S. L. (Eds.). (1994). *Handbook of psychotherapy and behavior change* (4th ed.). New York: Wiley.

Berman, E. (2000). Psychoanalytic supervision: The intersubjective development. *International Journal of Psychoanalysis, 81*, 273–290.

Berman, J. S., & Norton, N. C. (1985). Does professional training make a therapist more effective? *Psychological Bulletin, 98*, 401–407.

Bernard, J. M. (1979). Supervisor training: A discrimination model. *Counselor Education and Supervision, 19*, 60–68.

Bernard, J. M., & Goodyear, R. K. (2004). *Fundamentals of clinical supervision* (rev. ed.). Needham Heights, MA: Allyn & Bacon.

Beutler, L. E., & Clarkin, J. F. (1990). *Systematic treatment selection: Toward targeted therapeutic interventions.* New York: Brunner/Mazel.

Beutler, L. E., & Crago, M. (Eds.). (1991). *Psychotherapy research: An international review of programmatic studies.* Washington, DC: American Psychological Association.

Beutler, L. E., Crago, M., & Azrimendi, T. G. (1986). Research on therapist variables in psychotherapy. In S. L. Garfield & A. E. Bergin (Eds.), *Handbook of psychotherapy and behavior change* (3rd ed., pp. 257–310). New York: Wiley.

Beutler, L. E., Machado, P. P., & Neufeldt, S. A. (1994). Therapist variables. In A. E. Bergin & S. L. Garfield (Eds.), *Handbook of psychotherapy and behavior change* (4th ed., pp. 229–269) New York: Wiley.

Beutler, L. E., Malik, M., Alimohamed, S., Harwood, T. M., Talebi, H., Noble, S., & Wong, E. (2004). Therapist variables. In M. Lambert (Ed.), *Bergin and Garfield's handbook of psychotherapy and behavior change* (pp. 227–306). New York: Wiley.

Bloomfield, I. (1989). Through therapy to self. In W. Dryden & L. Spurling (Eds.), *On becoming a psychotherapist* (pp. 33–52). New York: Tavistock/Routledge.

Bonacci, J. (2000). Efficacy and cost effectiveness of psychotherapy. *Journal of Nervous and Mental Disorders, 188,* 389–390.

Bordin, E. S. (1979). The generalizability of the psychoanalytic concept of the working alliance. *Psychotherapy: Theory, Research, and Practice, 16,* 252–260.

Borys, D. S., & Pope, K. S. (1989). Dual relationships between therapist and client: A national study of psychologists, psychiatrists, and social workers. *Professional Psychology: Research and Practice, 20,* 283–293.

Botermans, J.-F. (1996). *The training of psychotherapists: Impact of confidence and mastery, self-efficacy, and emotional reactivity.* Doctoral dissertation. Université catholique de Louvain, Departement de Psychologie Clinique. Louvain-la-Neuve, Belgium.

Brady, J. L., Guy, J. D., & Norcross, J. C. (1995). Managing your own distress: Lessons from psychotherapists healing themselves. In L. Vandecreed & S. Knapp (Eds.), *Innovations in clinical practice: A source book* (Vol. 14, pp. 293–306). Sarasota, FL: Professional Resource Press.

Brady, J. L., Guy, J. D., Poelstra, P. L., & Brokaw, B. F. (1999). Vicarious traumatization, spirituality, and the treatment of sexual abuse survivors: A national survey of women psychotherapists. *Professional Psychology: Research and Practice, 30,* 386–393.

Burton, A. (1972). Healing as a lifestyle. In A. Burton (Ed.), *Twelve therapists* (pp. 1–27). San Francisco: Jossey-Bass.

Carson, R. C. (1969). *Interaction concepts of personality.* Chicago: Aldine.

Caspar, F. (1995). *Plan analysis: Toward optimizing psychotherapy.* Seattle, WA: Hogrefe & Huber.

Chaplin, J. (1989). Rhythm and blues. In W. Dryden & L. Spurling (Eds.), *On becoming a psychotherapist* (pp. 169–188). New York: Tavistock/Routledge.

Coster, J. S., & Schwebel, M. (1997). Well-functioning in professional psychologists. *Professional Psychology, 28,* 3–13.

Crits-Christoph, P., Barnackie, K., Kurclas, J. S., Beck, A. T., Carroll, K., Perry, K., et al. (1991). Meta-analysis of therapist effects in psychotherapy outcome studies. *Psychotherapy Research, 1,* 81–92.

Crits-Christoph, P., Siqueland, L., Chittams, J., Barber, J. P., Beck, A. T., Frank, A., et al. (1998). Training in cognitive, supportive–expressive, and drug counseling therapies for cocaine dependence. *Journal of Consulting and Clinical Psychology, 66,* 484–492.

Csikszentmihalyi, M. (1990). *Flow: The psychology of optimal experience.* New York: Harper & Row.

Csikszentmihalyi, M. (1996). *Creativity: Flow and the psychology of discovery and invention.* New York: HarperCollins.

Cushman, P. (1995). *Constructing the self, constructing America: A cultural history of psychotherapy.* Reading, MA: Addison-Wesley.

Davis, J. D., Elliott, R., Davis, M. L., Binns, M., Francis, V. M., Kelman, J. E., & Schröder, T. A. (1987). Development of a taxonomy of therapist difficulties: Initial report. *British Journal of Medical Psychology, 60,* 109–119.

Davis, J. D., Francis, V. M., Davis, M. L., & Schröder, T. A. (1987). *Development of a taxonomy of therapists' coping strategies: Initial report.* Unpublished manuscript.

Dent, J. K., & Furse, G. A. (1978). *Dimensions of the psycho-social therapies as revealed by the personalities of effective therapists* (DHEW Publication No. ADM 77-527). Washington, DC: U.S. Government Printing Office.

Derlega, V. J., Hendrick, S. S., Winstead, B. A., & Berg, J. H. (1991). *Psychotherapy as a personal relationship.* New York: Guilford Press.

Deutsch, C. J. (1984). Self-reported sources of stress among psychotherapists. *Professional Psychology: Research and Practice, 15,* 833–845.

Deutsch, C. J. (1985). A survey of therapists' personal problems and treatment. *Professional Psychology: Research and Practice, 16,* 305–315.

Dlugos, R. F., & Friedlander, M. L. (2001). Passionately committed psychotherapists: A qualitative study of their experiences. *Professional Psychology: Research and Practice, 32,* 298–304.

Doehrman, M. J. (1976). Parallel processes in supervision and psychotherapy. *Bulletin of the Menninger Clinic, 40,* 1–104.

Draguns, J. (2004). From speculation through description toward investigation: A prospective glimpse at cultural research in psychotherapy. In U. P. Gielen, J. M. Fish, & J. G. Draguns (Eds.), *Handbook of culture, therapy, and healing* (pp. 369–388). Mahwah, NJ: Erlbaum.

Dryden, W., & Spurling, L. (Eds.). (1989). *On becoming a psychotherapist.* London: Tavistock/Routledge.

Durkheim, E. (1951). *Suicide.* Glencoe, IL: Free Press. (Original work published 1897)

Durkheim, E. (1964). *The division of labor in society.* New York: Free Press. (Original work published 1893)

Eliot, T. S. (1952). Ash Wednesday. In *The complete poems and plays of T. S. Eliot* (p. 67). New York: Harcourt, Brace.

Elizur, A., Kretsch, R., Spaizer, N., & Sorek, Y. (1994). Self-evaluation of psychotherapeutic competence. *British Journal of Medical Psychology, 67,* 231–235.

Elkin, I. (1999). A major dilemma in psychotherapy outcome research: Disentangling therapists from therapies. *Clinical Psychology: Science and Practice, 6,* 10–32.

Elliott, R., Greenberg, L. S., & Lietaer, G. (2004). Research on experiential psychotherapies. In M. Lambert (Ed.), *Bergin and Garfield's handbook of psychotherapy and behavior change* (pp. 493–539). New York. Wiley.

Elliott, R., Orlinsky, D. E., Klein, M., Amer, M., & Partyka, R. (2004). Professional characteristics of humanistic therapists: Analyses of the Collaborative Research Network sample. *Person-Centered and Experiential Psychotherapies, 2,* 188–203.

Farber, B. A. (1983). The effects of psychotherapeutic practice upon psychotherapists. *Psychotherapy: Theory, Research, and Practice, 20,* 174–182.

Farber, B. A., & Heifetz, L. J. (1981). The satisfactions and stresses of psychotherapeutic work: A factor analytic study. *Professional Psychology, 12,* 621–630.

Fiedler, F. E. (1950). A comparison of therapeutic relationships in psychoanalytic, nondirective and Adlerian therapy. *Journal of Consulting Psychology, 14,* 426–445.

Flanagan, J. C. (1954). The critical incident techniques. *Psychological Bulletin, 51,* 327–358.

Frank, J. D. (1974). Psychotherapy: The restoration of morale. *American Journal of Psychotherapy, 131,* 271–274.

Frank, J. D. (1992). The Johns Hopkins psychotherapy research project. In D. K. Freedheim (Ed.), *History of psychotherapy: A century of change* (pp. 392–395). Washington, DC: American Psychological Association.

Frank, J. D., & Frank, J. B. (1991). *Persuasion and healing: A comparative study of psychotherapy.* Baltimore: Johns Hopkins University Press.

Fransella, F. (1989). A fight for freedom. In W. Dryden & L. Spurling (Eds.), *On becoming a psychotherapist* (pp. 116–133). New York: Tavistock/Routledge.

Freedheim, D. K. (Ed.). (1992). *History of psychotherapy: A century of change.* Washington, DC: American Psychological Association.

Freud, S. (1958). Recommendations to physicians practicing psycho-analysis. In J. R. Strachey (Ed.), *The standard edition of the complete psychological works of Sigmund Freud* (Vol. 12, p. 113). London: Hogarth Press. (Original work published 1912)

Freud, S. (1964). Analysis terminable and interminable. In J. R. Strachey (Ed.), *The standard edition of the complete psychological works of Sigmund Freud* (Vol. 23, p. 249). London: Hogarth Press. (Original work published 1937)

Garfield, S. L., & Bergin, A. E. (Eds.). (1978). *Handbook of psychotherapy and behavior change* (2nd ed.). New York: Wiley.

Garfield, S. L., & Bergin, A. E. (Eds.). (1986). *Handbook of psychotherapy and behavior change* (3rd ed.). New York: Wiley.

Gartner, A. (1976). *The preparation of human service professionals.* New York: Human Sciences Press.

Gay, P. (1986). *The tender passion. The bourgeois experience Victoria to Freud* (Vol. 2). New York: Oxford University Press.

Geller, J. D. (1994). The psychotherapist's experience of interest and boredom. *Psychotherapy, 31,* 3–16.

Geller, J. D., Lehman, A. K., & Farber, B. A. (2002). Psychotherapists' representations of their patients. *Journal of Clinical Psychology, 58,* 733–745.

Geller, J. D., Norcross, J. C., & Orlinsky, D. E. (2005). *The psychotherapist's own psychotherapy: Patient and clinician perspectives.* New York: Oxford University Press.

Gerin, P., & Vignat, J.-P. (1984). *L'identité des psychotherapeutes* [The identity of psychotherapists]. Paris: Presses Universitaires des France.

Goldberg, C. (1992). *The seasoned psychotherapist: Triumph over adversity.* New York: Norton.

Grater, H. A. (1985). Stages in psychotherapy supervision: From therapy skills to skilled therapist. *Professional Psychology: Research & Practice, 16,* 605–610.

Grawe, K. (2004). *Psychological therapy.* Göttingen, Germany: Hogrefe.

Gray, L. A., Ladany, N., Walker, J. A., & Ancis, J. R. (2001). Psychotherapy trainees' experience of counterproductive events in supervision. *Journal of Counseling Psychology, 48,* 371–383.

Green, J., Grosswald, S., Suter, E., & Walthall, D. (Eds.). (1984). *Continuing education for the health professions.* San Francisco: Jossey-Bass.

Guest, P. D., & Beutler, L. E. (1988). Impact of psychotherapy supervision on therapist orientation and values. *Journal of Consulting and Clinical Psychology, 56,* 653–658.

Gurman, A. S., & Razin, A. M. (Eds.). (1977). *Effective psychotherapy: A handbook of research.* New York: Pergamon.

Guy, J. D. (1987). *The personal life of the psychotherapist: The impact of clinical practice on the therapist's intimate relationships and emotional well-being.* New York: Wiley.

Guy, J. D., & Liaboe, G. P. (1986). The impact of conducting personal therapy on therapists' interpersonal functioning. *Professional Psychology: Research and Practice, 17,* 111–114.

Guy, J. D., Poelstra, P. L., & Stark, M. J. (1989). Personal distress and therapeutic effectiveness: National survey of psychologists practicing psychotherapy. *Professional Psychology: Research and Practice, 20,* 48–50.

Guy, J. D., Stark, M. J., & Poelstra, P. L. (1988). Personal therapy for psychotherapists before and after entering professional practice. *Professional Psychology: Research and Practice, 19,* 474–476.

Henry, W. E. (1954). The business executive: A study of the psychodynamics of a social role. In H. Brand (Ed.), *The study of personality: A book of readings* (pp. 551–559). New York: Wiley.

Henry, W. E., Sims, J. H., & Spray, S. L. (1971). *The fifth profession.* San Francisco: Jossey-Bass.

Henry, W. E., Sims, J. H., & Spray, S. L. (1973). *Public and private lives of psychotherapists.* San Francisco: Jossey-Bass.

Henry, W. P., Schacht, T. E., & Strupp, H. H. (1990). Patient and therapist introject, interpersonal process and differential psychotherapy outcome. *Journal of Consulting and Clinical Psychology, 58,* 768–774.

Henry, W. P., & Strupp, H. H. (1992). The Vanderbilt center for psychotherapy research. In D. K. Freedheim (Ed.), *History of psychotherapy: A century of change* (pp. 436–441). Washington, DC: American Psychological Association.

Heppner, P. P. (1989). Chance and choices in becoming a therapist. In W. Dryden & L. Spurling (Eds.), *On becoming a psychotherapist* (pp. 69–86). New York: Tavistock/Routledge.

Hess, A. K. (1987). Psychotherapy supervision: Stages, Buber, and a theory of relationship. *Professional Psychology: Research & Practice, 18,* 251–259.

Hill, C. E., Charles, D., & Reed, K. (1981). A longitudinal analysis of changes in counseling skills during doctoral training in counseling psychology. *Journal of Counseling Psychology, 28,* 428–436.

Hill, C. E., & Corbett, K. (1993). A perspective on the history of process and outcome research in counseling psychology. *Journal of Counseling Psychology, 40,* 3–24.

Hill, C. E., & O'Grady, K. E. (1985). List of therapist intentions illustrated in a case study and with therapists of varying theoretical orientations. *Journal of Counseling Psychology, 32,* 3–22.

Holloway, E. L. (1995). *Clinical supervision: A systems approach.* London: Sage.

Holmqvist, R., & Andersen, K. (2003). Therapists' reactions to treatment of survivors of political torture. *Professional Psychology: Research and Practice, 34,* 294–300.

Holt, R. R. (Ed.). (1971). *New horizon for psychotherapy.* New York: International Universities Press.

Holt, R. R., & Luborsky, L. (1958). *Personality patterns of psychiatrists* (2 vols.). New York: Basic Books.

Horowitz, L. M., Rosenberg, S. E., Baer, B. A., Ureno, G., & Villasenor, V. (1988). Inventory of interpersonal problems: Psychometric properties and clinical applications. *Journal of Consulting and Clinical Psychology, 56,* 885–892.

Horowitz, M. J. (1992). The Langley Porter projects. In D. K. Freedheim (Ed.), *History of psychotherapy: A century of change* (pp. 422–425). Washington, DC: American Psychological Association.

Houle, C. (1980). *Continuing learning in the professions.* San Francisco: Jossey-Bass.

Howard, K. I., Krause, M. S., & Vessey, J. (1994). Analysis of clinical trial data: The problem of outcome overlap. *Psychotherapy, 31,* 302–307.

Howard, K. I., Lueger, R., Maling, M., & Martinovich, Z. (1993). A phase model of psychotherapy: Causal mediation of outcome. *Journal of Consulting and Clinical Psychology, 61,* 678–685.

Howard, K. I., & Orlinsky, D. E. (1992). The Chicago Northwestern studies. In D. K. Freedheim (Ed.), *History of psychotherapy: A century of change* (pp. 408–412). Washington, DC: American Psychological Association.

Hughes, E., Thorne, B., DeBaggis, A., Gurin, A., & Williams, D. (1973). *Education for the professions of medicine, law, theology, and social welfare.* New York: McGraw-Hill.

Ivey, A. E., & Authier, J. (1978). *Microcounseling* (2nd ed.). Springfield, IL: Charles C Thomas.

Jennings, L., & Skovholt, T. M. (1999). The cognitive, emotional, and relational characteristics of master therapists. *Journal of Counseling Psychology, 46,* 3–11.

Jensen, J. P., & Bergin, A. E. (1988). Mental health values of professional therapists: A national interdisciplinary survey. *Professional Psychology: Research and Practice, 19,* 290–297.

Jensen, J. P., Bergin, A. E., & Greaves, D. W. (1990). The meaning of eclecticism: New survey and analysis of components. *Professional Psychology: Research and Practice, 21,* 124–130.

Joo, E., & Kim, J. (2000, June). *A qualitative study of master/expert counselors in Korea.* Paper presented at the 31st annual conference of the Society for Psychotherapy Research, Chicago.

Joo, E., Kim, H. A., & Orlinsky, D. E. (1995). The psychotherapeutic relationship in different cultures. In S.-H. Kang (Ed.), *Psychotherapy East and West: Integration of psychotherapies* (rev. ed., pp. 70–78). Seoul: Korean Academy of Psychotherapists.

Kagan, H., & Kagan, J. I. (1997). Interpersonal process recall: Influencing human interaction. In C. E. Watkins Jr. (Ed.), *Handbook of psychotherapy supervision* (pp. 296–309). New York: Wiley.

Keinan, G., Almagor, M., & Ben-Porath, Y. S. (1989). A reevaluation of the relationship between psychotherapeutic orientation and perceived personality characteristics. *Psychotherapy, 26,* 218–226.

Kelley, F. L., & Fiske, D. W. (1951). *The prediction of performance in clinical psychology.* Ann Arbor: University of Michigan Press.

Kiesler, D. J. (1983). The 1982 interpersonal circle: A taxonomy for complementarity in human transactions. *Psychological Review, 90,* 185–214.

Kiesler, D. J., Anchin, J. C., Perkins, M. J., Chirico, B. M., Kyle, E. M., & Federman, E. J. (1985). *The Impact Message Inventory: Form II.* Palo Alto, CA: Consulting Psychologists Press.

Kiesler, D. J., & Watkins, L. M. (1989). Interpersonal complementarity and the therapeutic alliance: A study of relationship in psychotherapy. *Psychotherapy, 26,* 183–184.

Kivlighan, D. M., Schuetz, S. A., & Kardash, C. M. (1998). Counselor trainee achievement goal orientation and the acquisition of time-limited dynamic psychotherapy skills. *Journal of Counseling Psychology, 45,* 189–195.

Knesper, D. J., Wheeler, J. R. C., & Pagnucco, D. J. (1984). Mental health services providers' distribution across counties in the United States. *American Psychologist, 39,* 1424–1434.

Kopta, S. M., Newman, F. L., McGovern, M. P., & Angle, R. S. (1989). Relation between years of psychotherapeutic experience and conceptualizations, interventions, and treatment plan costs. *Professional Psychology: Research and Practice, 20,* 59–61.

Kopta, S. M., Newman, F. L., McGovern, M. P., & Sandrock, D. (1986). Psychotherapeutic orientations: A comparison of conceptualizations, interventions, and treatment plan costs. *Journal of Consulting and Clinical Psychology, 54,* 369–374.

Kottler, J. A. (1993). *On being a therapist* (rev. ed.). San Francisco: Jossey-Bass.

Kramen-Kahn, B., & Hansen, N. D. (1998). Rafting the rapids: Occupational hazards, rewards, and coping strategies of psychotherapists. *Professional Psychology: Research and Practice, 29,* 130–134.

Kurzweil, E. (1989). *The Freudians: A comparative perspective.* New Haven, CT: Yale University Press.

Ladany, N., Friedlander, M. L., & Nelson, M. L. (in press). *Critical events in psychotherapy supervision: An interpersonal approach.* Washington, DC: American Psychological Association.

Ladany, N., Hill, C. E., Corbett, M. M., & Nutt, E. A. (1996). Nature, extent, and importance of what psychotherapy trainees do not disclose to their supervisors. *Journal of Counseling Psychology, 43,* 102–115.

Lakoff, G., & Johnson, M. (1980). *Metaphors we live by.* Chicago: University of Chicago Press.

Lambert, M. J. (1992). Psychotherapy outcome research: Implications for eclectic and integrative therapists. In J. C. Norcross & M. R. Goldfried (Eds.), *Handbook of psychotherapy integration* (pp. 94–129). New York: Basic Books.

Lambert, M. J. (Ed.). (2004). *Bergin and Garfield's handbook of psychotherapy and behavior change* (5th ed.). New York: Wiley.

Lambert, M. J., & Ogles, B. M. (2004). The efficacy and effectiveness of psychotherapy. In M. Lambert (Ed.), *Bergin and Garfield's handbook of psychotherapy and behavior change* (5th ed., pp. 139–193). New York: Wiley.

Lasch, C. (1979). *The culture of narcissism: American life in an age of diminishing expectations.* New York: Warner Books.

Leary, T. (1957). *Interpersonal diagnosis of personality.* New York: Ronald Press.

Lehman, A. K., & Salovey, P. (1990). An introduction to cognitive–behavior therapy. In R. A. Wells & V. J. Giannetti (Eds.), *Handbook of the brief psychotherapies* (pp. 239–259). New York: Plenum.

Lewinsohn, P. (1992). A program of clinical research on depression. In D. K. Freedheim (Ed.), *History of psychotherapy: A century of change* (pp. 417–421). Washington, DC: American Psychological Association.

Light, D. (1980). *Becoming psychiatrists: The professional transformation of self.* New York: Norton.

Lincoln, Y. S., & Guba, E. G. (1985). *Naturalistic inquiry.* Newbury Park, CA: Sage.

Lohser, B., & Newton, P. M. (1996). *Unorthodox Freud: The view from the couch.* New York: Guilford Press.

Lowenthal, M. F., Thurnher, M., & Chiriboga, D. (1975). *Four stages of life.* San Francisco: Jossey-Bass.

Luborsky, L. (1992). The Penn research project. In D. K. Freedheim (Ed.), *History of psychotherapy: A century of change* (pp. 396–400). Washington, DC: American Psychological Association.

Luborsky, L., Diguer, L., Seligman, D. A., Rosenthal, R., Krause, E. D., Haperin, G., et al. (1999). The researcher's own therapy allegiances: A "wild card" in comparisons of treatment efficacy. *Clinical Psychology: Science and Practice, 6,* 95–106.

Luhrmann, T. M. (2000). *Of two minds: The growing disorder in American psychiatry.* New York: Knopf.

MacDevitt, J. W. (1987). Therapists' personal therapy and professional self-awareness. *Psychotherapy, 24,* 693–703.

Macdonald, K. M. (1995). *The sociology of the professions.* London: Sage.

MacIntyre, A. (1981). *After virtue.* South Bend, IN: Notre Dame University Press.

Macran, S., & Shapiro, D. A. (1998). The role of personal therapy for therapists: A review. *British Journal of Medical Psychology, 71,* 13–25.

Macran, S., Stiles, W. B., & Smith, J. A. (1999). How does personal therapy affect therapists' practice? *Journal of Counseling Psychology, 46,* 419–431.

Mahoney, M. J., with Eiseman, S. C. (1989). The object of the dance. In W. Dryden & L. Spurling (Eds.), *On becoming a psychotherapist* (pp. 17–32). New York: Tavistock/Routledge.

Mahoney, M. J. (1997). Psychotherapists' personal problems and self-care patterns. *Professional Psychology: Research and Practice, 28,* 14–16.

Mahoney, M. J., & Craine, M. H. (1991). The changing beliefs of psychotherapy experts. *Journal of Psychotherapy Integration, 1,* 207–221.

Mallinckrodt, B., & Nelson, M. L. (1991). Counselor training level and the formation of the psychotherapeutic working alliance. *Journal of Counseling Psychology, 38,* 133–138.

Maslach, C., & Leiter, M. P. (1997). *The truth about burnout: How organizations cause personal stress and what to do about it.* San Francisco: Jossey-Bass/Pfeiffer.

Maslach, C., Schaufeli, W. B., & Leiter, M. P. (2000). Job burnout. *Annual Review of Psychology, 52,* 397–422.

Matarazzo, R. G. (1971). Research on the teaching and learning of psychotherapeutic skills. In A. E. Bergin & S. L. Garfield (Eds.), *Handbook of psychotherapy and behavior change* (1st ed., pp. 895–924). New York: Wiley.

Matarazzo, R. G. (1978). Evaluating the training of therapists. In S. L. Garfield & A. E. Bergin (Eds.), *Handbook of psychotherapy and behavior change* (2nd ed., pp. 941–966). New York: Wiley.

Matarazzo, R. G., & Patterson, D. (1986). Methods of teaching therapeutic skills. In S. L. Garfield & A. E. Bergin (Eds.), *Handbook of psychotherapy and behavior change* (3rd ed., pp. 821–843). New York: Wiley.

McGovern, M. P., Newman, F. L., & Kopta, S. M. (1986). Metatheoretical assumptions and psychotherapy orientation: Clinician attributions of patients' problem causality and responsibility for treatment outcome. *Journal of Consulting and Clinical Psychology, 54,* 476–481.

McNamara, J. R. (1986). Personal therapy in the training of behavior therapists. *Psychotherapy, 23,* 370–374.

Menninger, W. W. (1990). Anxiety in the psychotherapist. *Bulletin of the Menninger Clinic, 54,* 232–246.

Menninger, W. W. (1991). Patient suicide and its impact on the psychotherapist. *Bulletin of the Menninger Clinic, 55,* 216–227.

Morrow-Bradley, C., & Elliott, R. (1986). The utilization of psychotherapy research by practicing psychotherapists. *American Psychologist, 41,* 188–197.

Moskowitz, S. A., & Rupert, P. A. (1983). Conflict resolution within the supervisory relationship. *Professional Psychology: Research and Practice, 14,* 632–641.

Murtagh, M. P., & Wollersheim, J. P. (1997). Effects of clinical practice on psychologists: Treating depressed clients, perceived stress, and ways of coping. *Professional Psychology: Research and Practice, 28,* 361–364.

Najavits, L. M., & Strupp, H. H. (1994). Differences in the effectiveness of psychodynamic therapists: A process–outcome study. *Psychotherapy, 31,* 114–123.

Nelson, M. L., & Friedlander, M. L. (2001). A close look at conflictual supervisory relationships: The trainee's perspective. *Journal of Counseling Psychology, 48,* 384–395.

Nerdrum, P., & Rønnestad, M. H. (2002). The trainees' perspective: A qualitative study of learning empathic communication in Norway. *The Counseling Psychologist, 30,* 609–629.

Nerdrum, P., & Rønnestad, M. H. (2003). Changes in therapists' conceptualizations and practice of therapy following empathy training. *Clinical Supervisor, 22,* 37–61.

Neufeldt, S. A. (1999). *Supervision strategies for the first practicum* (2nd ed.). Alexandria, VA: American Counseling Association.

Nigam, T., Cameron, P. M., & Leverette, J. S. (1997). Impasses in the supervisory process: A resident's perspective. *American Journal of Psychotherapy, 51,* 252–272.

Norcross, J. C. (2000). Psychotherapist self-care: Practitioner-tested, research-informed strategies. *Professional Psychology: Research and Practice, 31,* 710–713.

Norcross, J. C, Geller, J. D., & Kurzawa, E. K. (2001). Conducting psychotherapy with psychotherapists II: Clinical practices and collegial advice. *Journal of Psychotherapy: Practice and Research, 10,* 37–45.

Norcross, J. C., & Guy, J. D. (1989). Ten therapists: The process of becoming and being. In W. Dryden & L. Spurling (Eds.), *On becoming a psychotherapist* (pp. 215–239). London: Tavistock/Routledge.

Norcross, J. C., & Prochaska, J. O. (1982). A national survey of clinical psychologists: Views on training, career choice, and APA. *The Clinical Psychologist, 56,* 3–6.

Norcross, J. C., & Prochaska, J. O. (1983). Clinicians' theoretical orientations: Selection, utilization and efficacy. *Professional Psychology, 14,* 197–208.

Norcross, J. C., & Prochaska, J. O. (1986a). Psychotherapist heal thyself: I. The psychological distress and self-change of psychologists, counselors, and lay persons. *Psychotherapy, 23,* 102–114.

Norcross, J. C., & Prochaska, J. O. (1986b). Psychotherapist heal thyself: II. The self-initiated and therapy-facilitated change of psychological distress. *Psychotherapy, 23*, 345–356.

Norcross, J. C., & Prochaska, J. O. (1988). A study of eclectic (and integrative) views revisited. *Professional Psychology: Research and Practice, 19*, 251–263.

Norcross, J. C., Prochaska, J. O., & DiClemente, C. C. (1986). Self-change of psychological distress: Laypersons' versus psychologists' coping strategies. *Journal of Clinical Psychology, 42*, 834–840.

Norcross, J. C., Strausser, D. J., & Faltus, F. J. (1988). The therapist's therapist. *American Journal of Psychotherapy, 42*, 53–66.

Norcross, J. C., Strausser-Kirtland, D., & Missar, C. D. (1988). The processes and outcomes of psychotherapists' personal treatment experiences. *Psychotherapy, 25*, 36–43.

Norcross, J. C., & Wogan, M. (1982). Relationship of behavior therapists' characteristics, activities, and clients to reported practices in therapy. *Professional Psychology: Research and Practice, 13*, 44–56.

Norcross, J. C., & Wogan, M. (1983). American psychotherapists of diverse persuasions: Characteristics, theories, practices, and clients. *Professional Psychology: Research and Practice, 14*, 529–539.

Norcross, J. C., & Wogan, M. (1987). Values in psychotherapy: A survey of practitioners' beliefs. *Professional Psychology: Research and Practice, 18*, 5–7.

Orlinsky, D. E. (1987). *How to do psychotherapy research without a grant.* Ulm, Germany: PSZ-Verlag Ulm.

Orlinsky, D. E. (1989). Researchers' images of psychotherapy: Their origins and influence on research. *Clinical Psychology Review, 9*, 413–441.

Orlinsky, D. E. (1994). Learning from many masters: Ansaetze zu einer wissenschaftlichen Integration psychotherapeutischer Behandlungsmethoden. *Psychotherapeut, 1*, 2–9.

Orlinsky, D. E. (1998, April 20). *The healing energy of the psychotherapist.* Plenary presentation at the Lindauer Psychotherapiewochen (Lindau Psychotherapy Weeks), Lindau, Germany.

Orlinsky, D. E. (2004). Der menschliche Kontext von Psychotherapien. Eine handlungstheorische Systemanalyse von Einflüssen auf therapeutische Prozesse und Ergebnisse (Teil 1, 2). [The human context of psychotherapies: An action-systems analysis of the influences on outcomes of therapeutic process (Part 1, 2)]. *Psychotherapeut, 49*, 88–100.

Orlinsky, D. E., Ambühl, H., Rønnestad, M. H., Davis, J. D., Gerin, P., Davis, M. L., et al. (1999). The development of psychotherapists: Concepts, questions, and methods of a collaborative international study. *Psychotherapy Research, 9*, 127–153.

Orlinsky, D. E., Botermans, J.-F., & Rønnestad, M. H. (1998, June). *Psychotherapeutic talent is the skill that therapists have already when they start training: An empirical analysis.* Paper presented at the 29th annual meeting of the Society for Psychotherapy Research, Snowbird, UT.

Orlinsky, D. E., Botermans, J.-F., & Rønnestad, M. H. (2001). Towards an empirically grounded model of psychotherapy training: Four thousand therapists rate influences on their development. *Australian Psychologist, 36,* 139–148.

Orlinsky, D. E., & Geller, J. D. (1993). Patients' representations of their therapists and therapy: A new research focus. In N. Miller, L. Luborsky, J. Barber, & J. Docherty (Eds.), *Psychodynamic treatment research* (pp. 423–468). New York: Basic Books.

Orlinsky, D. E., Geller, J. D., Tarragona, M., & Farber, B. A. (1993). Patients' representations of psychotherapy: A new focus for psychodynamic research. *Journal of Consulting and Clinical Psychology, 61,* 596–610.

Orlinsky, D. E., Grawe, K., & Parks, B. K. (1994). Process and outcome in psychotherapy—*Noch einmal.* In A. E. Bergin & S. L. Garfield (Eds.), *Handbook of psychotherapy and behavior change* (4th ed., pp. 270–376). New York: Wiley.

Orlinsky, D. E., & Howard, K. I. (1975). *Varieties of psychotherapeutic experience: Multivariate analyses of patients' and therapists' reports.* New York: Teachers College Press.

Orlinsky, D. E., & Howard, K. I. (1976). The effect of sex of therapist on the therapeutic experiences of women. *Psychotherapy: Theory, Research and Practice, 13,* 82–88.

Orlinsky, D. E., & Howard, K. I. (1977). The therapist's experience of psychotherapy. In A. S. Gurman & A. M. Razin (Eds.), *Effective psychotherapy: A research handbook* (pp. 566–589). New York: Pergamon Press.

Orlinsky, D. E., & Howard, K. I. (1978). The relation of process to outcome in psychotherapy. In S. L. Garfield & A. E. Bergin (Eds.), *Handbook of psychotherapy and behavior change* (2nd ed., pp. 283–329). New York: Wiley.

Orlinsky, D. E., & Howard, K. I. (1980). Gender and psychotherapeutic outcome. In A. Brodsky & R. Hare-Mustin (Eds.), *Women in psychotherapy* (pp. 3–34). New York: Guilford Press.

Orlinsky, D. E., & Howard, K. I. (1986a). Process and outcome in psychotherapy. In S. L. Garfield & A. E. Bergin (Eds.), *Handbook of psychotherapy and behavior change* (3rd ed., pp. 311–381). New York: Wiley.

Orlinsky, D. E., & Howard, K. I. (1986b). The psychological interior of psychotherapy: Explorations with the Therapy Session Reports. In L. Greenberg & W. Pinsof (Eds.), *The psychotherapeutic process: A research handbook* (pp. 477–501). New York: Guilford.

Orlinsky, D. E., & Howard, K. I. (1987). A generic model of psychotherapy. *Journal of Integrative and Eclectic Psychotherapy, 6,* 6–36.

Orlinsky, D. E., & Howard, K. I. (1994). Unity and diversity among psychotherapies: A comparative perspective. In B. Bongar & L. Beutler (Eds.), *Foundations of psychotherapy: Theory, research, and practice* (pp. 3–23). New York: Oxford University Press.

Orlinsky, D. E., Norcross, J. C., Rønnestad, M. H., & Wiseman, H. (2005). Outcomes and impacts of psychotherapists' personal therapy: A research review. In J. D. Geller, J. C. Norcross, & D. E. Orlinsky (Eds.), *The psychotherapist's own psychotherapy: Patient and clinician perspectives* (pp. 214–230). New York: Oxford University Press.

Orlinsky, D. E., & Rønnestad, M. H. (2003). *The psychotherapist's self-experience.* Unpublished manuscript, University of Chicago.

Orlinsky, D. E., Rønnestad, M. H., Ambühl, H., Willutzki, U., Botermans, J.-F., Cierpka, M., et al. (1999). Psychotherapists' assessments of their development at different career levels. *Psychotherapy: Theory/Research/Practice/Training, 36,* 203–215.

Orlinsky, D. E., Rønnestad, M. H., & Willutzki, U. (2004). Fifty years of psychotherapy process–outcome research: Continuity and change. In M. Lambert (Ed.), *Bergin and Garfield's handbook of psychotherapy and behavior change* (5th ed., pp. 307–389). New York: Wiley.

Orlinsky, D. E., Rønnestad, M. H., Willutzki, U., Wiseman, H., & Botermans, J.-F. (2005). The prevalence and parameters of personal therapy in Europe and elsewhere. In J. D. Geller, J. C. Norcross, & D. E. Orlinsky (Eds.), *The psychotherapist's own psychotherapy: Patient and clinician contributions* (pp. 171–191). New York: Oxford University Press.

Orlinsky, D. E., & Russell, R. L. (1994). Tradition and change in psychotherapy research: Some reflections on the fourth generation. In R. L. Russell (Ed.), *Reassessing psychotherapy research* (pp. 185–214). New York: Guilford Press.

Orlinsky, D. E., Willutzki, U., Meyerberg, J., Cierpka, M., Buchheim, P., & Ambühl, H. (1996). Die Qualität der therapeutishcen Beziehung: Entsprechen gemeinsame Faktoren in der Psychotherapie gemeinsamen Characteristika von PsychotherapeutInnen? [Qualities of the psychotherapeutic relationship: Do common factors in psychotherapy reflect common characteristics of psychotherapists?]. *Psychotherapie, Psychosomatik, medizinische Psychologie, 46,* 102–110.

Oxford English Dictionary. (1992). Oxford, England: Oxford University Press.

Parks, B. K. (1996). *Flow, boredom, and anxiety in therapeutic work: A study of psychotherapists' intrinsic motivation and professional development.* Unpublished doctoral dissertation, University of Chicago.

Parloff, M. B., & Elkin, I. E. (1992). The NIMH treatment of depression collaborative research program. In D. K. Freedheim (Ed.), *History of psychotherapy: A century of change* (pp. 442–449). Washington, DC: American Psychological Association.

Parloff, M. B., Waskow, I. E., & Wolfe, B. E. (1986). Research on therapist variables in relation to process and outcome. In S. L. Garfield & A. E. Bergin (Eds.), *Handbook of psychotherapy and behavior change* (2nd ed., pp. 233–282). New York: Wiley.

Parsons, T. (1964). Mental illness and "spiritual malaise": The role of the psychiatrist and the minister of religion. In *Social structure and personality* (pp. 292–324). New York: Free Press.

Parsons, T., & Bales, R. F. (1953). The dimensions of action-space. In T. Parsons, R. F. Bales, & E. A. Shils (Eds.), *Working papers in the theory of action* (pp. 63–109). Glencoe, IL: Free Press.

Piaget, J. (1950). *The psychology of intelligence*. London: Routledge & Kegan Paul.

Piaget, J. (1981). *Intelligence and affectivity: Their relationship during child development.* Palo Alto, CA: Annual Reviews Monograph.

Pines, A., & Maslach, C. (1978). Characteristics of staff burnout in mental health settings. *Hospital & Community Psychiatry, 29*, 233–237.

Pinsof, W. M. (1986). The process of family therapy: The development of the Family Therapist Coding System. In L. S. Greenberg & W. M. Pinsof (Eds.), *The psychotherapeutic process: A research handbook* (p. 220). New York: Guilford.

Polanyi, M. (1966). *The tacit dimension*. Chicago: University of Chicago Press.

Pope, K. S., Keith-Spiegel, P., & Tabachnick, B. G. (1986). Sexual attraction to clients: The human therapist and the (sometimes) inhuman training system. *American Psychologist, 41*, 147–158.

Pope, K. S., & Tabachnick, B. G. (1994). Therapists as patients: A national survey of psychologists' experiences, problems, and beliefs. *Professional Psychology: Research and Practice, 25*, 247–258.

Pope, K. S., Tabachnick, B. G., & Keith-Spiegel, P. (1987). Ethics of practice: The beliefs and behaviors of psychologists as therapists. *American Psychologist, 42*, 993–1006.

Pope, K. S., Tabachnick, B. G., & Keith-Spiegel, P. (1988). Good and poor practices in psychotherapy: National survey of beliefs of psychotherapists. *Professional Psychology: Research and Practice, 19*, 547–552.

Pope, K. S., & Vetter, V. A. (1991). Prior therapist–patient sexual involvement among patients seen by psychologists. *Psychotherapy, 28*, 429–438.

Prochaska, J., & DiClemente, C. C. (1982). Transtheoretical therapy: Toward a more integrative model of change. *Psychotherapy: Theory, Research and Practice, 19*, 276–288.

Prochaska, J., & Norcross, J. (1983a). Contemporary psychotherapists: A national survey of characteristics, practices, orientations, and attitudes. *Psychotherapy: Theory, Research and Practice, 20*, 161–169.

Prochaska, J., & Norcross, J. (1983b). Psychotherapists' perspectives on treating themselves and their clients for psychic distress. *Professional Psychology: Research and Practice, 14*, 642–655.

Prochaska, J. O., & Norcross, J. C. (1999). *Systems of psychotherapy: A transtheoretical analysis*. Pacific Grove, CA: Brooks/Cole.

Prost, A., & Vincent, G. (Eds.). (1991). *A history of private life: Riddles of identity in modern times*. Cambridge, MA: Belknap Press.

Rachelson, J., & Clance, P. R. (1980). Attitudes of psychotherapists toward the 1970 APA standards for psychotherapy training. *Professional Psychology, 11*, 261–267.

Radeke, J. T., & Mahoney, M. J. (2000). Comparing the personal lives of psychotherapists and research psychologists. *Professional Psychology: Research and Practice*, *31*, 82–84.

Raquepaw, J. M., & Miller, R. S. (1989). Psychotherapist burnout: A componential analysis. *Professional Psychology: Research and Practice*, *20*, 32–36.

Reichelt, S., & Skjerve, J. (2002). Correspondence between supervisors and trainees in their perception of supervision events. *Journal of Clinical Psychology*, *58*, 759–772.

Rieff, P. (1966). *The triumph of the therapeutic: Uses of faith after Freud*. New York: Harper Torchbooks.

Roberts, D. (2001). *Psychotherapy of severe mental illness: Therapist specialization and consequences of practice*. Unpublished master's thesis, University of Chicago.

Roe, A. (1954). Personality and vocation. In H. Brand (Ed.), *The study of personality: A book of readings* (pp. 377–386). New York: Wiley.

Rogers, J. L., Howard, K. I., & Vessey, J. T. (1993). Using significance tests to evaluate equivalence between two experimental groups. *Psychological Bulletin*, *113*, 553–656.

Rønnestad, M. H., & Orlinsky, D. E. (2000). Psykoterapiveiledning til besvær: Når veiledning hemmer og ikke fremmer faglig utvikling [Non-optimal supervision: When supervision inhibits professional development]. In A. Holte, G. H. Nielsen, & M. H. Rønnestad (Eds.), *Psykoterapi og psykoterapiveiledning* (pp. 291–321). Oslo, Norway: Gyldendal Akademisk.

Rønnestad, M. H., Orlinsky, D. E., Parks, B. K., & Davis, J. D. (1997). Supervisors of psychotherapy: Mapping experience level and supervisory confidence. *European Psychologist*, *2*, 191–201.

Rønnestad, M. H., & Skovholt, T. M. (1991). En modell for profesjonell utvikling og stagnasjon hos terapeuter og radgivere [A model of the professional development and stagnation of therapists and counselors]. *Journal of the Norwegian Psychological Association*, *28*, 555–567.

Rønnestad, M. H., & Skovholt, T. M. (1993). Supervision of beginning and advanced graduate-students of counseling and psychotherapy. *Journal of Counseling and Development*, *71*, 396–405.

Rønnestad, M. H., & Skovholt, T. M. (2001). Learning arenas for professional development: Retrospective accounts of senior psychotherapists. *Professional Psychology: Research and Practice*, *32*, 181–187.

Rønnestad, M. H., & Skovholt, T. M. (2003). The journey of the counselor and therapist: Research findings and perspectives on professional development. *Journal of Career Development*, *30*, 5–44.

Sampson, H., & Weiss, J. (1992). The Mt. Zion psychotherapy research group. In D. K. Freedheim (Ed.), *History of psychotherapy: A century of change* (pp. 432–435). Washington, DC: American Psychological Association.

Sandell, R., Carlsson, J., Schubert, J., Broberg, J., Lazar, A., & Blomberg, J. (2002). Varieties of therapeutic experience and their associations with patient outcome. *European Psychotherapy*, *3*, 17–35.

Schröder, T., & Orlinsky, D. E. (2003, June). *"You were always on my mind . . ."*
Therapists' preoccupations between sessions and therapeutic challenges. Paper pre-
sented at the 34th annual meeting of the Society for Psychotherapy Research,
Weimar, Germany.

Schwebel, M., & Coster, J. (1998). Well-functioning in professional psychologists:
As program heads see it. *Professional Psychology: Research and Practice, 29,* 284–
292.

Searles, H. F. (1955). The informational value of the supervisor's emotional experiences. *Psychiatry, 18,* 135–146.

Skovholt, T. M., & Jennings, L. (Eds.). (2004). *Master therapists: Exploring expertise
in therapy and counseling.* New York: Pearson/Allyn & Bacon.

Skovholt, T. M., Jennings, L., & Mullenbach, M. (2004). Portrait of the master
therapists: Developmental model of the highly functioning self. In T. M.
Skovholt & L. Jennings (Eds.), *Master therapists: Exploring expertise in therapy
and counseling* (pp. 125–146). New York: Pearson/Allyn and Bacon.

Skovholt, T. M., & McCarthy, P. (1988). Critical incidents: Catalysts for counselor
development. *Journal of Counseling and Development, 67,* 69–130.

Skovholt, T. M., & Rønnestad, M. H. (1992). Themes in therapist and counselor
development. *Journal of Counseling and Development, 70,* 505–516.

Skovholt, T. M., & Rønnestad, M. H. (1995). *The evolving professional self: Stages
and themes in therapist and counselor development.* Chichester, England: Wiley.

Skovholt, T. M., & Rønnestad, M. H. (2003). Struggles of the novice counselor
and therapist. *Journal of Career Development, 30,* 45–58.

Sloane, R. B., & Staples, F. R. (1992). The Temple psychotherapy project. In D. K.
Freedheim (Ed.), *History of psychotherapy: A century of change* (pp. 426–428).
Washington, DC: American Psychological Association.

Smelser, N. J., & Erikson, E. H. (Eds.). (1980). *Themes of work and love in adulthood.*
Cambridge, MA: Harvard University Press.

Smith, D. P., & Orlinsky, D. E. (2004). Religious and spiritual experiences among
psychotherapists. *Psychotherapy, 41,* 144–151.

Stiles, W. B. (1988). Psychotherapy process–outcome correlations may be mislead-
ing. *Psychotherapy, 25,* 27–35.

Stoltenberg, C. D., & Delworth, U. (1987). *Supervising counselors and therapists: A
developmental approach.* San Francisco: Jossey-Bass.

Street, E. (1989). Challenging the "white knight." In W. Dryden & L. Spurling
(Eds.), *On becoming a psychotherapist* (pp. 134–147). New York: Tavistock/
Routledge.

Strupp, H. H. (1955a). The effect of the psychotherapist's personal analysis upon
his techniques. *Journal of Consulting Psychology, 19,* 197–204.

Strupp, H. H. (1955b). Psychotherapeutic technique, professional affiliation, and
experience level. *Journal of Consulting Psychology, 19,* 97–102.

Strupp, H. H., Hadley, S. W., & Gomes-Schwartz, B. (1977). *Psychotherapy for
better or worse: The problem of negative effects.* New York: Jason Aronson.

Strupp, H. H., & Howard, K. I. (1992). A brief history of psychotherapy research. In D. K. Freedheim (Ed.), *History of psychotherapy: A century of change* (pp. 309–334). Washington, DC: American Psychological Association.

Sundland, D. M. (1977). Theoretical orientations of psychotherapists. In A. S. Gurman & A. M. Razin (Eds.), *Effective psychotherapy: A handbook of research* (pp. 189–219). New York: Pergamon.

Taylor, C. (1989). *Sources of the self: The making of modern identity*. Cambridge, MA: Harvard University Press.

The therapist as a neglected variable in psychotherapy research [Special series]. (1997). *Clinical Psychology: Science and Practice, 4*, 40–89.

Thorne, B. (1989). The blessing and the curse of empathy. In W. Dryden & L. Spurling (Eds.), *On becoming a psychotherapist* (pp. 53–68). New York: Tavistock/Routledge.

Toulmin, S. (1990). *Cosmopolis: The hidden agenda of modernity*. New York: Free Press.

Tracey, T. J., Hays, K. A., Malone, J., & Herman, B. (1988). Changes in counselor response as a function of experience. *Journal of Counseling Psychology, 35*, 119–126.

Turkle, S. (1978). *Psychoanalytic politics: Freud's French revolution*. New York: Basic Books.

Tyler, J. D., & Clark, J. A. (1987). Clinical psychologists reflect on the usefulness of various components of graduate training. *Professional Psychology: Research and Practice, 18*, 381–384.

van der Ploeg, H. M., van Leeuwen, J. J., & Kwee, M. G. (1990). Burnout among Dutch psychotherapists. *Psychological Reports, 67*, 107–112.

Vasco, A. B., & Dryden, W. (1997). Does development do the deed? Clinical experience and epistemological development together account for similarities in therapeutic style. *Psychotherapy, 34*, 262–271.

Wallerstein, R. (1992). The Menninger project. In D. K. Freedheim (Ed.), *History of psychotherapy: A century of change* (pp. 401–407). Washington, DC: American Psychological Association.

Wampold, B. E. (2001). *The great psychotherapy debate: Models, methods, and findings*. Mahwah, NJ: Erlbaum.

Watkins, C. E. (1994). The supervision of psychotherapy supervisor trainees. *American Journal of Psychotherapy, 48*, 417–432.

Watkins, C. E., Lopez, F. G., Campbell, V. L., & Himmell, C. D. (1986). Contemporary counseling psychology: Results of a national survey. *Journal of Counseling Psychology, 33*, 301–309.

West, J., Kohout, J., Pion, G. M., Wicherski, M. M., Vandivort-Warren, R. E., Palmiter, M. L., et al. (2001). Mental health practitioners and trainees. In R. W. Manderschied & M. J. Henderson (Eds.), *Mental health, United States, 2000* (pp. 279–315). Rockville, MD: U.S. Department of Health and Human Services.

White, R. W. (1975). *Lives in progress* (3rd ed.). New York: Holt, Rinehart & Winston.

Willutzki, U., Hernandez Bark, G., Davis, J., & Orlinsky, D. E. (1997, June). *Client outcome as a function of the therapist's difficulties and coping strategies in the course of psychotherapy: Initial results.* Paper presented at the 28th annual meeting of the Society for Psychotherapy Research, Geilo, Norway.

Willutzki, U., & Orlinsky, D. E. (2002, June). *Therapist competence and experience level in relation to outcome of therapy for patients with social phobia.* Paper presented at the 33rd annual meeting of the Society for Psychotherapy Research, Santa Barbara, CA.

Winnicott, D. W. (1965). *The maturational processes and the facilitating environment.* New York: International Universities Press.

Wiseman, H., & Egozi, S. (2002). Tipool ishi etzel yoatzot chinoochyot [Personal psychotherapy among school counselors]. *Hayeootz Hachinoochi [Journal of the Israel Association of Educational Counselors], 11,* 198–217.

Wiseman, H., & Orlinsky, D. E. (2003, June). *Therapists' intersession experiences and therapist characteristics.* Paper presented at the 34th annual meeting of the Society for Psychotherapy Research, Weimar, Germany.

Wiseman, H., & Shefler, G. (2001). Experienced psychoanalytically oriented therapists' narrative accounts of their personal therapy: Impacts on professional and personal development. *Psychotherapy, 38,* 129–141.

Worthington, E. L. (1987). Changes in supervision as counselors and supervisors gain experience: A review. *Professional Psychology: Research and Practice, 18,* 189–208.

Yeats, W. B. (1952). Among school children. In *The Collected Poems of W. B. Yeats* (p. 214). New York: Macmillan.

Yourman, D. B., & Farber, B. A. (1996). Nondisclosure and distortion in psychotherapy supervision. *Psychotherapy: Theory, Research, Practice, Training, 33,* 567–575.

AUTHOR INDEX

Abbott, A., 8, 20
Albee, G. W., 8
Almagor, M., 10
Ambühl, H., 10
Amer, M., 10
American Psychiatric Association, 35, 96
Ancis, J. R., 189
Andersen, K., 9, 65
Angle, R. S., 10
Anthony, N. A., 10
Ariès, P., 47
Arthur, A. R., 10
Auerbach, A. H., 10
Authier, J., 194
Aveline, M., 4
Azrimendi, T. G., 9

Bae, S.-H., 84n.4
Bales, R. F., 43
Baltes, Paul, 3, 6n.3
Bandura, A., 43
Barlow, D., 177n.2
Becker, H. S., 8
Bellah, R. N., 4, 47
Benjamin, L. S., 44n.1
Ben-Porath, Y. S., 10
Berg, J. H., 6
Berger, B., 5, 47
Berger, P., 5, 47
Bergin, A. E., 5, 10, 177n.2, 178
Berman, J. S., 10, 191
Bernard, J. M., 10, 178, 194
Beutler, L. E., 4–5, 8, 9, 10, 177n.2, 184
Bonacci, J., 8
Bordin, E. S., 55
Borys, D. S., 9
Botermans, J.-F., 10, 10n.5, 63n.2, 112, 137, 156, 176, 184n.1, 188n.2, 199
Brady, J. L., 9, 200
Brokaw, B. F., 9

Cameron, P. M., 190
Campbell, V. L., 10

Carson, R. C., 44n.1
Caspar, F., 108
Charles, D., 10
Chiriboga, D., 8
Clance, P. R., 188
Clark, J. A., 10
Clarkin, J. F., 4
Corbett, K., 4, 177
Corbett, M. M., 10, 189, 190
Coster, J., 195, 196, 198
Crago, M., 4–5, 9, 177n.2
Craine, M. H., 10
Crits-Christoph, P., 8, 9, 10
Csikszentmihalyi, M., 45, 57
Cushman, P., 47

Davis, J., 177, 206
Davis, J. D., 9, 10, 49, 51, 194
Davis, M. L., 51
DeBaggis, A., 8
Delworth, U., 10, 32
Dent, J. K., 9
Derlega, V. J., 6
Deutsch, C. J., 9
DiClemente, C. C., 9, 186
Dlugos, R. F., 9, 183, 195
Doehrman, M. J., 191
Draguns, J., 204
Dryden, W., 9, 10
Durkheim, E., 45

Egozi, S., 200
Eliot, T. S., 65
Elizur, A., 47
Elkin, I., 6, 6n.3
Elkin, I. E., 177n.2
Elliott, R., 6n.3, 9, 10, 188
Erikson, E. H., 8

Faltus, F. J., 9
Farber, B. A., 9, 12, 65, 189–190, 195
Fiedler, F. E., 9
Fiske, D. W., 5, 9

Francis, V. M., 51
Frank, J. B., 56, 172
Frank, J. D., 56, 170, 172, 177n.2
Freedheim, D. K., 177, 177n.2
Freud, S., 64, 66, 121
Friedlander, M. L., 9, 183, 189, 190, 195
Furse, G. A., 9

Garfield, S. L., 5, 178
Gartner, A., 8
Gay, P., 47
Geller, J. D., 6n.3, 9, 12, 16, 200
Gerin, P., 9
Goldberg, C., 116, 147
Gomes-Schwartz, B., 50n.5
Goodyear, R. K., 10, 178
Grater, H. A., 32
Grawe, K., 6n.3, 54, 178, 186
Gray, L. A., 189, 190
Greaves, D. W., 10
Green, J., 8
Greenberg, L. S., 6n.3
Grosswald, S., 8
Guba, E. G., 21
Guest, P. D., 10
Gurin, A., 8
Gurman, A. S., 9, 10
Guy, J. D., 9, 200

Hadley, S. W., 50n.5
Hansen, N. D., 9, 65, 195
Hays, K. A., 10
Heifetz, L. J., 9, 65, 195
Hendrick, S. S., 6
Henry, W. E., 5, 8, 8n.4, 9, 34
Henry, W. P., 173, 177n.2, 179
Herman, B., 10
Hernandez Bark, G., 177, 206
Hess, A. K., 32
Hill, C. E., 4, 10, 177, 189, 190
Himmell, C. D., 10
Holloway, E. L., 178
Holmqvist, R., 9, 65
Holt, R. R., 5, 8n.4, 9, 10
Horowitz, L. M., 44n.1
Horowitz, M. J., 177n.2
Houle, C., 8

Howard, K. I., 4, 6, 6n.3, 9, 12, 43, 55, 170, 177, 177n.2, 178, 180, 183, 186, 206
Hughes, E., 8

Ivey, A. E., 194

Jennings, L., 171, 200
Jensen, J. P., 10
Johnson, M., 5, 5n.1, 10, 107n.3
Joo, E., 84n.4

Kagan, H., 194
Kagan, J. I., 194
Kardash, C. M., 10
Keinan, G., 10
Keith-Spiegel, P., 9
Kelley, F. L., 5, 9
Kellner, H., 5, 47
Kiesler, D. J., 44n.1
Kim, H. A., 84n.4
Kivlighan, D. M., 10
Klein, M., 10
Knesper, D. J., 10
Kopta, S. M., 10
Kottler, J. A., 9
Kramen-Kahn, B., 9, 65, 195
Krause, M. S., 6n.3, 180
Kretsch, R., 47
Kurzawa, E. K., 9
Kurzweil, E., 8, 8n.4
Kwee, M. J., 9

Ladany, N., 10, 189, 190
Lakoff, G., 5, 5n.1, 107n.3
Lambert, M. J., 5, 50n.5, 56, 85n.5, 178
Lasch, C., 4, 47
Leary, T., 43, 55
Lehman, A. K., 9, 10
Leiter, M. P., 9, 110, 180, 195
Leverette, J. S., 190
Lewinsohn, P., 177n.2
Liaboe, G. P., 9
Lietaer, G., 6n.3
Light, D., 8, 10
Lincoln, Y. S., 21
Lohser, B., 64n.4

Schwebel, M., 195, 196, 198
Searles, H. F., 191
Shapiro, D. A., 4, 200n.9
Shefler, G., 199
Sims, J. H., 5, 34
Skjerve, J., 190, 194
Skovholt, T. M., 5, 9, 10, 16, 32, 58, 75,
        115, 128n.5, 137, 143, 147, 152,
        170, 171, 172, 178, 184, 185,
        187, 188, 197, 200
Sloane, R. B., 177n.2
Smelser, N. J., 8
Smith, D. P., 10n.5
Smith, J., 3, 6n.3
Smith, J. A., 9
Sorek, Y., 47
Spaizer, N., 47
Spray, S. L., 5, 34
Spurling, L., 9
Staples, F. R., 177n.2
Stark, M. J., 9
Stiles, W. B., 6n.3, 9
Stoltenberg, C. D., 10, 32
Strauss, A. L., 8
Strausser, D. J., 9
Strausser-Kirtland, D., 9, 16
Strupp, H. H., 4, 9, 47, 50n.5, 173, 177,
        177n.2
Sullivan, W. M., 4, 47
Sundland, D. M., 10
Suter, E., 8
Swidler, A., 4, 47

Tabachnick, B. G., 9, 16
Tarragona, M., 12
Taylor, C., 47
Thorne, B., 8
Thurnher, M., 8
Tipton, S. M., 4, 47

Toulmin, S., 5
Tracey, T. J., 10
Turkle, S., 8
Tyler, J. D., 10

van der Ploeg, H. M., 9
van Leeuwen, J. J., 9
Vasco, A. B., 10
Vessey, J., 6n.3, 180
Vetter, V. A., 9
Vignat, J.-P., 9
Vincent, G., 47

Walker, J. A., 189
Wallerstein, R., 177n.2
Walthall, D., 8
Wampold, B. E., 6n.3
Waskow, I. E., 9
Watkins, C. E., 10, 195
Watkins, L. M., 44n.1
Weiss, J., 177n.2
West, J., 10
Wheeler, J. R. C., 10
White, R. W., 8
Williams, D., 8
Willutzki, U., 6, 6n.3, 10n.5, 43, 54, 55,
        177, 177n.4, 178, 178n.5, 199,
        206
Winnicott, D. W., 56
Winstead, B. A., 6
Wiseman, H., 10n.5, 121, 199, 200
Wogan, M., 10
Wolfe, B. E., 9
Wollersheim, J. P., 9, 66, 195
Worthington, E. L., 194

Yeats, W. B., 6n.2
Yourman, D. B., 189–190

SUBJECT INDEX

DPCCQ. *See Development of Psychothera-pists Common Core Questionnaire* (DPCCQ)
Durkheim, Emile, 45

Early clinical practice, 184–185
Education. *See* Clinical education
Effective practice. *See* Practice patterns
Egypt, 204
Eliot, T. S., 65
Elkin, I. E., 177n.2
Elliott, R., 188
Emotivism, 4
Erkolahti, R., 204
Ethical conduct, 9
Ethical standards, 9
Evaluation, supervisory, 191–192
Experience level, 88–89, 119–120. *See also* Breadth and depth of case experience; Career cohorts
Experimental studies, psychotherapists in, 5–6

Factor analysis, 23, 109–110, 113–114
Family therapy, 35
Farber, B. A., 189–190
Felt therapeutic mastery, 113, 145–147, 164
Finland, 204
Flow, state of, 45. *See also* In-session feelings, of therapist
Flux, state of, 119, 164, 198, 198n.8
Focus group, for development of DPCCQ, 17
France, 33, 72
Francis, V. M., 51
Frank, J. D., 177n.2
Freedheim, D. K., 177n.2
Freud, Sigmund, 64–66, 121

Gender, 32–33, 69, 90, 119, 133, 183
Generality, across diverse groups, 21
Generalizability, from sample to parent population, 21–23
General Psychotherapeutic Model, 186
Generic Model of Psychotherapy, 186
Gerin, Paul, 16

Germany, 29, 33, 69, 74, 76, 78, 124, 126, 136, 140–141, 204–205
Goldberg, C., 147
Greece, 204
Group therapy, 35
Guneri, G., 204

Hakim, L. Z., 204
Handbook of Psychotherapy and Behavior Change, 178
Havik, O., 205
Hazard recognition, 198
Healing involvement, 63–65, 79, 81–82, 152, 162, 165, 167–170, 174. *See also* Stressful involvement
    for beginning therapists, 184–186, 193
    correlates of, 70–76
    and currently experienced growth, 122–124, 126, 129, 134, 138, 142, 167, 196
    and practice patterns, 82–83, 86
    and professional development, 138–140, 165–166
    and therapeutic bond, 179, 183
Henry, W. E., 34
Henry, W. P., 177n.2, 179
Hill, C. E., 189
Høglend, P., 205
Holding environment, 75
Horowitz, L. M., 44n.1
Horowitz, M. J., 177n.2
Howard, K. I., 177n.2

Iahns, Jean-François, 16
Impairment levels, client, 35–36, 96–97, 122
Individual therapy, 35
In-session feelings, of therapist, 42–43, 45, 57–58, 60, 63, 152. *See also* Healing involvement
    anxiety, 57–58
    boredom, 57–58
    flow, 57–58, 65
Interpersonal Process Recall, 194
Interrelations of work and development, 165–166
Interviews, use of, 16

Involvement, modes of, 161–162. *See also*
    Controlling involvement; Heal-
    ing involvement; Stressful
    involvement
Israel, 33

Johnson, M., 107n.3

Kassem, L., 204
Kazantzis, N., 203
Kiesler, D. J., 44n.1
Kim, K., 204
Knobloch-Fedders, L., 204
Kurzweil, E., 8n.4

Ladany, N., 189–190
Laireiter, A., 204
Lakoff, G., 107n.3
Lambert, M. J., 50n.5, 85n.5
Lampropoulos, G., 204
Lay analysts, 29
Lay therapists, 29
Leary, T., 43–45, 55
Lebow, J., 204
Lehtovuori, P., 204
Leiter, M. P., 180
Lewinsohn, P., 177n.2
Lippe, A. von der, 205–206
Lohser, B., 64n.4
Longitudinal analysis, 105, 107, 163,
    176n.1, 205
Luborsky, L., 177n.2
Luhrmann, T. M., 199
Lyngstad, G., 205

MacIntyre, A., 4
Malaysia, 204
Marital status, 33, 92
Maslach, C., 180
Maturation process, 171
Medical profession, 28–29
Meyerberg, J., 204, 206
Michalopoulos, I., 204
Microtraining, 194
Middle class, 34
Minnesota Study of Counselor and Thera-
    pist Development, 16
Monsen, J., 205

Morale, 180
Morrow-Bradley, C., 188
Moskowitz, S. A., 189
Motivation for continued development,
    124
    lack of, 173
Multiple-item scales, 23–24
Multiple-regression analysis (MRA), 25,
    70–72, 134, 138, 140

Narrative account, 19
Nationality, 33, 69, 149n.4
    American, 33, 69, 74, 76, 78, 124,
        126, 136, 140–141
    Danish, 33, 76
    French, 33, 72
    German, 33, 69, 74, 76, 78, 124,
        126, 136, 140–141
    Korean, 33, 69, 72, 74, 76, 78,
        84n.4, 123–124, 126, 133, 136,
        140–141
    Norwegian, 33, 69, 74, 76, 78, 124,
        126, 136, 140–141
    Portuguese, 33, 76
    Spanish, 33
    Swedish, 33
Nestoros, J., 204
Newton, P. M., 64n.4
New Zealand, 203
Ng, W.-S., 204
Norcross, J. C., 197–198
Norway, 33, 69, 74, 76, 78, 124, 126,
    136, 140–141, 204
Norwegian Multicenter Project for the
    Study of Process and Outcome of
    Psychotherapy, 205–206
Nursing, 29
Nutt, E. A., 189

Ogles, B. M., 50n.5, 85n.5
Openness to experience, 75
Orlinsky, David, 16, 177n.2, 177n.3
Outcome research, 6n.3
Outpatient setting, 34
Overall career development, 113. *See also*
    Cumulative career development

Parallel process, 191
Parks, B. K., 11

Parloff, M. B., 177n.2
Patterns, in therapists' experience, 61–63, 62n.1. *See also* Practice patterns; Current development patterns
Peer group interactions, 187–188, 198–199
Personal characteristics, 19, 32–34
Personal life, 47, 137, 183, 188
Personal therapy, 18, 121, 133, 136, 188, 199–200, 200n.9
Phenomenological approach, to study of professional development, 105–107
Portugal, 33, 76, 205
Practice characteristics, 34–36, 77, 133
Practice conditions, 92–97, 121–122
Practice difficulties, 42–43, 49–51, 58, 63, 65, 150–151
   frustrating treatment case, 50–51
   negative personal reaction, 50–51
   professional self-doubt, 50–51
Practice patterns, 82–85, 105, 122, 147–149, 162–163. *See also* Currently experienced depletion; Currently experienced growth; Healing involvement; Stressful involvement
   challenging practice, 83–85, 97, 122, 147–149, 162
   disengaged practice, 83, 85–86, 97, 122, 147–149, 162–163, 165
   distressing practice, 83, 85–86, 97, 122, 147–149, 162, 165, 185, 192, 198–200
   effective practice, 83–85, 97, 122, 147–149, 162, 165
Practice setting, 34–35, 95, 121–122, 133, 199
Premature closure, 172–173
Process–outcome research, 6n.3, 178
Prochaska, J., 186
Professional associations, 21
Professional background, 28–29, 119–120
Professional characteristics, 28–32
   and cumulative career development, 132–133
   and currently experienced development, 119–121
   and practice patterns, 86–90
Professional development, 12, 18, 103–108, 137–142, 163–165. *See also*

Career development; Cumulative career development; Currently experienced development
Professional experience, 10
Professional societies, 21–22
Professions, 67–68, 88, 204–205
   medicine, 28–29
   nursing, 29
   psychiatry, 29
   psychology, 29, 132
   social work, 29
Progress, sense of, 118–119, 164
Psychiatry, 29
Psychology, 29, 132
Psychosomatics, 29
Psychotherapeutic procedures, studies of, 4–5
Psychotherapists
   personal and demographic characteristics, 32–34
   practice characteristics, 34–36
   professional characteristics, 28–32
   recommendations for, 195–201
   research questions concerning, 7–8, 7n.4
   studies of, 3–7, 9–10, 177–180
   "typical" or "average," 36
Psychotherapy
   diversity of, 20–21
   in modern culture, 47
   nature of, 11
   as professional specialty or subspecialty, 28–29
Psychotherapy research, 4–7, 9–10, 177–180
Pursuit of happiness, 4

Qualifications, supervisory, 194–195

Rachelson, J., 188
Reconstructivity, 19
Reflection. *See* Continuous professional reflection; Self-reflection
Regress, sense of, 118–119, 164, 198–200
Reichelt, S., 190
Relational agency, 53–55, 63, 151
   baffled, 55
   efficacious, 54–55
   invested, 54–55

Theoretical breadth, 132–133, 140, 169–
    170, 186, 197
Theoretical orientation, 18, 29–31, 57,
    68, 78–79, 89–90, 120
  analytic–psychodynamic, 29–31
  behavioral, 29–31, 63n.3
  broad-spectrum, 31, 120
  cognitive–behavioral, 29–31, 120
  humanistic, 29–31, 63n.3, 120
  initial, 185–187
  systemic, 29–31,
  uncommitted, 120
Therapeutic bond, 55, 178–179
Therapeutic maturity, 147
Therapeutic sensibility, 4
Therapeutic work. *See also* Clinical skills;
    Coping strategies; Healing
    involvement; In-session feelings;
    Practice difficulties; Practice
    patterns; Relational agency;
    Relational manner; Stressful
    involvement; Treatment goals
  common elements in, 58–60
  diversification in, 197
  empirical findings for, 46–58
  facets of, 42–45
  as healing involvement, 167–170
  and stressful involvement, 172
Therapeutic work experience, 124, 134,
    136–142, 149–152, 161–163,
    165–166, 184–185
Therapeutic Work Involvement Scales,
    200–201
Therapist–patient relationship, 6–7, 6n.3,
    43–45, 178–179
Therapy Session Report questionnaire,
    206
Toukmanian, S., 204
Training, of psychotherapists, 10. *See also*
    Clinical education; Professions;
    Training programs

Training programs, 22, 194–195. *See also*
    Clinical education
Transferability of findings, 21
Transference, 49
Translations of DPCCQ, 20
Transtheoretical Model, 186
Treatment goals, 42–43, 46–47, 58,
    63n.3, 150
Treatment modalities, 35, 95, 186–187,
    197
Treatment models, 29–31. *See also* Theo-
    retical orientation
  analytic–psychodynamic, 29–31
  behavioral, 29–31
  cognitive, 29–31
  humanistic, 29–31
  "other," 29–31
  systemic, 29–31
Turkey, 204

United Kingdom, 203
United States, 33, 69, 74, 76, 78, 124,
    126, 136, 140–141

Vasco, A., 205

Wallerstein, R., 177n.2
Weiss, J., 177n.2
Willutzki, Ulrike, 16, 177n.4, 178n.5,
    205–206
Wisdom, 3
Work setting support, 187–188
  lack of, 173
Worried well, the, 35

Yeats, W. B., 6n.2
Yourman, D. B., 189–190

ABOUT THE AUTHORS

David E. Orlinsky, PhD, is a psychologist and professor of human development and social sciences at the University of Chicago and has won several awards for his contributions to the science and profession of psychotherapy (American Psychological Association Division of Psychotherapy, Society for Psychotherapy Research, Illinois Psychological Association). He wrote the pioneering study *Varieties of Psychotherapeutic Experience* (with K. I. Howard), recently coedited *The Psychotherapist's Own Psychotherapy: Patient and Clinician Perspectives* (with J. D. Geller and J. C. Norcross), and has authored dozens of influential journal articles and book chapters over the past 40 years (including reviews of process–outcome research in successive editions of Bergin and Garfield's *Handbook of Psychotherapy and Behavior Change*). He is a cofounder and past president of the International Society for Psychotherapy Research.

Michael Helge Rønnestad, PhD, is an award-winning Norwegian psychologist and a professor of clinical psychology at the University of Oslo. He has been honored by the American Counseling Association (Association for Counselor Education and Supervision Research Award), the Norwegian Psychological Association (Bjørn Christiansen Memorial Award), and the University of Iowa (Ida Beam Professorship). He coauthored a landmark qualitative study of therapist and counselor development, *The Evolving Professional Self* (with Thomas Skovholt) and has authored and edited several books in Norwegian on professional development, supervision, and clinical psychology, most recently *Det Kliniske Intervjuet* (*The Clinical Interview*; coedited with Anna von der Lippe). He has published numerous national and international journal articles and is a specialist in clinical psychology of the Norwegian Psychological Association.